Gender and
Conversational Interaction

Gender and Conversational Interaction

EDITED BY
Deborah Tannen

New York   Oxford
OXFORD UNIVERSITY PRESS
1993

Oxford University Press
Oxford   New York   Toronto
Delhi   Bombay   Calcutta   Madras   Karachi
Kuala Lumpur   Singapore   Hong Kong   Tokyo
Nairobi   Dar es Salaam   Cape Town
Melbourne   Auckland   Madrid

and associated companies in
Berlin   Ibadan

Published by Oxford University Press, Inc.
198 Madison Avenue, New York, New York 10016-4314

Oxford is a registered trademark of Oxford University Press, Inc.

Library of Congress Cataloging-in-Publication Data
Gender and conversational interaction /
edited by Deborah Tannen.
p.   cm. — (Oxford studies in sociolinguistics)
Includes bibliographical references.
ISBN 0-19-508193-5 (cloth). — ISBN 0-19-508194-3 (pbk.)
1. Language and languages—Sex differences.
2. Conversation.   3. Sociolinguistics.
4. Social interaction.
I. Tannen, Deborah.   II. Series.
P120.S48G46   1993   306.4'4—dc20   92-33401

4 6 8 9 7 5 3

Printed in the United States of America
on acid-free paper

To Robin Lakoff
pioneer, inspiration, mentor, friend

Acknowledgments

The place and peace to prepare this volume for publication, including writing the introduction, rewriting my own chapter, and editing the other chapters, were provided by the Institute for Advanced Study in Princeton, New Jersey. Editing of the copy-edited manuscript and page proofs was done while I was a fellow at the Center for Advanced Study in the Behavioral Sciences in Stanford, California. I am deeply grateful for the support of these two scholarly havens and for financial support provided through CASBS by the National Science Foundation SES-9022192.

Excerpts from *The Journal-Gazette*, Fort Wayne, Indiana, special section "The Flood of '82," March 19, 1982, p. 2, are reprinted with permission. Excerpts from the book *Mountain Language* by Harold Pinter, Copyright © 1988 by Harold Pinter. Used with the permission of Grove/Atlantic Monthly Press.

"Who's Got the Floor?" by Carole Edelsky appeared in *Language in Society* 10:3(1981):383–421 and is reprinted with the permission of Cambridge University Press. "Pickle Fights: Gendered Talk in Preschool Disputes," by Amy Sheldon; "Tactical Uses of Stories: Participation Frameworks within Boys' and Girls' Disputes," by Marjorie Harness Goodwin; "Cooperative Competition in Adolescent 'Girl Talk,'" by Penelope Eckert; and "Gender, Politeness, and Confrontation in Tenejapa," by Penelope

Brown originally appeared in a special issue of *Discourse Processes* (13:1 [Jan.–March 1990]) which I guest-edited and are reprinted by special permission of Walter J. Johnson, Ablex Publishing Corporation. I am grateful to Mr. Johnson for generously granting this permission. Moreover, I remain ever grateful to him and Roy Freedle for publishing my first books and articles.

Stanford, Calif.   D.T.
January 1993

Contents

III The Relativity of Discourse Strategies

IV Critical Reviews of the Literature

Gender and
Conversational Interaction

Editor's Introduction

DEBORAH TANNEN

This volume explores the relationship between gender and language through the analysis of discourse in interaction. Some chapters compare the discourse of females and males; others analyze interaction among females. All the analytic chapters both provide model analysis of conversational interaction and make significant theoretical contributions to the literature on gender and language.

Of the many methodological and theoretical approaches to this topic currently being pursued, the one embodied in this collection can be thought of as ethnographically oriented discourse analysis or, alternatively, interactional sociolinguistics. The chapters provide context-sensitive microanalysis based on observation, tape-recording, and transcription of language as it is used in interaction. The time is ripe for this approach, as gender and language research nears the close of its second decade.

The year 1975 can be regarded as having launched the field of gender and language. That year saw the publication of three books that proved pivotal: Robin Lakoff's *Language and Women's Place* (the first part appeared as an article in *Language in Society* in 1972), Mary Ritchie Key's *Male/Female Language,* and Barrie Thorne and Nancy Henley's edited volume *Language and Sex: Difference and Dominance*. These groundbreaking books made it possible to talk about—indeed, to see—systematic differences in the ways women and men tend to use language.

Lakoff's work in particular became a touchstone for subsequent research. Previous linguistic research had described the phenomenon of women and men using different forms of speech in American Indian langauges such as Yana (Sapir 1929) and Koasati (Haas 1944). Lakoff used this as a point of departure to describe patterns of language use that, according to her observations, distinguished women's and men's speech in American English. She arrayed these differences on the traditional linguistic paradigm: lexical, syntactic, and intonational levels. The succeeding generation of researchers (fewer of whom were from Lakoff's own field of linguistics than from sociology, psychology, anthropology, and speech communication) tested her observations about "women's language" in a variety of settings. Lakoff also examined language used about women and men—in other words, the way language uses us. For example, one of Lakoff's illustrations (as relevant now as it was then) identified the differing connotations of the word "aggressive" when it is applied to a man and a woman; in the first case fairly positive, in the second quite negative.

Since that watershed year the relationship between language and gender has become the focus of a vast multidisciplinary literature. Innumerable journal articles have been supplemented by review articles (e.g., Aries 1987, Eckert & McConnell-Ginet 1992, Gal 1991, McConnell-Ginet 1988, Philips 1980, Smith 1979, West & Zimmerman 1985), book-length edited collections (e.g., Coates & Cameron 1988, Dubois & Crouch 1976, McConnell-Ginet, Borker, & Furman 1980, Philips, Steele, & Tanz 1988, Thorne, Kramarae, & Henley 1983, Todd & Fisher 1988), and monographs (e.g., Baron 1986, Coates 1986, Hill 1986, Graddol & Swann 1989, Kramarae 1981, Preisler 1986, Smith 1985). The research reported in these sources covers aspects of language and gender such as language socialization in young children; lexical, phonological, and syntactic differences in the language used by women and men; discourse strategies; and language used to refer to women and men. In order to quantify features of women's and men's speech, many studies have been carried out in an experimental paradigm, and operational definitions have been devised to facilitate coding and counting. This volume is not intended to provide a cross section of such research. Rather, it presents a broad and in-depth sampling of work that combines anthropological, sociolinguistic, linguistic, and ethnographically oriented discourse analysis.

There has been a recent tendency to bifurcate the gender and language field into two camps, roughly conceived as the "dominance" approach and the "cultural" approach. The "dominance" approach is most often associated with the work of Nancy Henley, Cheris Kramarae, and Barrie Thorne. The "cultural" approach can be traced to an article by Daniel Maltz and Ruth Borker (1982) and is often associated with my own work (Tannen 1990, chapter 7 in this volume). This bifurcation is unfortunate because, like most bipolar representations, it belies the complexity of the issues and the subtlety of the scholars' research. I hope that the analyses and arguments contained in this volume will serve to obliterate this dichotomy. Those who take a "cultural" view of gender differences (many of the authors included here would fall into this group) do not deny the existence of dominance relations in general or the dominance of women by men in particular. Likewise, recognizing that men dominate women in our culture does not preclude the existence of patterns of communication that tend to typify women and men. What is needed—and what this volume contributes to—is a better understanding of the complex relationship between the cultural patterning of linguistic behavior and that of gender relations.

The "cultural" approach to gender usually refers to the proposal by Maltz and Borker that males and females can be thought of as belonging to two different cultural groups since they tend to socialize in primarily sex-separate peer interaction during childhood. Another aspect of cultural patterning that bears on gender and language is the recognition that gender is only one of many cultural influences affecting linguistic behavior. A number of chapters included in this volume investigate such cultural patterning. Penelope Brown's chapter is the most palpably anthropological in that it examines discourse recorded in a Mayan community in Mexico. Somewhat closer to home but still culturally diverse are the subjects of Marjorie Harness Goodwin's chapter describing discourse in an urban black neighborhood, Barbara Johnstone's analysis of conversational narratives of midwestern men and women, and my own chapter distinguishing the conversational styles of Americans of varying ethnic, regional, and class backgrounds.

All the analytic chapters examine actual discourse as it occurred in interaction. The chapters by Carole Edelsky and by me use the topic of gender differences as a starting point to explore theoretical issues in discourse and to demonstrate that they must be understood before questions about gender differences in language use can be addressed. A number of other chapters also emphasize the complexity of issues involved in theorizing gender, and the necessity of understanding them before differences in discourse styles can be understood. The final two chapters are particularly important in that they provide critical reviews of the literature on two topics that have been the subject of extensive investigation and debate. With the explosion of research on gender and language being carried out by scholars in a wide range of disciplines employing widely divergent methodologies, such efforts to bring the research into the view of a single lens are absolutely necessary.

Finally, this volume can be used as a kind of casebook for the field of interactional sociolinguistics since it demonstrates how work in the field addresses a particular sociolinguistic issue. The collection also sheds light on a central theoretical and methodological problem: the transcription of oral discourse. As discourse analysis has gained greater prominence, the complexity of the transcription process has received increasing attention. The question of transcription is not only methodological but also theoretical. This volume provides rich material for an investigation of the implications of the various transcription systems found in the chapters. For example, juxtaposing the nontraditional systems employed by Eckert and Edelsky with the more traditional but still individually unique systems used by the other authors would provide an unusually fruitful entry point to this topic.[1] Furthermore, Edelsky discusses in detail the reasons she found traditional transcription formats inadequate and potentially misleading, as well as how the system she developed for this study led her to questions about turn and floor that became the focus of her study.

This volume, then, provides an in-depth introduction to research on gender and language that has been carried out in the tradition that might be called ethnographically oriented discourse analysis or interactional sociolinguistics.

Overview of the Chapters

Part I of this volume examines conversational discourse, including two chapters focusing on the talk of adolescent girls. Chapter 1, Donna Eder's "'Go Get Ya a French!': Romantic and Sexual Teasing Among Adolescent Girls," represents the first extended treatment of the conceptually complex speech activity teasing among junior high school girls. Combining sociolinguistic and ethnographic methods, Eder taped the naturally occurring interactions of girls, and in some cases girls and boys, in a middle school at lunchtime. Eder observed the girls engaging in romantic and sexual teasing about boys they were interested in or "going with"—a relationship that could be as short as a few days in duration and might involve little or no direct contact. Eder shows that teasing provides the girls with ways of reinforcing bonds among themselves, experimenting with and reversing traditional gender roles, and managing newly experienced feelings of jealousy.

In chapter 2, "Cooperative Competition in Adolescent 'Girl Talk,'" Penelope Eckert draws on insights gained during two and a half years of participant observation in a suburban Detroit high school in order to analyze a discussion arranged, at her request, by six girls who had been part of the same group in junior high but have assumed different positions in high school. Three have found their place in the mainstream popular crowd, and three are involved in alternative social networks. Eckert examines their multitopic discussion to uncover its purpose and the verbal means by which that purpose is accomplished. Because the girls in high school, like women in society, gain "symbolic capital" and status on the basis of their character and relations with others rather than their accomplishments, possessions, or institutional status, they need to negotiate norms of behavior and balance conflicting needs for independence and popularity. Eckert shows how the girls accomplish this through group talk that expresses disagreement at the same time that it negotiates consensus.[2]

In chapter 3, "Community and Contest: Midwestern Men and Women Creating Their Worlds in Conversational Storytelling," Barbara Johnstone argues that differences between women's and men's conversational stories reflect and create women's and men's divergent worlds. Rather than seeing women's stories as reflections of women's powerlessness,

Johnstone finds in their narratives evidence that for them the community is a source of power. Analyzing naturally occurring conversational narratives, Johnstone finds that the women's stories tend to involve social power, as "disturbing or dangerous events are overcome through the power of interdependence and community." The men's stories involve "worlds of contest in which power comes from the individual acting in opposition to others." Accordingly, the men and women provide details about different elements: the men about places, times, and objects; the women about people and their speech. Finally, Johnstone examines written narratives relating to a flood that occurred in the town in which these stories were told. She finds that the flood story—a community story—has much in common with the women's narrative mode.

Part II is concerned with "Conflict Talk." Two of the authors whose chapters are included in this section, Penelope Brown and Marjorie Harness Goodwin, were pioneers in anthropological studies of gender differences in interaction: Brown's 1979 dissertation ("Language, Interaction and Sex Roles in a Mayan Community") and Goodwin's 1978 dissertation ("Conversational Practices in a Peer Group of Urban Black Children") were landmarks in using extended fieldwork and recorded interaction to address issues of gender and language use. Taken together, the chapters in this section lay to rest the frequently heard claim that only boys and men are competitive and frequently engage in conflict whereas girls and women are always cooperative and avoid conflict. At the same time they make clear that neither is it the case that females and males tend to engage in conflict to the same extent or in the same way.

The first two chapters of this section compare male and female styles, showing systematic differences in how the two groups use language in their play. Chapter 4, "Pickle Fights: Gendered Talk in Preschool Disputes," by Amy Sheldon, opens with an invaluable review of the literature on gender and language in general and gender differences in children's conflicts in particular. Sheldon then examines conflict talk among female and male triads of three-year-old friends. In the same kitchen corner of a day care center both groups (on different occasions) fight over possession of a plastic pickle. The gendered aspects of the disputes are made visible by interpreting them in terms of two models. Maltz and Borker's anthropological linguistic model characterizes feminine language style as affiliative and masculine style as adversarial. Gilligan's psychological framework, describing gender differences in reasoning about moral conflicts, characterizes the feminine orientation as focusing on the relationship and the masculine as focusing on the self. Sheldon finds the two dispute sequences she analyzes to be consistent with predictions that the boys' conflict process is more heavy-handed and their discourse strategies more controlling, whereas the girls' conflict is more mitigated and their discourse strategies more collaborative. Thus the study demonstrates the gendered nature of children's peer talk at ages as young as three. However, Sheldon emphasizes that although the boys' and girls' styles tend toward the gender-specific paradigm, they are not mutually exclusive. The children share the same discourse competencies, and there is overlap in their discourse choices.

Chapter 5, "Tactical Uses of Stories: Participation Frameworks Within Boys' and Girls' Disputes," by Marjorie Harness Goodwin, examines how children use narrative discourse to arrange and rearrange their social organization. Goodwin spent a year and a half observing and recording children ranging in age from four to fourteen playing in their West Philadelphia black working-class neighborhood. She finds that boys use stories to further an ongoing argument while transforming the participation structure of the event. The boys' stories function as a direct challenge in negotiating current status within a hierarchical social order. The girls use stories as part of an "instigating" routine by which talking behind someone's back leads to future confrontation—an early stage in an ongoing process of negatively sanctioning behavior the girls deem inappropriate. In this way a girl's story can elicit a promise to confront the offender and thereby spark a dispute that can mobilize the whole neighborhood. Whereas the boys' disputes are localized, the girls' disputes extend over time and can lead to ostracism from the group.

In chapter 6, "Gender, Politeness, and Confrontation in Tenejapa," Penelope Brown examines women's discourse in a court case, the only setting in which the peasant Mayan women among whom she did fieldwork are "authorized" to engage in direct confrontation. The two women involved in the case are the mothers of a bridal couple whose marriage ended when the wife left her new husband to live with another man. The groom's mother seeks to be repaid for the bridal gifts she had given her daughter-in-law, and the bride's mother seeks to avoid payment. The litigants dramatize their confrontation not only by flouting the turn-taking and kinesic rules for courteous interaction but also by exaggerating certain characteristically female forms of polite agreement through conventionalized irony, thereby transforming it into sarcastic agreement. In other words, linguistic forms associated with women's speech in contexts of cooperation and agreement are here used to express conflict, hostility, and disagreement. Brown argues that women can breach Tenejapan norms of polite behavior in this context because such public confrontation is a means of reestablishing one's public self-image or "face." Brown ends by discussing the nature of relations between language and gender. She argues that gender is, in a sense, a "master status" in Tenejapan society, but that the "relations between language and gender are context dependent." She therefore calls for research examining situation-specific speech events—a call that is answered in part, one might add, by this volume.

The theoretical discussion with which Brown concludes her chapter leads directly into Part III, "The Relativity of Discourse Strategies." This section reinforces one of the major tenets of the ethnographic approach: that linguistic forms must be examined in interactive context. The two chapters in Part III demonstrate that specific linguistic strategies cannot be aligned with specific interactional meanings. Rather, meaning varies with context in the broadest sense.

Chapter 7 is my own essay, "The Relativity of Linguistic Strategies: Power and Solidarity in Gender and Dominance." I demonstrate that the theoretical framework of power and solidarity is essential for understanding gender patterns in language use, and that gender and language is a fruitful site for investigating the dynamics underlying language choice, including such dimensions as power and solidarity. I use this framework to show that gender and language research cannot be approached as the mechanical search for specific linguistic devices. Analyzing examples from conversation as well as literary creations of conversations, I argue that each of the linguistic devices that have been claimed to show dominance can also show solidarity. For example, one can talk while another is talking in order to wrest the floor; this can be seen as a move motivated by power. Yet one can also talk along with another in order to show support and agreement; this must be seen as a move motivated by solidarity. The two, however, are not mutually exclusive. If both speakers are engaged in a ritual struggle for the floor, they might experience the entire conversation as a pleasurable one: an exercise of solidarity on the metalevel. My purpose, then, is not to question that particular linguistic devices, such as interruption, may be used to create dominance, but rather to argue that intention and effect may not be synonymous and that there is never a one-to-one relationship between any linguistic device and an interactive effect.

Chapter 8 is a very slightly revised version of a paper that has become a classic, Carole Edelsky's "Who's Got the Floor?" This chapter demonstrates that gendered patterns of interaction must be distinguished not only by speech event but by types of floor within a given event. Edelsky taped five complete meetings of a standing faculty committee composed of seven women (including herself) and four men. Although she initially set out to compare the women's and men's verbal behavior, she realized that she had to tackle a number of methodological and theoretical questions before she could address gender differences. Her focus therefore shifted to the nature of conversational turns and floors. Edelsky identified two types of floor: a singly developed floor in which one speaker holds forth while others listen or respond, and a collaborative floor in which several people seem to be either "operating on the same wavelength or engaging in a free-for-all." Gender differences could only be described in terms of these differing floors: Men took more and longer turns and did more of the joking, arguing, directing, and soliciting of responses during the singly developed floors; in the collaborative floors women and men talked equally, and women joked, argued, directed, and solicited responses more than men. Edelsky notes, however, that the women did not talk more during collaborative floors; rather, the men talked less. Finally she concludes that rather than asking how women and men use language to enact their different positions with respect to power, research must ask "*under what conditions* do men and women interact . . . more or less as equals and under what conditions do they not?" The implications of Edelsky's study are enormous and, despite the frequency with which it is cited, have not yet been adequately dealt with by researchers.

An insight that emerges from Edelsky's study as well as mine is that overlapping talk is not always uncooperative. Although it may be disruptive in singly developed floors, it is a constructive and indeed constitutive characteristic of collaborative floors. The phenomenon of overlapping talk is the focus of the first chapter in Part IV.

Part IV consists of two chapters that present critical reviews of the literature on two topics central to research on gender and language use: the questions of interruption and of who talks more. One of the most frequently cited claims in the literature is that men dominate women by interrupting them in conversation and by taking up more speaking time. In chapter 9, "Women, Men, and Interruptions: A Critical Review," Deborah James and Sandra Clarke tackle the question of whether it is true that men produce more interruptions than women in cross-sex—or same-sex—conversation. They find that of fifty-four studies, the great majority have, in fact, found women and men not to differ in number of interruptions. However, they point out that the research on interruptions has been seriously flawed by faulty assumptions (in particular, a failure to appreciate the extent to which simultaneous talk can function to show solidarity) and faulty methodology (studies have differed significantly in how interruptions were measured, have often used unreliable measures of interruption, and have taken insufficient account of a number of variables). They survey potential ways of determining whether men produce more specifically dominance-related interruptions than women, noting that no clear results emerge from the overall research based on any of these criteria. However, none of these criteria are entirely reliable. The authors suggest that to resolve this issue simultaneous talk must be examined in the framework of conversational analysis that takes into detailed account the larger context in which the simultaneous talk occurs. James and Clarke also note that some evidence does exist to suggest that women are more likely to produce cooperative overlapping talk than men—at least in all-female interaction.

In chapter 10, "Understanding Gender Differences in Amount of Talk: A Critical Review of Research," Deborah James and Janice Drakich examine the question of whether women or men talk more. The cultural stereotype holds that women are compulsive talkers who never let a man get a word in edgewise; however, as has been widely reported in the language and gender literature, most studies have found that men talk more. In their review of fifty-six studies, James and Drakich point out that there has nevertheless been considerable inconsistency in the research findings. While noting some methodological problems with the research similar to those outlined in chapter 9, they also propose that neither the "dominance" approach nor the "cultural" approach, considered separately, is adequate to account for the range of results with respect to amount of talk;

they argue that the best explanation is one which takes into account the overall social structure of the interaction, as informed by the difference in status between the genders and the differential cultural expectations about women's and men's abilities and areas of competence. As the social structure of the interaction changes, so do expectations and, consequently, women's and men's behavior with respect to amount of talk. Here James and Drakich adopt the approach of status characteristics theory (Berger, Fizek, Norman and Zelditch 1977). Both chapters 9 and 10 show that far more theoretical and methodological sophistication is required before key questions in language and gender can be answered.

It is the goal of this volume to contribute to such theoretical and methodological development. The strength of the interactional sociolinguistic or ethnographically oriented discourse analytic approaches is twofold: its focus on discourse as produced in interaction and its attention to context in the deepest sense. This volume provides a rich source of insight into studies that examine gender and language in interactional context. It points the way for a future generation of studies that will be based on more sophisticated understanding of how language works in conversational interaction; that will be sensitive to context in the broadest sense and will look at language holistically rather than as a bundle of isolated variables; that will take into account research done in a range of cultural settings; and that, ultimately, will broaden and deepen our understanding of gender, of language, and of the interaction between them.

NOTES

1. Edelsky cites a number of key papers discussing transcription. For recent discussions of the theoretical implications of transcription, see Edwards (1990) and Preston (1982, 1985).

2. This chapter, as well as the chapters by Sheldon, Goodwin, and Brown, were originally published in a special issue of *Discourse Processes,* which I guest-edited, entitled *Gender and Conversational Interaction* (13:1 [January–March 1990]). In summarizing these chapters, I have drawn heavily on the abstracts that preceded these articles in that journal.

REFERENCES

Aries, Elizabeth (1987). Gender and communication. In Phillip Shaver and Clyde Hendrick (Eds.) *Sex and Gender* (pp. 149–176). Newbury Park, CA: Sage.

Baron, Dennis (1986). *Grammar and gender.* New Haven, CT: Yale University Press.

Brown, Penelope (1979). Language, interaction and sex roles in a Mayan community. Ph.D. diss., University of California, Berkeley.

Coates, Jennifer (1986). *Women, men, and language.* New York: Longman.

Coates, Jennifer, & Cameron, Deborah (Eds.) (1988). *Women in their speech communities: New perspectives on language and sex.* London and New York: Longman.

Dubois, Betty Lou & Crouch, Isabel (Eds.) (1976). *The sociology of the languages of American women*. San Antonio, TX: Linguistics Dept., Trinity University.

Eckert, Penelope, & McConnell-Ginet, Sally (1992). Think practically and look locally: Language and gender as community-based practice. *Annual Review of Anthropology* 21:461–490.

Edwards, Jane (1990). Transcription in discourse. In *Oxford international encyclopedia of linguistics* (vol. 1, pp. 367–370). Oxford and New York: Oxford University Press.

Gal, Susan (1991). Between speech and silence: The problematics of research on language and gender. In Micaela DiLeonardo (Ed.), *Gender at the crossroads of knowledge: Feminist anthropology in the postmodern era* (pp. 175–203). Berkeley: University of California Press.

Goodwin, Marjorie Harness (1978). Conversational practices in a peer group of urban black children. Ph.D. diss., University of Pennsylvania.

Graddol, David, & Swann, Joan (1989). *Gender voices*. Oxford: Basil Blackwell.

Haas, Mary R (1944). Men's and women's speech in Koasati. *Language* 20:142–149.

Hill, Alette Olin (1986). *Mother tongue, father time: A decade of linguistic revolt*. Bloomington: Indiana University Press.

Key, Mary Ritchie (1975). *Male/female language: With a comprehensive bibliography*. Metuchen, NJ: The Scarecrow Press.

Kramarae, Cheris (1981). *Women and men speaking*. Rowley, MA: Newbury House.

Lakoff, Robin (1975). *Language and woman's place*. New York: Harper and Row.

Maltz, Daniel N. & Borker, Ruth A. (1982). A cultural approach to male-female miscommunication. In John J. Gumperz (Ed.) *Language and social identity* (pp. 196–216). Cambridge: Cambridge University Press.

McConnell-Ginet, Sally, Borker, Ruth, & Furman, Nelly (Eds.) (1980). *Women and language in literature and society*. New York: Praeger.

McConnell-Ginet, Sally (1988). Language and gender. In Frederick J. Newmeyer (Ed.) *Cambridge survey of linguistics* (vol. 4, pp. 75–99). Cambridge: Cambridge University Press.

Philips, Susan U (1980). Sex differences and language. *Annual Review of Anthropology* 9:523–544.

Philips, Susan U., Steele, Susan, & Tanz, Christine (Eds.) (1988). *Language, gender and sex in comparative perspective*. Cambridge: Cambridge University Press.

Preisler, Brent (1986). *Linguistic sex roles in conversation*. Berlin: Mouton de Gruyter.

Preston, Dennis R. (1982). 'Ritin fowklower daun 'rong: Folklorists' failures in phonology. *Journal of American Folklore* 95:304–326.

Preston, Dennis R. (1985). The Li'l Abner syndrome: Written representations of speech. *American Speech* 60:328–336.

Sapir, Edward (1929). Male and female forms of speech in Yana. In St. Wl. J. Teeuwen (Ed.) *Donum Natalicium Schrijnen* (pp. 79–85). Nijmegen-Utrecht. Reprinted in David Mandelbaum (Ed.) *Selected writings of Edward Sapir in language, culture, and personality* (pp. 206–213). Berkeley: University of California Press.

Smith, Philip M. (1979). Sex markers in speech. In Klaus Scherer & Howard Giles

(Eds.) *Social markers in speech* (pp. 109–146). Cambridge: Cambridge University Press.

Smith, Philip M. (1985). *Language, the sexes and society*. Oxford: Basil Blackwell.

Tannen, Deborah (1990). *You just don't understand: Women and men in conversation*. New York: Ballantine.

Thorne, Barrie, & Henley, Nancy (Eds.) (1975). *Language and sex: Difference and dominance*. Rowley, MA: Newbury House.

Thorne, Barrie, Kramarae, Cheris, & Henley, Nancy (Eds.) (1983). *Language, gender and society*. Rowley, MA: Newbury House.

Todd, Alexandra Dundas & Fisher, Sue (Eds.) (1988). *Gender and discourse: The power of talk*. Norwood, NJ: Ablex.

West, Candace & Zimmerman, Don H. (1985). Gender, language, and discourse. In Teun A. van Dijk (Ed.) *Handbook of discourse analysis* (vol. 4, pp. 103–124). London: Academic Press.

I
TALKING
AMONG
FRIENDS

1

"Go Get Ya a French!": Romantic and Sexual Teasing Among Adolescent Girls

DONNA EDER

There is no doubt that female-male relationships are of considerable significance to many adolescent females. During early adolescence many girls are becoming increasingly concerned with relationships with boys, often leading to conflicts with other girls (Schofield 1982). In later adolescence a focus on romance and femininity is particularly important for white working-class girls, who often base their rejection of academic values on this counterculture (McRobbie 1978, Kesseler et al. 1985, Griffen 1985).

Adolescence is also a time when humorous, playful activities are an essential part of peer culture (Willis 1977, Fine 1981, Everhart 1983, Griffen 1985). Through play children transform the familiar into something novel and create their own culture (Schwartzman 1978, Corsaro 1985). While this culture is based on the old culture, it has a freshness and uniqueness about it stemming largely from its playful nature. Thus, when adolescents playfully tease each other about female-male relationships, we find that it results in considerable transformation of traditional gender roles.

Teasing encompasses a broad range of playful interactions. Here teasing will be defined as any playful remark aimed at another person, which can include mock challenges, commands, and threats as well as imitating and exaggerating someone's behavior in a playful way. While the content of teasing would often be negative or hostile if taken literally, the playful meaning is determined in part by cues from the teaser indicating that the remark should be taken in a playful manner. These usually take the form of

17

metacommunication, because to be indirect is an inherent part of the playful nature of this activity. However, it is also possible for the target to respond in a playful manner to a comment that may have been meant to be quite serious and thereby keep the activity in a playful mode (Eder 1991).

Although teasing is an extremely common activity among children it has not been a frequent topic of research. In fact most of the sociolinguistic research on teasing has focused on adult-child interaction, where teasing has been found to serve a variety of social functions. For example, in cultures that are egalitarian teasing has been found to be a way to teach social norms and is often preferred to more authoritarian methods (Schieffelin 1986). It is also seen as a way to enhance solidarity and strengthen social bonds through the shared enjoyment that participants experience (Eisenberg 1986). Some working-class parents view teasing as a way to teach children how to defend themselves and control their hurt feelings (Heath 1983, Miller 1986). Miller (1986) also found that teasing activities teach children how to play with language and develop creative and novel responses. Finally a sociolinguistic study of teasing among adults found that teasing was often a mild and indirect type of reproof for overserious behavior such as bragging, complaining, and extolling (Drew 1987).

The few studies of teasing among children have been primarily ethnographic in nature. They have found that teasing is often an important means for initiating cross-sex interaction. Because of its ambiguous nature teasing is a safe way to communicate liking without being held accountable for one's feelings (Schofield 1982, Oswald et al. 1987). At the same time romantic teasing has also been found to be a technique for maintaining gender boundaries (Schofield 1982, Thorne 1985). Children will often tease other children for talking with or sitting next to someone of the other sex, implying there is a romantic attraction. As a result males and females often have limited contact with each other during the elementary and middle school years.

While these studies suggest that teasing is a common activity among adolescents with considerable significance for female-male relationships, it is difficult to analyze this complex activity relying solely on ethnographic methods. This study investigates romantic and sexual teasing activities among early adolescents using a combined ethnographic and sociolinguistic approach. When teasing is closely examined we see how it is used to accomplish multiple peer objectives, such as strengthening female friendships, communicating liking to males, and experimenting with gender roles. In the process we develop a better understanding of how adolescent females deal with jealousy and the tension it creates among group members. We also develop a better understanding of the way adolescent girls view traditional feminine and romantic behavior and of the socialization process in general.

An Ethnographic and Sociolinguistic Approach

This chapter reports on several findings of a larger study of adolescent peer relations and culture in a middle school setting (Eder 1985). Three female researchers observed peer group interaction during lunch periods and other informal school activities over a three-year period. The students in the groups we observed were between ten and fourteen years old and came from a variety of social backgrounds, ranging from middle-class to lower-class. While two of the groups included a black female, the rest of the students were white. Once rapport was established, we audiotaped approximately eight lunchtime conversations in each of the eight groups that we studied and videotaped three additional conversations in one of the groups. Altogether we have recorded data on fifty-nine students.

Because we did not want to be associated with adults in the school, we did not ask them to introduce us to students. Instead we started attending athletic practices and going to lunch, where we eventually found a range of peer groups to join. We purposely tried to sit with groups from a range of social backgrounds and status levels within the school. We also thought it was essential to spend a considerable amount of time with the peer groups to establish good rapport. After several weeks in the setting the students realized that we were not taking on adult authority roles and they began to swear openly in front of us and also to tell their friends that we were "okay." By the time we introduced recording equipment in the field they were very comfortable with our presence and when assured that no one they knew would hear their voices, they felt free to swear and talk naturally while the recorder was on.

There are a number of reasons for combining ethnographic and sociolinguistic methods. Through ethnography the most salient issues and activities of a group are allowed to emerge rather than be defined prematurely. The less structured nature of this approach allows the researcher to see more spontaneous behavior as well as ways in which participants actively construct their own culture. In addition, the more detailed language analysis can draw on a larger context in determining the meaning and significance of specific comments. Because this is what we naturally do in our conversations, this approach makes the sociolinguistic analysis more valid (Corsaro 1985).

Having a sociolinguistic analysis was also essential given the complexity of informal talk. While field notes are useful for identifying general patterns of speech activities, they do not allow one to identify more detailed patterns. Because teasing is a complex activity, it requires a detailed analysis to show how it is used to construct peer relations as well as peer knowledge. For example, we will see that teasing is a highly collaborative activity, where one person's talk often builds directly on previous talk. This is impossible to study without a detailed record of the talk. This detailed level of analysis often reveals more clearly the way in which peer culture is actively constructed and can add to our current understanding of adolescent culture.

Teasing About Romantic and Sexual Behavior

Teasing was a common activity among these adolescent girls. Overall the most common topics for teasing were female-male relationships, sexuality, and appearance. Other topics included female friendships, being "stuck-up," being "dumb," and speech styles. This chapter will focus only on teasing about female-male relationships and sexuality. These topics were especially popular in the groups of girls who interacted with males, which included six of the ten groups that we studied.

Interaction with males took a variety of forms in these six groups. Two of the eighth grade groups included several males who sat with the groups on a regular basis and had relatively long-term relationships with some of the girls, perhaps "going with" them for several months at a time. These groups also included several friends of each of the couples, some of whom went together for short periods.

In another pattern a single male sat with a female group for a shorter time. Usually he was currently "going with" one of the girls, had previously gone with one of them, or was interested in going with someone in the group. Occasionally a younger boy would sit with a group of females and while romantic teasing often occurred, it did not necessarily result in a romantic relationship.

In still another pattern boys stopped by and talked briefly with group members during the lunch period. These might be boys whom group members currently liked or were "going with." In other cases they were friends of boys who liked someone in the group or were contacts to boys whom some of the girls liked. This pattern was most common in seventh grade groups.

The term "going together" was widely used to describe a variety of female-male relationships in this school. In some cases the couples spent a lot of time together at school and the relationships were relatively long-term, lasting up to several months. This was quite rare, however, and group members were impressed by relationships that lasted as long as three weeks, considering that to be a long time to "go with" someone. Most of these relationships were quite brief, lasting from one day to two weeks. Some involved minimal or no contact between the couple, who had simply informed their best friends they were willing to go with each other and then left it to them to initiate the relationship. In one case, when asked about the last name of his girlfriend, a boy said, "I don't know but I'm going to find out." This comment indicates the relatively nonserious nature of many of these involvements.

In contrast to the instability of female-male relationships at this age, female relationships were much more stable and in many respects more central to females' overall self-esteem. Girls attached considerable significance to their popularity with other females (Eder 1985) and were very concerned about having a best friendship with another girl. They were also concerned about maintaining strong bonds within their female friendship groups. While one of the things which helped unite some of the groups was their common interest in boys, it is important to keep in mind that this interest in boys did not replace the strong interest in female friendships.

In general teasing is an important activity for strengthening female friendships in most of the groups we studied. As mentioned earlier, teasing can be an indirect way of expressing positive affect and through the experience of shared humor and the enjoyment of that humor can increase positive feelings among group members. Because of the common interest in boys in many of these groups, teasing about boys was an activity in which many groups members were likely to engage. In some cases girls who were fringe members of the group would initiate teasing activities as a way to enhance their solidarity with the group. This occurred in the first example,[1] where a group of seventh graders tease Mary about a boy she likes. Elaine, who is a fringe member of the group, begins the teasing activity by hinting at an activity in which Mary has been engaged, leaving it to Linda and Carol to supply the details.

Example One: Seventh Grade

1	Elaine:	You should have seen what Mary's been doing.
2	Mary:	Shut up.
3	Elaine:	Carol you should've been seen what Linda, see what Mary's been doing.
4	Linda:	Aw, she's been in the <u>stairwell</u>. Haven't // you Mary?
5	Mary:	I have <u>not</u>!
6	Carol:	She's been watching Wally's butt go up and down.
7	Nancy:	God. ((laughs))
8	Mary:	Uh. Oh you guys.
9	Linda:	Haven't you Mary?
10	Mary:	<u>Noooo</u>! //
11	Linda:	<u>Yes</u>

Teasing typically has many of the features shown here. Usually more than one group member joins in on the teasing activity, often expanding on it. While Elaine's initial comments hint at a potentially interesting activity, Linda supplies some of the details, saying, "Aw, she's been in the stairwell," and Carol expands further, saying, "She's been watching Wally's butt go up and down." As a result, all three girls share the enjoyment of teasing Mary, increasing the group solidarity.

In order for a teasing activity to remain playful the target of the teasing needs to respond in some nonserious manner. This can include an exaggerated denial or some other exaggerated response, such as extreme surprise.

It can also include joining in on the teasing by mocking one's self in some manner. Here Mary's response is one of exaggerated denial, shouting "I have *not!*" A little later her denial is somewhat less extreme. At this point Linda questions her again, saying, "Haven't you Mary?" to which Mary gives a more exaggerated response, shouting, "Nooo!" It appears that Linda wants to be sure that Mary is treating their comments in a playful way as that allows Mary also to participate in the shared enjoyment, and thus the increased solidarity.

In the next example the teasing also is clearly aimed at strengthening group solidarity. Prior to the teasing Marsha, Barbie, and Annie have all been staring at Ginny and trying to make her uncomfortable. They apparently are no longer interested in having Ginny in their group. However, Ginny chooses to stay and switches to a teasing activity which at least temporarily produces a high degree of solidarity among the group members. The teasing begins when Ginny pretends that Annie is alone with her boyfriend with a tape recorder on. Barbie and Marsha quickly join in and, much later, Annie does as well.

Example Two: Seventh Grade

1	Ginny:	You know what you guys are gonna say # Oh Bob # Annie # ( ) tape record (you're gonna listen to it) and say "Oh Bob it feels so good. ((laughter))
2	Annie:	// You ain't gonna hear that cause I ain't doin' nothin'.
3	Barbie:	( ) deeper! ((laughter))
4	Ginny:	Little bit higher Barbie # ( ) little bit higher # ( ) little bit higher.
5	Annie:	((loud groan))
6	Barbie:	What can I do?! Are we doin' it yet?! Uh # spread your legs a little more and ( ).
7	Marsha:	((makes a kind of sign to B)) Forever! ((a popular novel written for adolescents))
8	Barbie:	In and out # Forever!
9	Ginny:	Insert # outsert. (She goes - Annie.)
10	( ):	(In out in out.)
11	Annie:	( ) If she seems to be cryin' it's a moment of joy! ((laughter))

Annie's initial response to the teasing is a somewhat serious denial as well as groaning. It appears that the high level of sexual desire implied is embarrassing to her and prevents her from treating the teasing lightly. However, the teasing moves from making fun of male sexual incompetence to mocking the romantic view of sexual behavior by bringing up the title of a very popular romantic novel, *Forever,* which is then juxtaposed with the mechanical phrases "in and out" and "insert outsert." Now that the topic has switched from personal sexual feelings to a more impersonal topic, Annie gets over her embarrassment and joins in with a phrase that also makes fun of the romantic portrayal of sexual experience, saying, "If she seems to be cryin' it's a moment of joy!" As a result all of the girls are now united through their shared enjoyment of this activity.

This example shows one of the limits to successful female-male teasing, namely, intense embarrassment as the result of making sexual desire too explicit. It also shows how teasing allows girls to play with and transform traditional gender role concepts. Here they transform the traditional view of males as sexually competent as well as the traditional feminine view of sexuality as one based heavily in romance. By mocking both of these through their teasing play they signal both their knowledge of these traditional views and their current ability to detach themselves from them. Thus, teasing activities demonstrate both their awareness of traditional views and the areas which they currently feel free to make light of and detach themselves from.

Another aspect of female-male teasing which can limit the ability of the target to participate in a playful manner involves revealing her liking for a boy in his presence. Thus different norms apply to teasing when a boy is present as compared to when he's not. In the next example, which involves some of the same girls as the previous example, Marsha is teasing Annie about her current boyfriend, Wade, who is near the group. Later he joins the group and Josephine teases Barbie about still liking him in his presence.

Example Three: Seventh Grade

1	Marsha:	Go get ya a French!
2	Annie:	((pretends to push chair away)) Be back # no ((laughter))
3	Barbie:	He probably wouldn't.
4	Annie:	Yes he would
5	Barbie:	(Not) in the stairwell
6	Annie:	He did last night
7	Barbie:	Not in the stairwell
8	Josie:	Wade Wade # French her.
9	Wade:	No!
10	Annie:	She wants one ((referring to Josie))
11	Josie:	Nuh uh! Barbie does # Barbie wants to go back with you.
12	Barbie:	I do not.
13	Marsha:	Josie! # Don't man.

Marsha's initial comment detaches from traditional gender roles by transforming them when she casts Annie in the role of sexual initiator. "French" refers to a French kiss, a more sexual kiss involving the tongue. By telling Annie to go get such a kiss, Marsha is implying that she should seek out a sexual encounter. Annie plays along with the teasing by pretending to take

Marsha's advice and go look for Wade. After a serious debate on the actual nature of their sexual activity Annie's boyfriend comes closer to the group. When Josie begins to tease him, saying, "Wade Wade French her," Annie turns the teasing back on Josie by saying, "She [Josie] wants one." Josie gives an exaggerated denial and claims that Barbie wants one. She also adds, "Barbie wants to go back with you." This comment produces not only a serious denial from Barbie but also a strong sanction from Marsha, indicating how inappropriate it was. Not only is it embarrassing to have one's attraction revealed directly to a boy but since Wade is now Annie's boyfriend and may no longer like Barbie, it is even more embarrassing. Again we can see that while these adolescent girls can make light of traditional views regarding who initiates sexual behavior, they find it much more difficult to make light of their own current feelings of attraction toward certain boys.

Dealing with Multiple Social Concerns Through Teasing

Another interesting aspect of female-male relations was a tendency for several girls in a group to like the same boy. At first this was regarded as normal, similar to all liking the same girl or activity, and brought them even closer together. However, problems began to arise as they began to experience jealousy if another girl "flirted" with their boyfriend or if a boy they still liked began to show interest in one of their friends. These new feelings of jealousy became a source of tension and a threat to the solidarity of female friendships in some of the groups.

By the eighth grade jealousy had become an issue for some of the girls. This issue was most salient when a male spent time with the group and became the target of playful teasing. As mentioned earlier, teasing a boy can be a way to communicate affection indirectly. However, when teasing was used to communicate attraction to a boy it occasionally brought out underlying feelings of jealousy. Thus by eighth grade teasing is often a complex activity reflecting multiple peer concerns.

Given the complexity of teasing among eighth graders I will concentrate on one series of teasing episodes in one of the eighth grade groups. Three of the girls in this group, Natalie, Ellen, and Gwen, have been friends for several years and have very strong friendship bonds at this point. The other two girls, Pam and Allison, have been part of this group for much of the year. Jimmy has been sitting with this group quite often over the past few weeks and is the recipient of considerable teasing attention on this day.

Two weeks ago Natalie and Jimmy went together for two days (which Natalie reports is the shortest time she's ever gone with someone). When they broke up, Jimmy told Natalie that he liked her and wanted to go with her again but that he had some things he had to straighten out first. Natalie claims that Allison tried to take Jimmy away from her and that this is something which she always does. According to Natalie, Allison is not sincere when she does this and "has hurt about fifty boys this year," including the twenty boys that she liked. Allison does have another boyfriend at this point and has been warned by Natalie to "cool it" with Jimmy although he still continues to give her a lot of attention.

While Natalie is mainly jealous of Jimmy's attention to Allison, during these teasing episodes Pam and Gwen are giving Jimmy a lot of attention. Jimmy is sitting at the head of the table and Pam and Gwen are at either side of him so they are physically situated to have the most playful physical contact with him. Natalie and Ellen are seated in the middle of either side and Allison is at the far end of the table.

The first teasing episode is initiated by Natalie and targeted at Gwen. Gwen has just noticed a boy she knows walking past the table and gets his attention by saying "Oh Ted!" with a slight lilt in her voice. Natalie picks up on her intonation and mocks her by imitating her phrase, "Oh Ted," with a much higher and more flirtatious tone of voice. Immediately after that the other three girls begin imitating her phrase, using the same high tone of voice.

Example Four: Eighth Grade

1	Gwen:	Oh Ted! When do we have to have our pictures turned in?
2	Natalie:	Oh Ted! ((speaks in high, mocking, flirtatious tone, then giggles))
3	Pam:	[Oh Ted! ((same tone))
4	Ellen:	[Oh Ted! ((same tone))
5	Rhoda:	Ted. ((same tone))
6	( ):	Ted. ((same tone))
7	Jimmy:	Ted. ((same tone, putting a hand lightly on Gwen's shoulder))
8	Gwen:	Ohh Jimmy. ((touching Jimmy's arm, and mocking back))
9	Natalie:	((to Gwen, leaning across table and tapping her on arm)) You're not supposed to go, "Oh Jimmy"; you're supposed to go, "Ohhh, Jim!" ((gives words a more blatantly sexual emphasis. Leans back, claps hands together, and laughs giddily. Everyone else is laughing, too.))
10	Jimmy:	Oh man.
11	(Ellen):	That is
12	Jimmy:	ridiculous. ((poking Gwen under table))
13	Gwen:	Eek! ((slaps Jim on arm))
14	Natalie:	Sorry. ((still giggling))

This episode provides another example of females making fun of traditional feminine behavior, in this case the use of flirtatious behavior to get male attention. When Gwen participates, she uses the same high flirtatious tone that Natalie began mocking, thus making fun of herself along with traditional norms about feminine behavior. By making Jimmy the new target of the teasing, she also gives positive attention to Jimmy while increasing the general solidarity stemming from the mutual enjoyment of the activity.

However, by directing positive attention toward Jimmy, Gwen also appears to have set off Natalie's underlying feelings of jealousy as Natalie then escalates the teasing by saying, "You're not supposed to go, 'Oh Jimmy'; you're supposed to go, 'Ohhh, *Jim!*,'" with a strong sexual emphasis on the word "Jim." As in the second example this implies that Gwen has strong sexual feelings, and this is something which is embarrassing to these adolescents. It is clear to everyone that Natalie has taken the teasing too far. Jimmy and Gwen respond by saying, "Oh man. That is ridiculous," and Natalie apologizes. It appears that Natalie realizes that she was inappropriate in her behavior, and, in fact, it is likely that she purposely tried to end the teasing episode by taking the teasing too far. However, Jimmy immediately resumes a more playful manner by poking Gwen under the table, leading her to shout, "eek!" and playfully slap him back.

Shortly after this episode Pam and Gwen begin teasing Jimmy in a playful way with verbal comments as well as physical actions. Pam begins by telling Jimmy his hair is messed up and needs to be combed as she reaches over and playfully messes up his hair. When Jimmy pretends to leave, Gwen and Pam start a mock battle over Jimmy, pulling on him from both sides and ordering him to stay. Natalie again tries to end the teasing episode by making a serious command.

Example Five: Eighth Grade

1	Pam:	((to Jimmy)) Your hair's messed up. Gotta comb it. ((Tricia messes up Jimmy's hair with hand. Jimmy moves as if to leave))
2	Gwen:	Stay here, Jim. ((Jimmy and Pam begin to wrestle playfully))
3	Pam:	No! Stay here. ((laughing; both Pam and Gwen are pulling on Jimmy))
4	Natalie:	((to Gwen and Pam)) Leave his hair alone. // It's not your property. It's not mine either.
5	Jimmy:	((to Pam)) I've been insulted. I gotta go. I've been insulted. ((Jimmy is smiling, looking at Pam, and is waving his arms around as though trying to keep the girls away))
6	Gwen:	((grins at Natalie and then reaches under table and tickles Jimmy on thigh)) It's mine! ((laughing))
7	Jimmy:	Oh ho-ho.
8	Natalie:	I said it wasn't mine.
9	Gwen:	[It's my property. ((reaching out and touching Jimmy))
10	Pam:	[It's mine. ((Gwen pulls Jimmy's chair a little toward her and then puts hand on Jimmy's shoulder and pushes him to floor))
11	Jimmy:	((to Pam)) She made me sit on the floor. ((Jimmy gets up off floor and walks away.))

12	Gwen:	Jim, if you don't get up here ((pointing to chair he was sitting in)) I'll have someone kiss you // ( )
13	Natalie:	((whispering, in response to Gwen's comment)) I will.
14	Rhoda:	((to Jimmy)) Natalie will!

Even though Natalie tries to end the teasing by telling her friends that Jimmy is not their property, they resume their playful teasing by arguing playfully about whose property he is. Gwen then pushes Jimmy to the floor and he playfully responds by telling Pam, "She made me sit on the floor." When Jimmy leaves the group, Gwen starts a new teasing activity by threatening Jimmy with romantic behavior. However, instead of saying, "I'll kiss you," she says, "I'll have someone kiss you" to which Natalie adds, "I will." Gwen's wording supports the collective approach to teasing and may be Gwen's way of keeping the focus on the use of teasing to reinforce group solidarity. It is even possible that she is sensitive to Natalie's underlying jealousy and is trying to reinforce their collective playful pursuit of Jimmy as well to minimize the tension which Natalie's jealousy has created in this group.

Throughout these episodes we can see how these girls use teasing both to mock traditional female behavior and to experiment with nontraditional gender role behavior. By making fun of the use of a high, flirtatious tone to attract the attention of a male, these girls are showing their awareness of this traditional view of feminine behavior while also demonstrating their ability to detach from it and treat it lightly. In this episode the females continually engage in physically and verbally assertive behavior, pushing Jimmy around and verbally ordering him to stay put (see turns 1–3). By engaging in these less traditional feminine actions they are mocking traditional gender behavior while giving positive attention to Jimmy. These girls also transform the concept of ownership to one in which males are the property of females instead of vice versa (see turns 6–10). Finally, it is also possible that they are mocking the traditional notion that females are always competing for males, by pretending to be physically fighting over Jimmy. This is especially interesting because there is also real competition for Jimmy's attention in this group. However, some of the girls seem to be able to detach from and mock their own competitive behavior. There is some support for this interpretation of detachment on the part of Gwen because it seems unlikely that she would openly include others in her romantic threat toward Jimmy if she felt strongly competitive toward her friends. On the other hand, there is no evidence that Natalie is able to detach from her own competitive and jealous feelings at this point.

Shortly after this episode Gwen initiates another collective teasing episode. Jimmy has still not returned to the group, so Gwen first commands him to return and then threatens to start crying. After a complaint by Allison, Natalie joins in by pretending to whine as a way of getting Jimmy to comply. Finally Gwen joins in by ordering him and then giving him a sexual threat.

Example Six: Eighth Grade

1	Gwen:	((to Jim)) Get over here! ((puts fist on table for emphasis)) # I'll start to cryin'.
2	Rhoda:	((softly and urgently)) Gwen, would ya shut-up, you're getting us in trouble. Just // ( ) because of you.
3	Natalie:	((to Jimmy)) Come o'er here and sit down # Ple-e-ease. ((whining)) ((At this point all of the girls are looking in Jimmy's direction.))
4	(Rhoda):	Jim.
5	Ellen:	Jim, c'mere or I'll do some//thing. ((Gwen is tapping loudly on table with a pencil.))
6	( ):	Nothing
7	Natalie:	Please sit // down. ((spoken in higher intonation)) ((Jimmy walks back over.))
8	Ellen:	I'll ruin your family life. ((Jimmy sits down.))
9	Jimmy:	Oh! ((laughs with others))

In this episode the three closest friends in this group succeed in using teasing to deal with multiple peer concerns simultaneously. To begin with, all three girls communicate their liking of Jimmy by making him the target of their playful teasing. At the same time by participating in a shared enjoyable activity they reinforce their own friendship bonds. Finally all of their comments show some detachment from traditional gender roles, either mocking traditional feminine behavior such as crying and whining to get one's way (see turns 1 and 3) or reversing gender roles with females being sexually aggressive (see turn 8). Thus, at this moment these girls are able to express their common interest in boys while also maintaining their shared friendships for each other. One reason this may be successful at this point is that Gwen has been actively making teasing a collaborative activity, thereby showing Natalie that female friendship is a greater concern for her than competing for Jimmy's attention. It is likely that this has helped reduce Natalie's own feelings of jealousy and competition, allowing her to participate in a teasing episode even when it involves all three girls directing positive attention at Jimmy.

In summary, because teasing reflects a variety of peer concerns from communicating liking for a boy to reinforcing female solidarity, it was often a relatively complex activity by eighth grade when feelings of jealousy became most strong. Sometimes this resulted in conscious attempts to end a teasing episode if one girl became too jealous when other girls were giving positive attention to a boy through their teasing. However, this might also lead to one of the girls emphasizing the collaborative aspect of teasing as a way to minimize group tension resulting from jealousy. When this occurred, the girls were occasionally able to use teasing simultaneously to communicate affection toward a male and solidarity with each other and to experiment with traditional gender roles.

Discussion

These findings indicate that teasing activities among adolescent females share some of the same social functions previously found in studies of adult-child teasing. As in Eisenberg's (1986) study teasing is a way for females to strengthen social bonds through shared enjoyment. Also, as in Miller's (1986) study teasing gives females an opportunity to play with language and develop creative and novel responses. While this type of teasing is less relevant for teaching social norms, it does allow adolescents to experiment with and explore their own notions of gender roles.

One of the important findings from this analysis is the complex nature of jealousy among adolescent females. The perception of adolescent girls from ethnographic studies is that they are primarily focused on male relationships and often compete and fight with each other over boyfriends. Here it is clear that feelings of jealousy do exist among adolescent girls. However, it is also obvious that female friendships continue to be very important, and that some girls, such as Gwen in the last examples, actively try to defuse jealousy and competitive feelings while reinforcing their already strong female bonds.

Another important finding is the detachment that these girls have from many traditional gender roles. Working-class girls have often been described as rejecting school values through a focus on romance and femininity (McRobbie 1978, Kesseler et al. 1985). These data suggest that this focus is more complex and includes a detachment from traditional views of feminine and romantic behavior. Thus, rather than embracing and internalizing a set of traditional concepts, these girls feel free to use them as a resource for creating their own peer culture and specifically for creating humorous teasing episodes. It is even possible that this shared mocking of traditional gender roles further enhances feelings of solidarity among the females.

These findings provide additional support for a new approach to the study of socialization. As more and more researchers analyze actual episodes of peer interaction, it is becoming increasingly clear that children bring traditional and societal concepts to their activities, but primarily as a resource. Their actual behavior reflects these traditional concepts but frequently goes beyond them to include new and creative transformations (Corsaro 1987, Corsaro and Eder 1990). Through these studies one begins to develop a better sense of Mead's (1934) concept of the "I," or the spontaneous and innovative side of individual's behavior. It is also increasingly clear that while children and adolescents are aware of adult and societal expectations they do not completely determine their behavior.

Less clear are the implications of this research for adult behavior. This partly reflects a move away from the traditional model of socialization. If concepts and values are not being internalized, it is harder to predict the behavior of adults as well as children. Specifically it is unclear what implications these findings have for female-male relationships among adults. At the same time it is apparent that these adolescents are gaining experience in the creative use of language and humor which is likely to have long-term consequences. In other words those girls who develop the ability to play freely with language as adolescents may be more successful at doing this as adults. Likewise they may be more successful at detaching from traditional and societal gender roles through humor and verbal play. However, given the importance of collaboration and especially collaboration with other females, this is more likely to occur when females continue to have the opportunity to associate with other groups of females, either at work or in family gatherings.

NOTES

I would like to thank Cathy Evans and Stephanie Sanford for their help in collecting the data and Cathy Evans and Joyce Owens for transcribing the data. Cathy Evans and Janet Enke provided helpful comments on an earlier draft. An earlier version of this chapter was presented at a conference on Gender Roles Through the Life Span, sponsored by Ball State University, Muncie, Indiana. This research was supported by NIMH Grant No. 36684.

1. All names of people and places have been changed. The following notations are used in the transcripts:

((   )) = nonverbal behavior

(   ) = unclear utterance or unclear identification of speaker, used both when the transcriber has a possible sense of the utterance or identity of the speaker and when no sense of the utterance or speaker's identity can be made

// = point at which next speaker begins talking during someone's turn

[= speakers begin to talk at the same time

= brief pause during an utterance;

——— = louder tone of voice.

REFERENCES

Corsaro, William (1985). *Friendship and peer culture in the early years*. Norwood, NJ: Ablex.

Corsaro, William (1988). Routines in the peer culture of American and Italian nursery school children. *Sociology of Education* 61:1–14.

Corsaro, William & Eder, Donna (1990). Children's peer cultures. *Annual Review of Sociology* 16:197–220.

Drew, Paul (1987). Po-faced receipts of teases. *Linguistics* 25:219–253.

Eder, Donna (1985). The cycle of popularity: Interpersonal relations among female adolescents. *Sociology of Education* 58:154–165.

Eder, Donna (1991). The role of teasing in adolescent peer culture. In Spencer Cahill (Ed.) *Sociological studies of child development*, Vol. 4, pp. 181–197. Greenwich, CT: JAI Press.

Eisenberg, Ann (1986). Teasing: Verbal play in two Mexicano homes. In Bambi Schieffelin & Elinor Ochs (Eds.) *Language socialization across cultures*, pp. 182–197. Cambridge: Cambridge University Press.

Everhart, Robert (1983). *Reading, writing and resistance: Adolescence and law in a junior high school.* Boston: Routledge and Kegan Paul.

Fine, Gary A. (1981). Friends, impression management, and preadolescent behavior. In Steven Asher & John Gottman (Eds.), *The development of children's friendships,* pp. 29–52, Cambridge: Cambridge University Press.

Griffin, Christine (1985). *Typical girls? Young women from school to the job market.* London: Routledge and Kegan Paul.

Heath, Shirley Brice (1983). *Ways with words: Language, life, and work in communities and classrooms.* Cambridge: Cambridge University Press.

Kessler, S., Ashenden, D., Connell, R., & Dowsett, G (1985). Gender relations in secondary schooling. *Sociology of Education* 58:34–47.

McRobbie, Angela (1978). Working-class girls and the culture of femininity. In *Women take issue,* pp. 96–108. London: Hutchinson.

Mead, George Herbert (1934). *Mind, self, and society.* Chicago: University of Chicago Press.

Miller, Peggy (1986). Teasing as language socialization and verbal play in a white working-class community. In Bambi Schieffelin & Elinor Ochs (Eds.) *Language socialization across cultures,* pp. 199–212. Cambridge: Cambridge University Press.

Oswald, Hans, Krappman, Lothar, Chowdhuri, Irene, & von Salisch, Maria (1988). Gaps and bridges: Interactions between girls and boys in elementary school. In Peter Adler & Patti Adler (Eds.) *Sociological Studies of Child Development,* Vol. 2, pp. 204–224. Greenwich, CT: JAI Press.

Schieffelin, Bambi (1986). Teasing and shaming in Kaluli children's interactions. In Bambi Schieffelin & Elinor Ochs (Eds.) *Language socialization across cultures,* pp. 165–181, Cambridge: Cambridge University Press.

Schofield, Janet (1982). *Black and white in school: Trust, tension, or tolerance?* New York: Praeger Publishers.

Schwartzman, Helen (1978). *Transformations: The anthropology of children's play.* New York: Plenum Press.

Thorne, Barrie (1985). Girls and boys together, but mostly apart: Gender arrangements in elementary schools. In Willard W. Hartup and Zick Rubin (Eds.) *Relationships and development.* Hillsdale, NJ: Lawrence Erlbaum Associates.

Willis, Paul (1977). *Learning to labour.* London: Saxon House.

2

Cooperative Competition in Adolescent "Girl Talk"

PENELOPE ECKERT

> I think girls just talk too much, you know, they- they- talk constantly be-
> tween themselves and- about every little thing. Guys, I don't think we talk
> about that much. (*What kinds of things do you talk about?*) Not much.
> Girls ... cars, or parties, you know. I think girls talk about, you know, every
> little relationship, every little thing that's ever happened, you know.

As reflected in the foregoing quotation from an adolescent boy, it is commonly believed that girls and women regularly engage in long and detailed
personal discussions about people, norms, and beliefs and that boys and
men do not. Such speech events are frequently but inaccurately referred to
as gossip sessions. Although they often contain instances of gossip, they
also contain a great deal of other kinds of discussion. For want of a better
name, I will call these events by their alternative popular name, "girl talk."
This paper examines part of a girl talk event involving six adolescent girls,
with a view to uncovering its purpose as a gender-specific speech event
and the verbal means by which it accomplishes its purpose.

The real gender specificity of girl talk or its components is not altogether clear because we lack a systematic ethnographic account of the
verbal repertoires of men and women. As Goodwin (1980) shows, for
instance, gender differences in norms of interaction in one kind of speech
event (in this case norms concerning direct confrontation among black
elementary school girls) might not apply in another. And inasmuch as the
significance of gender is not uniform throughout society, one cannot assume that what holds in one set of observations is true of the society as a

whole. Indeed, gender differences in interaction must be studied within the context of the situations in which they are observed, with an understanding of the significance of those situations to men and women in that cultural group. There is some evidence that middle-class women in our society are more prone than men to pursue personal topics in discussion (Aries 1976). My own observations among adolescents and Wodak's (1981) data on therapeutic interactions show this to be less true for working-class, as compared with middle-class, speakers. Aries (1976) shows that in same-sex groups of college undergraduates, women talk about themselves, their personal feelings, and their relationships, and men engage in competitive conversation comparing knowledge and experience and recounting competitive exploits. There is also some evidence that women are more prone to share the floor than men, at least in same-sex interactions. Aries found a tendency in men's groups for an individual or individuals to gain control and dominate the group in the current and subsequent interactions, whereas the women tended to draw each other out, spreading the talk around. Writers frequently refer to women's conversational style as "cooperative"—women have been found, not only to encourage each other to participate, but also to build on each other's utterances and stories (Jones 1972, Kalčik 1975). However, because this is based primarily on the examination of women's behavior and not systematically compared with men's, the status of these differences remains highly speculative.

One obviously cannot conclude from the available evidence of sex differences in conversation that men do not engage in cooperative personal revelation, or women in impersonal competition. One might, rather, ask what competitive discussion of impersonal topics accomplishes in all-male groups and what personal and cooperative conversation accomplishes in all-female groups. The difference between male and female group dynamics is, I argue, based on differences in gender roles in society as a whole. The following discussion presents an analysis of some key aspects of personal and cooperative conversation among a group of white middle-class teenage girls.

Women and Symbolic Capital

The origins of gender differences in styles of interaction can be traced to the traditional roles that relegate women to the domestic realm and men to the economic marketplace, and although these roles have changed to some extent in our society, the social norms and the norms of interaction that have come to be associated with them remain to complicate and thwart social change. The domestication of female labor involves a strict division of roles, with men engaged in the public marketplace and women restricted to the private, domestic sphere (Sacks 1974). The man competes for goods and power in the marketplace in the name of the family and controls these within the family. Thus, although the woman is solely responsible for maintaining the domestic unit, she has no direct control over that unit's capital. Whereas a man's personal worth is based on accumulation of goods, status, and power in the marketplace, a woman's worth is based on her ability to maintain order in, and control over, her domestic realm. Deprived of power, women can only gain compliance through the indirect use of a man's power or through the development of personal influence.

Women can use men's power indirectly by winning men's cooperation through social manipulation or by borrowing men's status through the display and exploitation of connections with men. It is not, therefore, surprising that women are more concerned with the shape of their social networks, with their connections to people in those networks, and with their ability to understand and influence people. Although it is frequently said that women are more status conscious than men, it would be more accurate to say that they are more status *bound*.

Actual personal influence without power requires moral authority. In other words, women's influence depends primarily on the accumulation of symbolic capital (Bourdieu 1977): on the painstaking creation and elaboration of an image of the whole self as worthy of authority. This is not to say that men are not dependent on the accumulation of symbolic capital but to say that symbolic capital is the *only* kind that women can accumulate with impunity. And indeed, women's symbolic capital becomes part of their men's symbolic capital and, hence, part of the household's economic capital. Men can justify and define their status on the basis of their accomplishments, possessions, or institutional status, but women must justify and define theirs on the basis of their overall character and the kinds of relations they can maintain with others. Women, therefore, unlike men, are frequently obsessed with being the perfect spouse, the perfect parent, the perfect friend.

Whereas men compete for status in the marketplace, women must compete for their domestic status. The "better" woman gets the "better" domestic situation, the better deal in that situation, and ultimately greater access to the goods that men control. However, although the situation is inherently competitive, one cannot overtly compete in the accumulation of symbolic capital, for it is in the nature of symbolic capital that it should not appear to have been consciously accumulated. Because good personhood is supposed to be an inherent property, its possession specifically excludes competitiveness or the need for competition. Norms against women's competitiveness stem from two sources, therefore: Competition in the marketplace violates men's cultural prerogative, and competition in the personal realm contradicts the underlying definition of personal worth.

The marketplace establishes the value of men's capital, but women's symbolic capital must be evaluated in relation to community norms for women's behavior. The establishment and maintenance of these norms require regular monitoring, and, because it is women who must compete in relation to these norms, it is they who have the greatest interest in this monitoring. To the extent that they can control norms, women can increase their competitive edge. Girl talk, I will argue, is the major means by which they do this. Although it is certainly reasonable to assume, as is generally done, that this activity of women's is a conservative force, particularly the gossip that can enter into girl talk, I argue that gossip and girl talk not only keep track of individuals' behavior in relation to the norms but also keep track of the norms in relation to individuals' behavior. In this light, girl talk can be seen as an agent of social change, as well as of social control. By engaging in the negotiation of norms, women also increase their stake in the norms, simultaneously tying together the community and tying themselves to it. One might say that women's negotiation of norms is an important part of what makes communities. Harding (1975) characterizes much of women's talk as "climbing . . . the figurative fences between households" (p. 302), providing a flow of information that, in effect, maintains communication within communities.

The fact that women today are entering the marketplace does not change, but complicates, these dynamics. The strong norms associated with the domestication of women function to limit women's participation in the marketplace, and the verbal behavior that serves these norms takes on new significance, serving simultaneously as an adaptive strategy and as a barrier to access to the marketplace. For, as norms become more problematic, the need to negotiate them increases. It is reasonable, then, that girl talk should intensify with the double bind that marketplace participation imposes on women. However, at the same time, women's engagement in girl talk is taken as evidence of their unsuitability for the marketplace.

Female Symbolic Capital in the High School Setting

Girls in high school spend a great deal of time engaging in girl talk. They are at a life stage in which they are just coming to terms with women's roles and dealing with new and unfamiliar norms. In addition, the high school poses a double bind for many girls, for the emphasis on competitive status in the school institution conflicts with norms for women's behavior. Although there are any number of ways to function in high school, and certainly more than one context in which to achieve success and status (academics, music, ROTC, office assistance, etc.), there is a clear mainstream acknowledged, not only by the students, but by the school itself (Eckert 1989). Individuals of both sexes are expected to compete for personal mainstream success, which involves the accumulation of power through the domination of a small range of social, political, and athletic activities and membership in the social networks that dominate those activities. Although the importance of particular activities differs somewhat from school to school, the existence of a mainstream status group is common to public high schools across the country. Most high school students feel that the status system that defines mainstream success in the high school is unfair, even some of those who have benefited from it. But they are locked in an institution that supports this system and, as a result, must come to terms with it in some way.

Because the roles are arranged hierarchically and because there are few of them in relation to the size of the student population, school activities constitute a competitive marketplace. The terms of boys' and girls' competition in school are, however, very different. Central to this difference is the notion of popularity. Popularity is the community's joint recognition of an individuals' good personhood, in other words, a measure of her or his symbolic capital. In view of females' greater dependence on the accumulation of symbolic capital, it is reasonable that girls should be more concerned with popularity than boys and that they should compete for it. But, because popularity is accorded by the community as a whole, it requires not only likability but also sufficient, well-managed visibility to draw the community's attention to that likability. The visibility gained through elected office and other formal roles in the school activity marketplace thus increases one's access to popularity. This involves not only competition but also a certain measure of exclusivity (being associated with only prestigious people), to maximize visibility. The result is a double bind created by the conflict between competition and exclusivity on the one hand and likability on the other.

This conflict is played out in the instance of teenage girl talk to be presented here. This tape-recorded session took place in the course of two and a half years of participant observation in a Detroit suburban high school. During this time I followed one graduating class through their last two years of high school. The six girls involved in this interaction are all members of that graduating class. The analysis is based on the broader ethnographic context and on my relatively long-term and regular familiarity with the participants in this interaction and with many of their approximately six hundred classmates. This interaction did not occur spontaneously: I had asked one of the participants, Karen, to get together a bunch of friends after school to talk about "stuff." At the time of this interaction, the six participants, Karen, Betty, Miriam, Carol, June, and Pamela, were at the end of their junior year in high school.[1] All of them except June had been friends in Rover Junior High School, where they had been members of the same social cluster. June, who had gone to a different junior high school, was casual friends with all of the girls in this interaction and had been invited to come along to this session at the last moment as the girls were at their lockers getting ready. As a result, she said relatively little during the interaction, but she served as a kind of observer.[2]

The Rover girls had been part of the "active" group in junior high school, a fairly large network of boys and girls who dominated school activities and who pursued informal, large-group social activities outside school. These girls, like many of their peers in that group, agreed that ninth grade had been their "best year ever." When their class merged in high school with classes from two other junior high schools, the competition for status and opportunities in the new setting was fierce, and success required learning quickly who was who from the other schools and establishing contacts with them. There was, therefore, a race to get to know as many people from the other schools as possible and, in particular, to get to know the powerful people from the other schools. Ultimately, one had to run this race as an individual, and slower friends were typically left behind. Betty's account (on another occasion) of the history of her friendship with Karen, Miriam, and Pamela during this period of transition is a particularly poignant description of the process that yielded their current relations.

> We're pretty much alike. But as soon as we got into high school, which was kind of strange, we all just kind of drifted away, you know, and we were just like, you know, new friends here, new friends there, but then it just all came back together again, you know, because you can't really- you're never that much different . . . as soon as you get into high school, it's like popularity popularity- everybody's like, you know, you have to be popular, that's what- that's what's in you know, so you have to try to get the popular friends, the people who are really popular. Well if, you know, you feel that you really- the popular friends aren't too terrific, then, you know, you always fall back on just your friends that have been friends for so long.

The session under analysis is the first time these girls have gotten together as a group since junior high school, and this interaction, like any reunion, prompts them to measure their own progress in relation to each other's. Thus, it is inherently competitive: Each girl has a stake in showing herself and the others that she has "done well." The terms of this competition, however, are complex for two reasons. *First,* there is the conflict between their need to show that they have succeeded in the competitive marketplace and their need to show that they are likable. Thus, they must compete without appearing to. *Second,* to the extent that the girls in the interaction have been following different paths in high school, they need to negotiate what "doing well" is. In addition, they are competing, not only over status in the marketplace, but also over the very likability that makes it impossible for them to compete openly. Therefore, their noncompetitive performance in this interaction, which allows each girl to display her understanding of human nature and her ability to resolve conflict and create community, can be seen as part of the competition. The result is that the main activity of this interaction is the negotiation of a set of norms that allows equally for the accomplishments, behavior, and beliefs of all the girls involved.

The girls in this interaction are all good students with different measures of mainstream involvement and success in high school. None of them is a full-time member of the most popular and powerful group. Inasmuch as every one of these girls admits to having aimed for mainstream success in tenth grade, they have to account to themselves and to each other for both the things they did in seeking it (the likability issue) and their perceived success or failure to attain it (the status issue). Each girl has to either establish her own mainstream status or account for her lack of it. Establishing mainstream status involves the display of formal roles and/or social contacts, and almost all of the girls in this interaction make such displays in the course of this interaction.

One can account for lack of mainstream status by denying the value of mainstream success, by establishing the preferability of an alternative status system, and by affirming one's success in it. This is one main theme in the discussion, and it is linked to the issue of personal autonomy, another problematic issue for adolescents, particularly adolescent girls. Betty, Miriam, and June have taken the mainstream route, confining their interactions primarily to the network surrounding the mainstream popular crowd in their own graduating class and pursuing the school activities that bring mainstream status. Karen, Carol, and Pamela are involved in alternative networks in the junior and senior classes and pursue some less mainstream activities. Carol and Pamela, for instance, are involved in the band. They present themselves in the interaction as more autonomous or independent by virtue of their exploration of social alternatives and their transcendence of their own graduating class. In much of the discussion, Karen and Carol, on the one hand, and Betty and Miriam, on the other, form two sides in the discussion. Associated with the juxtaposition between mainstream and alternative networks is Karen and Carol's pride in their sophistication and their liberal outlook, whereas Betty and Miriam willingly cast themselves as the "innocents." (Their innocence stems from personal traits not necessarily associated with their mainstream identities.)

The Girl Talk

The main body of the discussion lasts one hour and fifty-five minutes and flows through a variety of topics. After everyone gets settled around the table, discussion begins with my asking a question about how they find things out in school. The discussion turns quickly to information management: preventing unfavorable information from getting out and promoting the dissemination of favorable information. This leads to a discussion of how girls can let boys know they "like" them, which introduces the section on boys. This section centers around relations with boys and ends in a discussion of who the popular boys are and what they are like. This leads to a discussion of popular people in general, popularity itself, and people who will do anything to gain popularity. A discussion of one girl who has been particularly responsive to peer pressure leads to the conclusion that she suffers from lack of family support. This leads into the discussion of family relations, in particular the need for mutual respect between parents and children. Further discussion of people who have bad relations with their parents leads Carol to tell about one such person who has been supported in her family difficulties by her religious faith. This leads to the discussion of religion, which ends with a discussion of the number of people in school that unexpectedly belong to church groups. This leads to a brief discussion of unguessable things about people, in particular popular people with family problems. Carol, Miriam, and Karen then tell a story each about past resolved conflicts with parents. After Karen's story, Carol points out how well Karen turned out in spite of this conflict because she has a basically strong relationship with her parents. This leads the conversation to how they have all changed since junior high school. This is an extremely important topic, because it deals explicitly with the covert agenda of the discussion. At this point, the discussion begins to move back and forth among topics already covered and ultimately leads to a discussion of their upcoming senior year, including the impending loss of their senior friends, the necessity of getting their own class together in senior year, and the responsibilities of being the school leaders (as a class). From here on, the conversation jumps quickly from topic to topic and, in a variety of ways, wraps up the entire conversation with implicit and explicit reference to earlier parts.

Shared norms imply community, and the negotiation of norms both reaffirms and requires community. The building of consensus is the building of community through the development of a shared account of themselves as a group. Communities build through repeated interactions among the individuals that constitute them, and each of these interactive events constitutes, in some sense, a temporary community of its own.[3] Each interaction builds an internal history as it progresses. Stories can be built on, points can be elaborated, and even a history of linguistic usage can develop, all of which can be invoked through the interaction. If the temporary community is sufficiently memorable, its participants may refer later either to the interaction as a whole or to community devices within it. The girl talk under consideration here is a prime example of the creation of community in an interaction. These girls are together for the first time after two years, and their separation has involved events and developments that continue to divide them. To be able to interact as friends, they need to become a community, but a temporary one, for they intend to resume their separation when they leave this interaction. They are not trying to recreate a community that existed earlier but a community that bridges the gap between their earlier relations and the present and that allows them to anticipate separating again without ill feeling or awkwardness. The particular value of this temporary community to each of them is to allow her to show herself and the others how far she has come and to demonstrate that her actions and choices have been worthy.

Disagreement is an important way of getting norms onto the table. Because these girls have followed somewhat different paths, and because each girl's claim to status depends on the group's recognition of her path, the paths themselves have to be worked into the consensus. To a great extent, therefore, the discussion is a long sequence of claims, counterclaims, and negotiated consensus. In these cases, a pattern is followed in which one girl makes a statement of opinion or belief, which someone else contradicts. Others might or might not take explicit sides at this initial stage, but then one or the other side presents support in the form of either an argument or an illustration. This might be countered by another argument or illustration, or consensus negotiation could begin immediately. Consensus is negotiated by finding a position that includes both positions presented or by refining one or both of the positions to eliminate the disagreement. Consensus is built not only through the accumulation of items, but also through a hierarchical development, with fairly trivial items of agreement combining to yield a broader item of agreement. As the girls discuss a given topic, each subtopic leads to a related subtopic. Discussion of each subtopic leads to some kind of consensus, and the progress through subtopics leads to the development of agreement on a higher level or a more general topic. It is clear at times that one or more of the participants finds herself stuck in a consensus that she probably does not really share, by virtue of having agreed to the earlier items of consensus and not being able to argue against the other participants' logic in building the higher level item.

Illustrations of behavior in relation to norms (what is normally referred to as gossip) are an important component of the history of a girl talk event. Gossip has been seen both as a means for building community and emphasizing community membership (Gluckman 1963) and as a means for personal advancement within communities (Paine 1967). It is perhaps in girl talk that the lack of contradiction between these two is the clearest. Within this interaction, gossip builds community in several ways. It provides stories that can be built on and referred to throughout the interaction, creating an interactional history. It also provides an opportunity for the group to align itself in relation to the people being discussed (or at least to their foibles, problems, or behavior), setting them off from the rest of the population as a temporary community. It allows the participants, singly and as a group, to display their compassion for the transgressors and maturity in analyzing the causes of the transgression. And it defines the community by virtue of the issues it raises. As Gluckman (1963) points out, one must be a member of a group to know how to gossip in it and to be allowed to. On the other hand, the same device provides opportunities for the teller to enhance her position in the interaction. Unlike a regular conversational turn, telling a story allows the individual a relatively long time slot. It thus allows the individual to expand on her point of view or to insert more information about herself than she could otherwise, without competing for the floor. Gossip also emphasizes the teller's individual network and information sources, and a personal story about a popular or powerful individual, for example, enhances the teller's claim to mainstream status. It is generally believed in our society that women are more likely than men to repeat confidences. I believe this to be true in certain circumstances, for where one's status depends on affiliation, repeating confidences is a way of displaying these affiliations. In most circumstances, women are more bound to prove affiliation than men.

It has been my observation that, in situations where the same is true of men, they do the same.

Illustrations can also be powerful in manipulating the point-by-point building of consensus discussed earlier, because illustrations are always specific and the use of items of consensus built on them is at times quite free. In the process of building consensus on a more general topic, therefore, illustrations allow the group to build consensus little by little, first by agreeing on the relatively nonthreatening interpretation of an individual example, then by gradually weaving the examples into a higher level and more general agreement that might, in fact, not be equally satisfactory to all.

Talk About Boys

The remainder of this chapter focuses on the first section of the girl talk event, the discussion of boys, because it contains illustrations of all of the devices and strategies just discussed and sets the tone for the entire interaction. It establishes the "sides" in the discussion, it establishes the norm of consensus negotiation, and it introduces what emerge as the two main themes of the entire interaction: popularity and independence. The underlying issues in the discussion of boys are (1) the issue of maturity and independence, as measured by the nature of one's relations with boys; and (2) the sticky issue of mainstream status, as measured by involvement with the popular boys.

The discussion can be divided into four episodes. It begins with issue (1), focusing on two issues concerning how to behave with boys: using go-betweens (Episode A) and asking boys out (Episode B). There is initial disagreement on both subjects, and each is resolved in turn. The process of resolution of each of these specific issues sets up Karen, Carol, and Pamela as more familiar with boys and as more mature and independent in their relations with them. Karen and Carol then close the discussion of handling boys by introducing what becomes a superordinate item of consensus: that one should not idolize boys. It becomes apparent in the course of the conversation that people are less likely to idolize boys if they know boys as *just people*. There is an implicit understanding that the girls who orient themselves toward popular boys have been denied this familiarity. By emphasizing the importance of not idolizing boys, therefore, Karen, Carol, and Pamela are leading the group into an endorsement of their involvement with nonmainstream boys. This sets the stage for Episodes C and D, in which the discussion turns to popular boys and the relative merits of different kinds of boys. The final resolution (in Episode D) is that nonmainstream boys and popular boys are desirable for different reasons. This is a major step toward resolving the differences between the girls' notions of "doing well."

Episode A: Third Parties. As already mentioned, this section of the discussion begins with the question of how girls can go about letting boys know that they "like" them. Carol and Pamela let the group know that they have one juicy story on this topic, but when they do not tell it right away, June tells a story about an unnamed person who made a fool of herself by having a friend act as go-between. The first disagreement comes as June finishes the story, saying that the strategy didn't work out. Karen denounces the use of go-betweens, or "third parties," and Miriam agrees (1).[4] Carol and Pamela then disagree and refer again to their own as yet untold story, which the others then beg them to tell (3–7).

1
June: . . . it just didn't work out.
Miriam: No they don't.
Betty:
Karen: Oh third parties NEVER work.
Carol:
Pamela:
Eckert:

2
June: I don't think so.
Miriam:
Betty: DON'T EVER use a third party.
Karen: They do SOMEtimes.
Carol: They do sometimes !!
Pamela:
Eckert:

3
June:
Miriam:
Betty: hhh   !!!
Karen: It's never worked for me. !!!
Carol: This is the voice of experience.
Pamela:
Eckert: Apparently it just worked over here.

4
June: Yeah I know !!
Miriam:
Betty: God now I'm dying to know !!!
Karen: yeah
Carol: ((cough))   ! yeah !!
Pamela: really?
Eckert:

5
June:
Miriam: Let's see here's gossip. We all=
Betty: ! ! ! ! ! ! ! ! ! ! ! ! ! ! ! ! ! !
Karen:
Carol:
Pamela: ! ! !
Eckert: Are are you dying to tell it or not?   ! !

6
June:
Miriam: =want to hear it. Come on, tell us.
Betty: ! ! ! ! ! !   ! !   Come on Pam !
Karen: ! ! !   Come on, Pamela.
Carol: Everybody just lean =
Pamela:
Eckert:

7
June:
Miriam: Yeah I know.
Betty: ! ! ! ! hhh
Karen: ! !
Carol: =forward.What was it? um Okay we might as well get it out.
Pamela: ((cough))   ! !   yeah right.
Eckert:

Carol and Pamela agree to tell the story together, and the telling begins jointly with Pamela helping Carol locate the incident in time (8–9). However, after their initial collaboration in establishing the approximate date of the incident in question, Pamela assumes a role as antagonist by virtue of her role as victim in the story by denying responsibility for the motives of Carol's action (13). Throughout the telling, the other girls, including Pamela, provide commentary on the story, jokingly challenging Carol's contention that she had acted spontaneously (16–17) and invoking external evaluations by filling in the boy's reactions (19–20). One might say that the group participation in the story in the form of laughter and comments implicates them all, already mitigating the disagreement that Carol's and Pamela's stance raised in the earlier discussion.

8
June:
Miriam:
Betty: !!!!!   snicker snicker hh
Karen: m hm
Carol: It was at a party earlier this year like   November   like was it
Pamela: m hm
Eckert:

9
June:
Miriam:
Betty:
Karen:
Carol: late   late October early November   and um =
Pamela: November
Eckert:

10
June:
Miriam:
Betty:
Karen:
Carol: =everybody's in REAL good mood from the party OK? and   two =
Pamela:
Eckert:

11
June:
Miriam:
Betty: hhh
Karen: ! !
Carol: =people are sitting there and I knew this one girl   who wanted to go to S-
Pamela:
Eckert: ! !   who=

12
June:
Miriam:
Betty: hh
Karen:
Carol: right wanted to go to Sadie Hawkins OK which=
Pamela:
Eckert: =will remain unnamed

13
June:
Miriam:
Betty:
Karen:
Carol: =is the girls ask
Pamela: not ALWAYS not really I was talked into it ! ! to go
Eckert: right

14
June:
Miriam:
Betty: hhh
Karen:
Carol: she   she wasn't sure she wanted to go   but   I was confident ! she did ! !
Pamela:
Eckert:

15
June:
Miriam: !
Betty: ((cough)) !
Karen:
Carol: and things just kept talking and so I asked the guy   you know we were=
Pamela: !!
Eckert:

16
June:
Miriam:
Betty:
Karen: just HAPPENED
Carol: =just   it just happened to come up in the conversation
Pamela: just HAPPENED?
Eckert:

17
June:
Miriam: ! ! !   sort of directed
Betty: hh ! !
Karen: !
Carol: yes. So we=
Pamela: she just happened to bring it up
Eckert:

18
June:
Miriam:
Betty:
Karen:
Carol:
Pamela: =were talking about it I said "so eh   John are you going to uh Sadie's?"
Eckert:

19
June:
Miriam:
Betty:
Karen: John   ! !
Carol: said "no"   said "would you like to go?"   he looks at me=
Pamela: he looks at her !
Eckert:

20
June:
Miriam: he goes "phew" no I'm only kidding !
Betty:
Karen:
Carol:
Pamela: =and I said "not with ME" goes "oh SURE I'd love to go"
Eckert:

21
June:
Miriam: I'm only joking ! ! !
Betty:
Karen:
Carol: and I go "Pamela wants to go with you" !
Pamela: hhhh   ((sniff))
Eckert:

```
22
June:
Miriam:
Betty:                                  hh                            ! ! !
Karen:
Carol:    =he goes "OH GREAT we'll go."   They've been going out ever since.
Pamela:                               hh                                    hh
Eckert:
```

At the end of the story, Miriam resolves the disagreement about third parties by refining Karen's original statement that third parties never work (1), making it compatible with Carol's story. According to Miriam's revised version, it would be all right for a third party to operate on her own, so long as it was not instigated by the first party (27). Now that the terms of consensus have been established, Carol continues with a further story about another girl who misused a third party (32–33). This extreme example gives everyone the opportunity to reaffirm the consensus by engaging in ridicule, aping, and laughter over this particularly ridiculous transgressor, uniting them as a group in opposition to the kind of people who do such silly things (34–36). The hilarity in this segment marks the end of the issue of third parties, which has now been resolved to everyone's satisfaction.

```
23
June:    So what did YOU do Pamela  did you know she was going to to say that=
Miriam:
Betty:   ! ! !
Karen:
Carol:
Pamela:
Eckert:
```

```
24
June:    =to him?
Miriam:
Betty:                                                                  hhh
Karen:
Carol:                                              she was sitting=
Pamela:    No I didn't                  YES I was sitting right next to him
Eckert:    You were sitting right there?
```

```
25
June:
Miriam:                                            !
Betty:
Karen:
Carol:    =right next  she was talking to somebody else though ! !
Pamela:                                           yeah
Eckert:                                                    so you=
```

26
June:
Miriam:
Betty: ! ! !   ! !
Karen: m hm
Carol: She ignored it
Pamela: Oh I HEARD it ! !   I heard it but it's just=
Eckert: =didn't hear it

27
June:
Miriam: Well those kind of third parties I think work when like=
Betty: hhhh
Karen: m hm   I know ! !
Carol:
Pamela: =OH GOD !
Eckert:

28
June:
Miriam: =someone would go up to someone and you didn't know they were=
Betty:
Karen: Oh that's that's silly.   It's too silly
Carol:
Pamela:
Eckert:

29
June:
Miriam: =saying it but um the one where like I would say to Karen, "would you=
Betty:
Karen:
Carol:
Pamela: m hm ((sniff))
Eckert:

30
June:
Miriam: =please tell this guy that I like him" or something   Those never-
Betty:
Karen: Oh that's=
Carol: Yeah.
Pamela: m hm
Eckert:

31
June:
Miriam: because yeah it just never get-
Betty:
Karen: =that's silly   it's too SILLY
Carol: Yeah yeah a friend of mine=
Pamela: right
Eckert:

32
June:
Miriam:
Betty:
Karen: juvenile and   turns you off.
Carol: = did that and   she's been doing it since uh last year and I think this=
Pamela:
Eckert:

33
June:
Miriam:
Betty:
Karen:
Carol: =guy is really getting sick of it   because she keeps telling him or she
              keeps telling all these other people   "well I really like him" and "kinda
              drop the hint that I like him"   I   I think I'd get turned off by that.=
Pamela:
Eckert:

34
June:
Miriam:
Betty:
Karen: =Oh yeah.   That's=
Carol: ((cough))   SAME GUY. yes.
Pamela:
Eckert: She's been dropping a hint about this one guy for a year?

35
June:
Miriam: And you eh you know he probably has gotten the hint. ! !
Betty: ! ! !   ! !   ! ! !!
Karen: =disgusting. ! !   I'm=
Carol:
Pamela: ! !
Eckert:

36
June:
Miriam: yeah
Betty: it's true ! !
Karen: =sure he's gotten it, yeah.   Ohh
Carol: And it hasn't been too subtle either.
Pamela: ! ! !   ! !
Eckert: Yeah right. ! !

The use of third parties is a key issue in relations with boys because of its
association with what the girls now see as the childish practices of junior
high school. In this consensus, the participants have all affirmed that they
are not silly about boys (as they might have been in ninth grade) and that
they know how to deal with them in a mature way. Carol's final story,
cementing the group's disapproval of immature dealings with boys, becomes a group story, which turns up later in this section.

Episode B: Asking Boys Out. Episode B continues directly from Episode A. Now that an end has been put to the issue of third parties, I ask whether they would ever ask a boy out (37). This question raises a new issue that results in a disagreement and conflict resolution sequence analogous to those in Episode A, continuing the general issue of know-how in relations with boys. In answer to my question, Miriam quickly says "never" and is contradicted by Carol's "yes" (37). (Of course, inasmuch as each is answering for herself, this is not so much a contradiction as a difference that must be resolved.) Negotiation of consensus on the issue of asking boys out is accomplished early on by Miriam's admission that she'd like to and Karen's mitigation of her statement that she has (38–39). Karen then expands on this subject, giving a rough description of the time she asked her current boyfriend out (39–45) and emphasizing the fact that she had been friends with her boyfriend before they started going out. This both introduces the fact that Karen has a boyfriend (which Carol and Pamela did not know) and shows her to have graduated from sex-segregated behavior with boys to more open, mature relationships.

```
37
June:
Miriam:                                       Never.   I WISH I could but I never would
Betty:                                                                              !
Karen:                                                             yeah
Carol:                              .               Yes.
Pamela:                                                             oh yeah NOW I do
Eckert:   Would you ever ask a guy out?


38
June:                          Betty!
Miriam:                                      ! ! Oh Betty!
Betty:     =NEVER AGAIN ! ! !                        ! !
Karen:                        hh                I have.    but I mean it=
Carol:                                             I have.
Pamela:              · ! !
Eckert:              ! ! !


39
June:
Miriam:
Betty:            !
Karen:     =was like after we knew each other      pretty well.      Not that=
Carol:                                             very well.
Pamela:                                  after            yeah ! after=
Eckert:


40
June:
Miriam:
Betty:     hhh            hhh
Karen:     =well but I mean it was like        we both   we both were like=
Carol:
Pamela:    =you'd been going out with him uh !
Eckert:
```

41
June:
Miriam:
Betty:
Karen: =said we were friends and stuff and it was a PLATONIC THING but=
Carol:
Pamela:
Eckert:

42
June:
Miriam: N:O it=
Betty: ! ! ! ! ! ! !
Karen: =I asked HIM out. so   no.!   !
Carol:
Pamela:
Eckert: and it stayed platonic.   oh.

43
June:
Miriam: =didn't !
Betty:
Karen: but it was for a while but it it's I did ask him out   it=
Carol: no. !
Pamela:
Eckert:

44
June:
Miriam:
Betty:
Karen: =was nothing and it was very relaxed. I was surprised. I thought I'd=
Carol:
Pamela:
Eckert:

45
June:
Miriam:
Betty:
Karen: =be so nervous.   but it was   it was good.
Carol: It's easier=
Pamela:
Eckert: yeah. m hm

At the end of Karen's turn, Carol joins her by supporting the importance of friendship (45–48) and denouncing "love at first sight" (48–49). By referring to Carol's story in Episode A, of the girl who kept sending hints, Karen then binds together the general subject of boy handling and allows them all to agree that one should not idolize boys (49–53). Carol's expansion of that story (53–54) allows the group to cement their agreement with vociferous contempt for those who have not transcended junior high school behavior with boys (54–57).

46
June:
Miriam: Mm hm
Betty: ((sniff))
Karen:
Carol: =it's easier when they build from like small friendships.
Pamela: friendship
Eckert:

47
June:
Miriam:
Betty:
Karen: Oh yeah and it's probably, you know, it'll STICK longer if it's a=
Carol:
Pamela:
Eckert:

48
June:
Miriam:
Betty:
Karen: =FRIENDSHIP instead of you know-
Carol: Yeah. Love at first sight=
Pamela:
Eckert: does that happen a lot?

49
June:
Miriam:
Betty: hh
Karen: No. It's not good either if one=
Carol: =Voom you know that's not good.
Pamela: hhh
Eckert:

50
June:
Miriam:
Betty:
Karen: =person IDOLIZES the other person. It's like the one girl said   she's been=
Carol:
Pamela:
Eckert:

51
June:
Miriam:
Betty:
Karen: =dropping hints and "oh God I just WANT to get to know him" well, you=
Carol: m hm
Pamela: ((cough))
Eckert:

52
June:
Miriam:
Betty:
Karen: = know, it's like "I worship you" and lalala and all of that sort of thing.
Carol:
Pamela:
Eckert:

53
June:
Miriam: I know
Betty:
Karen: HE can't relate to that.   uncomfortable
Carol: and the things that that make her so excited=
Pamela:
Eckert:

54
June:
Miriam: m hm
Betty: ! ! ! !   ! !
Karen: ! !
Carol: =are like "He SMILED at me today."   Whoopee
Pamela: Those things just OHH God
Eckert:

55
June:
Miriam: ! !   ! ! ! ! ! ! !
Betty: He gave me a GLANCE over ACROSS the room. ! ! !
Karen: yeah !
Carol:
Pamela:
Eckert: by mistake

56
June:
Miriam:
Betty: ! ! ! ! ! !
Karen: big mistake
Carol: yes ! ! !   the big one that I hate is "he bumped into me in=
Pamela:
Eckert: ! ! ! ! !

57
June:
Miriam:
Betty: uh huh
Karen: W:OOPS   Oh:
Carol: =the hall."   "hello:"   Oh you got a long way to . . .
Pamela: ((cough))   hello. mm
Eckert:

Episode C: Popular Boys. The girls have now agreed on appropriate behavior with boys, and Karen and Carol are assuming roles as authorities on boys. An important measure of mainstream success is familiarity with the popular boys. Karen, Carol, and Pamela are on friendly terms with boys who are not part of the popular crowd, whereas June, Miriam, and Betty are more oriented toward the popular boys, who, by virtue of their status, are generally available on only the most casual basis. There arises a tension, therefore, between the value of popular contacts, on the one hand, and close experience with boys such as Karen and Carol have displayed, on the other. The issue of the desirability of popular boys takes longer and is more complex than the issue of how to behave with boys.

Following the discussion of girls who idolize boys, I ask which boys girls tend to idolize. This sparks a somewhat confused disagreement about whether people look up to older boys, leading to the following segment that starts with June's pronouncement on which boys people in general look up to (1). This elicits the expected lineup of opinion: agreement from Miriam and Betty and disagreement from Karen, Carol, and Pamela (1–2). Karen and Carol then begin to expand on their view of popular boys, while Pamela says that she doesn't know them (2–4). My question, along with Miriam's answer (5), can be seen as a challenge to Carol's assertions that popular boys have big heads and no personality, and she quickly backs down (5). Karen, however, saves her position for her (6) by saying that "it CAN be true." Carol then disavows contact with these popular boys, with humorous support from Miriam and Pamela, and with June providing the reason (7–11). More discussion ensues of what makes boys popular (such as sports, student government, looks, well-roundedness).

```
1
June:     mostly your   BIG POPULAR people.
Miriam:                                   Yeah, I think so too, just like   you=
Betty:                                              Yeah.              hh
Karen:                                                     I don't think so at=
Carol:
Pamela:    ! !
Eckert:


2
June:
Miriam:  =know                    I-        Looking up?
Betty:                       hh
Karen:   =ALL It's different for me.                              -pular
Carol:       I find that that turns me off.      the big   No. The big popular
Pamela:     those  I don't know them.      yeah                big popular
Eckert:


3
June:
Miriam:
Betty:
Karen:                      whoo         h              turnoff. h
Carol:   macho guy. That's one thing that I just do NOT like.
Pamela:                      ooh                 no           I can't=
Eckert:
```

```
4
June:
Miriam:
Betty:                                                              hh
Karen:
Carol:            Yes.              It's the big heads and no personality.
Pamela:  =stand it.
Eckert:               Why not?

5
June:
Miriam:                                      Not all the time.
Betty:         no comment hh
Karen:   Yeah                      I-
Carol:                               no it's not. I think that's just a=
Pamela:    mm hmm
Eckert:            Is that really true?

6
June:
Miriam:
Betty:         I think it's a front. yeah
Karen:   =stereotype                              It CAN be true=
Carol:             stereotype        I don't have a lot of oh
Pamela:
Eckert:

7
June:
Miriam:
Betty:
Karen:   =though
Carol:         a lot of watchacallit           No uh  well that's the word but=
Pamela:                         interaction
Eckert:

8
June:
Miriam:                    relationships   friendships          hh
Betty:
Karen:                                !  !              m ! ! !
Carol:   =it's not the one I                   Action.  ! ! ! I don't=
Pamela:                      I know                    ! !
Eckert:                                              ! ! !

9
June:
Miriam:
Betty:
Karen:                                         yeah          oh see I
Carol:   =have a lot of exposure to a lot of those guys.   I just don't see them.
Pamela:
Eckert:
```

10
June: You're not a cheerleader you're not   you're not=
Miriam:
Betty:
Karen:
Carol: I don't talk to a lot of those guys.
Pamela:
Eckert:

11
June: =involved with them.
Miriam:
Betty:
Karen: No.
Carol:
Pamela:
Eckert:

Episode D: Flaws. Episode D begins when I ask who exactly these popular boys are that they are talking about. Two boys are mentioned (1), who serve as the focus of the ensuing conversation. Karen cuts off the naming of popular boys (1) with a disavowal of contact with such boys (1–4) and an introduction of her alternative network. There ensues a short competition between Karen and Pamela over which of them has less to do with popular boys (4–6). At this point, Miriam comes out in defense of popular boys, at the same time displaying her familiarity with them (6–10). Carol supports her, first by providing the key word for her utterance (*change*) (9), then by repeating Miriam's evaluation (10). She then displays her own familiarity with Al Jones (10–12).

1
June:
Miriam: John Smith.
Betty: Al Jones !
Karen: See now I'm I'm around=
Carol: Al Jones.
Pamela: Al Jones
Eckert:

2
June:
Miriam:
Betty:
Karen: =the guys who are more inTELLIgent when- they're seniors and=
Carol:
Pamela:
Eckert:

3
June:
Miriam: yeah
Betty: hh   that's true.
Karen: =BOY they're a LOT NICER ! !   Yeah I don't really=
Carol: m hm Yeah   uh huh.
Pamela:
Eckert:

4
June:
Miriam:
Betty:
Karen: =even MESS with these guys I mean
Carol: Oh I don't either. I-
Pamela: I don't know them.
Eckert:

5
June:
Miriam:
Betty: yeah
Karen: I don't even know=
Carol:
Pamela: I mean I know them by face and-
Eckert:

6
June:
Miriam: but you know, Al Jones-
Betty: =their FACES I've just heard so much aBOUT them
Karen:
Carol:
Pamela:
Eckert:

7
June:
Miriam: everybody looks up to him.   I mean you know, as we were=
Betty:
Karen:
Carol:
Pamela: mm m
Eckert:

8
June:
Miriam: =saying,   falling all over him and he- at first his appearance to me
         that he was really   you know big head and that, but when I met
         him it was it=
Betty:
Karen:
Carol:
Pamela:
Eckert:

9
June:
Miriam: =was so   such a refreshing-   change that he was not like that=
Betty: uh exactly
Karen: hh
Carol: change
Pamela:
Eckert:

10
June:
Miriam: =at all. He was really nice.
Betty: he IS nice
Karen:
Carol: He IS. He's a very nice guy. I've worked=
Pamela: I don't=
Eckert:

11
June:
Miriam: yeah.
Betty:
Karen:
Carol: =with him on makeup for one of the plays   and he was=
Pamela: =know him.   m hm
Eckert:

12
June:
Miriam: looks
Betty:
Karen:
Carol: =really nice.
Pamela: looks
Eckert: How do people GET into that position? how-

When I ask how boys get popular (12), Miriam, Pamela, and Karen agree that "looks" are important, but then Miriam brings up John Smith's broader qualities (13–14) and finds support from the others (13–15).

13
June:
Miriam: I think   hmmmm
Betty: HIS case is looks but like there there's like John Smith's case where=
Karen: lot is looks
Carol:
Pamela: looks   he's smart
Eckert:

14
June:
Miriam:
Betty: =it's just like sports and smartness and   good personality   yeah
Karen:
Carol:
Pamela: sports and smart   he's a
Eckert:

15
June:
Miriam:
Betty: ! ! ! ! !
Karen: an apple pie face.
Carol:
Pamela: he's a basic   all around American guy.
Eckert:

If consensus is to cover each girl's behavior, it must allow for the desirability of both the popular boys and the boys that Karen, Carol, and Pamela are involved with. It is Karen who offers the terms of consensus. Her description of John Smith as having an "apple pie face" (15) provides a transition to her evaluation of popular boys as too perfect (16). Her humorous expression of affection for flaws (17–18) brings the others into participation in her preference for nonmainstream boys. Miriam, who until now has been the greatest defender of popular boys, expands on Karen's statement, explicitly raising the theme of individuality for the first time (20–21), and Carol's observation that there is a lot of individuality in the band (22) brings this topic home. The girls have now agreed that nonmainstream activities and networks have a special quality. The orchestration of the discussion of faults allows all the girls to agree on the perfection of the popular boys, the importance of individuality, and the frequent disjunction between the two.

16
June:
Miriam:
Betty: right. apple pie face ! !
Karen: I don't know - but they're so perfect.
Carol:
Pamela: mm
Eckert:

17
June:
Miriam: and it's it's-
Betty: They ARE.   It IS pathetic
Karen: you just wouldn't-   Yeah, the people that are=
Carol: It's pathetic.
Pamela:
Eckert:

18
June:
Miriam: Yeah. m
Betty: m hmm
Karen: =more appealing are the people with the flaws.
Carol:
Pamela:
Eckert:

19
June:
Miriam:
Betty: ! !
Karen: I- I really go for like a a big nose. ! ! ! I DO. Things that are WRONG=
Carol:
Pamela: ! !
Eckert:

20
June:
Miriam: It just- they so- you know what it is, they're individual
Betty: ! !
Karen: =are GOOD.   It's so-   Oh yeah
Carol: yes
Pamela: ((cough)
Eckert:

21
June:
Miriam: individualized by that and it's so much more-
Betty: so much-
Karen: Individuality is a =
Carol:
Pamela:
Eckert:

22
June:
Miriam:
Betty:
Karen: ts ahh
Carol: =good thing you can find in uh band. Now see I don't   when when I I=
Pamela: yeah yes
Eckert:

23
June:
Miriam: m hm
Betty:
Karen: m hm
Carol: =came to Belten I was not appealed by any of the big jocks and I found=
Pamela:
Eckert:

24
June:
Miriam:
Betty:
Karen:
Carol: =myself not in any group. . .
Pamela:
Eckert:

It is at this point that one could consider the issue of boys to be resolved, and indeed the discussion turns immediately to popular girls. The smaller issues resolved in the discussions of third parties and asking boys out combine to give the higher level agreement that boys are just people and not to be worshipped. This discussion also establishes Karen and Carol as ahead of at least some of the others in "normal" relationships with boys. The affirmation of the merits of popular and alternative boys allows for all six girls to justify their preferences because they have acknowledged the validity of a choice of independence over the "popularity route."

Conclusion

The themes of independence and popularity continue throughout the interaction, as do the verbal strategies for their negotiation and the personal alignments. Consensus on the issue of independence becomes increasingly broad, and, during the discussion on parents, the general consensus develops that, ultimately, one must make her own decisions about values and behavior. This consensus, now built on a solid and expanding consensus about the importance of independence, takes an interesting twist in the discussion of religion. Early in the discussion, Miriam comes out against mixed marriages, on the grounds that the family must have a single religion if the children are to develop strong values. At the end of the discussion, however, because of the differences in religious background and opinion in the group, Carol offers the resolution, once again, that each person must ultimately make his or her own decision, this time about religious choice. Miriam is forced into an uneasy participation in this consensus by her participation in all the previous steps that led to it. The flimsiness of this consensus emphasizes the strikingly constant negotiation of consensus in the interaction. The development of common norms for the group is sufficiently crucial to the maintenance of the group and its interaction that not one topic is allowed to conclude without an expression of consensus.

The norms that govern this interaction are clearly derived from the place that women and girls find themselves in in society. Their need to define themselves in terms of their overall character and the constraints placed on their participation in the world at large create a need to explore and negotiate the norms that govern their behavior. In fact, their ability to create freedom to function in the world depends on their understanding of, and control over, these norms, and girl talk events like the one described here are a major source of that understanding and control.

NOTES

This research was funded by grants from the National Science Foundation (BNS-8023291) and the Spencer Foundation. This chapter originally appeared in *Discourse Processes* 13 (1990):1.91–122.

1. All names are fictitious.

2. One could say that this interaction had five members, one inside observer (June), one outside observer (me), and six mechanical observers (tape recorders). Each girl wore a lavalier microphone attached to a separate tape recorder. The girls controlled their own tape recorders, turning them on and off and turning and changing the tapes. Although it is common in sociolinguistics to try to make taping as unobtrusive as possible, to reduce the speakers' self-consciousness, I have found that, in group sessions where individuals were implicated in their own recording, there was less awareness of the machines than otherwise.

3. I owe a great deal in this section to discussions with Charlotte Linde.

4. To represent as clearly as possible the relations among different participants'

utterances, I have organized the transcript as a musical score, with each speaker represented at all times. Overlaps in speech are indicated as precisely as possible within the limitations of uneven orthographic length. Successive uninterrupted lines of speech (i.e., lines representing the speech of all six participants) are numbered sequentially, and it is these numbers that are referred to in parentheses in the text. Transcription conventions within this format are similar but not identical to those commonly used in conversation analysis. Although there is a good deal of variation in actual pronunciation, all speech is represented by standard orthography, to avoid the frequently misleading or stereotypic character of common conventions for representing vernacular features of speech. An equal sign (=) at the end and beginning of subsequent lines indicates latching. Blank spaces within and at the limits of lines are rough indications of pause length. Exclamation points represent laughter, while *h*'s represent inhaled laughter. A hyphen (-) at the end of a word or word fragment indicates an incomplete utterance as signaled by level pitch. Emphatic stress is indicated by printing the entire word in uppercase letters.

REFERENCES

Aries, Elizabeth (1976). Interaction patterns and themes of male, female and mixed groups. *Small Group Behavior* 7:7–18.

Bourdieu, Pierre (1977). *Outline of a theory of practice.* Cambridge: Cambridge University Press.

Eckert, Penelope (1989). *Jocks and burnouts.* New York: Teachers College Press.

Gluckman, Max (1963). Gossip and scandal. *Current Anthropology* 4:307–315.

Goodwin, Marjorie Harness (1980). Directive/response speech sequences in girls' and boys' task activities. In Sally McConnell-Ginet, Ruth Borker & Nelly Furman (Eds.) *Women and language in literature and society* (pp. 157–173). New York: Praeger.

Harding, Susan (1975). Women and words in a Spanish village. In Rayna Reiter (Ed.) *Toward an anthropology of women* (pp. 283–308). New York: Monthly Review Press.

Jones, Deborah (1980). Gossip: Notes on women's oral culture. In Cheris Kramarae (Ed.) *The voices and words of women and men* (pp. 193–198). Oxford: Pergamon Press.

Kalčik, Susan (1975)". . . like Ann's gynecologist or the time I was almost raped." Personal narratives in women's rap groups. *Journal of American Folklore* 88:3–11.

Paine, Robert (1967). What is gossip about?: An alternative hypothesis. *Man* 2:278–285.

Sacks, Karen (1974). Engels revisited: Women, the organization of production and private property. In Michelle Zimbalist Rosaldo & Louise Lamphere (Eds.) *Woman, culture, and society* (pp. 207–222). Stanford, CA: Stanford University Press.

Wodak, Ruth (1981). Women relate, men report: Sex differences in language behaviour in a therapeutic group. *Journal of Pragmatics* 5:261–285.

3

Community and Contest: Midwestern Men and Women Creating Their Worlds in Conversational Storytelling

BARBARA JOHNSTONE

It has often been noted (Labov 1972, Polanyi 1985, Johnstone 1990b) that the anecdotes Americans tell about their lives in the course of ordinary conversations tend to have a climactic structure. The plots of spontaneous oral narratives, like those of traditional folktales and many literary stories, center around disturbances in the usual flow of events, which must be overcome or lived through. Situations become dangerous or embarrassing, failure looms, unusual people or supernatural apparitions are encountered. Protagonists manage these disturbances, in their stories about them, by calling on various sources of strength. In some stories, disturbances are resolved as a result of individual characteristics of the protagonist: willpower, cleverness, or physical prowess. In others the power to overcome or understand disturbances is communal: the help and advice of friends or neighbors, the law, or the dictates of religion. Still other stories involve supernatural sources of power. Each of these choices about how to present disturbances and their resolutions involves the creation, in the story, of a world: a world of contest in which individuals act alone to overcome challenge or threat, or a world of community in which disturbances in the status quo are managed jointly, or a world in which supernatural forces and personalities can create and resolve disturbances.

The story I call "When I Was Really in Shape" illustrates the first of these options. Its teller, a white, twenty-five-year-old student, is talking to a friend of the same age who is taping the conversation for a class project. They are in Dave's apartment. The friend, Ron, has just been talking about accidentally scaring a coworker, and Dave responds with a reminiscence about a longtime friend and former roommate, "Mr. McCoy," and a mis-aimed karate kick.[1]

When I Was Really in Shape

Dave: When I was really in shape (I'd) throw kicks at him all the time,
        shit that was when I could kick to my Adam's apple.
        Used to practice at home?
        Had this light cord hanging down you know?
        Just .. practice kicking it up in the air.
        I'd .. kick at him one time I kicked him.
        He was closer than what I thought he w-,
        well he wasn't *closer,*
        yeah he was.
        Kicked his goddamn bowl of .. soup out of his hand,
        just reaction he [slaps hand] *turned around and* HIT *me man,*
        [gesture of turning around as he hits fist against palm]
        and it backed me ⎡ *up against the goddamn* ⎤ reFRIgerator,
Ron: ⎣   [laughs]   ⎦
Dave: and WOW .. *what* IS *this shit?* .. 'cause Mister McCoy MELLOW you
        know,
Ron: Yeah, ⎡ [laughs] ⎤
Dave: ⎣ Oh man ⎦ he felt bad as hell about that for a *long* time.
        He finally told me he said,
        "Yeah I don't feel too sorry about that no more." [imitating deeper
        voice]
        [laughter]

The disturbance of normality around which this story revolves is Dave's accidentally kicking his roommate's soup bowl out of his hand. Dave delivers the next few lines in a voice ranging from loud to shouted, accompanied with iconic gestures of hitting and being "backed up," and punctuated with "goddamn," "wow," and "shit." These heavily evaluated lines call maximum attention to how Mr. McCoy resolves the disturbance: by hitting Dave, "just reaction," hard enough to "back [him] up against the goddamn refrigerator." Although he is referred to by his last name in the story, McCoy is an old friend of Dave's, and for a time he feels "bad as hell" about the accident. But eventually, in the only words Dave presents him as actually saying, McCoy announces that he doesn't "feel too sorry about that no more." "When I Was Really in Shape" is a story about friends; it is in fact an illustration of friendship. But friendship, in the world Dave creates in this story, expresses itself in contest of the most elemental kind: kicks and punches. Neither of the friends regrets the inadvertent fight for very long, and their relationship survives intact.

The second option, resolution of disturbance by means of community, is illustrated in "The Gift Box," another story about friends. The storyteller is Ruby, a white twenty-three-year-old housewife with some high school education. She is part of a group consisting of her husband, Fred; her brother, Rob; and her sister-in-law, Sammie, all in their early twenties, who are sitting in her living room chatting about childhood antics. Sammie made the recording.

The Gift Box

Ruby: Now when we were younger,
           me and Ann my sister,
           and Ellen and Marlene the neighbor kids,
           used to go out,
           and like we at first we started out with just purses.
           We'd hide in these shrubs that were along the road,
           and we'd set a purse out there with a piece of fish string tied *to* it.
               [laughing]
           Well we'd always get a dollar and stick out of it,
           and this was you know,
           right around sunset where it was getting kind of dark,
           and we'd .. hide in those bushes, [laughs]
           and then cars would go by you know,
           and they'd see that purse laying in the middle of the road,
           sprung open here was a dollar hanging out of it you know,
           and they'd ... stop and they'd back up,
           and while they were backing up,
           we'd pull the purse back in, [laughs]
           and here they'd be out a-looking you know in the road,
           knowing they'd seen that you know.
           And we'd do this and do this,
           and then finally,
           One . you know that got kind of boring after while,
           so we found this box, [laughs]
           and Ann said ... "Let's set this out in the middle of the road,"
           well (1.0) she said "Let's fill it with all the trash we can find."
           Well she'd just went in the bathroom and used the bathroom,
           and she goes "Oh I didn't even flush the toilet." [laughs lightly]
           Well she took this spoon and started
               scooping=

Sammie: =*Oh gross*=

Ruby: =this stuff out, [laughing]
           and putting it ⌈ in this   ⌉ box?

Fred: ⌊ Only Ann. ⌋

Ruby: And then we went outside to Ellen and Marlene's dog Happy,
           and gathered up *his* turds, [laughs]

Sammie: *Oh God,*

Ruby: and put them in there. [laughs]
           And we put old chicken bones,

Fred: (   )

Ruby: grease ... old food,
           everything we could think of that was nasty and awful into this
               box,
           and then we took it and gift-wrapped it and put this big bow on
               it, [laughs]
           and a little card.

Well we set it out in the road,
and waited and waited you know and nobody ever came by.
(1.5)
And at this time also,
there was these Mexicans that lived down the road from Ellen.
And she kind of looked Mexican herself and his name was Javier,
     [laughs lightly]
and he was you know really such a lover, [laughs lightly]
and he'd go . go by "Mu mu mu" [kissing noise] to that Ellen you
     know, [laughing]
"Eh baby eh baby" [imitating Javier; laughing] always to her.
Well who would pull up in that van *but Javier.* [laughs]
We about lost it you know. [laughs]
We about gave ourselves away from laughing so hard. [laughs]
And here he comes you know,
"*Aeee aeee,*" [imitating Javier]
talking in this Spanish as fast as he could seeing that box there.
     [laughs lightly]
Him and this other ... *Sancho* ... ⌈ was with him. ⌉
     [laughs] | |
                                       ⌊ [laugh]   ⌋

Fred,
Sammie:

Ruby: You know and here they come,
               and stuff and they get out buddy and grab that box,
               you know excited as can be, [laughs]
               you know thinking they've really found something here. [laughs]
               Well ... [laughing] they get that thing in the van and the van
                    stops,
               and we're laughing so hard we can't hardly control it,
               and all of a sudden man we hear them start this loudest Spanish
                    talking ever,
               growing louder and louder and all of a sudden, [laughing]
               this box comes a-flying out of that van all,
               they're a-cussing in Spanish, [laughs]
               and that stuff is scattered all over the road. [laughs]
               We were er you know here we were scared to death they were
                    gonna hear us a-laughing in these bushes and come and get us.
               [laughs]
                       ⌈ [draws in breath] ⌉
Fred, Sammie: ⌊ [laugh]   ⌋
Ruby: But it was just wild. [laughs]

The disturbance in "The Gift Box" occurs when Javier, the irritating
but also somewhat alluring Hispanic, happens to stop with his friend
Sancho to take the girls' gift box bait. What was meant as a harmless, if
disgusting, joke to be played on strangers suddenly looks like a personal
insult to a "lover" and his friend, who could "come and get" the girls.
Though Ruby has presented Javier's sexual baiting of Ellen in light parody
("He'd go 'Mu mu mu' . . . 'Eh baby eh baby'"), the girls know they need
to keep themselves hidden: they "were scared to death [the men] were
gonna hear [them] a-laughing in these bushes." The disturbance is resolved (the girls don't get caught) through their mutual attempts to con-

trol their laughter. Throughout the story, the girls are a team; the story's protagonist is almost always the communal *we*, never an individual *I*, and an individual *she* (Ann) only in the three lines of the bathroom episode. Ruby uses her friends' names repeatedly in the story, as well as the name of the neighbor's dog and those of the men, and key parts of the story, such as the girls' decision to fill the gift box, Javier's history of sexual harassment, and the men's reaction to the gift, are represented as actual speech.

A third option for a storyteller is to create a world in which disturbances can be resolved in supernatural ways. White, middle-class Americans seem rarely to create such a world in personal-experience stories: "ghost stories" are about often apocryphal others, and stories involving the teller's being spooked usually end with a rational explanation of the incident.[2] "The Presence of a Presence," told by a businessman about a distant relative of his, is thus somewhat unusual.

The Presence of a Presence

In 1976 my aunt's mother-in-law died,
she lived in Rockville Indiana,
and my aunt and her two daughter-in-laws went to this woman's house to clean
    out her possessions.
After a hard day's work she bedded down in the downstairs bedroom with her
    young grandson Robert,
the two daughter-in-laws were sleeping upstairs.
As she was drifting off to sleep,
she was aware of the presence- of a presence at the foot of her bed.
(4.0)
It was a tall man dressed in black with a beard.
She wasn't frightened at all,
because he had a sweet beneficent smile on his face.
(4.0)
And she waved him off,
and told him to go away,
that she was tired.
And then ... uh went uh ... to sleep.
In the morning she chuckled to herself,
thinking that this was all a dream,
and how silly it was,
then at breakfast,
(4.0)
her grandson Robert asked her "Grandma who was that man in black in our room
    last night?"
and she dropped her fork.
They went through the family album that day,
and found ... that the man ... was the father of the dead woman,
and he had died in that room.
(5.0)
And they found his picture,
it matched perfectly with the vision seen the night before.

"The Presence of a Presence" is a well-rehearsed, writerly presentation of a story, quite dissimilar from the two personal-experience narratives. The disturbance in this story, the apparition of the man in black, is resolved the next day when the family figures out whose ghost it was. The world created in this story is one in which the supernatural has a part, even if people are skeptical at first.

To recapitulate, then, personal-experience stories can create worlds of various kinds. Some of these "talerealms" (Young 1987) center around contest; others around community; others, less commonly created in white, middle-class Americans' stories, around the supernatural. "When I Was Really in Shape" exemplifies the first of these possibilities—a world of contest. This story was created by a man. "The Gift Box" exemplifies the second—a world of community. This is a woman's story. In the remainder of this essay, I explore this correlation between gender and story type.[3]

To do this, I examine a corpus of spontaneous personal experience stories which includes "When I Was Really in Shape," "The Gift Box," and "The Presence of a Presence," stories told by white, middle-class mid-western men and women. I explore whether there are any systematic differences between these men and women with regard to the worlds they create in their stories and with regard to the linguistic resources they use in doing so. Specifically, I examine the plots to which the men and women adapt their experience; the men's and women's use of details to create social and physical worlds in their stories; and the men's and women's representation of their own and others' speech.

I have two aims in doing this. My first aim is to contribute to the empirical, descriptive study of the discursive practices of a group of female Americans who are rarely studied: white, middle-class, urban mid-westerners. These are women who would identify themselves, as they are identified by others, as members of the "mainstream"; they are women of the "silent majority" of the "heartland" of America, with whom women of various minority groups are often implicitly—but much more rarely explicitly—compared.[4] I show that women's personal experience stories, in the Indiana city I have been studying, do in fact tend to revolve around joint action by communities of people, whereas men's stories tend to be about acting alone, and that women's stories include more details about people than do men's, more reported talk, and different ways of talking about talk. I also examine a story created about and by the community in which these women and men live: a story that belongs to the city of Fort Wayne. I show that community stories like this are in some ways more like women's stories than like men's.

My second aim is a theoretical one, which bears on the study of women and language in a more general way. I am interested in the relationship between the social world created *in* a story by means of a teller's linguistic choices and the social world that *gives rise* to the story. I suggest that women and men make the choices they do in storytelling not simply because they have different psychologies or participate in different subcultures, if they do, and not simply because their stories reflect their differential access to power in the real social world, but also because they are actively creating different worlds in and through their stories, worlds which are at the same time reflective and constitutive of men's and women's psychological, social, and cultural worlds outside their stories.

~ *Discourse, Gender, and World*

Evidence of a variety of kinds suggests that men and women do not—or do not always—use and interpret language the same way. As discourse analysis and sociolinguistics have become increasingly sophisticated, early descriptions of "women's language" (Lakoff 1975) based on intuition and informal observation have inspired empirical studies of how men and women interpret others' speech (Tannen 1982) and how women use language, in conversation with men (Zimmerman & West 1975, Fishman 1978, Maltz & Borker 1982, West & Zimmerman 1983) and among themselves (Harding 1975, Kalčik 1975, Jones 1980, Rakow 1986), in joking (Mitchell 1985), in public image making (Adams & Edelsky 1988), and in the writing (Warshay 1972, Flynn 1988) and telling of personal stories (McLaughlin et al. 1981, Baldwin 1985, Mills 1985, Jahner 1985, Silberstein 1988). As has much other work in discourse analysis and sociolinguistics, work on language and gender in the United States has tended to be about well-educated middle- to upper-middle-class women, who are white and either Jewish or Christian. Universal claims about what women and men do based on research about a subset of women and men must be examined critically; however, since I am explicitly interested in the white middle class, much previous research is potentially relevant to mine.

Explanations for gender differences in language use have been of several kinds. Some scholars see the differences between men's talk and women's as reflections of psychological differences (Gilligan 1982, Boe 1987). Others claim that the differences are social in origin, based in differential status and prestige (O'Barr & Atkins 1980, Kramarae, Schulz, & O'Barr 1984). Others attribute language-use differences to cultural differences, noting that girls and boys are socialized, in same-sex peer groups, into different forms and functions of talk (Maltz & Borker 1982, Tannen 1990). These approaches are by no means mutually exclusive, of course. All could be subsumed under the general claim that men and women live in different worlds, be these affective and/or cognitive psychological worlds; social worlds involving relationships of prestige, power, and status; or worlds of belief and knowledge created by culture; and that the world in which a person lives helps to shape the person's talk.

But talk and world are connected in a variety of ways. Talk is certainly often about the world and reflects what the world is like. At the same time, though, worlds are created in talk. This is in fact most obviously true of narrative talk, since stories, by means of introductory abstracts, summary codas, and other linguistic framing devices, explicitly take teller and audience out of the "storyworld" in which their conversation takes place into a "talerealm" in which the narrative takes place (Young 1987:19–68).

Many students of personality suggest that stories are central to people's identities. As Ursula K. LeGuin (1989) puts it:

> Narrative is a central function of language. Not, in origin, an artifact of culture, an art, but a fundamental operation of the normal mind functioning in society. To learn to speak is to learn to tell a story. . . . [Narrative is] an immensely flexible technology, or life strategy, which if used with skill and resourcefulness presents each of us with that most fascinating of all serials, The Story of My Life. (39, 42)

Telling one's story is at the heart of the psychoanalytic process, which, according to Roy Schafer (1981), is about "the self as telling." Jerome Bruner (1986) argues that while natural reality can be understood by means of logical rationality, human reality is essentially narrative: people make sense of human actions by telling stories about them.

The sociocultural world is also at least partly constituted through talk. Victor Turner (1981) points out that "social dramas" and tellings about them both reflect the same underlying process: stories take the form of social life and social life takes the form of stories. People use stories not simply to perpetuate social reality but also to create it and manipulate it (Johnstone 1987). Stories are not merely—if they are at all—icons of a preexisting extratextual world of cultural norms and social relations. The worlds created in stories do provide evidence of how psychological and social reality constrains people's tellings about it, but in addition, and more interestingly, the social worlds created in stories provide evidence about the nature of the creative power wielded by people who talk.

Men's and Women's Narrative Worlds

I now turn to fifty-eight personal experience narratives, all of which arose in the course of spontaneous conversation among familiars. All were told by white middle-class Americans from in and around an Indiana city of about 300,000 inhabitants. Thirty-three stories were told by women and twenty-five by men; the tellers' ages range from fourteen to around seventy. I will move from general observations about what these men's and women's personal experience stories tend to be about to increasingly specific claims about what sorts of social worlds the women and men create in their stories and how they make differential use of the resources of English to do this.

On the most general level the women's stories tend to be about community, while the men's tend to be about contest. The men tell about human contests—physical contests such as fights as well as social contests in which they use verbal and/or intellectual skill to defend their honor. They tell about contests with nature: hunting and fishing. Stories about contests with people or animals can take the form of tall tales, which are themselves a kind of contest between a teller and an audience. When a male storyteller is not the protagonist in his story, the protagonist is a man; men rarely tell stories involving women.[5]

The women's stories, on the other hand, revolve around the norms of the community and joint action by groups of people. The women tell about incidents in which they violate social norms and are scared or embarrassed as a result; about people helping other people out of scrapes; about sightings of apparent ghosts which are then explained by others; about meeting their mates and acquiring their cats. The women tell about peculiar people, dramatizing their abnormal behavior and setting it implicitly in contrast with social norms. They tell stories about themselves, about other women, and about men.

Looking in more detail at the plots of stories in which the teller is the protagonist—in other words, people's stories about themselves—one finds striking differences in how often male and female protagonists act alone and how often they act in concert with others, and what the outcome is in each case. Table 3.1 summarizes the figures to be mentioned.

Of a total of twenty-one men's stories about themselves, thirteen are about men acting alone, in such situations as these:

> A young man is hassled by another man in a bar but says the right threatening thing to put an end to the situation; he is with others, but no one else is involved in this interchange.

> The players on a semiprofessional softball team pour ice water on the club's public relations director, as a sort of initiation ritual; the victim responds in just the right clever way, by breaking into the song "Stormy Weather."

> By calling on his own willpower, a high school boy enables himself to beat forty or fifty other contestants in a cattle-judging competition.

When men act alone, the outcome is usually positive, as in these examples.

Of the twenty-six women's stories, protagonists act alone in only ten. In seven out of these ten, the outcome is bad: embarrassment, fright, pain, or failure. In one case, not consulting others is explicitly the reason for the bad outcome:

> A woman pays respects to the wrong corpse at a funeral home, and, worse, signs the visitors' book, a gaffe she could have avoided by asking someone for directions.

Table 3.1   Individual vs. Joint Action by Protagonists

	Men's Stories (N = 21)	Women's stories (N = 26)
Protagonist acts alone		
with bad outcome	3	7
with good outcome	10	3
TOTAL	13	10
Protagonist acts with others		
others are just there	4	5
others help and advise	4	11
TOTAL	8	16

In the other three stories in which female protagonist/tellers act alone, they are successful.

Eight men's stories are about acting in concert with others. Of the eight, however, four have men doing things together, but not advising or helping each other: deer hunting, training to be pilots, hunting for fishing worms, and fishing. Only four out of a total of twenty-one men's stories about themselves involve their actively helping or being helped or advised. In one (a tall tale), the protagonist asks for advice after he inadvertently shuts a cat in a freezer. In another, a mechanic sends his assistant to help with a car that won't start (though the mechanic himself is the one who eventually solves the problem). In another, a soldier and his buddies survive being stranded with a broken-down vehicle in a remote part of Germany, all working together. In the other, a driver prevails on a sheriff who has providentially arrived on the scene to do something about an erratic tailgater.

Sixteen women's stories have the woman acting in concert with others. In five of these, people are simply doing things together: trashing a laundromat, throwing crabapples at cars, joyriding in a friend's brother's car, vacationing in Europe, visiting socially. In the other eleven, though, the outcome depends crucially on cooperation with others. Examples are these:

> What could have been an embarrassing mistake (saying "Good God" instead of "Good morning" in Spanish) is shrugged off when the Spanish speaker being addressed laughs about it, because he's such a nice fellow.

> A woman trying to rescue her drowning nephew almost drowns too, but her sister borrows a life raft and saves both.

> A woman deals with the aftermath of a frightening skid in the snow with the help of neighbors, who give helpful advice, and the local police officer, who accompanies her back to the scene of the accident to retrieve her license plate and check for damage.

To summarize, the men's stories tend to be about contests in which the protagonist acts alone and is successful. When groups of men act in concert, they tend not to stand in relationships of advice or support, but rather simply to act as copresent buddies. The women, on the other hand, tell stories which stress the importance of community. When women's protagonists act alone, they tend not to be successful, and when groups of women act together, they do so in mutually supportive ways.[6]

Language and Storyworld

In addition to the thematic choices I have just described—choices about which events to narrate, about who does what in a story, and about how it comes out in the end—the men and women use a variety of strategies for how to talk—discourse choices—as they create their worlds of contest and community. I examine two of these here: extrathematic detail and reports of speech, both direct and indirect.

In many of the stories, both men's and women's, the teller includes more detail than is strictly necessary to move the story's plot along or provide minimal identification of its setting and characters. I call this type of detail "extrathematic."[7] When there is extrathematic detail in a story, it can take the form of extra specifications of place or time, titles of events like movies, descriptions of objects such as cars, or people's names—even sometimes when the storyteller's audience does not recognize the names. Table 3.2 shows what types of extrathematic detail occur in the men's and women's stories.

While the men specify place and time more often than do the women, the women use personal names more than twice as often as do the men. The figures in the table do not include unsuccessful attempts to recover proper names—sentences like "Now let's see, what was his name?" or "I wish I could remember his name." Attempts like these are made only by the women.

An additional type of extrathematic detail consists of reports of speech events that take place in the background—details like "we were just talking and visiting," "there they mostly spoke English," "he would sit and talk to my mother," or "I'm talking to, you know, somebody." While six of the women's stories mention such background talk, only two of the men's stories do. Especially interesting in this regard is one man's story, in which talk is rather conspicuously *not* mentioned as one of the things that went on during a long Saturday on a hunting trip:

The Saturday of that weekend,
we just did a lot of shooting,
and actually just lounging around camp a lot.
Did a little bit of hunting,
really just ... took it good and easy that day.

Hunting trips are, in fact, traditionally silent events, I am told; stories like this help create and perpetuate that tradition.

Table 3.2 Types and Numbers of Occurrences
of Extrathematic Detail in Stories

Type of Detail	Women's Stories	Men's Stories
specifications of place	11	18
specifications of time	3	7
descriptions of objects	1	5
titles of events	2	1
people's names	15	7
narrated reports of speech acts	6	2

Choices of detail, then, and especially choices of extrathematic detail, help create different worlds in the men's and the women's stories. People in the women's stories have names, and they sit around and talk; people in the men's stories are more often nameless, and their environment is more silent.

Talk is not just a possible background activity in these stories. Story plots sometimes revolve crucially around talk: saying the right thing can defuse a dangerous situation, for example, or a person's verbal response to an event can create the humor in a story. Perhaps because reported speech serves as an evaluative device (Labov 1972) in narrative, underscoring the point of a story by creating drama, and because the drama created through "constructed dialogue" helps establish rapport between storyteller and audience (Tannen 1986, 1989:98–133), both the male and the female storytellers use reported speech at least once in over half of their stories, as is shown in Table 3.3.

But while there is little difference between the men and the women in the percentage of *stories* that include reported speech, there is a notable difference in the percentage of breath-group *lines* that report speech. As Table 3.4 shows, half again as many women's story lines report speech as men's.

This is to say that when the women report speech in their stories, they do so at greater length and more often in the story. This is related to the observation reported previously that talk seems to be a more salient sort of detail for the women than for the men. Female tellers are sometimes frustrated when the exact words of their characters don't come to mind: "and I said ... I wish I could remember what I said!" One woman creates words in a foreign language she doesn't know (the Hispanic men who receives the disgusting package in "The Gift Box" are described as saying "Aeee, aeee"), and, in one story, a woman uses direct discourse to report words she—fortunately—*didn't* say to a patient delivering a large urine sample at her husband's rural medical office:

> So I was .. I was saved from *terrible* embarrassment,
> because I *hadn't* actually said,
> 'My husband will sure enjoy this,
> he *loves* cider!"

To report speech that wasn't spoken is clearly a creative choice. Maybe more obviously than most but no differently from any other, this story-

Table 3.3 Men's and Women's Stories
Including Reported Speech

	Men's Stories (N = 25)	Women's Stories (N = 33)
Reported speech present	15 (60%)	24 (73%)
No reported speech	10 (40%)	9 (27%)

Table 3.4   Total Number of Lines in Men's and Women's
Stories Reporting Speech

	Men's Stories (N = 25)	Women's Stories (N = 33)
Total no. lines	1,538	1,885
Lines with reported speech	129 (8.3%)	242 (12%)

teller is creating a world, not just reporting about one. This woman's world is like the worlds many women create in their stories: a world in which what you don't say is as important as what you do say; a world in which linguistic interaction is crucial.

A Community Story

I now turn to an illustration of the use to which stories like the women's can be put in a larger social context. In the spring of 1982 there was severe flooding in the city in which (or around which) these stories were collected. Thousands of people had to leave their homes, and millions of dollars worth of property was damaged. In the course of the two-week-long disaster a public story about it was created in the local and national news media. What began as reports of water-level and evacuation statistics turned into a well-developed narrative, with animate characters (the water as calculating enemy, the city as war-weary hero), consistent imagery (both militaristic and Christian), and a clear moral. This story was told and retold in various guises. The version which follows is from a special souvenir tabloid section of the evening newspaper, which appeared after the crisis was over (Fort Wayne *Journal-Gazette,* special section "The Flood of '82," March 19, 1982, p. 2):

> They are charming rivers some springs. Their banks green with budding plants and trees, the three waterways glide gracefully past homes and parks in Fort Wayne, a delight for fishing, canoeing or a moment's peaceful contemplation.
> But in the spring of 1982, the Maumee, the St. Marys and the St. Joseph rivers became an awesome and devastating natural force when the worst possible weather conditions—a record winter's snow and ice, heavy rain and a rapid thaw—sent tons of water pouring into their channels.
> In a disaster that was heard about around the world, the bloated rivers outgrew their banks and burst their streams, reclaiming thousands of acres of lowlands and plundering cars, homes, farms and lives.
>
> . . .
>
> "When I went to sleep Saturday night, there wasn't any water," said one stunned Nebraska resident. "When I woke up Sunday morning, it was at the front door."
> Nebraska neighbors—and later, those along Sherman Boulevard and Superior Street—clung to their homes until the rising rivers began pouring into their streets and basements, bursting up through sewers with a force

that popped off manhole covers and bubbled into houses through drains and toilets.

. . .

And then the two rivers gushed into the backed-up Maumee at the confluence in the heart of Fort Wayne. By March 18, when it crested at 1 a.m., the Maumee had become a 25.93-foot wall of treacherous water, straining the city's aging dikes and holding 4,000 neighbors in the Lakeside area and 2,000 others who were evacuated for precautions in suspense for days.

Only *the superhuman labors of hundreds of other neighbors,* most of them teen-agers, saved the graceful, old neighborhoods. With water seeping through the muddy mound of the Pemberton Drive dike on the city's northeast side on the night of March 17, *the volunteers swallowed their fears and strained under the weight of 25,000 sandbags an hour* to bolster the sagging dikes.

. . .

But The Flood of '82 left a mark on Fort Wayne that the cleanup effort can't erase. After two years of morale-beating recession and unemployment, *Fort Wayne warmed the nation's soul—and surprised itself in the measure—with an outpouring of care and help from its citizens.*

The estimated 60,000 volunteers, serving meals, filling sandbags, building dikes, *turned the battle against the rivers into a triumphant celebration of neighborly love.* In a city that celebrates the three rivers each July, the flood fight lent new eloquence to the meaning of the Festival of the Three Rivers.

This story presents elements of contest and community both. The contest is that of the city against the rivers. But the city is a collectivity: it is the fact that people worked together that allowed the city to prevail in this contest. This is a story, then, in which community overcomes contest.[8] The segments I have italicized highlight this theme. People are referred to as "neighbors" or "volunteers" who have to "swallow their fears" and "strain" to save the city. They "care" and "help." What starts out as a contest—a battle with the rivers—ends up as "a triumphant celebration of neighborly love." This celebration of community allowed the story to be used, later, as the basis for a very effective public relations campaign for the city, designed around the slogan "The City That Saved Itself." The city thus created itself as a world and presented itself to the world in the terms of a story of community.

Discussion

This analysis of some midwestern men's and women's personal experience stories has shown that there is a tendency for the women's stories to involve social power: disturbing or dangerous events are overcome through the power of interdependence and community. Accordingly the women tend to include more details about people than do the men and more reported conversation. The men, on the other hand, tend to create worlds of contest in which power comes from the individual acting in opposition to others. The men tend to use more details about places, times, and objects than do the women, and they tend to report less of others' speech.

I have argued that neither of these two strategies for resolving the disturbances that give rise to narrative is inherently more powerful or reflective of greater power than the other. To make this point, I showed how the story that arose out of a disturbance in the life of the city in which these men and women live invoked the power of community most often represented in the women's stories as well as the power of contest most often represented in the men's. The theme of the flood story is the theme of many American stories, including the American Revolution as it exists in the popular mind: a beleaguered group of citizens acts as a community to defeat an unjust force from outside.

I have also suggested that women's and men's narratives are not simply the products of women's and men's worlds. People create worlds in discourse, as they create selves, communities, and places (Johnstone 1990b). The women storytellers I have been talking about often present themselves, as individuals, as powerless: things happen to them, and when they act alone they are unsuccessful. The women need other people, and when they act in concert with others they overcome the challenges they tell stories about. The community is thus the source of the women's power, and this social power is tapped through discourse—through real talk among named people. I see the women's stories, then, not as examples of powerless discourse or of women's discourse about their powerless worlds. I find it more useful to see these women's stories as statements about the world-creating power of discourse.

NOTES

I am grateful to the men and women whose stories I analyze here, and to the student field workers who collected them. Versions of this chapter were presented at the "Discourses of Power" conference held at Arizona State University in October 1988 and at the "Georgetown University Bicentennial Conference on Women in America" held in April 1989; audiences at both conferences made useful suggestions, as has Deborah Tannen. Delma McLeod-Porter passed along some relevant articles uncovered in her research on girls' and boys' written narratives.

1. The stories discussed in this chapter were collected between 1981 and 1984 by students at Indiana University–Purdue University, Fort Wayne. The field workers taped ordinary, casual conversations among their families and friends and later transcribed stories that had been told during the conversations. See Johnstone (1990b:12–14) for a description of the project.

The transcription system used here is fairly conventional. Stories are transcribed in lines, each of which corresponds to a breath group and ends with final rising or falling intonation. This way of transcribing oral narrative and the rationale for transcribing this way are described in Chafe (1980). Rising intonation is indicated with a question mark. Falling intonation is indicated with a comma, if the line ends with an intermediate drop in volume and pitch, or a period, if it ends with a sentence-final drop. Hesitations of less than a second are marked with from one to three dots; hesitations of more than a second with the number of seconds, in parentheses. Nonverbal accompaniments to the talk are described in square brackets. Overlap (simultaneous speech or laughter) is indicated with brackets connecting the overlapping segments. Talk that follows immediately on another's talk is indicated with equals signs connecting the relevant turns. Raised volume is indicated with italics, and especially loud talk is in small capital letters. Unfilled parentheses, in one place, show that what was said is not intelligible on the tape.

2. This is not the case, for example, for Thais (Neill 1987), whose stories about personal experience often include supernatural explanations for events.

3. Stories about the supernatural are, as I have mentioned, relatively rare in the corpus of narrative with which I am working. When they are told, they often sound more like rehearsed recitations than spontaneous anecdotes. More are told by women than by men—"The Presence of a Presence" is an exception—but there are not enough of them to support generalizations. I will not discuss stories of this type in what follows.

4. The "mainstream" is not, of course, a monolithic whole, and the data I am discussing are not to be taken as representative of all of mainstream culture. As I show elsewhere (Johnstone 1990a, b), these stories are closely and in many ways tied to the community in which they were told. Whether they are representative of the narrative style of any larger group is an empirical question, with which I have not been primarily concerned. As Senta Troemmel-Ploetz has pointed out to me, my concern with maintaining a specific, particularlistic stance vis-à-vis these data mirrors, in a way, the concern of the women storytellers with specific, named people, and with real talk. It also reflects my theoretical orientation toward the "linguistics of particularity" (Becker 1984, 1988).

5. Mills (1985) finds the same pattern in oral narratives of women and men in Afghanistan: "men tend to tell stories about men, whereas women tell stories about women and men" (187).

6. In a study of 236 written narratives by white midwestern college students, Warshay (1972) found that the males involve themselves more in relation to events than do the females, locating events in a personal sphere of activity and making less reference to others than do females. Females, on the other hand, locate events in an interacting community, "seek[ing] satisfaction in primary relations in the local community" (8). Warshay's findings are strikingly similar to the results of the analysis reported here, as are those of Flynn (1988), who analyzes four student narratives and finds that "the narratives of the female students are stories of interaction, of connection, or of frustrated connection. The narratives of the male students are stories of achievement, of separation, or of frustrated achievement" (428). Flynn's students are probably midwesterners (they are first-year students at a Michigan college); their race is not identified. McLeod-Porter (1991) finds similar distinctions in an analysis of written stories by black and white adolescents in east-central Texas.

7. Extrathematic detail is discussed in greater detail in Johnstone (1990a).

8. There is a great deal more that could be said about this story, some of which I have tried to say elsewhere (Johnstone 1990b:109–125).

REFERENCES

Adams, Karen, and Edelsky, Carole (1988). Male and female styles in political debates. In Kathleen Ferrara, Becky Brown, Keith Walters & John Baugh (Eds.) *Linguistic change and contact: Proceedings of NWAV XVI (Texas Lin-*

guistics Forum, Vol. 30) (pp. 18–24). Austin: University of Texas, Department of Linguistics.

Baldwin, Karen (1985). "Woof!" A word on women's roles in family storytelling. In Rosan A. Jordan & Susan J. Kalčik (Eds.) *Women's folklore, women's culture* (pp. 149–162). Philadelphia: University of Pennsylvania Press.

Becker, A. L. (1984). The linguistics of particularity: Interpreting superordination in a Javanese text. In Claudia Brugman & Monica Macaulay (with Amy Dahlstrom, Michele Emanatian, Birch Moonwomon & Catherine O'Connor) (Eds.) *Proceedings of the Berkeley Linguistics Society, Tenth Annual Meeting* (425–436). Berkeley, CA: Berkeley Linguistics Society.

Becker, A. L. (1988). Language in particular: A lecture. In Deborah Tannen (Ed.) *Linguistics in context: Connecting observation and understanding* (pp. 17–35). Norwood, NJ: Ablex.

Boe, S. Kathryn (1987). Language as an expression of caring in women. *Anthropological Linguistics* 29:271–285.

Bruner, Jerome (1986). *Actual minds, possible worlds.* Cambridge, MA: Harvard University Press.

Chafe, Wallace (1980). The deployment of consciousness in the production of a narrative. In Wallace Chafe (Ed.) *The pear stories: Cognitive, cultural, and linguistic aspects of narrative production* (pp. 1–50). Norwood, NJ: Ablex.

Fishman, Pamela (1978). Interactions: The work women do. *Social Problems* 25:397–406.

Flynn, Elizabeth A. (1988). Composing as a woman. *College Composition and Communication* 39:423–435.

Gilligan, Carol (1982). *In a different voice: Psychological theory and women's development.* Cambridge, MA: Harvard University Press.

Harding, Susan (1975). Women and words in a Spanish village. In Rayna Reiter (Ed.) *Towards an anthropology of women* (pp. 283–308). New York: Monthly Review Press.

Jahner, Elaine (1985). Woman remembering: Life history as exemplary pattern. In Rosan A. Jordan & Susan J. Kalčik (Eds.) *Women's folklore, women's culture* (pp. 214–233). Philadelphia: University of Pennsylvania Press.

Johnstone, Barbara (1987). "He says . . . so I said": Verb tense alternation and narrative depictions of authority in American English. *Linguistics* 25:33–52.

Johnstone, Barbara (1990a). Variation in discourse: Midwestern narrative style. *American Speech* 65(3):195–214.

Johnstone, Barbara (1990b). *Stories, community, and place: Narratives from middle America.* Bloomington: Indiana University Press.

Jones, Deborah (1980). Gossip: Notes on women's oral culture. In Cheris Kramarae (Ed.) *The voices and words of women and men* (pp. 193–198). Oxford: Pergamon Press.

Kalčik, Susan (1975). ". . . like Ann's gynecologist or the time I was almost raped." In Claire R. Farrer (Ed.) *Women and folklore* (pp. 3–11). Austin: University of Texas Press.

Kramarae, Cheris, Schulz, Muriel & O'Barr, William M. (1984). Introduction: Toward an understanding of language and power. In Cheris Kramarae, Muriel Schulz & William M. O'Barr (Eds.) *Language and power* (pp. 9–22). Beverly Hills, CA: Sage.

Labov, William (1972). The transformation of experience in narrative syntax. In

Language in the inner city (pp. 354–396). Philadelphia: University of Pennsylvania Press.

Lakoff, Robin (1975). *Language and woman's place*. New York: Harper and Row.

LeGuin, Ursula (1989). *Dancing at the edge of the world*. New York: Grove Press.

Maltz, Daniel N. & Borker, Ruth A. (1982). A cultural approach to male-female communication. In John J. Gumperz (Ed.) *Language and social interaction* (pp. 196–216). Cambridge: Cambridge University Press.

McLaughlin, Margaret C., Cody, Michael J., Kane, Marjorie L. & Robey, Carl S. (1981). Sex differences in story receipt and story sequencing behaviors in dyadic conversation. *Human Communication Research* 7:99–116.

McLeod-Porter, Delma (1991). Gender, ethnicity, and narrative: A linguistic and rhetorical analysis of adolescents' personal experience stories. Diss., Texas A&M University.

Mills, Margaret (1985). Sex role reversals, sex changes, and transvestite disguise in the oral tradition of a conservative muslim community in Afghanistan. In Rosan A. Jordan & Susan J. Kalčik (Eds.) *Women's folklore, women's culture* (pp. 187–213). Philadelphia: University of Pennsylvania Press.

Mitchell, Carol (1985). Some differences in male and female joke-telling. In Rosan A. Jordan & Susan J. Kalčik (Eds.) *Women's folklore, women's culture* (pp. 163–186). Philadelphia: University of Pennsylvania Press.

Neill, Catherine R. (1987). Sources of meaning in Thai narrative discourse: Grammar, rhetoric, and socio-cultural knowledge. Diss., Georgetown University.

O'Barr, William M. & Atkins, Bowman K. (1980). "Women's language" or "powerless language"? In Sally McConnell-Ginet, Ruth Borker, & Nelly Furman, *Women and language in literature and society* (pp. 93–110). New York: Praeger.

Polanyi, Livia (1985). *Telling the American story: A structural and cultural analysis of conversational storytelling*. Norwood, NJ: Ablex.

Rakow, Lana F. (1986). The telephone and women's talk: An ethnographic study. Paper presented at Speech Communication Association Annual Conference, Chicago, Nov. 1986.

Schafer, Roy (1981). Narration in the psychoanalytic dialogue. In W.J.T. Mitchell (Ed.) *On narrative* (pp. 25–49). Chicago: University of Chicago Press.

Silberstein, Sandra (1988). Ideology as process: Gender ideology in courtship narratives. In Alexandra Dundas Todd & Sue Fisher (Eds.) *Gender and discourse: The power of talk* (pp. 125–149). Norwood, NJ: Ablex.

Tannen, Deborah (1982). Ethnic style in male-female conversation. In John J. Gumperz (Ed.) *Language and social interaction* (pp. 217–231). Cambridge: Cambridge University Press.

Tannen, Deborah (1986). Introducing constructed dialogue in Greek and American conversational and literary narrative. In Florian Coulmas (Ed.) *Direct and indirect speech* (pp. 311–332). Berlin, New York, Amsterdam: Mouton de Gruyter.

Tannen, Deborah (1989). *Talking voices: Repetition, dialogue, and imagery in conversational discourse*. Cambridge: Cambridge University Press.

Tannen, Deborah (1990). *You just don't understand: Women and men in conversation*. New York: Ballantine.

Turner, Victor (1981). Social dramas and stories about them. In W.J.T. Mitchell (Ed.) *On narrative* (pp. 137–164). Chicago: University of Chicago Press.

Warshay, Diana W. (1972). Sex differences in language style. In Constantina Safilios-Rothschild (Ed.) *Toward a sociology of women* (pp. 3–9). Lexington, MA: Xerox College Publications.

West, Candace & Zimmerman, Don H. (1983). Small insults: A study of interruptions in cross-sex conversations between unacquainted persons. In Barrie Thorne, Cheris Kramarae, & Nancy Henley (Eds.) *Language, gender, and society* (pp. 102–117). Rowley, MA: Newbury House.

Young, Katharine Galloway (1987). *Taleworlds and storyrealms*. Boston: Martinus Nijhoff.

Zimmerman, Don H. & West, Candace (1975). Sex roles, interruptions and silences in conversation. In Barrie Thorne & Nancy Henley (Eds.) *Language and sex: Difference and dominance* (pp. 105–129). Rowley, MA: Newbury House.

II

CONFLICT TALK

4

Pickle Fights:
Gendered Talk in
Preschool Disputes

AMY SHELDON

Introduction

Conversations are a fundamental, yet mysterious, part of our lives.
Through them we learn to express ourselves as female or male. This chapter is concerned with the connections between language and the development of gender identity in early childhood. What is the effect of gender on
how children construct the oral texts that embody their everyday social
interactions? Does the language that young children use in conflict episodes reflect gender socialization and, if so, in what way? I present a close
analysis of two long disputes that occurred during the spontaneous play of
three-year-old friends in same-sex groups. The chapter contains four sections. The first section is a survey of gender socialization in childhood
through language socialization by adults and peers. Gender differences in
dispute management are also discussed. The second section is a description
of two frameworks for thinking about how gender is reflected in the ways
that language is used. The third section is a description of the study of two
disputes over a plastic pickle, one in a girls' group and the other in a boys'
group. The fourth section contains concluding remarks.

Gender Socialization Through Language

Gender Socialization Through Language Socialization

Expectations about appropriate gendered behavior are powerful. Feminist
scholars and others have pointed out that gender is "the primary category

by which the social world is organized" (Eagly 1987, Goffman 1979, Hare-Mustin 1988; see also Kessler & McKenna 1978). However, thinking about gender is complicated. Thorne (1980, 1986) argues for an approach that analyzes the way gendered behavior is shaped and constrained by the situation and the context. According to Deaux and Kite (1987), research on gender is moving more in this direction. In addition, feminist scholars in a variety of disciplines have argued that discussions of gender must be broadened to include factors such as class, race, and ethnicity. Thus, the study of the interconnectedness of language and gender depends as much on what we understand the characteristics of gendered behavior to be as it does on which aspects of language and which aspects of situations we choose to study.

Language is a part of culture and an instrument for transmitting and perpetuating implicit, historically situated, and culture-bound principles of social order and systems of belief that define and assign unequal social value to femininity and masculinity. Not surprisingly, recent sociolinguistic research in various cultures has found gender differences in the speech styles of adults (e.g., Philips, Steele & Tanz 1987, Thorne, Kramarae & Henley 1983). From this we can expect that language is a major influence on what and how children learn about gender and that gender is a major influence on the way children use language in everyday life. Language functions not only to initiate novices but also to perpetuate and enforce asymmetrical gendered behavior by means of reconstructing social relations between and among females and males in countless ordinary daily conversations over a lifetime.

The process by which children and other novices learn to use language in ways that fit a culture's norms of appropriate feminine and masculine behavior is called *language socialization* (Schieffelin & Ochs 1986). The influence of language as a powerful tool of *gender* socialization has, until recently, been largely overlooked in child language research. In a review of the language acquisition literature, Klann-Delius (1981) declares that studies that test whether or not there are gender differences in children's language are in "dire need of being developed." Such studies are beginning to appear.

Interaction with adults is one way that children are "socialized through language and socialized to use language" (Schieffelin & Ochs 1986:2) according to the local gender ideology and norms. Sociocultural information about gender is encoded in the organization of discourse. Thus adults influence children by providing models of women and men talking to each other (Fishman 1983), as well as to children (Freedle & Lewis 1977, Gieason 1987, Lewis & Cherry 1977), that children can identify with and learn from.

Gender Role Socialization Through Peer Talk and Peer Play

Children spend much time in the company of other children. So, in addition to language socialization by adults, we can expect language socialization by peers. In a review of cross-cultural studies of child development, Whiting and Edwards (1988) conclude that patterns of interpersonal behavior are most influenced by the company that one keeps and the organization of activities performed with that company. If girls and boys frequently engage in different activities, which evoke different forms of social organization, then there will be differences in their behavior. We would expect this to be true for language behavior, although research has just begun to study this question.

Just how much children play with same-sex companions, given the chance to do so, and what sorts of activities same-sex groupings prefer, are important questions for understanding the nature of peer talk in childhood. Same-sex play increases the opportunity to learn about, try out, reproduce, and solidify gender-appropriate styles of language use. Whiting and Edwards (1988:81) claim that the "emergence of same-sex preferences in childhood is a cross-culturally universal and robust phenomenon." Their cross-cultural research and the work of others found that children begin to show preferences for same-sex companions around the age of two or three years. Same-sex play increases with age and is more prevalent in the peer group than in the mixed-age group. The robustness of same-sex play shows up even in mixed-sex play, where a child's nearest companion will often be of the same sex. Cahill (1986) notes that same-sex play co-occurs with children's inclination to regard members of the other sex with "benign hostility," as if they were tainted. Thorne (1986) found that working-class elementary school children defined girls as "polluting," and it is more taboo for a boy to play with a girl than vice versa. This gender mythology heightens children's awareness of sexual boundaries and, presumably, strengthens their belief in its importance.

Given the possible universal preference for same-sex play starting in very early childhood, how do female and male play groups differ? In what ways does same-sex play in childhood constitute an experience of growing up in different conceptual, social, and linguistic environments? Do girls and boys have different experiences of common events such as conflict? How do girls' groups and boys' groups function in ways that produce predictably different speech events?

Female and male play groups in the United States have been found to differ in marked ways that exert powerful influences in shaping behavior (Brooks-Gunn & Matthews 1979, Cahill 1986, Ellis, Rogoff & Cromer 1981, Maccoby 1986, Thorne 1986). Of particular relevance to this paper is the observation by Jennings and Suwalsky (1982) that white, middle-class, three-year-old girls in dyads spent more time in sustained, mutual play, whereas boys spent more time in solitary play, interactions with others that were not sustained, or interactions in which they pursued their own activity or attempted to impose their own ideas. McLoyd (1983) reports that lower class boys in same-sex groups who play-acted domestic script fantasies (e.g., playing "mommy," "daddy," and "baby") did so less frequently than girls and for a shorter time. Such group play turns into solitary play or play alongside another child with toys such as trucks, in which they create individual fantasy scripts.

Maccoby (1986) notes that, although there is considerable overlap between boys and girls on individual social characteristics, as a group their social behaviors are highly differentiated by sex. Thorne (1980, 1986), on the other hand, emphasizes that situations constrain behavior. Girls' and boys' behavior may be more a function of the particular context of their play activities than of intrinsic gender attributes. Goodwin and Goodwin (1987) stress the same point in the study of children's speech. Finally, Maccoby (1986:271) points out that "we have a clearer picture of what girls' groups do *not* do than what they *do* do," so there is a need for a "more clearly delineated account of interaction in female social groups."

Gender Differences in Dispute Management

In this chapter I use the definition of *conflict* proposed by Eisenberg and Garvey (1981:150): "an interaction which grows out of an opposition to a request for action, an assertion, or an action . . . and ends with a resolution or dissipation of conflict." The disputes discussed in this paper are mutual oppositions, rather than an opposition raised by just one child.

Observing children's conflict management provides a lens on the social and linguistic context of development. C. Shantz (1987) suggests that conflicts are an important part of getting to know other people. Conflicts arise because of incompatibility in wants, goals, and behavior. Successful resolution requires the participants to adapt to each other. Goodwin and Goodwin (1987) point out that conflicts provide an opportunity for children to demonstrate and learn a variety of discourse skills. Miller, Danaher, and Forbes (1986) frame two perspectives on conflict: the first is to see it foremost as a contest, a "competition of viewpoints," and to focus on the tactics used for persuasion and control; the second perspective considers the emotionally threatening aspects and focuses on tactics that restore interpersonal function and harmony. Thus, each conflict has the potential of being aggravated and escalated or of being mitigated and resolved with a sense of community restored. Seen in this way, it is not surprising that nonaggressive conflict doesn't block friendships in childhood; Green (1933:251) found that, in childhood, "mutual friends are more quarrelsome, and mutual quarrelers are more friendly than the average." Moreover, in some cultures, conflict is a form of sociability and a display of solidarity (Schiffrin 1984).

Studies of conflict in the child development literature, however, have been largely about aggressive conflict that injures or threatens to injure another person. Boys' play is more physically aggressive than girls' (DiPietro 1981, Maccoby & Jacklin 1974, 1980). Nevertheless physical force accounts for a small percentage of the strategies that children use to manage conflict (Eisenberg & Garvey 1981). Preschool girls have more nonaggressive conflicts than preschool boys do (D. Shantz & Schomer 1977), fighting more often over issues of personal control, whereas boys fight more over objects. Considering such differences, it seems reasonable to ask whether there are other differences in girls' and boys' disputes and, if so, how they affect girls' and boys' characteristic verbal strategies for conflict management.

Two Models of Gendered Styles in Children's Talk

A research program that aims to describe and eventually explain the acquisition and cultural transmission of gender through language is faced with the question of how to theorize gender. How is femininity different from masculinity? To look at verbal conflict through a gendered lens, we need a model of gender and an idea of what features of language use differentiate the sexes.

Affiliative Versus Adversarial Styles

Maltz and Borker (1982) present a model of gender-marked language use. They hypothesize that, between five and fifteen years of age, American children learn conversational rules from same-sex peer groups with different results. However, it is clear that even the speech of children younger than five can be differentiated by gender (Garcia-Zamor 1973, Haas 1979, Leaper 1991, Meditch 1975, Sachs 1987). Maltz and Borker claim that boys' and girls' speech is thought to have different content and to serve different purposes. Male speech can be characterized as *competition oriented*, or *adversarial*. Boys' (and men's) groups are thought to be hierarchical and competitive. Boys play in larger groups (Brooks-Gunn & Matthews 1979), and their play is rougher than girls' (DiPietro 1981). Maltz and Borker (1982:207) state that boys use speech to "1) assert one's position of dominance, 2) attract and maintain an audience, and 3) assert oneself when other speakers have the floor."

On the other hand, female speech can be characterized as *collaboration oriented*, or *affiliative*. DiPietro (1981), Fishman (1983), Goodwin (1980), Kalčik (1975), Leaper (1991), and Maccoby (1986) claim that girls (and women) use language more cooperatively, sharing turns to speak more often than boys, showing more verbal organization of group behavior, acknowledging what others have said, and expressing agreement more. They show more interest in what other people are saying by responding to and elaborating on what others have said, by making more supportive comments, by asking more questions, and by working harder to keep conversations going. Closeness has been proposed as a developmental theme for girls, whereas separation is a theme for boys (Bakan 1966, Chodorow 1978, Eagly 1987). Maltz and Borker (1982:205) claim that girls learn to use words: "1) to create and maintain relationships of closeness and equality; 2) to criticize others in acceptable ways; and 3) to interpret accurately the speech of other girls."

James and Drakich (this volume) observe that white, middle-class American women's affiliative orientation makes it difficult for women to assert status or dominance. Consistent with this is the popular belief that an assertive woman is "pushy" or a "bitch" but an assertive man is "manly." Competition has even been called a "taboo" for women (Miner & Longino 1987). Girls criticize other girls for being "bossy" or "mean" if they tell others what to do. Presumably what is being objected to is the creation of inequality through a dominance hierarchy. Lever's (1976) study has often been referred to in discussions of females and conflict. She found that fifth-grade girls' play and games did not tolerate or resolve conflict but disbanded instead. Subsequent work by Goodwin (1980) and Goodwin and Goodwin (1987) shows that urban, working-class black girls do engage in conflict and can be even more skillful at it than boys. They frequently have conflicts and exchange ritual insults without disrupting their play. In this study, arguments were as common for girls as they were for boys and could even be more extensive. Girls also were skillful in legalistic debate. On the other hand, Goodwin (1980) found that the social organization of the girls' group was more egalitarian than the boys', with minimal negotiation of status. This group's activity was linguistically organized by syntactic forms that enabled joint decision making and joint action. Requests were presented in the context of what the situation or the group required, rather than of what a group member was obligated to do. The structure of the boys' group was more hierarchical. The boys were more self-serving and negotiated status more. Their requests for action were usually issued in the form of direct commands.

In a study in which dominant and subordinate middle-class children were paired as play partners, Camras (1984) found that dominant boys were much less polite than either dominant girls or subordinate girls and boys. On the other hand, older dominant girls were as polite as or more so than their subordinate partners or than younger dominant girls. Camras (p. 263) interprets these results as showing that these dominant girls "are gradually socialized to mask their exercise of power during conflicts with use of polite language." Goodwin (1980) also found that, in certain activities, girls mitigated their attempts to control other girls and avoided the *appearance* of hierarchy. Thus girls and women are forced by gender prescriptions to avoid or limit *direct* self-assertion during competition and conflict, at least in certain situations.

Focus on the Relationship Versus Focus on the Self

Another perspective on gender and conflict that is concerned with the themes of affiliation and independence comes from the work of Gilligan (1982, 1987, 1988) and her associates. This work looks at how females and males differ in reasoning about hypothetical and real-life moral conflict. Gilligan's model makes predictions that are relevant to young children's verbal management of conflict. Gilligan claims that people approach the resolution of moral conflict from "care" and "justice" orientations. Women are most likely to focus on the care orientation and men on the justice orientation. However, both orientations are used by women and men, although only one is focused on at a time. Neither orientation belongs to just one sex. The following discussion transposes Gilligan's care and justice orientations into a hypothesis about young children's everyday conflict styles.

Female-Associated Conflict Style: Focus on the Relationship

The care orientation focuses on maintaining the connection between oneself and others in intimate groups, on defining the self in the context of the relationship (Gilligan 1987). Terms used by others to describe this focus are *communion, affiliation, empathy, interdependence,* and *involvement* (Bakan 1966, Eagly 1987, Leaper 1991). This perspective pays more attention to the needs of others. The following characteristics of this perspective, presented in Gilligan (1987), might also be associated with girls' dispute management. A person who operates from the care orientation (1) assumes connection between the self and others, frames conflict resolution in terms of the relationship; (2) shows greater tolerance of, compassion for, and responsiveness to others; (3) emphasizes understanding and communication through listening and speaking, hearing, and being heard; (4) seeks agreement and tries to respond to everyone's needs; (5) shows less legalistic elaboration; (6) shows willingness to make exceptions to rules; (7) appeals more to a particularistic understanding of others and less to a universal point of view.

Recent research on girls' language use is consistent with these predictions. Miller et al. (1986:543) claim that their female subjects were more concerned with maintaining interpersonal harmony during conflict than boys were. Observing racially and socioeconomically mixed five- and seven-year-olds playing in mixed-sex groupings, they found that girls used significantly more tactics that mitigated conflict, such as compromise and peaceful acquiescence, than boys did. They also used less heavy-handed persuasion tactics. Leaper (1991) found that collaborative speech acts were more frequent than controlling speech acts in the dyads of middle-class, educationally advantaged girls aged four to nine years. Girls also showed greater positive reciprocity. Other studies that do not have conflict as their focus support the theme of mitigation as a female-associated behavior. Preschool girls give directives and otherwise regulate the behavior of peers using mitigated and indirect speech (Sachs 1987). They learn to "say it with a smile." Differences in directness in the speech of American women and men have been noted by Gleason (1987).

Male-Associated Conflict Style: Focus on the Self

The justice orientation focuses on autonomy (Gilligan 1987). Terms used to describe this focus are *agency, self-assertion, individuality* (Bakan 1966, Eagly 1987, Leaper 1991). This orientation tends to appeal to a universal point of view, rather than to the particular concerns and needs of others and of one's relationship with them. The following characteristics of this perspective, discussed in Gilligan (1987), may also be associated with boys' dispute management. A person who operates from the justice orientation (1) frames conflict in terms of individual rights that must be respected in the relationship; (2) values detachment, independence, and autonomy; (3) assumes separation and the need for an external structure of connection; (4) steps back from the situation and appeals to a rule or reasons from a principle to resolve conflict, valuing logic, rationality, and control and often losing sight of the needs of others; (5) attends to rights and respect.

Recent research on boys' language use is consistent with these predictions. Miller, Danaher & Forbes (1986:543) claim that the boys in their study were more "forceful" in pursuing their own agenda than the girls were. Boys also had more conflict episodes than girls did, as also noted by Dawe (1934). They engaged in the more heavy-handed tactics of threats and physical force. Boys' dyads have shown greater amounts of controlling speech acts and more negative reciprocity (Leaper 1991). Sachs (1987) found more unmitigated requests and prohibitions in the speech of preschool boys. These results are consistent with those of Lever (1976), who found that fifth-grade boys' games involved continual quarrelling and that they seemed to enjoy legalistic disputes about rules.

The Pickle Fights

Method

The conversations to be examined here are from an extensive research project with three- to five-year-old children at a day-care center in a large midwestern city. The children were grouped into twelve same-sex triads on the basis of friendship and age. The groups were formed after consultation with the children's teachers. The participants in this study were educationally and socially advantaged, middle-class, urban children who were predominantly white. The children attended the day-care center for full days, year round, and had known each other for one to three years.

The triads were videotaped during the regular day-care day in one of the children's usual play areas, which was separate from the larger group. The only children in the room were those being filmed. They were not supervised by an adult, although an assistant and I sat somewhat out of sight in a play loft above and behind the children's play area. The children knew we were there. They were videotaped on three separate occasions, each time playing at one of three types of activities. Each group was videotaped for a total of approximately seventy-five minutes (twenty-five minutes per session).

The choice to group in triads rather than dyads was made on the assumption that this would produce more talk. It also produces greater complications in recording and transcribing because the three voices must be identifiable. To solve this problem, each child wore a vest that had a lavalier microphone attached to the front and a wireless microphone transmitter in a pocket on the back. An audio technician, who was out of sight, recorded each child's voice on a separate audio cassette at the same time that the three voices were mixed onto the videotape sound channel. Later, during transcription, if it was unclear which child was speaking, the transcriber could verify by playing back that child's individual audiotape.

This chapter examines extended disputes that arose in two of the twelve triads: one in a girls' group and the other in a boys' group. The girls' ages were 3.0, 3.7, and 3.11 years; the mean was 3.7 years. The boys' ages were 3.8, 3.9, and 4.0 years; the mean was 3.8 years. All but one (Lisa) were firstborn children.

The conflicts both come from housekeeping sessions. For this activity the room was set up with a number of props for dramatic play. There was a housekeeping area that had a toy stove and sink, a basket of lifelike plastic food items, cooking pots, plastic eating utensils, and paper plates and cups. Nearby was a child-size dining table with three chairs. A doll's high chair was placed on the fourth side. In a nearby area there was a telephone next to a child-size easy chair. There was also a doll's bed with dolls and blankets in it. Close by was a doctor's kit. There was an area with dress-up clothes and a mirror.

These two sessions produced two long disputes. Both were fights over one of the food items, a plastic pickle, that had become part of one child's play. The girls' conflict lasted one minute and forty-five seconds and contained forty turns. The boys' conflict lasted five minutes and contained seventy turns. In a study of nearly two hundred preschool children, grouped into dyads, Eisenberg and Garvey (1981) found that 92% of conflict episodes were shorter than ten turns and 66% were shorter than five. The average length of children's conflicts has been computed across a number of studies to be twenty-four seconds (C. Shantz 1987). The greater length of the disputes discussed here could have come from a variety of factors, such as the facts that they occurred in a triad; they were not monitored by an adult who, in other circumstances, might have stepped in and terminated them; the participants were friends; and the dispute was over an object that was the only one of its kind.

Differences in the Use of the Pretend Frame by the Girls and the Boys

The number of themes involved in the girls' and boys' fantasy play in the full session was similar: five themes for the boys and seven themes for the girls. However, a more interesting pattern emerges if one looks at the number of times that the children changed the theme of their play. There were seven theme shifts for the girls and seventeen theme shifts for the boys. Shifts were from pretend play themes like preparing food, talking on the telephone, taking a trip, and dressing up. In addition, two of the shifts out of a pretend play theme for the boys involved unresolved conflicts or competition for resources. These shifts served as transitions out of the conflict. They provided temporary resolution of the dispute, but conflict resurfaced in the next play frame. There were no shifts out of a play theme and into another for the girls as a result of conflict. Play theme shift was not the mechanism that the girls used to resolve their dispute.

The different number of play theme shifts in the two groups reflects the different balance struck in each group between (a) involvement in the joint construction of pretend play and (b) opposition that prevented the joint construction of pretend play. The girls' agenda appeared to be that of jointly inventing and sharing play. Their conflict episodes did not prevent the rich elaboration of their pretend play. In fact, each girl used the pretend frame to try to convince the other girl to let her have the pickle. On the other hand, the boys' agenda seemed to be to oppose one another. Their strategies escalated the conflict. They used the pretend frame less than the girls. The result was that their pretend play was much less developed, each play theme lasted for a shorter time, and there were many more play frames attempted.

The Girls' Session: Preliminary Discussion

The girls' disputes in this housekeeping session were characterized by the participants' ability to find (or acquiesce to) resolutions, to maintain their pretend play themes through the dispute, and to maintain group cohesion. Three strategies in particular that helped maintain group cohesion during conflict were characteristic of this group: compromise, clarification of intent, and evasion (see Eisenberg & Garvey 1981, Miller et al. 1986). Despite some physical aggression (pushing a child down, grabbing for the pickle), the pickle fight did not break up the pretend play frame of preparing food.

A degree of harmony in play was established before the pickle fight. The following discussion describes the context preceding that dispute. Two interconnected pretend play scenarios have been going on in adjacent areas since the session began eleven minutes before the girls' pickle fight. Mary and Lisa are absorbed in playing with dolls at the doll bed. Nearby, Sue is preparing food for everybody in the kitchen area. Sue keeps Mary and Lisa involved in her pretend frame of food preparation by describing what she is doing and checking back with Mary and Lisa about what food they want to eat. She is taking the role of the mother and has indicated that she considers Mary and Lisa her children. Meanwhile Mary and Lisa are taking care of their babies. Both subdivisions of the triad have stayed with their own theme since the beginning of the session, using language to maintain connection between the two groups. An effective strategy for doing this that they frequently use is for one girl to ask for clarification of another's feelings or intent and to clarify her own behavior in connection with their pretend play. Miller et al. describe this as a conflict mitigating strategy, but it also functions in nonconflictual interactions, as shown in the following example of interaction that takes place in overlapping pretend frames. This example took place prior to the pickle fight.

Sue is in the kitchen area preparing food; Mary and Lisa are playing with the dolls at the doll bed. Sue keeps including Mary and Lisa in her pretend play frame, despite their absorption in their own, by telling them what she is doing *and* asking about their wishes. (In the transcriptions below overlapping utterances are indicated by a caret [∧] at the place where the subsequent phrase starts to overlap. The line numbering is from the original transcript. Some lines from the transcript were omitted because they are not related to the topic; omission is indicated by ellipses. A hyphen indicates a break in the utterance. An increase in volume is marked by underlining. The children's names are fictional.) In the following segment simultaneous talk is represented vertically; one conversation has a food theme and the other has a doll theme.

	FOOD THEME		DOLL THEME
26	Sue:	(*to Mary and Lisa*) I'm gonna cook sandwiches. We're gonna eat them for supper. We're	
27		gonna have milk, right?	
28	Lisa:	Yeah, we're gonna have milk.	
29	Sue:	(*setting out plates*) One for Mary.	Mary: (*to Lisa*) And this baby
30		I'm gonna set up the table, ok?	know what, my baby has
31		One plate for Lisa.	to go to bed.
32			Lisa: (*to Mary*) Oh, your baby has to go to bed?

Mary leaves the doll play with Lisa and comes over to Sue who is at the kitchen table. Sue and Mary converse (lines 40–44) while Lisa talks to herself (lines 41–44).

40	Sue:	I'm setting up the table, you want some eggs?	
41	Mary:	No, I want, um,	Lisa: Oh, this shirt is too
42		cauliflower.	big for baby. Oh, this
43			shirt is really too big
44	Sue:	Cauliflower.	for baby.
45	Mary:	(*to Sue about the cauliflower*) That's big, I can't eat it.	
46	Sue:	Lisa, do you want eggs?	
47	Lisa:	I want eggs, yeah, eggs are really good.	
48	Mary:	∧ I want eggs	
49	Sue:	Okay.	

In this example, Sue announces to the others what she is doing ("I'm gonna cook sandwiches," "I'm setting up the table"). At 27 and 30 she asks tag questions that are directed to either Mary or Lisa ("We're gonna have milk, right?"), and at 40 and 46 she asks each one if she wants some eggs. Asking is a way of keeping tabs on one another and of including

Mary and Lisa in her pretend play. In addition, both Mary and Lisa do their part in maintaining a connection with Sue. Mary responds with a thoughtful reply about the cauliflower and Lisa is enthusiastic about eggs. This conversation is representative of other sequences in the girls' session in which connection was maintained by asking for or giving clarification about behavior, wishes, or intent. Use of this strategy is congruent with Maltz and Borker's claim that girls learn to create and maintain relationships of closeness and equality. It is also consistent with Gilligan's "care" orientation, which focuses on the relationship.

The Girls' Pickle Fight

The pickle fight is the longest series of oppositions in the girls' session. While Mary and Lisa were playing with the dolls, Sue was preparing food for all of them by herself. She has been involving them in her play thoughout their own play, as seen in the preceding example. But now, Mary has left Lisa at the doll bed and has joined Sue with the intention of choosing food herself. Both Mary and Sue are choosing things to eat from the food basket at the stove and bringing the food to the table where Lisa is now sitting. Mary moves into Sue's role of food preparer/mommy and makes a decision about what is for dinner. Sue opposes, and each in turn grabs for the pickle. This is the beginning of the pickle fight. The fight is presented in sections. It is described in terms of conflict-management strategies based on those proposed by Eisenberg and Garvey (1981) and Miller, Danaher & Forbes (1986).

213 Sue: And strawberries are for dinner, right?
214 Mary: And the- and this is for dinner. (*Mary puts the pickle into a pot on the stove*)
215 Sue: And the pickle. Do you like pickle? (*Sue takes the pickle out of the pot*)
216 Mary: And this (*the hamburger*) is for dinner. (*Mary pulls the hamburger and pickle out of Sue's hand and puts them back into the pot*)
217 Sue: No, they aren't for dinner, no, Lisa wants pickles. (*Sue tries to grab the
218   hamburger and pickle back from Mary but she holds on and puts them back into the pot*)

Both Mary and Sue have used or attempted physical force to get possession of the pickle. At 216 Mary grabs it from Sue and at 218 Sue tries unsuccessfully to grab it back. At 217 Sue contradicts Mary's assertion that the hamburger is for dinner. She invents a reason for why she should get the pickle, arguing not in terms of what she wants, but in terms of what Lisa wants, even though Lisa herself has not made her wishes known yet.

At 219 Sue continues to oppose Mary and insists that Lisa wants the pickle. Mary replies with a counter reason, that Lisa has something already, and she seems to be suggesting that there has been a fair distribution of food.

219 Sue: No, Lisa wants pickle. (*Sue tries to grab the pickle again*)
220 Mary: She gots (*unintelligible*).

At 221 Sue goes over to Lisa at the table and asks for clarification of what she wants. Sue is presumably asking for confirmation of her claim that Lisa wants the pickle, and Lisa provides it.

221 Sue: You want pickle, Lisa?
222 Lisa: Mmmhm. (*Mary brings the pickle over to Lisa at the table*)
223 Sue: Lisa says she wants pickle.

At 223 Sue again insists that the pickle should go to Lisa and cites as evidence the fact that Lisa said she wants it. Lisa confirms Sue's claim, making an alliance with her. Mary accepts this, but she still wants the pickle.

At 224 Mary invents a compromise, using the pretend frame, saying that she will "cut" the pickle. Lisa rejects this. Mary insists on her proposal, giving as justification that she "needs" to. Meanwhile Sue has gotten involved in looking for other food and either avoids or ignores the discussion or is too preoccupied to join in. At 228 Mary takes the pickle off the table near Lisa and puts it back into the pot on the stove once again. At 230 Sue takes it out of the pot.

224 Mary: I'll cut it in half.
225 Lisa: No, that's not fair!
226 Sue: (*looks for other food*) And the oranges.
227 Mary: I need, I need to cut it in half, one for dessert and one for you. (*Mary
228 takes the pickle back to the stove and puts it into a cooking pot*)
229 Sue: 'kay, another one.
230 Lisa: Orange. (*Sue takes the pickle out of the pot*)

At this point there is a struggle and both girls use physical force. At 232 Mary continues to insist on her compromise of cutting the pickle and at 234 she insists on her rights to the pickle. Sue holds her ground and insists in turn.

231 Sue: And this is a pickle. (*Mary pushes Sue down and struggles with her
for the pickle. Sue holds it away from Mary. Mary tries to grab it.*)
232 Mary: No, no, I- I- I cut it in half, and I'm going to
233 Lisa: No.
234 Mary: put it in the pan now, I- I had it first.
235 Sue: No, Lisa wants it. Lisa wants it!
(*Sue gives the pickle to Lisa*)

Now Mary tries another compromise that also utilizes the pretend frame.

236 Mary: I'm cutting it in half. (*she takes the pickle off the table and pretends
to cut it with the plastic knife*)
237 Lisa: (*to Mary*) Look what you did with it!
238 Sue: No, Lisa wants it.
239 Lisa wants it!
240 Mary: (*holds on to pickle*) I cut it in half. One for Lisa, one for me, one
for me.
241 Sue: But, Lisa wants a <u>whole</u> pickle!

242 Mary: Well, it's a whole <u>half</u> pickle.
243 Sue: No, it isn't.
244 Mary: Yes, it is, a whole <u>half</u> pickle.

At 236 Mary tries to find a mathematical solution that will satisfy everyone. She is not successful. Sue rejects her plan. Mary continues to pursue
her imaginative resolution, pretending to cut the pickle in half and explaining how the pickle will be distributed ("One for Lisa, one for me, one
for me"). When Sue challenges her solution ("But Lisa wants a <u>whole</u>
pickle!), Mary explains how, in the pretend frame, she can accommodate
Lisa ("It's a whole <u>half</u> pickle"). Sue rejects this attempt at compromise.
Mary insists. At 245 Sue counters by inventing what she thinks is a better
alternative. Pointing to some food on the table, she says,

245 Sue: I'll give her a whole half- I'll give her a <u>whole</u>,
246   <u>whole</u>, I gave her a whole one. (*she touches the pickle on the table*)

At this point the alliance between Sue and Lisa dissolves. Lisa moves
out of the pretend frame, criticizes Sue, and rejects her proposal.

247 Lisa: No, that's not a whole half, that's a <u>egg</u>! (*disparagingly*)

At 248, without an ally, Sue pulls back from the fight. She turns away from
facing Mary and Lisa, which takes some of the force out of her opposition.
She uses the pretend frame to further mitigate her opposition. Her tone
softens. She clarifies her intent, which also has the force of insisting on the
pretend logic.

248 Sue: I'm pretending I gave you one. (*She turns away from Mary and Lisa.*)
249 Lisa: (*pause*) No. (*surprised, doesn't accept this explanation*)
250 Mary: (*pause*) No. (*surprised, doesn't accept this explanation*)

At 251 Sue appears to avoid quarreling. She evades, offering a different
food.

251 Sue: Do you want the oranges?
                          ∧
252 Lisa: I need one.
253 Mary: Orange.

The following section is a transition out of the dispute, a prelude to the
resolution of the fight. In it the girls *jointly* reflect on what just happened.
They step out of the pretend frame and try to clarify each other's behavior.
They describe or excuse the quarrel as just play ("just pretending"). This is
a patching-up process that brings them to a face-saving resolution. Their
commentary on the play frame dissipates the opposition and forms a basis
of agreement among them.

254 Mary: (*to Sue*) You were just pre- (*to Lisa*) she was just pretending.
             (*ameliorating tone*)

255 Sue: You were just pretending it was tomato. (*agreeing in an ameliorating tone*)

. . .

257 Sue: It was a orange.
258 Mary: Yeah.
259 Lisa: Ok, and I get the pickle. (*takes the pickle off the table*)

The pickle fight is over quickly at 259. Sue gets her way, Lisa gets the pickle, and Mary gives in. The food preparation fantasy continues. However, one effect of the conflict is that a new role for Mary and Lisa in the food play is getting negotiated. The power in the group gets redistributed right after the pickle fight. Sue is no longer exclusively in charge of preparing the food. She now has to share this role. She no longer can act as if she is the mother and Mary and Lisa are the children. At 260 she tells them which food they are having. Mary resists her idea at 262–263 by telling her that the food will be for dessert and then ending the utterance with a tag question asking for Sue's agreement. At 264 Sue acquiesces to the redistribution of power in the group. The acquiescence continues at 277, 279, and 281, where Sue shifts from *telling* Mary what food will be served to *asking* her.

260 Sue: And here's one for you.

. . .

262 Mary: No, that is going to be for dessert.
263 This is gonna be for dessert, ok?

264 Sue: Oh.   Yes, it is.

. . .

272 Mary: There. Here's some- or- here's some pepper for me. Here's lots of strawberries.

. . .

277 Sue: Can you give Lisa one? Give Lisa one.
278 Mary: I'll give her all of them.
279 Sue: All of them?
280 Mary: Just those.
281 Sue: Those? Can I have one of them?

In conclusion, the girls' pickle fight contains a number of opposition-insistence-opposition sequences. However, the girls also use a variety of tactics and reasons to elaborate on their resistance to each other's opposition and to *negotiate* a resolution. Mary is persistent in using the pretend frame to argue for a compromise to satisfy everyone who wants the pickle ("I'll cut it in half, one for Lisa, one for me, one for me"). The girls' conflict process maintains interconnectedness among the group members and stability of the play theme.

The Boys' Session: Preliminary Discussion

There were a number of features that differentiated the boys' dispute from the girls'. The boys' fight was a more extended struggle for control of the pickle. It lasted two and a half times longer than the girls' fight. It was principally between two of the boys, Kevin and Nick. However, Nick was able to make an ally of the third boy, Joe, who alternately stepped in for him and escalated the fight or moved out of it and played by himself. Neither Kevin nor Nick was willing to give in to the other. Their insistence on getting their own way escalated and extended the fight. Eisenberg and Garvey (1981) note that insistence is the least adaptive strategy for ending conflict. The use of more heavy-handed dispute tactics and the more adversarial quality of boys' interactions have also been noted in studies with larger data samples discussed earlier. The boys' fight was temporarily concluded by inventing and switching to a new pretend theme, taking a trip "to another nation," which didn't require the pickle. (The idea for taking this trip came about because Nick had just gone to a local Festival of Nations that featured activities, crafts, and foods from many nations.)

Another difference in the boys' pickle fight, compared with the girls', is that it disrupted the boys' play. In fact, throughout their twenty-five-minute play session disputes frequently erupted over control of various objects, such as who got to push the buttons and talk on the telephone. Connected to this is the fact that there were seventeen theme shifts. It is not clear what the frequent theme shifts and shorter pretend play episodes were due to. Perhaps it was the nature of the play resources in the house-keeping situation. Resources that are more associated with boys' play preferences, such as trucks (see Connor & Serbin 1977), might produce more extended pretend play scenarios. As mentioned earlier, shorter pretend play scenarios in boys' groups have also been noted by Jennings and Suwalsky (1982) and McLoyd (1983).

There were two aspects of the boys' pickle fight that were unique to their conflict process: (1) the appeal to rules to settle the dispute and (2) the threat of separation as a way to solve the conflict. Both were ways in which they tried to establish control. In addition, the heavy-handed tactics of physical intimidation and threats of physical force played a major role in their fight. The two main combatants, Kevin and Nick, did not use mitigating strategies like clarification of intent, ignoring, or acquiescence. Compromise tactics were tried by Nick, without success. Finally the boys' fight did not result in a redistribution of power as the girls' fight did; instead it resulted in a stalemate.

Two separate play themes have been in progress since this session began twelve minutes before the boys' pickle fight: food preparation and telephone play. During this time each of the boys has changed the theme of their play at least once, moving back and forth between the telephone and the kitchen area. Joe and Kevin are at the telephone. Nick has left them and is sitting at the table preparing the food. Throughout their telephone play he has been describing what he is doing, but they have not paid attention to him. In part, this is because Kevin and Joe have been quarreling about how to play with the phone. Like Sue, before the pickle fight, Nick plays with the food while the rest of the group plays with other resources. However, in the examples to follow, Nick's *statements* report what he is doing. They neither elicit nor receive a response from the others ("I'm having dinner," "I'm cutting the cauliflower"). Contrast this with Sue's *questions* to Mary and Lisa about what they want, which elicit replies in lines 40–49 (Sue: "Lisa, do you want eggs?" Lisa: "I want eggs, yeah, eggs are really good"). The boys' verbal interaction is not designed to, and does not, connect the group across the two play themes as the girls' does.

	FOOD THEME		TELEPHONE THEME
105	Nick: *(at table)* I'm having dinner.	Kevin:	*(on phone)* Hi, oh yeah. This is
106			Kevin and this my friend Joe.
107			Oh, yeah. Okay. Bye-bye. Okay.
108		Joe:	*(to Kevin who is still on the phone)* Now can I call again?
109	Nick: I'm gonna have-	Kevin:	*(still on the phone)* Oh, sure,
110			that's great. Okay. Bye-bye.
111	Nick: I'm gonna have cauliflower.	Joe:	*(to Kevin)* Now, I'll do it. *(makes a call)*
112	Nick: And pickles	Kevin:	*(to Joe)* Okay. You- No, I'll
113			push the buttons.
114		Joe:	I will!
115		Kevin:	*(pushes the buttons)* There! Now the person's there you wanted.
			. . .
129	Nick: I'm cutting the cauliflower.	Joe:	*(to Kevin)* Then I can *(i.e., it will be*
130			*Joe's turn)* and then you push the
131			buttons. I'll push one more button.
			. . .
137	Nick: I'm cutting the cauliflower.	Kevin:	*(on the phone)* Oh boy. Your
138	I'm cutting the cauliflower		phone is broken too. I know it.
139	with my knife.		Oh, bye-bye.

The Boys' Pickle Fight

Nick has been playing with the food at the table and intermittently watching Kevin and Joe. Now Kevin leaves the phone and approaches the table. The food is spread out in front of Nick, who has turned to watch Joe on the phone.

148   Kevin: *(at the table)* Pickle. *(takes the pickle)*

Nick turns back, continues cutting the cauliflower, starts to reannounce that fact, and then sees that Kevin has the pickle.

149   Nick: I'm cutting- I'm cutting- No, I have to cut that!
            (Nick tries to take the pickle back from Kevin)
150   Kevin: No, I cut it.
151   Nick: No! No, no, no! You're the children!
152   Kevin: No, I'm not!

At 149 Nick insists on his right to continue to play with the pickle. Kevin rejects his reason. Nick counters with a reason in a pretend frame ("You're the children!"), which presumably vests him, as the parent, with the right to prepare the food. Kevin denies being "the children."

Nick continues to angrily insist, citing as reasons that he "has to" and "wants to" cut the pickle. He also claims the right of possession.

153 Nick: (*screams*) Kevin, but the, oh, I have to cut! I want to
154   cut it! It's mine! (*in a whining voice*)

Nick is not successful in getting the pickle back. He complains to Joe, who has been using the phone. Joe's strategy for solving the dispute is to threaten physical force, a win-lose plan that pits Nick and Joe in an alliance against Kevin. This aggravates the competition over the pickle and perhaps distracts Kevin from reasoning with Nick. Kevin gets into an opposition-insistence-opposition sequence with Joe and Nick.

155 Nick: (*whining to Joe*) Kevin is not letting me cut the pickle.
156 Joe: (*joins conflict and says to Nick*) Oh, I know! I can pull it away
157   from him and give it back to you. That's an idea!
158 Kevin: Joe!
159 Nick: I can pull it, take it away from you and put it in the oven.

     (*Kevin runs away with the pickle and Nick chases him.*)
160 Kevin: Don't, Joe, don't, don't, don't,
161   don't!

At 162 Nick invents an imaginary reason to get the pickle, an apparent compromise that utilizes the pretend frame, expressed as an order to Kevin. He and Kevin again get into an opposition-insistence-opposition sequence. Joe has gone back to the phone.

162 Nick: You have to make a pickle salad! So I'll put it in the pot.
163 Kevin: Don't.
164 Nick: You have to make a pickle salad, Kevin. (*Nick follows Kevin around
         the room*)
165 Joe: (*on the phone*) Hello. What? Bye.
166 Kevin: Don't (*Joe returns to the dispute*)

167 Joe: You have to make a pickle salad.
168 Kevin: Don't, Nick. I'm gonna have-

At 169 Joe again threatens physical force. He shows his anger, faces Kevin, points at him, and uses a mild curse word. He orders Kevin to give the pickle back and threatens force if Kevin doesn't comply. Kevin continues to resist. At 174 he rejects Joe's proposal, stating outright that he doesn't like it.

169 Joe: Oh, you get it back and bring it to Nick! I'll get it!
170   Darn you Kevin! (*Joe gets more agitated, plants his feet, clenches his
         fists, and spreads two rigid arms out to his sides as if to block Kevin.*)
171 Kevin: No, Joe!

172 Joe: I'll give it back to Nick, if you don't! I'll get it
173   away and give it back to Nick if you don't. (*Joe lifts and spreads his arms down rigid again*)
174 Kevin: Joe!   Joe!   That's
175   not a way to solve the problem Joe, because I don't like that.
176   (*Kevin pushes the back of Joe's arm with the blade of his plastic knife*)

At 177 Nick proposes another imaginative resolution, an ad hoc alternative that is compatible with his pretend play; he will get the pickle after Kevin cuts it. Kevin orders Joe to stop bothering him. Joe and Nick again insist that Nick "needs" the pickle. Kevin insists on "cutting" the pickle first.

177 Nick: I'll- after you cut it, I'll put it back together and I'll cut it.
179 Kevin: No. Joe, don't.
180 Joe: Well, Nick needs it.
181 Nick: (*conciliatory*) I really need it to make a pickle salad.
182 Kevin: Nick. Can't cut it now.
183   I'm going to.

Joe again proposes physical force. Nick also tries to get the pickle from Kevin, and when Kevin orders him to stop and walks away from him, Nick screeches, begs, and continues to insist that he "needs" the pickle. Kevin continues to refuse.

184 Joe: Well, I'll get it away! (*Joe gets up to go to Kevin*)
185 Kevin: No, I just cut it. (*rubs plastic knife on pickle*)
186 Joe: (*turns to Nick*) Nick, I'll get your pickle back.
188 Kevin: (*moves away*) I'm sorry, I already cut it, in half
189   I'm sor-
190 Nick: I'll get it, I'll get it! (*goes to Kevin*)
191 Kevin: Don't! (*goes away from Nick*)
192 Nick: (*screeches*) I need it! Oh. (*begs*) Please give it back to me. (*Nick walks after Kevin, who scampers away*)
193   (*Joe appears uncomfortable, looks at the camera, and leaves the area*)
194 Nick: I need it.
195 Kevin: No.

Nick again proposes physical force and Kevin again opposes him.

196 Nick: (*Nick chases Kevin*) I'll grab it from you.
197 Kevin: No. (*runs away from him*) Don't, Nick. I'm not gonna let you have it,
198   if you're not gonna let me- if you're not gonna tell me.

Nick follows up on the pretend alternative that he proposed in 177. Joe has left the quarrel and plays with the telephone.

200 Nick: (*conciliatory tone*) I need- I need to get that pickle back.
201   Cause I'm gonna put it back together.

Kevin, still holding the pickle, goes over to the phone and grabs it from
Joe. They get into an opposition-resistance-opposition sequence over the
phone.

202 Joe: (*at the telephone*) I'll call one more person.
203 Kevin: No, I'm gonna call a person. (*Kevin grabs the phone from Joe*)
204 Joe: Ow! I will.

Kevin, who now holds the phone, hands the pickle to Nick without a
word. Nick, however, *continues* the opposition. At 205 his strategy is an
appeal to an ad hoc rule. The rule also fits in with the pretend frame. Kevin
joins in with him in pretending to cut the pickle, and Nick appeals to
another rule, in a pretend frame, to try to stop him. When Kevin doesn't
pay attention to that admonition, Nick invokes the pretend frame again to
tell Kevin that he can't cut the pickle because he, Nick, has already "cut" it.
Joe continues to stay out of their fight, playing alone and talking to
himself.

205 Nick: But you- but our rule is put it back together. (*he pretends to cut the pickle*)
206   Cut, cut, cut, cut, cut, cut, cut, cut, cut, cut, cut.
207 Kevin: (*sitting next to Nick, looks up from the phone and also pretends to cut
             the pickle with his knife*) Cut, cut, cut, cut, cut.
208 Nick: No, no! No, no! (*pulls pickle off table, holds it away from Kevin*)
210 Nick: You can't, Kevin. Our rules is you can't, Kevin, with a sharp knife.
211 Kevin: (*reaches over to the pickle with his knife, trying to cut it*) I can't cut.
212 Nick: You really can't cut this pickle. I already cut it in half. (*Kevin keeps
213   reaching with his knife to cut it*)
214 Kevin: I'll put it back together. Putting back together. (*sing-song*)
                                             . . .
219 Nick: (*starts to pretend to cut the pickle again*) Cut, cut, cut, cut, cut, cut!
220 Kevin: (*starts to pretend to cut the pickle too*)   Cut, cut, cut,
             cut, cut, cut, cut!

Then Nick appeals to a principle that preschoolers often hear, namely,
to "be cooperative," and threatens Kevin with separation from "the family." Perhaps thinking that he is still the parent, he assumes the right to
decide who stays and who goes. When this doesn't work Nick threatens to
send him away again, to bed this time.

221 Nick: (*pulls the pickle away from Kevin*) No, no, no! I'll, I'll make-
             (*Kevin pushes Nick in the chest*) you have to go out of this family
222   if you don't co- roperate with this family.
223 Kevin: Joe! no, Joe, no! (*Joe has stood up behind
             Kevin, and Kevin turns around apparently surprised*)
224 Nick: Well, then I'll send you to bed and you'll never have a sweet- your dinner.
225   All right?

This starts another opposition sequence between Kevin and Nick. At
226 Kevin counters Nick's proposal by inventing a new play theme in
which he tells Nick that he is going to leave him. Nick picks up on this and
orders him to go away. Kevin reverses himself and refuses. This precipi-

tates another cycle of oppositions in which Nick orders Kevin to leave and Kevin refuses.

226	Kevin:	I'm not- I'm not- I'm not gonna be with you.
227		I'm gonna go to drive somewhere else.

. . .

229	Kevin:	I'm going to another place if you're not gonna do this.
230	Nick:	Go to another country.

. . .

232	Kevin:	No, I won't.

233   Nick: Go to another country, go to another nation.

. . .

235	Kevin:	No, I won't. I'm here. (*holds the phone*)
236	Nick:	Drive off to another nation.
237	Kevin:	No, I won't.

At 238 Nick decides to pursue the idea of going away himself. He develops the new pretend theme, announcing his intentions to the others.

238	Nick:	I'll tell part of my family I'm gonna
239		take a trip to another nation.

. . .

241	Nick:	(*goes over to Joe*) I'm gonna take a trip to another nation.
242	Joe:	(*unintelligible*)
243	Nick:	What? With my baby, all right? All right. With my baby. (*gets a doll from the doll crib*)
244	Kevin:	(*on the phone*) Hello? Oh, well, I bet they can.
245	Nick:	(*sing-song, boasting*) I- I'm taking a trip to another nation.

Nick sits down with the doll on a foam chair next to where Kevin is playing with the phone. At 247 Kevin opposes him for the chair.

247   Kevin: No, this is mine. No this is my car. That's my car.
          (*Kevin stops talking on the phone and pulls on the chair*)

At 249 there is a transition out of their quarreling. There is a détente, or respite, when Nick, who is sitting on the chair, offers Kevin a place on it.

249	Nick:	Okay, well you can sit by me. (*very conciliatory tone*)
250	Kevin:	(*sits down on foam chair next to Nick*) Sure, okay.

At 251 Nick and Kevin move into a new pretend frame. Nick announces it and Kevin agrees.

251	Nick:	We're going to another nation.
252	Kevin:	Yeah.
253	Nick:	So we won't be with this family so much. Right?
254	Kevin:	(*no verbal response*)

At 253 Nick comments retrospectively on the dispute that happened in the previous play frame while they are in the new one of taking a trip "to another nation." Nick indirectly refers to their dispute by criticizing "this family," as if it is something outside themselves. This is also an indirect

acknowledgment of the unpleasantness of their fight. There is a momentary truce. Unlike the girls, they don't seek to retrospectively understand the others' actions during the dispute (e.g., Mary to Lisa: "She was just pretending"; Sue to Mary: "You were just pretending"). Rather, by attributing their quarreling behaviors to "this family," they distance themselves from their own actions. Leaving the "family" is a way to leave their quarreling selves behind. They move on, and at 255 they change to another theme, dressing up.

255   Kevin: (*jumps up from the chair*) Oh boy, what did I forget? I forgot my coat! (*goes over to dress-up clothes*)
256   Joe: I forgot my coat. This is my coat. (*goes over to dress-up clothes*)
                    . . .
259   Nick: Oh, look what I forgot. I forgot my coat! (*goes over to dress-up clothes*)

In conclusion, the boys' dispute is escalated and stretched out by many more rounds of opposition-insistence-opposition in which they resist doing what the other wants them to do. They use more directive speech and coercive physical tactics such as threats and physical intimidation (chasing, blocking.) Although Nick made two proposals—one at 162 ("You have to make a pickle salad! So I'll put it in the pot") and the other at 177 ("after you cut it, I'll put it back together")—the boys do not *jointly negotiate* a resolution. All of this contributes to the greater rigidity and tension in this fight. Even when Kevin gives the pickle back to Nick at 205 and turns his attention to controlling the phone, Nick still tries to dominate him and Kevin continues to oppose Nick, as if their play agenda is one of opposition.

Conclusion

The analysis of the two disputes reveals similarities and differences. Both disputes are complex because of their length and the range of strategies the participants used. Both make use of pretend and real elements in interesting ways. Both are precipitated by a child's attempt to maintain control over a resource that he or she was playing with and that a playmate has become interested in. There are quarrels over an object, as well as quarrels over interference in one's ongoing activity. Finally, in both disputes an alliance was formed between one of the disputants and the third child (the bystander).

The way the children conduct the pickle fights is consistent with generalizations in recent studies of young children's sex-related strategies for negotiating conflict (Miller, Danaher & Forbes 1986) and other forms of discourse (Leaper 1991), which involved a total of 162 children and the analysis of more than 1,000 conflict episodes. In these studies boys were found to engage in more conflict. Their conflict is described as more heavy-handed and more controlling. Girls' negotiation of conflict is described as more mitigated than boys', and their discourse is characterized as more collaborative, suggesting greater (apparent) interpersonal harmony.

In addition, when the pickle fights are interpreted in terms of Maltz and Borker's model and Gilligan's "different voices" framework, they do not look like random events. The two dispute processes are congruent with the predictions made by these frameworks. The boys' pickle fight fits Maltz and Borker's claim that boys use language "to assert one's position of dominance." The girls' pickle fight fits their claim that girls use language "to create and maintain relationships of closeness and equality" and "to interpret accurately the speech of other girls." When the pickle fights are interpreted through Gilligan's framework, the girls' focus on the relationship shows through in their *negotiations,* which serve to enhance communication and respond to the needs of others. Negotiation through clarification of intent, compromise, and evasion mitigates opposition and works through conflict to find a resolution. The girls' real interest appeared to be in jointly constructing and maintaining their pretend play. Their conflict process kept them on that track. In the boys' pickle fight, the focus on the self shows through in their insistence on getting their way, their appeal to self-serving rules and threats of separation, and their *lack* of joint negotiation. The boys' longer and more insistent conflict process made it difficult to develop their pretend play scenarios very much, although, as mentioned, Nick tried some proposals. Gilligan's model has been proposed to account for gender differences in adult and adolescent moral reasoning processes. This study indicates that Gilligan's model is useful for interpreting face-to-face verbal conflict management by children as young as three years of age.

In regard to the discussion of gender socialization in the first section, there are questions this study has not addressed and that we need to understand better. In what ways are "gendered" behaviors due to the activities and social organization of female and male groups? Although features of the pickle fights are consistent with what previous research labeled *feminine* and *masculine,* this should not be taken to mean that girls or boys *only* function in these ways, that their styles are mutually exclusive, or that these are essential, intrinsic, and biologically determined attributes. Gender and situation are confounded. Gendered behavior is situationally dependent. Some work has already shown this (e.g. Goodwin 1980, Thorne 1986), but we need to do much more. In a different play activity, for example, a boy-associated activity like playing with trucks (Connor & Serbin 1977), these girls and boys might interact differently. In addition, conflict in triadic interaction may be different for girls or boys from conflict in larger groups or in dyads. Future research needs to address these and other issues concerning the systematic variation of girls' and boys' language behavior.

In conclusion, the pickle fights provide insight into the negotiation skills that three-year-old children are developing through the process of constructing a world of shared fantasy. The ways that conflicts are resolved, or whether they are resolved at all, have immediate consequences for the continued construction of the oral texts that embody their social interactions. This study, then, is as much about how very young children construct a world of meaning with their friends as it is about their arguments. The pretend play framework is sensitive to opposition. Pretending can be derailed by conflict, and it can be creatively enriched and developed by conflict. Observing children's arguments can show us just how fragile—and how resilient—their process of constructing shared meaning is.

NOTES

The larger study of which this chapter is a part required the help of numerous individuals. I am grateful to the children and parents of the University of Minnesota Child Care Center who participated. I have benefited from the advice, insights, cooperation and generous support given by their teachers and other staff members at the Center, particularly Patty Finstad, Mary Widlund, Bobbie Williams, Karen Eherenman, Bev Krehbiel, Mary Leinfelder, Shirley Morton, Mina Shafizadeh, Susan Alexander, Mary Johnson, Kelli Kern, Judy Seefeldt, and Mary Berg. Financial support was provided by the following units at the University of Minnesota: a Small Grant and two Undergraduate Research Opportunity grants from the Educational Development Program; a grant from the Center for Research in Learning, Perception, and Cognition; and a CLA/McMillan Travel grant. Recording assistance and equipment were provided by the University of Minnesota Media Resources and the Media Resources Engineering Departments, the Learning Resource Center (COLP), the Department of Linguistics, and the Institute for Child Development. I also wish to thank Jim Gregory for his technical advice; Kathleen McVey, Tracy Thomas, Sarah Tjornhom, and Michelle Bennett, who transcribed tapes and produced transcripts; Claire Harkness, who made creative contributions to the study and assisted during the filming; and Sally McConnell-Ginet and Deborah Tannen for their encouragement and support.

A version of this chapter was read at the Tenth Annual National Women's Studies Association Meetings in Minneapolis, June 1988. Comments were given by colleagues at Cornell University when I was in residence as a Fellow during 1988–89 at the Society for the Humanities. I thank the Society for providing the time necessary for writing and research. The following people are also to be thanked for their comments on drafts: Katie Salter Goodell, Marjorie Harness Goodwin and Deborah Tannen.

This chapter originally appeared in *Discourse Processes* 13(1990):1.5–31.

REFERENCES

Bakan, David (1966). *The duality of human existence: An essay on psychology and religion*. Chicago: Rand McNally.

Brooks-Gunn, Jeanne & Matthews, Wendy S. (1979). *He & she: How children develop their sex-role identity*. Englewood Cliffs, NJ: Prentice-Hall.

Cahill, Spencer (1986). Language practices and self definition: The case of gender identity acquisition. *Sociological Quarterly* 27(3):295–311.

Camras, Linda (1984). Children's verbal and nonverbal communication in a conflict situation. *Ethology and Sociobiology* 5:257–268.

Chodorow, Nancy (1978). *The reproduction of mothering: Psychoanalysis and the sociology of gender.* Berkeley, CA: University of California Press.

Connor, Jane M. & Serbin, Lisa A. (1977). Behaviorally based masculine- and feminine-activity-preference scales for preschoolers: Correlates with other classroom behaviors and cognitive tests. *Child Development* 48:1411–1416.

Dawe, Helen C. (1934). An analysis of two hundred quarrels of preschool children. *Child Development* 5:139–157.

Deaux, Kay & Kite, Mary E. (1987). Thinking about gender. In Beth Hess & Martha Marx Ferree (Eds.) *Analyzing gender: A handbook of social science research.* Newbury Park, CA: Sage.

DiPietro, Janet Ann (1981). Rough and tumble play: A function of gender. *Developmental Psychology* 17(1):50–58.

Eagly, Alice H. (1987). *Sex differences in social behavior: A social-role interpretation.* Hillsdale, NJ: Lawrence Erlbaum.

Eisenberg, Ann R. & Garvey, Catherine (1981). Children's use of verbal strategies in resolving conflicts. *Discourse Processes* 4:149–170.

Ellis, Shari, Rogoff, Barbara & Cromer, Cindy C. (1981). Age segregation in children's social interactions. *Developmental Psychology* 17(4):399–407.

Fishman, Pamela M. (1983). Interaction: The work women do. In Barrie Thorne, Cheris Kramarae & Nancy Henley (Eds.) *Language, gender and society* (pp. 89–101). Rowley, MA: Newbury House.

Freedle, Roy & Lewis, Michael (1977). Prelinguistic conversations. In Michael Lewis & Leonard A. Rosenblum (Eds.) *Interaction, conversation and the development of language* (pp. 157–185). New York: John Wiley and Sons.

Garcia-Zamor, M. A. (1973). Child awareness of sex-role distinctions in language use. Paper presented at the meeting of the Linguistic Society of America Meeting, San Diego.

Gilligan, Carol (1982). *In a different voice: Psychological theory and women's development.* Cambridge, MA: Harvard University Press.

Gilligan, Carol (1987). Moral orientation and moral development. In Eva Feder Kittay & Diana T. Meyers (Eds.) *Women and moral theory* (pp. 19–33). Totowa, NJ: Rowman & Littlefield.

Gilligan, Carol (1988). Two moral orientations: Gender differences and similarities. *Merrill-Palmer Quarterly* 34(3):223–237.

Gleason, Jean Berko (1987). Sex differences in parent-child interaction. In Susan U. Philips, Susan Steele, & Christine Tanz (Eds.) *Language, gender, and sex in comparative perspective* (pp. 189–199). Cambridge: Cambridge University Press.

Goffman, Erving (1979). *Gender advertisements.* New York: Harper & Row.

Goodwin, Marjorie Harness (1980). Directive/response speech sequences in girls' and boys' task activities. In Sally McConnell-Ginet, Ruth Borker & Nelly Furman (Eds.) *Women and language in literature and society* (pp. 157–173). New York: Praeger.

Goodwin, Marjorie Harness & Goodwin, Charles (1987). Children's arguing. In Susan U. Philips, Susan Steele & Christine Tanz (Eds.) *Language, gender, and sex in comparative perspective* (pp. 200–248). Cambridge: Cambridge University Press.

Green, Elise H. (1933). Friendships and quarrels among preschool children. *Child Development* 4:237–252.

Haas, Adelaide (1979). The acquisition of genderlect. In Judith Orasanu, Mariam K. Slater, & Leonore Loeb Adler (Eds.) *Annals of the New York Academy of Sciences: Language, sex and gender* 327:101–113.

Hare-Mustin, Rachel T. (1988). Family change and gender differences: Implications for theory and practice. *Family Relations* 37:36–41.

Jennings, Kay D. & Suwalsky, Joan T. D. (1982). Reciprocity in the dyadic play of three-year-old children. In John Loy (Ed.) *The paradoxes of play,* (pp. 130–140). West Point, NY: Leisure Press.

Kalčik, Susan (1975). ". . . like Ann's gynecologist or the time I was almost raped": Personal narratives in women's rap groups. *Journal of American Folklore* 88:3–11.

Kessler, Suzanne J. & McKenna, Wendy (1978). *Gender: An ethnomethodological approach.* Chicago: University of Chicago Press.

Klann-Delius, Gisela (1981). Sex and language acquisition: Is there any influence? *Journal of Pragmatics* 5:1–25.

Leaper, Campbell (1991). Influence and involvement: Age, gender, and partner effects. *Child Development* 62:797–811.

Lever, Janet (1976). Sex differences in the games children play. *Social Problems* 23:478–487.

Lewis, Michael & Cherry, Louise (1977). Social behavior and language acquisition. In Michael Lewis & Leonard A. Rosenblum (Eds.) *Interaction, conversation and the development of language,* (pp. 227–245). New York: John Wiley and Sons.

Maccoby, Eleanor E. (1986). Social groupings in childhood: Their relationship to prosocial and antisocial behavior in boys and girls. In Dan Olweus, Jeanne Block, & Marian Radke-Yarrow (Eds.) *Development of antisocial and prosocial behavior* (pp. 263–284). San Diego: Academic Press.

Maccoby, Eleanor E. & Jacklin, Carol N. (1974). *The psychology of sex differences.* Stanford, CA: Stanford University Press.

Maccoby, Eleanor E. & Jacklin, Carol N. (1980). Sex differences in aggression: A rejoinder and reprise. *Child Development* 51:964–980.

Maltz, Daniel & Borker, Ruth (1982). A cultural approach to male-female miscommunication. In John Gumperz (Ed.) *Language and social identity* (pp. 196–216). Cambridge: Cambridge University Press.

McLoyd, Vonnie (1983). The effects of structure of play objects on the pretend play of low-income preschool children. *Child Development* 54:626–663.

Meditch, Andrea (1975). The development of sex-specific speech patterns in young children. *Anthropological Linguistics* 17:421–433.

Miller, Patrice, Danaher, Dorothy & Forbes, David (1986). Sex-related strategies for coping with interpersonal conflict in children aged five and seven. *Developmental Psychology* 22(4):543–548.

Miner, Valerie, & Longino, Helen (1987). *Competition: A feminist taboo?* New York: Feminist Press.

Philips, Susan U., Steele, Susan & Tanz, Christine (Eds.) (1987). *Language, gender, and sex in comparative perspective.* New York: Cambridge University Press.

Sachs, Jacqueline (1987). Preschool boys' and girls' language use in pretend play. In Susan U. Philips, Susan Steele & Christine Tanz (Eds.) *Language, gen-*

der, and sex in comparative perspective (pp. 178–188). Cambridge: Cambridge University Press.

Schieffelin, Bambi & Ochs, Elinor (1986). *Language socialization across cultures.* New York: Cambridge University Press.

Schiffrin, Deborah (1984). Jewish argument as sociability. *Language in Society* 13:311–335.

Shantz, Carolyn Uhlinger (1987). Conflicts between children. *Child Development* 58:283–305.

Shantz, David W. & Schomer, Joyce (1977). Interpersonal conflict in preschoolers: A naturalistic study. Paper presented at the Fifth Biennial Meeting of the Southeast Regional Meeting of the Society for Research in Child Development, Atlanta.

Thorne, Barrie (1980). Gender . . . How is it best conceptualized? Revision of paper presented at the 1978 meeting of the American Sociological Association, San Francisco.

Thorne, Barrie (1986). Girls and boys together . . . but mostly apart: Gender arrangements in elementary schools. In Willard Hartup & Zick Rubin (Eds.) *Relationships and development* (pp. 167–184). Hillsdale, NJ: Erlbaum.

Thorne, Barrie, Kramarae, Cheris & Henley, Nancy (Eds.) (1983). *Language, gender, and society.* Rowley, MA: Newbury House.

Whiting, Beatrice Blyth & Edwards, Carolyn Pope (1988). *Children of different worlds.* Cambridge, MA: Harvard University Press.

5

Tactical Uses of Stories: Participation Frameworks Within Girls' and Boys' Disputes

MARJORIE HARNESS GOODWIN

Introduction

Stories are often treated as artifacts that can be abstracted from their local circumstances and examined in terms of their internal features (Labov 1972). Here, instead, I want to look at how they are deeply embedded within larger social processes. My concern is with how children use stories as a constitutive feature of the activities they are engaged in and as powerful tools to arrange and rearrange the social organization of a group. In this paper I examine stories within a particular context, the organization of dispute.

My primary concern is with the participation frameworks that stories provide, allowing children to *construct and reconstruct their social organization on an ongoing basis*. I examine how boys and girls, in their same-sex groups, make use of features of stories to accomplish and restructure social identities within encounters. To investigate how stories constitute tools for accomplishing social tasks I look at how they structure situations within one particular domain, argumentative sequences, a fruitful site for investigating the intersection of genres. As noted by Turner (1986:39–43) a world of theater is often created while redressing grievances, as conflict provides the quintessential arena in which "the structures of group experience (*Erlebnis*) are replicated, dismembered, re-membered, refashioned, and mutely or vocally made meaningful" (p. 43). When stories are used in dispute processes they permit the playing out of an event in full dramatic regalia; through a multiplicity of voices (Goffman 1974), the teller of the story and her hearers animate principal figures in the story and offer commentary upon the unfolding action and characters.

Using the same story and dispute resources, boys and girls construct quite different types of events. Boys use stories as a way of continuing an ongoing argument while reshaping the domain in which dispute takes place; by switching from a sequence of counters to a story, a speaker may radically reformulate the participation structure of the moment. Girls, in contrast, use stories to restructure alignments of participants, not only in the current interaction, but also at some future time. Stories can generate in listeners who are offended parties statements of future plans to confront an offending party, which result in confrontations that mobilize the entire neighborhood. I examine how each gender group manages its social organization through storytelling.

Fieldwork and Theoretical Approach

The present study is based on fieldwork among a group of children in a black working-class neighborhood of West Philadelphia whom I encountered during a walk around my neighborhood. I observed them for a year and a half (1970–1971) as they played in their neighborhood, focusing on how the children used language within interaction to organize their everyday activities.[1] The children (whom I will call the Maple Street group) ranged in age from 4 through 14 and spent much of the time in four same-age and same-sex groups:

Younger Girls	Ages 4–9	5 children
Younger Boys	Ages 5–6	3 children
Older Girls	Ages 9–13	15 children
Older Boys	Ages 9–14	21 children

Here I am concerned principally with older children, ages nine to fourteen. Specific ages of the children who are included in the groups reported on in this paper are listed in Appendix A.

As the children played on the street after school, on weekends, and during the summer months, I audiotaped their conversation. In gathering data, I did not focus on particular types of events that I had previously decided were theoretically important (for example, games or rhymes) but instead tried to observe and record as much of what the children did as possible, no matter how mundane it might seem. Moreover I tried to avoid influencing what the children were doing. The methods I used to gather data about the children were thus quite different from those characteristically used in psychological and sociological studies of children's behavior; in such studies efforts are typically made to systematically collect in a carefully controlled fashion particular types of information deemed to be theoretically important. Rather than being based on a laboratory model, the methodology I used was ethnographic, designed to capture as accurately as possible the structure of events in the children's world *as they unfolded in the ordinary settings where they habitually occurred.*

The tapes I collected preserved a detailed record of the children's activities, including the way in which their talk emerged through time. In all, over two hundred hours of transcribed talk form the corpus of this study. The approach used in this chapter, conversation analysis, constitutes an approach to the study of naturally occurring interaction developed within sociology by the late Harvey Sacks and his colleagues.

Stories Within Disputes of Boys

Within the boys' group, games in which points are scored or activities in which there are winners and losers provide a way of distinguishing group members with respect to relative rank. Boys' pastimes permit a range of comparisons in terms of skill and ability, and boys proclaim and protest how they stand in a series of activities. For example, boys discuss ranking in terms of skill displayed in games and contests.

(1)

| William: | I could walk on my hands better than *any*body out here. Except him. And Freddie. *Thom*as can't walk. |

(2)

	((Discussing ranking of go-cart members))
Malcolm:	I'm the *driv*er.
Tony:	He's the driver. // You know he drives it.
Malcolm:	I know what // that- Archie can't *drive* that good.
Archie:	See- I'm number *three* driver. I'm number *three* driver.
Malcolm:	And *Dave* can't drive that good,=
Tony:	I'm number // *two* driver.
Archie:	I'm number *three* driver.

In addition, boys compare one another in contests of verbal repartee, as in the following fragments, which occur during a slingshot-making session. Nine boys, aged nine through fourteen, are making slingshots in the backyard of Malcolm and Tony Johnson. The boys have informally divided themselves into two teams, one under the direction of Malcolm (aged thirteen), and the other led by Tony (aged fourteen).[2]

Disputes Built Through Reciprocal Counters

Looking at example 3, it can be observed that argument proceeds through a sequence of **reciprocal counters:** two-turn sequences in which a first challenge or threat is answered by a counter to it. Data are transcribed according to the system developed by Jefferson and described in Sacks, Schegloff, and Jefferson (1974:731–733). A simplified version of this transcription system appears in Appendix B.[3]

(3)

1	Tony:	*Gi*mme the ***things***.
2	Chopper:	You sh:ut up you ***big*** lips. (Y'all been
3		hangin around with thieves.)
4	Tony:	(***Shut*** up.)
5	Chopper:	Don't gimme that.=I'm not ***talk***in to
6		you.
7		(1.4)
8	Tony:	I'm talkin to ***y:ou***!
9	Chopper:	Ah you better sh:ut ***up*** with your
10		little- ***di***:ngy sneaks.
11		(1.4)
12	Tony:	I'm a ***din***gy your hea:d.=How would you
13		like ***that***.

Using such couplets to build an argument shapes the interaction of the moment in distinctive ways. First, it both focuses talk and restricts participation in the debate. Each subsequent challenge selects prior speaker as next speaker. Thus, though nine people are present, only two parties speak in the sequences. Second, the protagonists in this sequence talk in relatively short turns that, typically, are not interrupted.

Within the context of the event that has been in progress, this is striking. The boys have divided themselves spatially into two separate teams, each making its own ammunition in preparation for the slingshot fight, and, during most of this work, parties within each group have been carrying on separate conversations. The effect of this has been considerable simultaneous talk.

The emergence of the dispute sequence creates a point of focus for all present. It thus provides organization not only for those who talk within it, but also for the others present, who become ratified overhearers to it. In brief, argumentative sequences built from paired counters shape in distinctive ways both the interactions of the moment and the talk occurring within it.

Looking at line 9 of example 4, we find that, at a certain point, Tony simply disattends Chopper and turns to other activities.

(4)

1	Tony:	Why don't you get out my yard.
2	Chopper:	Why don't you ***make*** me get out the yard.
3	Tony:	I ***know*** you don't want that.

```
 4 Chopper:    You're not gonna make me get out the yard
 5             cuz you can't.
```

```
 6 Tony:       Don't force me.
 7 Chopper:    You can't. Don't force me to hurt you.
 8             ((snickering)) Khh Khhh!
```

```
 9 Tony:       ((to his team)) Now you gotta make
10               ⌜your noodles.
11 Chopper:   [[ You hear what I said boy?
```

Thus, despite the fact that Chopper wants to pursue the sequence—note his "You hear what I said boy?" in line 11—he is unable to do so without Tony's continuing coparticipation. Moreover, though an extended dispute occurs here, there is no clear demonstration that one of the protagonists has gotten the upper hand over the other.

One might ask how a speaker in the midst of a sequence of this sort could design talk that would prevent a move such as the one made by Tony. For example, would it be possible to build a participation framework in which such a unilateral exit would no longer be a strong possibility?

Using a Story to Restructure a Dispute

Example 5 is a continuation of the "I'm a dingy your head" dispute seen in (3).

(5)

```
12 Tony:      I'm a dingy your hea:d.=How would you
13            like that.
14               (0.4)
```

```
15 Chopper:   No you won't you little-*h Guess what.
              └──────────────────┘↑ └──────┘
                 Recognizable    Self    Story
                 Counter to   Interrupt  Preface
                   Prior
```

```
18               (0.4)
19 Chopper:   Lemme~tell~ya.=Guess what. (0.8) We
20            was comin home from practice, (0.4)
21            and, three boys came up·there (.) and
22            asked~us~for~money~and~Tony~did~like~
23            this. (0.6)
24            *hh ((raising hands up))
25            "I AIN'T GOT n(h)(hh) ⌜o (°m(h)oney)."
26 Pete:                          [ Ah~hih~ha,
27            *hh Hah~hah!
28 Chopper:   ((snicker)) khh
```

```
29 (    ):      (°      look ┌good.
30 Pete:                     └*hh
31 Tokay:       You di:┌d, ((smile intonation))
32 Pete:               └Aw:,
33 Chopper:     ((snicker)) *hhh~Khh ┌°Hey Poo(h)chie.
34 Malcolm:                           └Ah~ha~aa~aa Ah~ha//ha
35 Tokay:       You there Malcolm,
36 Chopper:     ((snickering)) *hhKh He was the(hh)re.
37 Tokay:       What'd he say Chopper. ((smile
38              intonation))
39 Chopper:     ((snicker)) *hKh Yeah.=
40 Tony:        =You was there ┌Tokay!
41 Chopper:                    └*hih *hih
42 Chopper:     Lemme~tell ya, An h(h)e sai(hh)d,
```

In line 15 Chopper starts a counter to what Tony has just said but breaks it off before it reaches completion.

No you won't you little-

He then produces a prototypical story preface, "Lemme tell ya. Guess what" and, subsequently, in lines 19–25 tells a story about Tony. With his preface he signals that he has a multiutterance unit to complete that will extend over several turns. Although, generally, following such a preface a recipient provides a warrant for the telling by responding at that point, here the storyteller launches quickly into a story.

Participant Frameworks Invoked by the Story

Introducing a story at this point has a range of consequences. First, since the utterance containing Chopper's counter is not brought to completion, Tony is not given the opportunity to respond to it. The return and exchange sequence has, in effect, ended, and participants are no longer within that frame. Second, the story invokes a *participation framework* that is quite different from that provided by the aborted counter. The counter locates Tony as its specific addressee—for example, with the second person pronoun in line 15 ("you little-")—and makes relevant particular types of next actions, such as return counters, from him and not others. Dialogue is restricted to two persons. Though others are present, they are positioned as *onlookers* to the dispute between Chopper and Tony.

By way of contrast the story is addressed to all present and, indeed, Tony, who is now referred to in the third person, is no longer the exclusive, or even the principal, addressee. Rather than being situated as onlookers to a dispute that does not concern them, others present now become the *audience* to the story. Moreover insofar as members of the audience are active coparticipants in the production of a story (C. Goodwin 1984, 1986), they gain rights to participate in the telling in distinctive ways.

Within the story, Chopper portrays Tony as cowardly. In addition, Chopper proposes that Tony's behavior be evaluated in a particular way, specifically as **laughable:** In line 25, as Chopper speaks the words "no(h)(hh)o m(h)oney," he starts to embed laugh tokens in the talk being quoted. This laughter is not heard as part of Tony's words but rather as Chopper's current *comment on* those words. Here, rather than simply reporting what Tony said, Chopper enacts Tony's behavior at the moment of climax; indeed as Vološinov (1971) has argued, one never simply reports an action but, rather, takes up a position with regard to what she or he is saying. First, with the phrase "Tony did like this," Chopper announces that an enactment is to follow. He then marks the talk that follows as an enactment through animation cues such as increased volume (indicated by capital letters) and emphasis (italicized words, the italicization marking high pitch), which result in focus upon the initial part of the reported denial *"I AIN'T* GOT." Other work (M. H. Goodwin 1980b) has demonstrated that such heightened dramatizations in the midst of speech function to obtain enhanced responses from recipients. Thus rather than treating people other than Tony as overhearers, Chopper is now inviting them to participate in the talk of the moment. Moreover, in animating (Goffman 1974:516–544) Tony's talk and drawing attention to it through increased loudness, Chopper proposes that it should be evaluated in a particular way—as laughable. Jefferson (1979) has demonstrated that such laugh tokens can solicit recipient coparticipation in the laugh, and, indeed, that is what happens here. In response to Chopper's talk, Pete (lines 26–27) and Malcolm (line 34) produce laughter. Before Chopper's animation has reached its conclusion, Pete is laughing with him. Shortly afterward, Malcolm (line 34) also laughs, thereby displaying an affiliation and agreement with the mode of argument Chopper is presenting.

In brief switching to a narrative *about* Tony creates a participation framework into which others now have rights to enter with their evaluations of the events heard in the story. Rather than treating people other than Tony as overhearers, Chopper is now inviting them to participate in the talk of the moment.

Audience Alignment Toward Opponent/Story Character

Recipients may, of course, respond in a number of different ways, depending on their structural positions with respect to the story: (1) Recipients occupying the identity of prior participant in the recounted event can assist the teller in providing details of the event, (2) a prior participant whose actions are negatively portrayed may counter the claims made against his character, (3) participants absent from the event being discussed can provide requests that lead to expansion of the story or replaying of its key scenes.

In what follows, Tokay not only requests information concerning specifics of the story but also displays intense interest in the report and, with smile intonation, aligns himself with Chopper:

(6)

25	Chopper:	"*I AIN'T* GOT n(h)(hh) o (°m(h)oney)."
26	Pete:	⌈Ah~hih~ha,
27		*hh Hah~hah!
28	Chopper:	((*snicker*)) khh
29	(ei2):	(° look good.
30	Pete:	⌈*hh
31	Tokay:	→ You *di*: d, ((*smile intonation*))
32	Pete:	⌈Aw:,
33	Chopper:	((*snicker*)) *hhh~Khh °Hey Poo(h)chie.
34	Malcolm:	⌈Ah~*ha*~aa~aa Ah~*ha*/ha
35	Tokay:	→ You there *Mal*colm,
36	Chopper:	((*snickering*)) *hhKh He was the(hh)re.
37	Tokay:	→ What'd he say *Chop*per. ((*smile*
38		*intonation*))
39	Chopper:	((*snicker*)) *hKh Yeah.=
40	Tony:	=*You* was there Tok*ay*!
41	Chopper:	⌈ *hih *hih
42	Chopper:	Lemme~tell ya, An h(h)e sai(hh)d,

Tokay's talk is first answered by Chopper, who intercepts a request directed to Malcolm ("*You* there *Mal*colm") and requests for elaboration ("What'd he say *Chop*per"). Second, it is answered by protagonist Tony, who argues that Tokay's asking questions into the story is inappropriate ("*You* was there Tok*ay*!") in line 40.

Tony elaborates a defense against the portrait being presented of him in lines 45–51; he argues that he didn't, in fact, raise his hands up in cowardice.

(7)

42	Chopper:	Lemme~tell ya, An h(h)e sai(hh)d,
43	Tokay:	*WH:EN*!=
44	Chopper:	="*I* ain't got no(h) mo (h)ney."
45	Tony:	⌈Member=
46	Pete:	Whew::,
47	Tony:	⌈ that night when we was goin there,
48	Chopper:	⌈((*snicker*)) Khh
49	Tony:	and them boys came down the street,
50	Chopper:	⌈((*snicker*)) Khhh!

```
51  Tony:     →  I ain't rai:sed my hands  up.
52  Chopper:                              [Go
53             ahead.=You're gonna say it- I know:.
54             *hh Didn't he g'like this? (0.4)
55             "I ain't go(hh)t
56             no(hh)n (h)e."
57  Malcolm:          [Ah~ha~ha~ha~ha~ha~ha
58  Chopper:   ((snicker)) *hkh
59  Malcolm:   Aw::::
60  Chopper:   ((snicker)) *KHH
61  Malcolm:   ((baby voice)) "I ain't got no money."
62             Ah~ ha~ha.
63  Chopper:       [((snicker)) Khhhhheh!
```

This move is useful to the ongoing development of Chopper's characterization of Tony. Chopper counters Tony's defense: "*Y*ou was there To*kay*!" and then explicitly requests confirmation ("*D*idn't he g'like this?") of his quote of Tony, which he recycles once again in lines 55–56.

Afterward Chopper's talk receives renewed laughter (line 57), as well as recycling of the refrain ("I ain't got no money") in mocking intonation (line 61) from Malcolm. Refutations are used to Chopper's benefit in the elaboration of the story that he wants to tell. Though Tony repetitively produces counters, these are defensive answers to Chopper's stories rather than first moves in counter sequences. Throughout the storytelling, when Tony attempts to defend himself, he gets himself into greater and greater trouble. Counters result in three further descriptions that instance Tony's cowardice. Recipients ratify Chopper's depiction through laughter and through recyclings of the quote "I ain't got no money" (which gets used as a refrain indexing Tony's cowardice) until Chopper finally entraps Tony.

Building a Multiparty Consensus

Though the introduction of the story constitutes a marked transformation of the dispute, it remains very relevant to it. Of crucial importance is the way in which the story allows Chopper to create a visible multiparty consensus against Tony. Chopper moves to a structure that provides parties not initially designated as ratified participants the opportunity to participate. Maintaining and shaping their participation in particular ways, Chopper is able to demonstrate publicly that his characterization of Tony is one that others share. Through their laughter Pete and Malcolm affiliate themselves with Chopper's position.

Throughout the encounter the story remains a point of focus to which others can return. More important, the rearrangement of argument mode also calls into play a different configuration for social organization. The event shifts from one designating only two parties to the dispute (others present being ratified overhearers but not full-fledged contributors) to one inviting the participation of all those present. In that others may become contributing participants in the activity, even without being officially summoned as witnesses, they may align themselves with a particular side of the dispute, and their participation may display whose version has more support.

The structure of the recounting itself allows for displays of appreciation, both laughter and repetition of lines in Chopper's story produced in a mocking tone of voice, as well as requests for elaboration of the story, which grant Chopper a warrant to develop his line.

Girls' Stories

In contrast with boys, girls do not generally utilize direct methods in evaluating one another. They seldom give one another bald commands or insults, and making explicit statements about one's achievements or possessions is avoided. Such actions are felt to indicate someone who "thinks she cute" or above another, thus violating the egalitarian ethos of the girls. These different cultural perceptions concerning evaluating oneself in the presence of others lead to different ways in which stories that are part of dispute processes are built by the teller and involve others in the process of storytelling. Rather than directly confronting one another with complaints about inappropriate behavior, girls characteristically discuss their grievances about someone in that party's absence. Through an elaborated storytelling procedure called "instigating," girls learn that absent parties have been talking about them behind their backs, and they commit themselves to future confrontations with such individuals.

The activity of reporting to a recipient what was said about her in her absence constitutes an important stage preliminary to the confrontation event. It is the point where such an event becomes socially recognizable as an actionable offense. The party talked about may then confront the party who was reportedly talking about her "behind her back," producing an utterance of the following form:

Bea to Ann:	**Kerry said you said that (0.6)** **I wasn't gonna go around *Pop*lar no more.**
Bea—>Ann |	**Bea is speaking to Annette** **in the present**
Ker—>Bea |	**about what Kerry told Bea**
Ann—>Ker |	**that Annette told Kerry**
Bea	**about Bea**

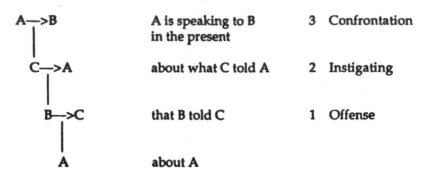

A—>B	A is speaking to B in the present	3 Confrontation
C—>A	about what C told A	2 Instigating
B—>C	that B told C	1 Offense
A	about A	

Informing leading up to the confrontation typically is accomplished through use of stories by a girl who stands as neither accuser nor defendant. This type of storytelling, as noted, is called "instigating" by the children. The instigator may initiate a sequence of events that leads to conflict as part of a process of negatively sanctioning the behavior of a girl who steps outside the bounds of appropriate behavior or as a way of demonstrating her ability to orchestrate such events.

The larger framework of the he-said-she-said dispute provides organization for the storytelling process in several ways.

1. It provides structure for the cited characters and their activities within the story.
2. It influences the types of analysis recipients must engage in to appropriately understand the story.
3. It makes relevant specific types of next moves by recipients: for example, evaluations of the offending party's actions during the story, pledges to future courses of action near the story's ending, and rehearsals of future events at story completion and upon subsequent retellings.

Structure in Telling and Listening to Instigating Stories

Bringing about a future confrontation has direct bearing upon the way a speaker structures her instigating story and recipients respond to it. Through dramatic character development, the speaker skillfully guides her recipients to interpret the events she is relating in the way she wants them to and attempts to co-implicate hearers in forms of future activity. Recipients' responses to instigating stories are differentiated, depending upon the identity relationship of listeners to figures in the story.

Bea tells two stories dealing with Kerry. Bea's first story recounts to both Julia and Barbara what Kerry said about Julia. Julia then leaves, and Bea starts a new set of stories in which she tells Barbara what Kerry said about *her* (Barbara).

The description of the past is organized so as to demonstrate that the events being recounted constitute *offenses*. Moreover, the presentation of past events is carefully managed, so as to elicit from its recipient, now positioned by the story as an *offended party,* pejorative comments about the party who offended her, without this appearing as the direct intent of the speaker's story.

I start by examining the initiation of Bea's first story, recounting what Kerry said about Julia.[4]

(8)

11	Bea:	*How- how-* h- um, uh h- h- how about me
12		and *Ju*lia, *h and all them um, and
13		*Ke*rry, *h ⌈and all them-
14	Julia:	⌊*Isn't Kerry mad* at
15		*me* or *s:om*p'm,
16		(0.4)
17	Bea:	*I'on'* kn//ow.
18	Barb:	Kerry~*al*ways~mad~at somebody.
19		°*I* ⌈'on' care.
20	Julia:	⌊Cuz- cuz cuz I wouldn't, cu:z she
21		ain't put my *name* on that *pa*per.
22	Bea:	*I* know cuz OH yeah. *Oh* yeah.

This story beginning has the form of a reminiscence. Bea requests that others remember with her a particular event: "*How- how-* h- um, uh h- h- how about me and *Ju*lia, *h and all of them um, and *Ke*rry." The numerous stutterings in her speech contribute to the highly charged framing of this talk. The proposed story concerns negative attributes of Kerry. The telling of pejorative stories, especially in the context of the he-said-she-said, poses particular problems for participants. That is, such stories constitute instances of talking behind someone's back, the very action at issue in a he-said-she-said.

A party who tells about another runs a particular risk: Current recipient might tell the absent party that current speaker is talking about her behind her back. The activity of righteously informing someone of an offense against her can itself be taken and cast as an offense. Are there ways in which a party telling such a story can protect herself against such risk? One way might be to implicate her recipient in a similar telling so that both are equally guilty and equally vulnerable. However, this still poses problems: Specifically, it would be most advantageous for each party if the other would implicate herself first. This can lead to a delicate negotiation at the beginning of the story: In lines 11–13, when Bea brings up Kerry's offenses toward Julia, she requests the opinion of others, while refusing to state her own position. In response, Julia asks a question that describes her relationship to Kerry in a particular way: "*Isn't Kerry mad* at *me* or *s:om*p'm" (lines 14–15). If Bea in fact provides a story at this point demonstrating how Kerry is mad at Julia, Bea will have talked pejoratively about Kerry before Julia has co-implicated herself in a similar position. Bea subsequently passes the opportunity to tell such a story by saying "*I'on'* know" (line 17). Then Julia provides an answer to her own question: "Cuz- cuz cuz I wouldn't, cu:z she ain't put my *n*ame on that *pa*per" (lines 20–21). Only after Julia implicates herself does Bea begin to join in the telling (line 22).

Cited Characters and Current Participants

Instigating stories concern others within one's neighborhood group of friends who are judged to have behaved in an inappropriate fashion. Such stories have certain features in common:

1. The principal character in the story is a party who is not present.
2. The nonpresent party performed actions directed toward some other party.
3. These actions can be seen as offenses.
4. The target of the cited offenses is the present hearer.

The placement of present recipient within the story as a principal figure provides for her involvement in it and, consequently, for the story's rather enduring life span, by comparison with other recountings.

Some evidence indicates that the four features just listed are oriented to by the teller in the construction of her instigating stories. In the data being examined, Bea's initial stories (line 20 in Appendix D) involve offenses Kerry committed toward Julia. These include having said that Julia was acting "stupid" and inappropriately when girls were telling jokes and having intentionally excluded Julia's name from a "hall pass." During these stories both Julia and Barbara are present. However, Julia then departs, leaving only Barbara as audience to Bea. Bea now starts a new series of stories (line 21) in which Barbara is the target of a different set of offenses by Kerry. Thus, when one hearer (Julia) leaves (prior to the beginning of line 21), the speaker modifies her stories. In both sets of stories the absent party who commits the offenses, Kerry, remains constant. However, the recipient of her actions is changed so that the target of the offense remains the present hearer. Through such changes the speaker maintains the relevance of her story for its immediate recipient. What happens here demonstrates the importance of not restricting analysis of stories to isolated texts or performances by speakers but, rather, of including the story's recipients within the scope of analysis, since they are consequential to its organization.

Stories may also be locally organized with respect to the person selected as the offender. The fact that Kerry is reputedly the agent of offensive talk in the story to Julia may well be why she is selected as a similar agent in the stories to Barbara several minutes later.

Larger political processes within the girls' group might also be relevant to the selection of Kerry as offender in these stories. Gluckman (1963:308) notes that gossip can be used "to control aspiring individuals." In the present data, Kerry is the same age as the other girls but has skipped a year in school, and they are annoyed at her for previewing everything that will happen to them in junior high school. The structure of the immediate reporting situation, as well as larger social processes within the girls' group, is thus relevant to how past events are organized within these stories and the way in which particular members of the girls' group become cited figures (Goffman 1974:529–532).

In replaying past events, the teller animates (Goffman 1974) the cited figures within her stories in ways that are relevant to the larger social projects within which the stories are embedded. In a variety of ways the absent party's actions toward the current hearer are portrayed as offensive. Thus, in describing what Kerry said about Julia, Bea (lines 26–31) reports that Kerry characterized Julia as having acted "stupid."

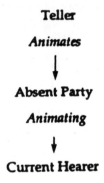

Teller

Animates

↓

Absent Party

Animating

↓

Current Hearer

(9)
```
26  Bea:      She said, She said that um, (0.6)
27            that (0.8) if that girl wasn't
28            there=You know that girl that always
29            makes those funny jokes, *h Sh'aid if
30            that girl wasn't there you wouldn't be
31            actin, (0.4) a:ll stupid like that.
```

Continuing on, Bea (lines 35–36) animates Kerry's voice as she reports that Kerry said that Julia had been cursing.

(10)
```
35  Bea:      and she said that you sai:d, that,
36            "Ah: go tuh-" (0.5) somp'm like tha:t.
```

As Bea further elaborates her story about Kerry, she relates how Kerry attempted to exclude Julia's name from a "hall pass" (a permission slip to go to the bathroom). At the same time that she describes Kerry's actions as offensive, she portrays Julia as someone whose actions were appropriate and exemplary (lines 64–66) and herself as someone who stood up for Julia (lines 68–69).

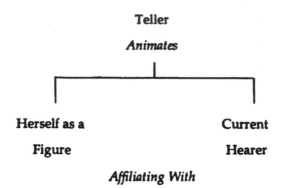

Teller

Animates

Herself as a	**Current**
Figure	**Hearer**

Affiliating With

(11)

64	Bea	An m- And Julia w'just sittin
65		up there actin- actin:, ac- ac- actin
66		sensible. An she up- and she up there
67		talking bout, and she- *I* said, I s'd I
68		s'd I s'd "This is how I'm- I'm gonna
69		put Julia *na*:me down here." Cu- m- m-
70		Cuz she had made a pa:ss you know. *h
71		She had made a *pa*:ss.

Throughout her talk, Bea's stuttering adds to the dramatic quality of her talk as she expresses excitement about what she is relating. As Bea animates Kerry's voice, she colors her talk with a whiny high-pitched defensive tone, enacting Kerry's distaste for having to include Julia's name. Immediately following, however, Bea again portrays herself as someone who *defended* the position of her present hearer against the offender.

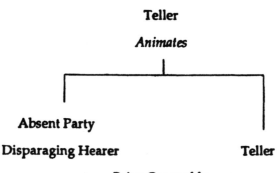

Teller

Animates

Absent Party	
Disparaging Hearer	**Teller**

Being Opposed by

(12)

93	Bea:	But she ain't even put your *na*me down
94		there. *I* just put it *down* there. Me
95		and Martha put it down.=An I said, and

96	she said "*Gi*mme-that-paper.=I don't
97	wanna have her *name down* here." I s- I
98	s- I s- I said "She woulda allowed *you*
99	name."

Quite different forms of affect and alignment toward Julia's perspective are conveyed by Bea's animation of Kerry and of herself. Kerry was eager to remove Julia's name from the hall pass, so that she would not be included in the group of girls exiting from the classroom together. Bea, in contrast, stood up for Julia and argued that, had Julia been in a similar situation, she would have included Kerry.

Recipient Responses

In responding to talk, participants pay close attention to the differential access they have to the events being talked about. Briefly, parties who both were present when the action described occurred and are figures in the story may participate in its telling, denying and countering the absent offending party's statements about them. Recipients who were not present at the past event and are not characters in the story may provide general comments on the offender's character, referring to ongoing attributes of the offender in the present progressive tense, for example:

(13)

18	Barb:	Kerry~*al*ways~mad~at somebody.
19		°*I* 'on' care.

(14)

40	Barb:	Kerry *al*ways say somp'm.=When you
41		*jump* in her *face* she gonna de*ny* it.

In response to listeners' evaluations of events, the speaker acts upon any indication by recipient of her alignment toward the absent party. For example, when Julia makes an evaluative comment, "OO: r'mind me a-you old b:aldheaded Kerry" (lines 109–110) at the close of the story about Kerry's actions toward Julia, Bea states, "*I* should say it in fronta her face. (0.8) Bal: head" (lines 111–112). Bea presents a model of how she herself would confront the offending party and invites the recipient to see the action in question as she herself does, as an action deserving in return an aggravated response such as an insult.

Suggestions for how to act toward absent party may also take the form of stories in which *speaker,* rather than recipient, appears as principal character reacting to actions of offending party. Briefly the speaker makes her suggestions by telling her present recipient the kinds of actions that *she herself* takes against the offender, these actions being appropriate next moves to the offenses described in the informing stories.

Teller

Animates

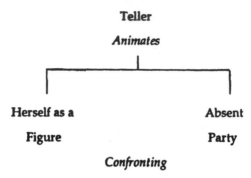

Herself as a   Absent

Figure   Party

Confronting

(15)

142	Bea	*h And she was leanin
143		against- I- I said, I s'd I s'd I s'd I
144		said, "**Hey** girl don't lean against that
145		thing cuz it's **weak enough**." *h And
146		she said and she said *h she- she did
147		like that.=She say, "Tch!" ((*rolling*
148		*eyes*)) // like that. I s'd- I said "You
149		c'd **roll** your eyes all you **want** to.
150	Barb:	Yeah if somebody do that to her-
151		And if ⌈ you know what?
152	Bea:	⌊ Cuz I'm **te**llin you. (0.5)
153		**Te**llin- I'm not **ask**in you." (0.4) An I
154		ain't say no **plea**:se **ei**ther.

In this story, Bea tells how she confronted Kerry with marked insult forms, issuing a direct command to her: "Cuz I'm **te**llin you. (0.4) **Te**llin- I'm not **ask**in you" (lines 152–153). The bald, on-record nature of the command is highlighted by placing it in contrast with a more mitigated form that was not said: "An I ain't say no **plea**:se **ei**ther" (lines 153–154).

Evaluation through descriptions of past activities is consequential for the process of eliciting from the recipient a promise to confront the offender in the future. On the one hand pejorative actions performed by the absent party can be interpreted as explicit offenses against the current recipient. On the other hand, a speaker's description of her own actions in response to such offenses, that is, confronting the offender, can provide a recipient with a guide to how she should act toward that party. Thus Julia's statement that she will confront Kerry occurs right after Bea has described how she confronted Kerry about having excluded Julia's name from the bathroom pass.

(16)

87	Julia:	I'm a- I'm a **tell** her about herself.

Offended parties' responses that constitute plans to confront the offending party are made in the presence of witnesses; they thus provide displays of someone's intentions to seek redress for the offenses performed against her. Failure to follow through with a commitment statement such as "I'm a *t*ell her about herself" can be remarked on as demonstrating inconsistencies in a person's talk and actions, thus reflecting negatively on her character. Indeed, when Julia later fails to confront Kerry, others use her actions in the present exchange to talk about the way in which she had promised to tell Kerry off but then did nothing.

(17)

Bea:	Yeah and Julia all the time talking
	bout she was gonna tell what'shername
	off. And *she* ain't do it.

Alignments taken up in the midst of an exchange such as this can thus be interpreted as **commitments** to undertake future action for which parties may be held responsible by others. People who refuse to confront once they have reported their intentions are said to "swag," "mole," or "back down" from a future confrontation. The fact that a statement about future intentions can be treated as a relevantly absent event at a future time provides some demonstration of how responses to instigating stories are geared into larger social projects.

Thus, through a variety of activities—passing the opportunity to align herself with a definitive position before the hearer does at story beginning, presenting herself as having defended the offended party in the past, and portraying how she boldly confronted the offending party—the speaker carefully works to co-implicate her present recipient in a next course of action. Though the report is reputedly a narrative account of past events involving teller and offending party and speaker's alignment of righteous indignation toward these acts, it may also function to suggest future courses of action for present recipient.

A Comparison of Boys' and Girls' Dispute Stories

The forms of participation made available in boys' and girls' dispute stories may now be compared. The girls' and boys' stories examined here share several features: (1) The principal topic is offenses of another, and (2) one of the characters in the story is a present participant. In the case of boys' stories, cited offenses deal with wrongdoings of a *present participant*. Among girls, however, offenses concern *reported deeds of absent parties*. Such differences have consequences for the trajectory of dispute in girls' and boys' groups; whereas boys can deal directly with an offender, girls must wait to confront the offending party at a future time.

Within boys' and girls' dispute stories *hearer who is a character in the story* is portrayed in different ways. Whereas in Chopper's story Tony has performed objectionable actions in the past as a coward, in girls' instigating stories the present hearers (Julia and Barbara) are said to have performed exemplary actions in the past that sharply contrast with the reportedly objectionable actions of an absent party (Kerry). Among the girls, storyteller skillfully works to align hearer *with teller against an absent third party*. A coalition of what the girls call "two against one" (teller and hearer against absent party) is established in the immediate interaction. From the teller's perspective, the offended party's alignment is important for bringing forth a future confrontation. From the recipient's perspective the fact that at least two parties agree on a particular version of an event provides a warrant for bringing action against a third party. By way of illustration, consider the following speech that Vettie (age eleven) makes to her adversary during a confrontation:

(18)

> Vettie: Well I'm a get it straight with the people.
> What *Kerry*, (1.4)
> it's between Kerry, and you, (1.0)
> See *two* (0.5) two against one. (0.7)
> Who wins? The one is two.=Right? (0.5)
> And that's Joycie and and Kerry. (0.5)
> They both say that you said it.
> And you say that you didn't say it.
> Who you got the *proof* that say that
> you *did*n't say it.

In contrast the teller in the boys' stories constructs a situation of conflict, not at some future time, but instead between teller and recipient, who is the principal character in the immediate interaction; boys who are hearers (and can be co-tellers of the story) align themselves *with the teller against the present principal character*.

Response from parties other than those who are principal figures in the story are similar in both girls' and boys' stories; such parties aid in the teller's depiction of the offending party by providing comments on the offender's character. Responses of offended parties, however, differ in girls' and boys' groups. Although offended parties in both girls' and boys' groups oppose reported descriptions, they oppose different identities. Boys who are offended parties direct counters to *principal storyteller*, but girls direct counters to *cited figures* who offended them in the past.

The portrayal of characters and events within dispute stories has consequences for the form and timing of interaction that ensues. Thus, whereas boys' dispute stories engender disagreements that permit contesting in the *immediate setting*, girls' stories engender alignments of "two against one" against an absent third party who will be confronted *at some future time*. In that the offending party is absent from the instigating event, girls cannot resolve their disagreements in the present interaction. Girls' he-said-she-said disputes, in contrast with those of boys, may be extended over several days.

An offended party in girls' stories reacts by stating not only that she disapproves of the offending party's actions toward her in the past, but also that she is prepared to confront her offender. When the offended party confronts the plaintiff, she does so with indirect, rather than direct, speech, in that the offenses at issue have been learned about through a third party. Girls' stories constitute a preliminary stage in a larger process of negatively sanctioning inappropriate behavior. After the instigating session, girls replay reactions of offended parties to the stories and rehearse future possible scenarios for confrontation with friends (M. Goodwin 1988b). Following the confrontation, serious offenders of the girls' moral code may be ostracized; the degradation ceremony of ridicule and teasing that results can extend over several weeks. Whereas boys' stories have little motive power beyond the present situation, girls' instigating stories are embedded within a larger social process, the he-said-she-said, a speech event providing for the involvement of participants in multiple phases of activity.

The present study has relevance for theories regarding not only the relationship of speech activities to larger social processes but also gender differences in children's social organization and culture. Whereas boys' arguments display an orientation toward social differentiation and principles of hierarchy, within he-said-she-said disputes girls display a form of organization based on what has been called "exclusiveness," reportedly more characteristic of American girls' groups than of boys'(Douvan & Adelson 1966:200–202, Eder & Hallinan 1978, Feshbach & Sones 1971, Lever 1976, Savin-Williams 1980:348, Sutton-Smith 1979). Girls affirm the organization of their social group through assessing the behavior of absent parties. The alliances they form in the process of discussing others mark who is included and excluded from the social group of the moment, rather than relative rank.

It is sometimes argued that girls avoid direct competition and are little interested in "negotiational involvements" (Gilligan 1982, Lever 1976, Sutton-Smith 1979). Girls' tendency to be more nurturant than boys is felt to result in relatively less conflict in their same-sex peer group (Miller, Danaher, & Forbes 1986:547). Within certain domains (M. H. Goodwin 1980a, 1988a) girls do select accounts for their actions that more closely reflect what Gilligan (1982:62–63) terms an ethic of care (as contrasted with an ethic of justice) and appear more concerned with a self "delineated through connection," than with a "self defined through separation" (Gilligan 1982:35) or differentiation from others. Such forms of behavior, however, must be interpreted as situated presentations of self, sensitive to the contexts in which they occur. As the data presented here vividly show, within the he-said-she-said storytelling event, girls react with righteous indignation when they learn their character has been maligned. They display an intense interest in initiating and elaborating disputes about their rights (not to be talked about behind their backs) that differentiate offending and offended parties. Alignments taken up during such disputes clearly demarcate who stands within the bounds of an inner circle of friends, as well as who is relegated to that circle's periphery. Stories thus provide arenas for each gender group to negotiate concerns central to each group's notions of social organization.

Appendix A: The Children

	Boys			Girls	
Name	Age	Grade	Name	Age	Grade
Tony	14	8th	Barbara	13	8th
Archie	13	8th	Bea	12	7th
Pete	13	8th	Martha	12	7th
Malcolm	13	8th	Julia	12	7th
Tokay	12	7th	Kerry	12	8th
Dave	12	7th	Annette	10	5th
Chopper	12	7th	Rochele	9	4th
William	10	5th			
Tommy	9	5th			

Appendix B. Transcription

The following example has been constructed to contain a variety of relevant transcription devices in a brief example. It is not an accurate record of an actual exchange. Features most relevant to the analysis in this paper are identified after it.

**Example
Number**
↓
(16)

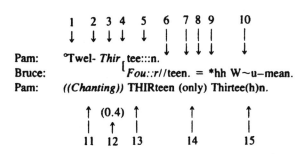

```
              1  2  3 4   5   6  7 8 9    10
              ↓  ↓  ↓ ↓   ↓   |  | | | |   |
                                ↓  ↓ ↓ ↓   ↓
Pam:     °Twel- Thir tee:::n.
                      [
Bruce:                 Fou::r//teen. = *hh W~u–mean.
Pam:     ((Chanting)) THIRteen (only) Thirtee(h)n.

         ↑  (0.4)  ↑          ↑            ↑
         |    ↑    |          |            |
         11   12   13         14           15
```

1. **Low Volume:** A degree sign indicates that talk it precedes is low in volume.
2. **Cutoff:** A hyphen marks a sudden cutoff of the current sound. In the example, instead of bringing the word *twelve* to completion, Pam interrupts it in midcourse.
3. **Italics:** Italics indicate some form of emphasis, which may be signaled by changes in pitch and/or amplitude.
4. **Overlap Bracket:** A left bracket marks the point at which the current talk is overlapped by other talk. Thus, Bruce's *"Thir*teen"

begins during the last syllable of Pam's *Four*teen." Two speakers beginning to speak simultaneously are shown by two left brackets at the beginning of a line.

5. **Lengthening:** Colons indicate that the sound just before the colon has been noticeably lengthened.

6. **Overlap Slashes:** Double slashes provide an alternative method of marking overlap. When they are used, the overlapping talk is not indented to the point of overlap. In the example, Pam's last line begins just after the *"Four"* in Bruce's *"Four*teen."

7. **Intonation:** Punctuation symbols are used to mark intonation changes, rather than as grammatical symbols:
   • A period indicates a falling intonation contour.
   • A question mark indicates a rising intonation contour.
   • A comma indicates a falling–rising intonation contour.

8. **Latching:** The equal signs indicate "latching"; there is no interval between the end of a prior turn and the start of a next piece of talk.

9. **Inbreath:** A series of *h*'s preceded by an asterisk marks an inbreath. Without the dot, the *h*'s mark an outbreath.

10. **Rapid Speech:** Tildes (~) indicate that speech is slurred together because it is spoken rapidly.

11. **Comments:** Double parentheses enclose material that is not part of the talk being transcribed, for example, a comment by the transcriber if the talk was spoken in some special way.

12. **Silence:** Numbers in parentheses mark silences in seconds and tenths of seconds.

13. **Increased Volume:** Capitals indicate increased volume.

14. **Problematic Hearing:** Material in parentheses indicates a hearing that the transcriber was uncertain about.

15. **Breathiness, Laughter:** An *h* in parentheses indicates plosive aspiration, which could result from events such as breathiness, laughter, or crying.

16. **Citation:** Each example is preceded by a citation that locates the tape and transcript where the original data can be found.

Appendix C. Boys' Dispute Story

(19)

1 Tony:	*Gi*mme the ***things***.
2 Chopper:	You sh:ut up you ***big*** lips. (Y'all been
3	hangin around with thieves.)
4 Tony:	(***Shut*** up.)
5 Chopper:	Don't gimme that. =I'm not ***talk***in to
6	you.

```
 7                    (1.4)
 8 Tony:      I'm talkin to y:ou!
 9 Chopper:   Ah you better sh:ut up with your
10            little- di:ngy sneaks.
11                    (1.4)
12 Tony:      I'm a dingy your hea:d.=How would you
13            like that.
14                    (0.4)
15 Chopper:   No you won't you little- ⌜*h Guess what.
16 Jack:                               ⌊(°foul) foul
17            thing.
18                    (0.4)
19 Chopper:   Lemme~tell~ya.=Guess what. (0.8) We
20            was comin home from practice, (0.4)
21            and, three boys came up there (.) and
22            asked~us~for~money~and~Tony~did~like~
23            this. (0.6)
24            *hh ((raising hands up))
25            "I AIN'T GOT n(h)(hh)⌜o °m(h)oney."
26 Pete:                          ⌊Ah-hih-ha,
27            *hh Hah-hah!
28 Chopper:   ((snicker)) khh
29 (     ):   (°         look ⌜good.)
30 Pete:                      ⌊*hh
31 Tokay:     You di:⌜d, ((smile intonation))
32 Pete:             ⌊Aw:,
33 Chopper:   *hhh~ ((snicker)) Khh ⌜°Hey Poo(h)chie.
34 Malcolm:                         ⌊Ah~ha~aa~aa Ah~ha//ha
35 Tokay:     You there Malcolm,
36 Chopper:   ((snicker)) *hhKh He was the(hh)re.
37 Tokay:     What'd he say Chopper. ((Smile
38           Intonation))
39 Chopper:   ((snicker)) *hKh Yeah.=
40 Tony:      =You was there ⌜Tokay!
41 Chopper:                  ⌊*hih *hih
42 Chopper:   Lemme~tell ya, An h(h)e sai(hh)d,
43 Tokay:     WH:EN!=
44 Chopper:   ="I ain't got no(h) mo⌜(h)ney."
45 Tony:                          ⌊Member=
46 Pete:      =⌈⌊Whew::,
47 Tony:       that night when we was goin ⌜there,
48 Chopper:                                ⌊((snicker)) Khh
49 Tony:      and ⌜them boys came down the street,
50 Chopper:       ⌊((snicker)) Khhh!
51 Tony:      I ain't rai:sed my hands ⌜up.
52 Chopper:                             ⌊Go
```

```
53              ahead.=You're gonna say it- I know:.
54              *hh Didn't he g'like this?  (0.4)
55              "I ain't go(hh)t
56              no(hh)n⌐(h)e."
57  Malcolm:               Ah~ha~ha~ha~ha~ha~ha
58  Chopper:    ((snicker)) *hkh
59  Malcolm:    Aw::::
60  Chopper:    *H ((snicker)) KHH
61  Malcolm:    ((baby voice)) "I ain't got no money."
62              Ah-⌐ha-ha.
63  Chopper:        ((snicker)) Khhhhheh!
64  Tony:       If he had money.  If ⌐he had money
65  Chopper:                         *hihh
66  Tony:    ⌐⌐and he said he didn't=
67  Chopper:  *hih
68  Tony:       =them boys kicked his b'hi(hh)nd. °eh heh
69  Chopper:    I ain't had no mon- I only had a penny
70              they didn't even find it.
71                  (0.4)
72  Jack:       °mmYeah.
73                  (0.8)
74  Chopper:    At least I didn't go up there and say,
75                  (1.2)
76  Chopper: ⌐⌐"I ain't got none."
77  Tony:       Well there'd be some problems if he
78              came found it didn't it.
79  Chopper:    Nope.  And ⌐guess what Mal⌐colm.
80  Malcolm:                 °He said        said
81              ((baby voice)) "I ain't got no money."=
82  Chopper:    =Guess what Malcolm.=Them boys out
83              there said, *hh "Your football player
84              ca:n't, play," And guess where To:ny
85              was.  (0.6)  All the way ar(h)ound the
86              cor(hh)n(h)er.  (0.5) *hih ⌐Remember=
87  ( ):                             °What?
88  Chopper:    =that night?  Them little boys said
89              "That little p:unk can't fight?"  And
90              Tony started runnin across the s:treet.
91  Jack:       Hey:⌐:,
92  Chopper:        Not e⌐ven waitin for em.=
93  Ray:                 eh~heh~heh.
94  Tony:       =WHAT?!
95  Chopper:    Member that time, (0.5) Lemme see we
96              got about- where we was playin
97              basketball at?  (1.2)  And // you had
98  Tony:       Where who w'playin basketball at.
99  Chopper:    You know, where we were playin
```

100	basketball? And you wasn't even waitin
101	for us, you was up there r:unnin,
102	Until you got way around the
103	corner.=Them boys said, those boys kep,
104	those boys kept on (*I* said,) "Hey Tony
105	what you runnin for." He said "*I* ain't
106	runnin." That boys woulda come next to
107	*me* I(h) woul(hh)da, ((snicker)) *hKkh I woulda
108	k:icked their *ass*. And // Tony was
109	was all the way ar(h)ound the corner.
110 Tony:	I don't know what *you talkin* bout.
111 Jack:	°Talkin // bout bein *kick*ed. That's
112	what it // is.
113 Pete:	Member that time,
114 Tony:	I don't remember // what *you talk*in
115	about.
116 Pete:	that we was goin around the corner on
117	Poplar?
118 Chopper:	"*I ain*'t got no(hh) mo(hh)ney."
119 Pete:	That boy down there
120 Malcolm:	((baby voice)) "*I ain*'t got no money."
121	"I ain't got no money."
122 Tokay:	Remember when that boy down in the
123	park, °that time, when he was talkin
124	to ┌Tony for
125 Tony:	└What he- When is he talkin ┌about.
126 Chopper:	└OH YEAH!
127	(0.5)
128 Chopper:	"I *know* you ain't talkin to
129	*me*!" Down in the park! ((snicker)) Khh~heh!
130 Pete:	eh~heh~heh.
131 Chopper:	*hh We was down the park, (0.7) and we
132	was- (0.6) and wh- wh- what was he
133	*do*in,=
134 Tony:	=You can ask *Ralph* what happened down
135	the *park* Malcolm Johnson cuz *this*
136	sucker *lie* too much.
137 Chopper:	*Uh* UH. we was playin- (0.3) we was
138	makin a *darn raft*, (0.5) and them
139	boys (.) was throwin things at Tony,
140	(0.7) And *he* said, (0.6) "Boy!" And-
141	lemme tell.=(*They*) were talkin to that
142	*lit*tle boy. Th'he said, "Boy you
143	better watch them *things!*" That big
144	boy said,
145 Tony:	°What ones.=
146 Chopper:	="I *know* (he ain't talkin to *me*!)" I

147		said (0.4) and he said-
148		"NO: not ⌐you: du(hh)mmy-"
149	Tony:	⌐What things.
150	Pete:	Ah:~*heh*~heh~⌐heh.
151	Chopper:	"The *little* bo:(hh)y."
152		Eh~heh~heh. ((snicker)) *hKh
153	Malcolm:	That-
154	Chopper:	That big boy woulda kicked his butt!
155	Malcolm:	That *li*⌐ttle boy.
156	Tony:	That's a lie *too* Chopper.
157	Chopper:	Why you talk to that *little* boy.
158		(1.0)
159	Tony:	*I* said *what*?
160	Chopper:	Got you got you *got* you!
161		(1.2)
162	Chopper:	Say Hey heh *heh*
163		heh, Hey hey HEY! HEY HEY *HEY*! "I
164		ain't go(h)t no(h)" (0.8) Da:g!

Appendix D. Girls' Dispute Story

(20)

((Bea, Barbara, and Julia are sitting on Julia's steps discussing substitute teachers during a teacher's strike.))

1	Barb:	*Teach* us some little *six*th grade work.
2		(0.4) *That*'s how these volun*teers* doin
3		now. A little um, *h *Ad*din 'n all
4		that.
5	Bea:	*Y*ahp. *Y*ahp. // Yahp. An when
6		we was in the-
7	Barb:	Twenny and twenny is // forty an all
8		that.
9	Bea:	*How* bout when we was in-
10	Barb:	Oo I *hate* that junk.
11	Bea:	*How*- *how*- h- um, uh h- h- how about me
12		and *Ju*lia, 'h and all them um, and
13		*K*erry, 'h ⌐and all them-
14	Julia:	*Is*n't Kerry *mad* at
15		*me* or s:*omp*'m,
16		(0.4)
17	Bea:	*I'on*' kn//ow.
18	Barb:	Kerry~*al*ways~mad~at somebody.

19		°*I* ['on' care.
20	Julia:	Cuz- cuz cuz I wouldn't, cu:z she
21		ain't put my *name* on that *pa*per.
22	Bea:	*I* know cuz [OH yeah. *Oh* yeah.
23	Barb:	[An next she,
24		(0.3)
25	Barb:	[[talk~bout~*peo*ple.
26	Bea:	*She* said, *She* said that um, (0.6)
27		that (0.8) if that *girl* wasn't
28		there=*You* know that girl that always
29		makes those funny jokes, 'h Sh'aid if
30		that *girl* wasn't there *you* wouldn't be
31		*ac*tin, (0.4) a:ll *stu*pid like that.
32		[[°Sh-
33	Julia:	But *was* I actin stupid w[ith them?
34	Bea:	[Nope, no,=And
35		she- and she said that *you* sai:d, that,
36		"*Ah*: go tuh-" (0.5) somp'm like [tha:t.
37	Julia:	[°No I
38		didn't.
39	Bea:	She's- an uh- somp'm like *that*. She's-
40	Barb:	Ke[rry *al*ways say somp'm.=When you=
41	Bea:	[She-
42	Barb:	=*jump* in her *face* she gonna de*ny*
43		it.
44	Bea:	Yah:p Y[ahp.=An she said, 'h An- and
45	Julia:	[°Right on.
46	Bea:	she said, hh that *you* wouldn't be *ac*tin
47		*like that* aroun- around *peo*ple.
48	Julia:	So: *she* wouldn' be *ac*tin *like that*
49		wi' that *oth*er girl.=*She* the one picked
50		*me* to *sit* wi'them.='h She said ["Julia you
51	Bea:	[Y:ahp.
52	Julia:	sit with her, 'h and I'll sit with her,
53		'h an Bea an- an Bea an-
54		an an [Martha sit together."
55	Barb:	[SHE TELLIN Y'ALL WHERE TA SIT
56		AT?
57		(0.2)
58	Bea:	An so *we* sat together, An s- and s- and
59		so Julia was ju:st s:ittin right
60		there.=An the girl, an- an- the girl:
61		next to her? 'h and the girl kept on
62		getting back up. 'h Ask the teacher
63		can she go t'the bathroom. An Julia
64		say she don' *wan*na go t'the bathroom

65		w'her. An m- And Julia w'just sittin
66		up there actin- actin:, ac- ac- actin
67		sensible. An she up- and she up there
68		talking bout, and she- *I* said, I s'd I
69		s'd I s'd "This is how I'm- I'm gonna
70		put Julia *na*:me down here." Cu- m- m-
71		Cuz she had made a pa:ss you know. 'h
72		She had made a *pa*:ss.
73		(0.2)
74	Bea:	[For all us to go down to the bathroom.
75	Barb:	Y'all go down t'the bathroom?
76	Bea:	For ALLA- yeah. Yeah. For u:m, (0.4)
77		for- for alla us- t'go to the
78		bathroom.=I s'd- I s'd "*How*: *co*:me you
79		ain't put Julia name down here." *h So
80		she said, she said ((*whiny defensive tone*))
81		"That other girl called 'er so,
82		she no:t *wi*:th *u*:s, so,"
83		That's what she said too. (0.2) So *I*
84		said, s- so I snatched the paper
85		wi'her. I said wh- when we were playin
86		wi'that paper?
87	Julia:	I'm a I'm a *tell* her about herself
88		to*da*[y. Well,
89	Bea:	[Huh? huh remember when we're
90		snatchin that [paper.
91	Barb:	[An she gonna tell you
92		another story *anyway*. // (Are you gonna
93		talk to her today?)
94	Bea:	But she ain't even put your *na*me down
95		there. *I* just put it *down* there. Me
96		and Martha put it down.=An I said, and
97		she said "*Gi*mme-that-paper.=I don't
98		wanna have her *name down* here." I s- I
99		s- I s- I said "She woulda allowed *you*
100		name (if you star:ted)."
101		(1.0)
102	Julia:	I said Kerry "°How come you ain't put my
103		name."
104	Barb:	Here go B//ea, "uh uh uh well-"
105	Julia:	"You put that *other* girl (name down)
106		didn't you. I thought *you* was gonna
107		have- owl: a hall pass with that *other*
108		girl." That's °what Kerry said. I said
109		(What's~her~problem.) OO: r'mind me a-
110		you old b:aldheaded Kerry.
111	Bea:	*I* should say it in fronta her *face*.

112		(0.8) Bal: head.
113	Barb:	Hey member when what we did th(h)e
114		o(h)ther ti(*h*)me.

(21)

((*The following occurs 45 seconds later after Julia has gone inside.*))

1	Bea:	She shouldn't be *writ*in things, about
2		me. (0.5) An so- An so- so she said
3		*Bar*bara, Barbara need ta *go*
4		somewhere.
5		(1.0)
6	Barb:	Well you *t*ell her to *c*ome say it in
7		front of my fa:ce. (0.6) And *I*'ll *p*ut
8		*her* somewhere. (3.8) An Barbara
9		ain't got nuttin t'do with *what.*
10	Bea:	*Write*- um doin um, ⌈that- that thing.
11	Barb:	⌊What do y'*all*
12		got ta do with it.
13	Bea:	Because because um, *I* don't know what
14		we got to do with it. Bu⌈t she said-
15	Barb:	⌊W'll *she*
16		don't know what *she* *talk*in bout.
17	Bea:	But- but she- but we *di:d* have somp'm
18		to do because we was *ma:d* at *her*.
19		Because we didn't *like* her no more.
20		(0.6) And *that's* why, (0.6) Somebody
21		the one ⌈that use-
22	Barb:	⌊So, she got anything t'say she
23		come say it in front of my face. (1.0)
24		I better not *see Kerry* today. (2.5) I
25		*ain*'t gonna say- I'm~a~say "Kerry *what*
26		*you say* about m⌈e. She gonna say
27	Bea:	⌊((whiny)) (Nyang)
28	Barb:	I ain't *say* nuttin."
29	Bea:	(behind her face) she meant- sh'ent You
30		know you- you know what. She- she
31		chan⌈gin it.
32	Barb:	⌊If I *wro:*te somp'm then I *wrote*
33		it.=Then I got somp'm to do with
34		it.=W'then I *wrote* it.
35		(0.5)
36	Bea:	And *she* said, an- an- she u:m ah
37		whah.(I'm sorry oh.) I'm a walk you
38		home. *She* said that um,
39	Barb:	She get on my *nerves*.

40	Bea:	She said that um,=
41	Barb:	=*Nown* I got somp'm ta write about her
42		*now*::.
43		(0.5)
44	Bea:	Oh yeah.=She sai:d tha:t, (0.4) that
45		um, you wouldn't have nuttin ta do with
46		it, and every*thing*, and *plus*, (0.5)
47	Bea:	⌜um,
48	Barb:	WELL IF I WROTE SOME'N *I* HAD SOMP'M
49		T'*DO* with it.
50	Bea:	An she said, *I* wanna see what I was
51		gettin read ta say, (2.0) °And um,
52	Barb:	She gonna de*ny* every *word*.=Now *watch*.
53		I c'n put more up there for her the:n.
54		(2.0)
55	Bea:	⌜*What*,
56	Barb:	An in magic marker °so there.
57		(0.6)
58	Bea:	Oh yeah, oh yeah.=*She* was, *she*- w's
59		*she* was in Rochele: house you know, and
60		she said that um, that- I heard her
61		say um, (0.4) um um uh uh "*Jul*ia said
62		y'all been talking behind my back."=I
63		said I'm a- I'm a say "H:oney, I'm gla:d.
64		that *you* know I'm *talk*in be*hind your*
65		*back*. Because *I*- because *I meant*
66		for you to know *any*way." An she said,
67		I- said "I don't have to talk behind
68		your back.=I can talk in front of your
69		*face too*." // And she said-
70	Barb:	That's all I write. I didn't
71		write that. *I* wrote *that*.
72		(1.2)
73	Bea:	Over here. *I* write *this*- I cleared it
74		*off*. Because *Lan*da *wrote*
75		and I- *h⌜ and *I* made it *big*ger.
76	Barb:	Mmm,
77		(0.2)
78	Bea:	So she said, ⌜That first-
79	Barb:	And the other I did with
80		my finger on the cars ⌜and all that.
81	Bea:	An- so- *I* said,
82		an- an so we were playin *school* you
83		know at Rochele's house? And *boy we*
84		*tore* her *all*- we said, I got
85		uh y'know ⌜I was doin some signs?
86	Barb:	I better *not* go around an

87		catch Kerry.
88	Bea:	And Ro*chele* called her *bald*headed
89		right~in~fronta~her face. She said "You
90		*bald*headed *thing*." Because she was
91		messin with Rochele.=I said, and so she
92		said, you know we were playin around
93		with her? And she said "You *bald*headed
94		thing."=She said, "Rochele YOU DON'T
95		LIKE IT?" I said I said ⌐that's why-
96	Barb:	└Yeah she gonna
97		base in some little kid's ⌐face.
98	Bea:	└Yeah. And
99		she said, // I said AND I SAID= I said I
100		said "What~are~ya doin to her."
101	Barb:	I better not see Kerry to*day*. I'm a
102		say "Kerry *I* heard *you* was talkin bout
103		me."
104	Bea:	I a s⌐ay-
105	Barb:	└Then she gonna say "I ain't- *What*
106		*I* say about you." I say "Ain't none
107		yer *bus*iness what you said.=You come
108		say it in front a my *face* since what=
109		you been tell everybody *else*." (0.4)
110		*((falsetto))* OO:, And I can put more
111		and I'm a put some- some °bad words in
112		to*day*.
113		(0.5)
114	Bea:	*She* said, and *she* was saying,
115		⌐she said-
116		└*Now*:
		n I got somp'm to write ⌐ab*out*.
117	Bea:	└*I* said,
118	Barb:	I better not catch you t'day.=I'm a
119		*tell her butt o*:ff.
120		(0.4)
121	Barb:	An if she //get *bad* at me:*e*: I'm a,
122		punch her in the eye.
123	Bea:	*I* said, *I* s- *I* said, I said, Hey
124		Barbara I said, "Why don't you" um, I
125		s- I- I- I- and "*Why* don' you stop
126		messing with her." And she said she
127		said "She called me baldheaded."
128		=I said,
129	Barb:	That's right.
130	Bea:	=⌐An so-
131	Barb:	└That's her name so call her name back.
132	Bea:	*Guess* what. *Guess* what. Uh- we- w-
133		an we was up finger waving?=And I said,

134		I said, I said I said *((does motion))*
135		like that.=I did.
136		hh An ⌜just like that.='h and I said=
137	Barb:	⌞OO::,
138	Bea:	an I an I was doin all those *sig:*ns in
139		her face and everything? (0.5) 'h And
140		she said that um, (1.0) And then she-
141		an you- and she s- °She- roll her eye
142		like that. 'h And she was leanin
143		against- I- I said, I s'd I s'd Is'd I
144		said, "*Hey* girl don't lean against that
145		thing cuz it's *weak* e*nough.*" *h And
146		she said and she said 'h she- she did
147		like that.=She say, "Tch!" *((rolling*
148		*eyes))* // like that. I s'd- I said "You
149		c'd *roll* your eyes all you *want* to.
150	Barb:	Yeah if somebody do that to her-
151		And if ⌜you know what?
152	Bea:	⌞Cuz I'm *tell*in you. (0.5)
153		*Tell*in- I'm not *ask*in you." (0.4) An I
154		ain't say no *plea:*se *ei*ther.
155	Barb:	mm hmm.
156	Bea:	*((chews fingers))*
157	Barb:	*Don'*t do that. (1.5) W'll I'm tellin ya
158		*I* better not catch *K*erry to*day.* Cuz if
159		I catch her I'm gonna give *her* a wor:d
160		from my *mou*th. (0.6) An if she *j*ump in
161		my *f*ace I'm a punch her in her *f*a:ce.
162		(1.5) And she can talk behind my ba:ck
163		she better say somp'm in front of my
164		face.
165		(1.5)
166		*((Boy walks down the street))*
167	Barb:	OO: there go the *Tack.* 'h 'hh 'hh Eh
168		That's your na(h)me.
169		(1.5)
170		*((Barbara starts down the street))*
171	Barb:	°h See y'all.
172	Bea:	*See* you.

NOTES

This chapter originally appeared in *Discourse Processes* 13(1990):1.35–71.

1. For a more complete description of this fieldwork see M. H. Goodwin (1990).

2. A more extensive analysis of the formation of teams, as well as speech activities, occurring in this encounter appears in C. Goodwin and M. H. Goodwin (1990).

3. The complete cycle of stories from which these data were selected appears in Appendix C. Subsequent line numbers related to this example refer to line numbers in the expanded version of this story in Appendix C.

4. The series of stories from which these data were taken appears in Appendix D. Line numbers in this fragment correspond to line numbers in the more expanded sequence of which this story is a part, which appears in Appendix D.

REFERENCES

Douvan, Elizabeth & Adelson, Joseph (1966). *The adolescent experience*. New York: John Wiley & Sons.

Eder, Donna & Hallinan, Maureen T. (1978). Sex differences in children's friendships. *American Sociological Review* 43:237–250.

Feshbach, Norman & Sones, Gittelle (1971). Sex differences in adolescent reactions toward newcomers. *Developmental Psychology* 4:381–386.

Gilligan, Carol (1982). *In a different voice: Psychological theory and women's development*. Cambridge, MA: Harvard University Press.

Gluckman, Max (1963). Gossip and scandal. *Current Anthropology* 4:307–315.

Goffman, Erving (1974). *Frame analysis: An essay on the organization of experience*. New York: Harper & Row.

Goodwin, Charles (1984). Notes on story structure and the organization of participation. In Max Atkinson & John Heritage (Eds.) *Structures of social action* (pp. 225–246). Cambridge: Cambridge University Press.

Goodwin, Charles (1986). Audience diversity, participation and interpretation. *Text* 6(3):283–316.

Goodwin, Charles & Goodwin, Marjorie Harness (1990). Interstitial argument. In Allen Grimshaw (Ed.) *Conflict talk* (pp. 85–117). Cambridge: Cambridge University Press.

Goodwin, Marjorie Harness (1980a). Directive/response speech sequences in girls' and boys' task activities. In Sally McConnell-Ginet, Ruth Borker & Nelly Furman (Eds.) *Women and language in literature and society* (pp. 157–173). New York: Praeger.

Goodwin, Marjorie Harness (1980b). Processes of mutual monitoring implicated in the production of description sequences. *Sociological Inquiry* 50:303–317.

Goodwin, Marjorie Harness (1988a). Cooperation and competition across girls' play activities. In Sue Fisher & Alexandra Dundas Todd (Eds.) *Gender and discourse: The power of talk* (pp. 55–94). Norwood, NJ: Ablex.

Goodwin, Marjorie Harness (1990). *He-said-she-said: Talk as social organization among black children*. Bloomington, IN: Indiana University Press.

Goodwin, Marjorie Harness (1990–91). Retellings, pretellings and hypothetical stories. *Research on Language and Social Interaction* 24:263–276.

Jefferson, Gail (1979). A technique for inviting laughter and its subsequent acceptance/declination. In George Psathas (Ed.) *Everyday language: Studies in ethnomethodology* (pp. 79–96). New York: Irvington.

Labov, William (1972). The transformation of experience in narrative syntax. In

William Labov, *Language in the inner city: Studies in the black English vernacular* (pp. 354–396). Philadelphia: University of Pennsylvania Press.

Lever, Janet (1976). Sex differences in the games children play. *Social Problems* 23:478–487.

Miller, Patrice, Danaher, Dorothy & Forbes, David (1986). Sex-related strategies for coping with interpersonal conflict in children aged five and seven. *Developmental Psychology* 22:543–548.

Sacks, Harvey, Schegloff, Emanuel A. & Jefferson, Gail (1974). A simplest systematics for the organization of turn-taking for conversation. *Language* 50:696–735.

Savin-Williams, Richard (1980). Social interactions of adolescent females in natural groups. In H. C. Foot, A. J. Chapman, & J. R. Smith (Eds.) *Friendship and social relations in children* (pp. 343–320). New York: John Wiley and Sons.

Sutton-Smith, Brian (1979). The play of girls. In Claire B. Kopp & Martha Kirkpatrick (Eds.) *Becoming female* (pp. 229–257). New York: Plenum.

Turner, Victor W. (1986). Dewey, Dilthey, and drama: An essay in the anthropology of experience. In Victor W. Turner & Edward M. Bruner (Eds.) *The anthropology of experience* (pp. 33–44). Urbana, IL: University of Illinois Press.

Vološinov, Valentin Nikolaevic (1971). Reported speech. In Ladislav Matejka & Krystyna Pomorska (Eds.) *Readings in Russian poetics: Formalist and structuralist views* (pp. 149–175). Cambridge: M.I.T. Press.

6

Gender, Politeness, and Confrontation in Tenejapa

PENELOPE BROWN

This chapter examines some interactional details of a court case that took place in the Mexican community of Tenejapa, a community of peasant Mayan Indians who speak a language called Tzeltal, and compares it with Tzeltal verbal interaction in other contexts. In particular I want to contrast women's speaking style in amicable cooperative 'ordinary' Tzeltal conversation with their speech in angry confrontation in a Tzeltal court case, the *only* context in this society in which face-to-face angry confrontation is authorized for women.

The purpose of this study is to explore how relations between language and gender are context dependent, with respect to both the kind of discourse—in this case cooperative versus confrontational interaction—and the speech event and the particular norms governing talk within it. Yet, despite this context dependency, women's characteristic concerns, and the ways of speaking characteristic of women in this society that derive from those concerns, put their stamp on interactions with radically different interactional goals, so that gender is, in some senses, a "master status" transcending contexts in this society.

Specifically, what I want to claim is that, in many ways, the interactional conduct of a Tzeltal court case, a formal arena for face-to-face confrontation with the aim of settling disputes between people, is the *inverse* of interactional conduct in ordinary conversation in Tenejapan society. That is, ordinary conversational structures and interactional norms are systematically violated in a public display of indignation and anger. Nevertheless, in this context, certain features pervasive in women's speech in ordinary

144

amicable conversation—features used to convey positive affect, empathy, agreement, sympathetic understanding—are here carried over but are used to convey the *opposite:* negative affect, hostility, contradiction.

In short, even when women *aren't* being polite—emphatically the opposite—their characteristically female "ways of putting things" indirectly, using irony and rhetorical questions for positive politeness, carry over but with inverted functions: to emphatically contradict or disagree.

In what follows I first give a brief indication of some current issues in language and gender research to which this study is oriented. Second, I describe conversational structures employed in ordinary Tzeltal conversation, as well as the norms governing Tzeltal interaction in general and women's normal public demeanor in particular. Third, I describe the organization of Tzeltal court cases and show how interaction in the courtroom flouts certain of these norms systematically. Finally, I draw some conclusions about (1) the nature of dispute settlement in Tenejapa, (2) how gender meanings can get transformed in different contexts, and (3) implications for language and gender research in other contexts and societies.

Current Themes in Language and Gender Research

Out of the past fifteen years of cross-linguistic and cross-cultural research into aspects of the relationship between language and gender has gradually emerged the perspective into which I want to place the data discussed in this chapter. This perspective, which has been promoted in my own work (Brown 1979, 1980, Brown & Levinson 1979, 1987) and more recently cogently argued for in, for example, McConnell-Ginet (1988), Philips, Steele, and Tanz (1987), and Ochs (1992), has several basic tenets:

1. Although gender-based differences in language are, for most languages examined to date, fairly minimal in language structure, they are pervasive in language use, especially in clusters of linguistic features that differentiate male and female *communicative styles.*
2. For the most part, gender is not marked directly, but gender indexing is *indirect,* via other connections between gender and habitual uses of language (speech acts, speech events, social activities, interactional goals, and strategies).
3. Gender indexing is *context dependent* in very interesting, patterned ways.

In this view, the study of language and gender is part of the more general study of relations between language and social meaning (Ochs 1992). We have to think in terms of a complex web of social meanings being conveyed when individuals speak, gender being only one, and not necessarily always a relevant one, of these social meanings.

What is needed is a much better understanding of both gender, as a social attribute, and how social meanings like gender are expressed in speech. What kind of a thing is gender? Is it a master status, omnirelevant in all situations? How is it related to social roles, to activities and speech events? To what extent do gender norms constrain people's behavior even in situations in which gender should be irrelevant? How do different social meanings (for example, professional identity versus gender identity) interact? How do these reflect speakers' perceptions of their social relationships?

The study reported here is oriented to these sorts of questions; it aims to illustrate with an example from my own work in southern Mexico what I think is a profitable approach to the problem of trying to understand the ways in which gender influences language use and is reflected in that use. To the extent that gender influences the social meanings that people express when they speak, these can be discovered by conversation-analytic techniques applied to interactions in different social contexts, where language is being used to achieve different purposes.

This paper takes up this banner in one particular domain, comparing gender influences on language usage in casual cooperative conversation with those in angry confrontation. The Tzeltal case exemplifies the approach originally promoted by Garfinkel (1967): If you want to understand social norms, look at how they are breached and how the management of breaches reinstates the norms.[1]

Ethnographic Background

Tenejapa is a peasant Mayan community in the Chiapas highlands of southern Mexico, about twenty miles from the town of San Cristóbal de las Casas. It is a corporate community of Tzeltal-speaking Indians, in a populous rural area where there are many other Indian communities of Tzeltal or Tzotzil speakers, each of which maintains a strong ethnic identity distinguishing it from the others and from the dominant Ladino (Mexican national) culture.

As a corporate community Tenejapa has its own hierarchy of civil-religious officials who run the local political system with a large degree of autonomy, although it is subject to the Mexican laws and policies in some arenas (schooling and health, principally). In law Tenejapa can settle its own disputes, except for very serious ones such as murder, which go to the Mexican court in San Cristóbal.

The community consists of dispersed hamlets, connected by a dense network of foot trails, and a ceremonial center, where local political and religious ceremonies are based and where people holding political or religious offices live during their tenure. Here there are a large church, the locus of the community's religious ceremonies, and a town hall (Cabildo), which is the locus of political activities; it is here that our court case takes place.

Norms of Interaction

My 1972–1973 fieldwork in Tenejapa focused on gender differentiation in this community, in particular male-female styles of interaction (Brown

1979, 1980). In this work it became clear that, on many indices, women can be seen to be "more polite" than men; men are more direct and straightforward in their speech. Thus, compared with men, women are more positively polite to intimates and familiars, expending more interactional effort in reassuring their interlocutors of their interest in, and appreciation of, their conversational contributions. They are also more negatively polite in public, where they are normally self-annihilating kinesically and operate under very stringent interactional constraints including strong inhibitions against public displays of emotion or public confrontation, which do not apply to nearly such an extent for men. Self-control and self-humbling are crucial aspects of a woman's public presentation of self; sanctions against behaving otherwise include ridicule by one's peers and potential physical punishment by fathers, elder brothers, or husbands.

Women's demeanor in public is highly constrained; eye contact tends to be avoided, and deference to or social distance from unfamiliars is indicated by using a very high-pitched register. Among familiars, "positive politeness" imbues most interaction with elaborated expressions of sympathy, approval, and interest. Rhetorical questions and ironies are a conventionalized mode of expression among women. They are used to stress shared understandings and values, emphatic empathy and agreement, as in these two examples taken from natural conversation in relaxed situations.[2]

1   A: . . . mak ma wan sc'ahubotik ta stamel ʔin c'i
           . . . perhaps it's not possibly that we get tired from bending over to pick
           (coffee, that has fallen to the ground) then! (conveys sympathetic
           understanding: of course, it's tiring!)
   B: mak bi yuʔuni ma sc'ahub.
           Perhaps why don't (we) get tired. (conveys: We sure do!)
   A: yak mak.
           Yes, perhaps. (We do!)

2   A: mak ban yaʔwil ʔaʔba
           Perhaps where do we see each other?
           (conveys: Nowhere, we never get a chance to see one another.)
   B: huʔu
           No (agrees with implicature: No, nowhere.)

Women use this form of expression notably more than men do; indeed, it seems to be a highly conventionalized form of feminine positive politeness in this society (see Brown 1979:chap. 4, and Brown, in press, for more details).

Casual Conversational Style

Tzeltal conversation is archetypally two-party, with speaker and respondent roles distinguished. Turn-taking rules apply quite rigidly; overlap is relatively rare and covers relatively short segments of the utterance at speaker-transition points. The floor is passed back and forth at regular short intervals, and interruptions are relatively few. Even during the telling of a story or anecdote (where one interlocutor has all the information and is trying to impart it to the other), the respondent takes up each point with a response indicating interest, understanding, an appropriate emotional reaction, or simply the Tzeltal equivalent of "yeah, I hear you, go on." These, essentially back channel, comments occupy a full turn; they normally do not overlap with the storyteller's running speech as they often do in English conversations. Smiles, nods, or other nonverbal attempts to respond might accompany, but cannot supplant, a verbal response.

These responses often take the form of repeating part of the prior speaker's utterance, elaborated with appropriate prosodic indications of surprise, interest, or agreement. These repetitions structure Tzeltal conversations into neat little sequences of utterance, plus repeat-response, plus optional repeat of the repeat (or part of it), and so on, resulting in interchanges like the following, which illustrates this highly characteristic structure of Tzeltal conversation:

3   (from a conversation between an elderly woman (GM) and her visiting
      granddaughter (GD), who is explaining how it is that she has come vis-
      iting so late in the day)
      GD: ha?te ha? ye z'in ?a ka?yix tal ha?al ho?otike
           But so it was, we-excl. got rained on (on the way here)
      GM: eh! la?wa?yix tal z'in
           Oh! you got (rained on) then
                                    [
      GD: la!
                                    (we) did!
      GM: la ha? in sab i
           That was this morning.
      GD: ha?
           It was.
      GM: ha?
           It was.
      GD: ha?
           It was.
      GM: ha?te hic suhtat nix tal ?a z'in
           But so thus you've just returned (from hot country) then.
      GD: suht nix z'in
           So (we) have just returned.
      GM: suht
           Returned.
      GD: suht
           Returned.

The conversational uses of such repeats as responses to an utterance have been reported for other languages and societies (see, for example, Tannen 1987, 1989, for English; Haverkate 1989:402 for Spanish), but in Tzeltal these are conventionalized as the normal way to respond to an interlocutor's narrating or explaining something. Men in Tenejapa do this too, in casual speech, but their repeat cycles tend in general to be shorter and less affectively positively polite.

Arenas for Conflict

Women in daily interaction tend to suppress conflict. It is veiled, even in private, and, between nonintimate women, openly angry confrontation rarely occurs. Interaction is simply avoided, and gossip, mockery, and backbiting against the object of one's anger are expressed to sympathetic intimates.

Anger between women who are intimates (for example, members of one's own household, family, or neighbors) is normally expressed through controlled "leakage," in which silence, nonresponsiveness, or terse replies (clipped pronunciation and abrupt timing) to proffered utterances can indicate restrained anger. There might also be kinesic distancing, avoidance of smiling, of eye contact, and of physical contact, which contrast with normal relaxed behavior to suggest anger. It is common to declare stiffly, if questioned, that one is not angry, to insist that nothing is wrong, and, if pressed, to launch into a tirade of self-abuse, saying, in effect, "I'm a terrible person, a no-good, a bum." In this context it is overwhelmingly obvious that the person is angry, but there are strong constraints on overtly admitting it to the object of one's anger.[3]

Men, in contrast, can and do express conflict overtly in relatively private contexts; both verbal and physical abuse from husband to wife are routine in some households. In public arenas men are likely to express open conflict only if drunk.

Procedures for dispute settlement operate at various levels. They might be worked out through family mediation or taken up in front of a local hamlet arbitrator, in informal meetings with the two sides both presenting their points of view; the arbitrator (a schoolmaster or church leader, for example) has, however, no authority to impose a settlement.

The forum of last resort for irresolvable conflicts is the Tenejapan court; this is resisted by most, as here private quarrels (and their embarrassing or humiliating details) are exposed to public view. That is what happened in the case we're going to examine here.

A Tenejapan Court Case

Format and Procedures

The format of a typical court case at this community level is a hearing in the Cabildo, presided over by the Tenejapan president or judge, either of whom can act as judge for the case. The "plaintiff" (the person who originated the case with a complaint to the judge) and the "defendant" (the accused party, who has been summoned to the court) appear, and each is given a chance to present his or her case.[4] This is done in a special named speech style, (*col k'op* "explaining speech"), which is a sequential presentation of argument (with features similar to those of narrative in casual conversation) laying out the source and details of the dispute from the speaker's point of view.[5] A number of Tenejapan officials who have an interest in the case, or who have nothing else to do, may be present as audience to the transaction, though they rarely participate. The judge presides, listens, asks questions, and eventually decides what ruling to make. This ruling is discussed, and may be modified, until all participants agree to it. Then it is typed up by the Ladino secretary in an official document (an *acta*), which is signed by all three; copies are retained by each participant and a copy goes into the court record.

This process is set in motion by a complaint, when the plaintiff comes to the president or the judge, or to one of the officials representing the plaintiff's local hamlet, and asks for the defendant to be summoned to court. The officials representing the defendant's hamlet go to his or her house and fetch the defendant to the town, where a hearing takes place in the Cabildo (or at the president's house). People who are afraid or ashamed to appear may get someone to appear for them—a representative who is deemed good at speaking in public. Friends of the court, family supporters, witnesses, and casual bystanders may all be present, may wander in and out, and may contribute to the discussion. Normally the defendant pays the fee exacted by the officials for the summons; in addition, fines or jail or a period of community service (for example, work on church repairs) might be imposed. In cases involving moral breaches, a lecture might be given to the wrongdoer by the judge. The procedure ends with the signing of the *acta* by all three parties.

The majority of issues tried in this forum are domestic quarrels, including adultery, physical violence such as wife-beating and drunken attacks, child support, divorce and property settlement. They can also involve land disputes and inheritance disagreements, debts, property damage or (rarely) theft, interactional hostilities (drunken insults, character assassination), and witchcraft.[6]

The procedure, then, is straightforward: When the opponent is not present in the courtroom (because he or she couldn't be found or is already in jail, for example), the plaintiff "explains" his or her complaint in a long narrative detailing the cause and conduct of the dispute. The judge asks questions, then makes a ruling. The tone of the court cases we observed with no opponent present was generally earnest, calm, and self-righteous. When the opponent is present, however, as is normally the case, blatant interactional confrontation can occur between the two, in which the interaction violates, point by point, the interactional norms of cooperative discourse, resulting in a display of confrontation for rhetorical (and perhaps cathartic) ends.

The Case of the Runaway Daughter-in-Law

In the case we are considering here, a woman, the principal plaintiff, complains that her former daughter-in-law owes her a lot of money. The background of this complaint is as follows: The daughter-in-law married her son after a normal Tenejapan courtship, stayed with him in his parents' household for five months, then ran away and married another Tenejapan man without any divorce proceedings first. This breach of social relations, outrageous by Tenejapan standards, is not the subject of this case, however; in fact it only comes up obliquely in the forty minutes of the proceedings. The complaint is that the daughter-in-law, while living with her first husband's family, received a number of gifts from her husband and his parents. These gifts were things normally (but not obligatorily) given to new brides and included a corn-grinding machine, a skirt, a red belt, a white belt, some meat, and some thread for weaving. The plaintiff has no (official) complaint against this girl for leaving her husband, but she claims that she should be paid for all these items that were given to the bride, in good faith, as a new daughter-in-law.

The defendant pleading here isn't the wife who remarried, but her *mother*. The daughter doesn't appear in court (she was too ashamed, because of her "bad" behavior, it was said). The claims are against her natal family, represented here by her mother.

The case takes place in the Cabildo, around a large central table. The judge is seated at one side; the litigants take up standing positions at the end near the door. The Ladino secretary is typing business letters (unrelated to this case) at the far end of the room. Around the table on benches against the wall are seated about ten Tenejapan officials and litigants from preceding cases, as well as a number of bystanders (plus the two ethnographers, filming and taping the event). The case begins when the judge addresses the plaintiff and asks her to explain her complaint (she has previously entered, greeted the judge, and stood waiting at the end of the table while another case was presented). The plaintiff presents her claims, and the defendant (the runaway wife's mother) vociferously argues against these claims. There is a lot of disagreement, simultaneous speech between the defendant and the plaintiff, and overt expression of hostility, anger, and contempt—quite extraordinary by Tenejapan standards. The interaction alternates between sections in which the judge poses questions and the plaintiff or the defendant replies, in an orderly fashion, and those in which they take off in mutually oriented antagonistic tirades while the judge quietly listens. Eventually the judge succeeds in getting them to agree that the defendant will pay the plaintiff nine hundred pesos for the gifts and that she will bring the money to court the following Sunday. This solution represents a compromise between the amount of money the plaintiff claimed (totaling some twelve hundred pesos) and the amount the defendant concedes is due (somewhat less than nine hundred pesos), as well as in the amount of time she is given to come up with the money. The local official is paid for his summons by the defendant, and the case ends (to be followed immediately by another one) when the two women leave the courtroom.

Interaction in the Courtroom Context

Here I focus on specific contrasts between courtroom behavior and ordinary interaction.

Speech Event Demarcation. There are no clear boundaries to the event. Minimal greetings are given by the plaintiff, none by the defendant, and no farewells at all. And, although the case is started by the judge's saying to the plaintiff, "So I'll listen to your speech now ma'am," it is readily interrupted when he is called to attend to other business, and, although the two parties may carry on their presentation, the judge isn't listening.[7]

Participants. There are three main participants (plaintiff, defendant, and judge), with a large audience of about ten officials and several litigants from other cases, including a number of men from the neighboring Indian community of Chamula. With this "audience" (or, more strictly, "copresent bystanders," not necessarily attending) under other circumstances the behavior of Tenejapan women would be extremely circumspect. Members of the audience frequently engage in background conversation not addressed to the case at hand. Periodically the judge is drawn into this background conversation, especially when required to say ritual greetings or farewells to men who are entering or leaving the courtroom, but the litigants in our case ignore this entirely.[8]

Roles of speaker and addressee are fluid and rapidly switched, and the large degree of overlapping speech means that both the plaintiff and the defendant can be both speaker and addressee simultaneously. The judge's institutional role as adjudicator is operated with restraint; he does not heavy-handedly push the parties toward a resolution but allows them to work toward one themselves with minimal interference. And his role as listener is not rigidly upheld; although some of the time he does conscientiously display his attentiveness with hms, uhuhs, and the like, at several points he turns to other business. The audience takes no part in the argument or discussion of this case.

Although the judge is the monitor of the proceedings, except at the beginning when he invites the plaintiff to begin and asks her some questions, he rarely exercises his right to choose the next speaker. Generally, turn taking operates as a local management system, as in ordinary casual conversation.

Turn-Taking Structure. The most interesting features of the interaction are in the management of turn taking, which has two distinctive characteristics:

1. An overall dyadic structure is imposed on what is, in principle, a three-party interaction.
2. Periodically the normal turn-taking rules are suspended in interaction between the two women, and they speak simultaneously.

First, despite the fact that there are three main participants, the interaction overwhelmingly displays a dyadic structure, with two of the three participants addressing one another (in an A-B-A-B-A-B sequential structure). The third party frequently tries to gain the floor and participate in the dialogue but either fails entirely (is ignored by the two) or succeeds in gaining only one addressee, and the dyadic structure is retained with different members constituting the dyad. Thus, over the entire event, speech alternates among the judge-plaintiff dyad, the plaintiff-defendant dyad, and the judge-defendant dyad.

Speech in ordinary conversation also shows a marked tendency toward dyadic exchanges, but the clearly demarcated roles of speaker and respondent, with the respondent replying with encouraging repetitions of the speaker's utterances, is almost entirely absent in the courtroom.

The most surprising feature of this interaction, compared with speech in other contexts, is the simultaneous speech of the plaintiff and the defendant for extended periods. As a result of persistent attempts to gain the floor by the party not included in the dyad of the moment, there are frequent interruptions and a great deal of overlap, which in extreme instances consists of the plaintiff and the defendant speaking simultaneously *at* one another for as much as half a minute. Sometimes their utterances, though heavily overlapping, are responding to one another's remarks and challenges; at other times they are apparently totally independent tirades.

Thus, the basic dyadic structure of the interaction is continually being challenged by the party left out at any moment, but the successful challenge only succeeds in shifting the constitution of the dyad. Interactional orderliness is also maintained to some degree by the judge exercising his monitoring role; periodically he interjects questions to break up a dyadic interchange and redirect the topic. Frequently, however, his attempts fail, as illustrated in (4), where the judge makes two unsuccessful tries before finally capturing P's attention (at line 324) on his third attempt (→ marks turns where J tries to enter the conversation):

4	Judge's attempts to monitor			
	(D = defendant P = plaintiff J = Judge)			
	(P is in the middle of her explanation to J about the background to her claims against D)			
302	P:	ha? ye z'i (. . .) waxakeb to k'al ?a kuc'tik te pox		
		So it was for 8 days we drank the booze together		
		[ ] [ ]		
303 →	J:	bweno		
		OK,		
304	J:		ha? nax bal ?a z'i bi =	
			That was how it was, eh?	
305	(J)	=yu? me ya?-		
		because if you-		
		[ ]		
306	D:	ehhh cuhkilal=		
	(to P)	Eh, the belt-		

307   (D)   peru bi yu?un ha? nax ya?toy ?a?ba
                  but why is it you just pride yourself
                = [   ]
308   P: ha? (.) waxakeb k'al ?a kuc' ho?tik ?a poxe (.)
   (to D)   It is so. For 8 days we drank the booze that time,
309   (P)   (ba kuzi) k'amal ba ya slekot z'in te=
                  ?   where it was made good then, at
                  [[   ]
      J: ((laughs))
311   D (to P)   ehhh:
312   (P):   = pask'ue
                  Easter
                      [   ]
313 → J: yu? nax z'i ha? nax bal z'i ya stikun te-
                     Just because, so is it just that he sent-
                                   [   ]
314   D (to P)   mac'a lah: (.)
                                   Who, was it said
315   (D)   mac'a xkucoh ?ocel (teklum) (.)
                  who had carried (it) entering town?
316   (D) tatik ya- ?a scelbet ?a?ba mac'a ?a skucoh (. . .)=
           the man, he ?-ed for you, the one who had carried
                      [ ]   [   ]
317   P: hoo
                  Huh.
318   P: mak ha? z'i kerem ku?un
                               Perhaps it was my boy, eh
319   (D): =pepsi c'e =
            the Pepsis, eh?!
                  [ ]
320   J: hoo
                  Huh.
321   P: =ha? bal z'i kerem ku?uni=
   (to D)   Was it my own boy then?
322 → J: =ya   na wan z'i stolik   ?in te   pox c'e
           They perhaps paid for this booze then, eh?!
                  [   ]
323   D (to P);   xk'otok (cikin) bi mak
                     His (ear?) returned perhaps, eh?
324   P (to J);   hai?
                  What?
325   J: ya wan ?a (st- kurik na)
             Perhaps he (?)
                  [   ]
326   P: ma niwan s?os stikun bel ?a huc stukel=
                  Perhaps he didn't send away (for it)
327   (P)   =ya?wa?y z'in pox yan z'in te ha? nax kalat . . . .
            you see then, the booze, or rather it's just as I tell you,
                  [   ]
328   J: hoo
                  Yeah
(P continues her explanation to J)

This refusal to yield the floor is extremely marked behavior by two women to a male official; he, however, treats the interchanges as a normal and expected part of the proceedings, not as an extraordinary breakdown.

The simultaneous speech of the women and their refusal to yield the floor are important vehicles for their expression of antagonism. The mood of dynamic confrontation that permeates this interaction is also carried more explicitly by their aggressive kinesics, direct eye contact, and aggressive gestures that suggest contempt or disgust. Occasionally there are overt insults and abusive words, but prosodic indication of anger and emphasis is rampant throughout.

In short, interactional antagonism is carried to a large extent in breakdowns and manipulations of the turn-taking rules: in interruptions, overlaps, and speech that is simultaneous and nonresponding. In contrast, the plaintiff's and defendant's interchanges with the judge are much more orderly and slow, with fewer overlaps and interruptions. Both the plaintiff and the defendant occasionally use the Tzeltal "respect voice" (very high pitch) to the judge, though never to each other.

Irony and Rhetorical Questions. A final realm for the display of antagonism is in the very noticeable absence of preference for agreement; indeed, in direct contradictions of one another's claims, especially via an exploitation of women's typical positive politeness agreement strategy—rhetorical questions and ironies—which are here done sarcastically, as challenges. Let's look at some of these in detail.

5   Irony and rhetorical questions as confrontation
    (P has been listing her claims; J has just said "wait a minute" and begun to write them down, one by one).

231	J:	te: um=
		the, um
232	P:	=hm
		umhm
233		(1.5)
234	J:	zekel z'i
		(for the) skirt, then
235	P:	hm (.) ox-cehp z'in zekele (1.5) ca'cehp cuhkilal
		Hm, three hundred then for the skirt, two hundred for the belt.
236 →	D:	bi yu?un ma ha?uk z'in mak yu? ma ho?winikuk (sti) =
		Why wasn't it then, perhaps it wasn't one hundred or so
		(ironic: conveys: it *was* only worth 100 pesos)
237	(D)	=mak bit'il ta? ya stoytik yu? mak ha? te sle bi xan ?ae
		how is it that they overstate (the price of the belt) because perhaps it's that she (P) is looking for something more (from me)!
238		(1)
239	(D)	(. . . . . hobe . . . .) =
		[ ]
240	P:	ya stak xa?leben (.)
		You can look for (it- the belt) for me,
241	(P)	ya stak xa?leben shol teme hice
		you can look for a replacement for it if that's the way it is. (i.e., if you think that was a cheap belt, get a better one!)
		[ ]
242 →	D:	=ha? yu? wan ha? z'i baz'il szozil z'i mak ma ha?=
		It's that, perhaps it's that it's real wool then perhaps! (Conveys: It *wasn't* of real wool; i.e., it was cheap!)

243   (D)   =(tay z'in men)
                  (perhaps it's not then)
                        [ ]
244 → P: mancuk ?a z'in mak yu? ma toyoluk k'uxel z'i=
                            So what about that then, perhaps it's not that it was ex-
                            pensive then (conveys: It *was* expensive!)
245 → D: =toyol nanix stukel ?a z'i bi mak
                  Really expensive, (it is) itself then, perhaps, eh? (conveys sarcasm:
                  It was *really* cheap!)

The effectiveness of this ironic phrasing of agreement, sarcastic agreement, to convey disagreement relies on the conventional use of irony to
agree, and the disagreement is thereby made more poignant, more dramatic, taking place as it does against the background of feminine positive
politeness. By the same token, the occasional sarcastic use of normally
respectful address forms underlines the women's hostile intent.

Conclusion

This Tzeltal court case is a paradigm example of verbal interaction in one
social context (a court case) being played out in opposition to the norms
for verbal interaction in another social context (everyday public interaction), in order (partially) to reinforce those first-context norms (appropriate gender behavior) and, as I now argue, where face is threatened, in
order to restore face. For the case under discussion is indeed partly about
money but largely about face, and personal reputation. In the buildup to
this confrontation, appropriate female role behavior and affinal behavior
have been grossly transgressed; both parties have been publicly shamed.
The conduct of the court case is, to a large extent, oriented toward rein-
stating them in the community.

Two distinct things are at issue in this court case:

1. A dispute about financial outlays, requiring a monetary settlement
2. Face, as implicated in female roles, especially in the female in-law
   relationships

In aid of the substantive dispute is the content of the argument in
court, which is overtly about the rights and wrongs of financial outlays:
whether they occurred, whether they legitimately were part of the marriage ceremonies or part of subsequent in-law relationship obligations,
and, therefore, whether they should be reimbursed due to the breakdown
of the in-law relationship. In aid of face-support is the whole style of the
courtroom proceedings: the plaintiff's portrayal of innocent outrage, indicating a generalized message to the effect that "this person has so rent the
social fabric that I'm justified in breaking the norms of propriety governing female behavior" (specifically, nonconfrontation). By successfully displaying her outrage, she (1) reestablishes her face, (2) influences the financial outcome of the case, and (3) gets cathartic release from long-term
pent-up anger. The defendant, by responding with a display of innocent

outrage, casts doubt on the authenticity of the plaintiff's outrage and gains certain concessions in the financial outcome.

In Tenejapa, then, despite the strong constraints against public displays of anger, there is an institutionalized context (and mode) for confrontation: a dramatized outrage played against the backdrop of appropriate norms for female behavior. The very excessiveness of the hostility expressed suggests that, in Tenejapa, litigation involves a form of *drama* in which the litigants are given scope to dramatize their antagonism, to display their anger and outrage in direct face-to-face confrontation, in ways almost unheard of in other contexts. The forum of the courtroom provides a frame for this display that makes it interactionally manageable; such open display of anger outside the courtroom would be, for women, unthinkably dangerous, provoking accusations of witchcraft. The protagonists here are breaking the norms (in a controlled manner), in order to affirm the norms of appropriate female behavior.

I do not mean to suggest that all women in Tenejapan court cases behave in this confrontational manner, nor that men never do, but only that in court such behavior is not only sanctioned but actually necessary to reestablish one's besmirched reputation.

The courtroom solution results in a compromise, negotiated between the two protagonists, that reinstates both in the community with some face left. Gossipers can now have a field day with the details of the dispute; nonetheless, by going through the court procedure the plaintiff reestablishes herself as "not exploited and shamed," and the defendant reestablishes herself as having paid for her daughter's flouting of social norms.

But here we find the paradox at the heart of Tzeltal litigation. If the display and revelation in the courtroom interaction accomplish the working out of anger and the reinstatement of public "face," at the same time they work against one of the most cherished Tenejapan values: self-protection through emphatic insistence on privacy. Privacy is an overwhelming concern in Tenejapan social life; in this small, gossip-ridden community people are extremely sensitive to what others know about them, as well as to what they can learn, and infer, about others from their behavior. Hiding the details of one's personal effects and social relations from prying eyes is a dominant concern in interpersonal conduct.[9] In this context it is astonishing that cases are ever brought to court at all, and indeed, public exposure of one's private affairs in court is much feared. Litigation is a form of mutual punishment, at least potentially, through which the air is cleared. Face is saved by face being thrown to the winds.

That in a small-scale, face-to-face, nonhierarchical peasant society where privacy is a dominant concern disputes are settled in a confrontational display is perhaps not too surprising. And that they are likely not to remain settled is perhaps an obvious consequence of their agonistic display.

What can we conclude from all this about gender and language in Tenejapa? The norms of gender-appropriate behavior are clear: Politeness, restraint, and circumspection are enjoined. Nonetheless, in one kind of social context, litigation, whether at the local level or in the official Tenejapa court, where a woman's reputation is on the line inverted behavior occurs: Women are given license to excel in public demonstrations of anger and outrage. Indeed, such a display seems part of the very process of, and essential to, clearing one's stained reputation, reestablishing one's public face.[10]

This provides clear evidence, for Tenejapan society, that gender is not a unified one-dimensional feature of one's social identity; one's gender has different applicability (and different effects) in different kinds of situations. We do find (in Tenejapan society, at any rate) gender-characteristic patterns of speaking across contexts—even contexts as contrastive as those we've been considering—that indicate that gender-specific "ways of putting things" can operate across contexts, and this is perhaps especially so when one's face qua woman (or man) is implicated in the different contexts.

In a recent paper, Elinor Ochs (1992) puts forward an analysis of how gender is indexed that can help us understand what is happening in Tenejapa. Ochs argues that the relation of language to gender is not a straightforward mapping of linguistic form onto the social meaning of gender but is constituted and mediated at least partly by the relation of language to what she calls *stances:* general interactional poses having to do with how one presents oneself to others, for example, hesitation/aggression, or coarseness/delicacy, or accommodation versus nonaccommodation to the addressee. I think that the ironies and rhetorical questions that proliferate in Tenejapan women's speech are manifesting a characteristic female stance, emphasizing in-group solidarity expressed through ironic agreement and displays of shared values; women's joking and humor in Tenejapa also often take the form of irony. In amicable interactions, women's positively polite ironic phraseology assumes and stresses shared values and norms, cooperation, mutual sympathy and understanding. In the courtroom confrontation this stance is evoked, but from a distance, ironically, in the sarcastic politeness of hostile pseudoagreement.

As Ochs (1992:341–342) puts it,

> the relation between language and gender is mediated and constituted through a web of socially organized pragmatic meanings. Knowledge of how language relates to gender is not a catalogue of correlations between particular linguistic forms and sex of speakers, referents, addressees and the like. Rather, such knowledge entails tacit understanding of 1) how particular linguistic forms can be used to perform particular pragmatic work (such as conveying stance and social action) and 2) norms, preferences and expectations regarding the distribution of this work *vis à vis* particular social identities of speakers, referents, and addressees.

She goes on to argue that we need to understand, then, (1) how particular linguistic forms can be used to perform particular pragmatic work and

(2) what are the norms, expectations, and preferences about the distribution of this work across gender categories. Continuity in women's verbal practices across diverse situations is due to habitual gender differences in things like stance and social action (for example, confirmation checks), which carry over from situation to situation.

The Tenejapan case is a beautiful example of this, for it is the exception that proves the rule: Even when women are *not* being polite, characteristic female strategies of indirectness and politeness are manifested in their speech.

This suggests that, for a deeper understanding of language and gender, we need to take very detailed looks at gender behavior in different situations. One situation casts light on others, especially if one (like confrontation) is defined in opposition to the other (ordinary courteous interaction). By looking at how gender meanings get transformed in contexts of confrontation, we can explore the complex situational variability in what speakers, male or female, are aiming at when they speak. For example, is it cooperation, harmony, the "we" code that is being evoked, or is the interaction one of conflict or self-defense, in the idiom of "I versus you"?

Most significantly, the Tenejapan case suggests how we might try to make sense of the widespread finding in language and gender research that women interact more cooperatively than men do, at least on the surface; that a patina of agreement is put over women's interactions in many contexts and in different societies. With the Tenejapan women, this cooperative ethos spills over into their noncooperative discourse. The result is sarcastic cooperation and sarcastic indirectness: exploiting mutual knowledge and shared agreement strategies to emphasize disagreement. In Tenejapa (as well as in Japan, it has been suggested)[11] this particular stance is a woman's forte, and it makes the criticism/disagreement all the more painful, as the superficial amicability in which it is couched adds an additional barbed element to the contrast.

One would hope that close attention to these situation-specific kinds of speech events will improve our understanding of how and when gender is implicated in interaction and, when it is, just how it affects women's and men's ways of speaking. Only then will we be in a position to address the more general comparative sorts of questions posed by Ochs (1992): What kinds of meanings (social, pragmatic) are women and men likely to index in their speech in different kinds of societies, and how do such gender meanings relate to the positions and the images of men and women in society?

NOTES

In previous incarnations, this chapter was given as a paper at the Australian Anthropological Society meetings in August 1981 and at seminars at the Australian National University; at Sussex University, England, in 1983; at the University of Colorado, Boulder and at the Max Planck Institute for Psycholinguistics in Nijmegen, Holland, in 1988. I am grateful for the many comments that improved my thinking about the issues herein addressed. The fieldwork on which this paper is based was conducted by Stephen Levinson and me in July–August 1980, when four court cases in addition to the one analyzed here were tape-recorded and filmed with Super-8 equipment, in a project funded by the Department of Anthropology, Research School of Pacific Studies, The Australian National University. This chapter originally appeared in *Discourse Processes* 13(1990):1.123–141.

1. This study is pertinent not only as an exploration of language and gender, the emphasis in this chapter, but also as a contribution to the literature on the organization of courtroom speech, as contrasted with speech in other contexts (see, for example, Atkinson & Drew 1979, Lakoff 1989), and to the recently burgeoning interest in how face-to-face confrontation is managed (for example, Goodwin & Goodwin 1987, Haviland 1989, Grimshaw 1990).

2. The Tzeltal data cited here come from films and/or tape recordings of natural interactions in Tenejapa. Transcription conventions: Square brackets [] indicate overlapping speech; = indicates speech tied to that on the next line with no pause; dots in parentheses (. . .) indicate material omitted; a single dot in parentheses (.) indicates a micropause; numbers in parentheses, for example (1.5), indicate approximate pauses in seconds; words in parentheses () indicate sections where transcription is uncertain; an arrow → draws attention to a line of transcript under discussion. The Tzeltal transcription is roughly phonemic: c represents the sound spelled in English *ch*, *x* corresponds to English *sh*, *z* represents English *ts*, ? indicates a glottal stop, and ' indicates that the preceding consonant is glottalized. Speakers' initials are in parentheses when the line following is a continuation of a turn begun on a prior line. Question mark ? in translation indicates translation uncertain.

3. There are, of course, personality differences among individuals. I am describing a general cultural constraint on the mode of expression of anger, which individuals may differentially bow to.

4. I use the labels "plaintiff" and "defendant" in these restricted senses here, although these are very unsatisfactory terms insofar as they carry all the connotations of Western legal practice, which are inapplicable in the Tenejapan case. The summons-initiator, who lodges the original complaint, and the summons-recipient, who is the object of the complaint, might well switch complainer-complainee roles in the course of the proceedings: Plaintiff might become the accused and defendent the accuser, and indeed, the original plaintiff might be the one who is hauled off to jail.

5. Despite this named style, Tzeltal speakers themselves do not categorize speech in the courtroom as different in kind from that taking place in other contexts. Conversation in Tzeltal is a form of ?*ac k'op* "new speech," covering all the secular and modern genres of speech (joking, conversing, word play, speechmaking), as distinct from the special genres of *poko k'op* "ancient speech," which cover the sacred and ritual uses of words and music. The speech in a court case is a kind of ?*ac k'op*, with structural features similar in most respects to those of casual conversation (?*ayanel*); it is not a specialized genre (see Stross 1974), and "explaining speech" in other contexts is also called *col k'op*.

6. Serious crimes under Ladino law, especially murder, are not tried in the Tenejapan court but are sent to a Ladino court in San Cristóbal. Major crimes (murder, by violence or witchcraft, and major theft) often do not come to court at

all. The culprit flees and lies low for a while, possibly for years; then he or she may return and all may be, if not forgotten, ignored.

7. It should be noted that Tenejapan cases differ in this respect from the case reported by Nash (1970) for the nearby Tzeltal community of Amatenango, which was much more formally structured and bounded. See also Collier's (1973) description of Tzotzil courts in Zinacantan.

8. They also completely ignore the camera, two tape recorders, and the two foreign ethnographers in the room. At no point do their eyes meet the camera, and they appear oblivious to it. (This was not the case during our filming of casual interaction.)

9. This is even more true in the neighboring community of Zinacantan (Haviland & Haviland 1983). There women are apparently much more circumspect about entering into court cases at all (Devereaux 1988).

10. This is particularly clear in cases where the charge is an assault on a girl's sexual reputation. In one hearing I observed at the hamlet level, a girl who had been publicly accused by a woman of "wanting to marry the woman's son," produced an hour-long tirade violently protesting her innocence, outrage, and humiliation at the unjust slander. Her reputation as a "good" girl was thereby publicly reinstated, a matter of some importance in a society where the sullying of an unmarried girl's reputation, whether justified or not, can provoke beatings from her father and/or brother.

11. The connection between Japanese women and ironic politeness as rudeness was suggested to me by a Japanese student at one of the seminars in which this material was presented. In Brown (1979) I illustrated Tenejapan women's ironic stance in much more detail and made the suggestion that an ironic stance is perhaps especially the ploy of the downtrodden or underprivileged.

REFERENCES

Atkinson, J. Maxwell & Drew, Paul (1979). *Order in court: The organisation of verbal interaction in judicial settings.* London: Macmillan.

Brown, Penelope (1979). Language, interaction and sex roles in a Mayan community: A study of politeness and the position of women. Ph.D. diss., University of California, Berkeley.

Brown, Penelope (1980). How and why are women more polite: Some evidence from a Mayan community. In Sally McConnell-Ginet, Ruth Borker & Nelly Furman (Eds.) *Women and language in literature and society* (pp. 111–149). New York: Praeger.

Brown, Penelope (in press). Politeness strategies and the attribution of intentions: The case of Tzeltal irony. In Esther Goody (Ed.) *Implications of a social origin for human intelligence.* Cambridge: Cambridge University Press.

Brown, Penelope & Levinson, Stephen C. (1979). Social structure, groups, and interaction. In Klaus Scherer & Howard Giles (Eds.) *Social markers in speech* (pp. 291–341). Cambridge: Cambridge University Press.

Brown, Penelope & Levinson, Stephen C. (1987). *Politeness: Some universals in language usage.* Cambridge: Cambridge University Press.

Collier, Jane F. (1973). *Law and social change in Zinacantan.* Stanford, CA: Stanford University Press.

Devereaux, Leslie (1988). Gender difference in Zinacantan. In Marilyn Strathern (Ed.) *Dealing with inequality: Analysing gender relations in Melanesia and beyond* (pp. 89–111). Cambridge: Cambridge University Press.

Garfinkel, Harold (1967). *Studies in ethnomethodology.* Englewood Cliffs, NJ: Prentice-Hall.

Goodwin, Marjorie Harness & Goodwin, Charles (1987). Children's arguing. In Susan Philips, Susan Steele & Christine Tanz (Eds.) *Language, gender and sex in comparative perspective* (pp. 200–248). Cambridge: Cambridge University Press.

Grimshaw, Allen (Ed.) (1990). *Conflict talk.* Cambridge: Cambridge University Press.

Haverkate, Henk. (1988). Towards a typology of politeness strategy in communicative interaction. *Multilingua* 7(4):385–409.

Haviland, John B. (1989). Sure, sure: Evidence and affect. In Elinor Ochs & Bambi Schieffelin (Eds.) *Discourse and affect,* Special issue of *Text* 9(1):27–68.

Haviland, Leslie K. & Haviland, John B. (1983). Privacy in a Mexican village. In S. I. Benn & G. F. Gauss (Eds.), *Public and private in social life* (pp. 341–361). London: Croom Helm.

Lakoff, Robin (1975). *Language and woman's place.* New York: Harper & Row.

Lakoff, Robin Tolmach (1989). The limits of politeness: Therapeutic and courtroom discourse. In Sachiko Ide (Ed.) *Linguistic politeness II. Multilingua* 8:2–3.

McConnell-Ginet, Sally (1988). Language and gender. In Frederick J. Newmeyer (Ed.) *Cambridge survey of linguistics:* Vol. 4 (pp. 75–99). Cambridge: Cambridge University Press.

Nash, June (1970). Rhetoric of a Maya Indian court. In *Estudios de cultura maya: Vol. VIII.*

Ochs, Elinor (1992). Indexing gender. In Alessandro Duranti & Charles Goodwin (Eds.) *Rethinking context* (pp. 335–358). Cambridge: Cambridge University Press.

Philips, Susan U., Steele, Susan & Tanz, Christine (1987). *Language, gender and sex in comparative perspective.* Cambridge: Cambridge University Press.

Strecker, Ivo (1988). *The social practice of symbolization: An anthropological analysis.* London: Athlone.

Stross, Brian (1974). Speaking of speaking: Tenejapan Tzeltal metalinguistics. In Richard Bauman & Joel Sherzer (Eds.) *Explorations in the ethnography of speaking* (pp. 213–239). Cambridge: Cambridge University Press.

Tannen, Deborah (1987). Repetition in conversation: Toward a poetics of talk. *Language,* 63(3):574–605.

Tannen, Deborah (1989). *Talking voices: Repetition, dialogue, and imagery in conversational discourse.* Cambridge: Cambridge University Press.

III

THE RELATIVITY
OF DISCOURSE
STRATEGIES

7

The Relativity of Linguistic Strategies: Rethinking Power and Solidarity in Gender and Dominance

DEBORAH TANNEN

Introduction

In analyzing discourse, many researchers operate on the unstated assumption that all speakers proceed along similar lines of interpretation, so a particular example of discourse can be taken to represent how discourse works for all speakers. For some aspects of discourse, this is undoubtedly true. Yet a large body of sociolinguistic literature makes clear that, for many aspects of discourse, this is so only to the extent that cultural background is shared. To the extent that cultural backgrounds differ, lines of interpretation and habitual use of many linguistic strategies are likely to diverge. One thinks immediately and minimally of the work of Gumperz (1982), Erickson and Shultz (1982), Scollon and Scollon (1981), and Philips (1983). My own research shows that cultural difference is not limited to the gross and apparent levels of country of origin and native language, but also exists at the subcultural levels of ethnic heritage, class, geographic region, age, and gender. My earlier work (Tannen 1984, 1986) focuses on ethnic and regional style; my most recent work (Tannen 1990b) focuses on gender-related stylistic variation. I draw on this work here to demonstrate that specific linguistic strategies have widely divergent potential meanings.[1]

This insight is particularly significant for research on language and gender, much of which has sought to describe the linguistic means by which men dominate women in interaction. That men dominate women as a class, and that individual men often dominate individual women in interaction, are not in question; what I am problematizing is the source

165

and workings of domination and other intentions and effects. I will show that one cannot locate the source of domination, or of any interpersonal intention or effect, in linguistic strategies such as interruption, volubility, silence, and topic raising, as has been claimed. Similarly, one cannot locate the source of women's powerlessness in such linguistic strategies as indirectness, taciturnity, silence, and tag questions, as has also been claimed. The reason one cannot do this is that the same linguistic means can be used for different, even opposite, purposes and can have different, even opposite, effects in different contexts. Thus, a strategy that seems, or is, intended to dominate may in another context or in the mouth of another speaker be intended or used to establish connection. Similarly, a strategy that seems, or is, intended to create connection can in another context or in the mouth of another speaker be intended or used to establish dominance.

Put another way, the "true" intention or motive of any utterance cannot be determined from examination of linguistic form alone. For one thing, intentions and effects are not identical. For another, as the sociolinguistic literature has dramatized repeatedly (see especially McDermott & Tylbor 1983, Schegloff 1982, 1988, Erickson 1986, Duranti & Brenneis 1986), human interaction is a "joint production": everything that occurs results from the interaction of all participants. A major source of the ambiguity and polysemy of linguistic strategies is the paradoxical relationship between the dynamics of power and solidarity. This is the source that I will explore here.

Overview of the Chapter

In this chapter I first briefly explain the theoretical paradigm of power and solidarity. Then I show that linguistic strategies are potentially ambiguous (they could "mean" either power or solidarity) and polysemous (they could "mean" both). Third, I reexamine and expand the power and solidarity framework in light of cross-cultural research. Finally, I demonstrate the relativity of five linguistic strategies: indirectness, interruption, silence versus volubility, topic raising, and adversativeness (that is, verbal conflict).

Theoretical Background

Power and Solidarity

Since Brown and Gilman's (1960) introduction of the concept and subsequent elaborations of it, especially those of Friedrich (1972) and Brown and Levinson ([1978]1987), the dynamics of power and solidarity have been fundamental to sociolinguistic theory. (Fasold [1990] provides an overview.) Brown and Gilman based their framework on analysis of the use of pronouns in European languages which have two forms of the second-person pronoun, such as the French *tu* and *vous*. In English the closest parallel is to be found in forms of address: first name versus title-last name. In Brown and Gilman's system, power is associated with nonreciprocal use of pronouns; in English, the parallel would be a situation in which one speaker addresses the other by first name but is addressed by title-last name (for example, doctor and patient, teacher and student, boss and secretary, building resident and elevator operator). Solidarity is associated with reciprocal pronoun use or symmetrical forms of address: both speakers address each other by *tu* or by *vous* (in English, by title-last name or by first name). Power governs asymmetrical relationships where one is subordinate to another; solidarity governs symmetrical relationships characterized by social equality and similarity.

In my previous work exploring the relationship between power and solidarity as it emerges in conversational discourse (Tannen 1984, 1986), I note that power and solidarity are in paradoxical relation to each other. That is, although power and solidarity, closeness and distance, seem at first to be opposites, each also entails the other. Any show of solidarity necessarily entails power, in that the requirement of similarity and closeness limits freedom and independence. At the same time, any show of power entails solidarity by involving participants in relation to each other. This creates a closeness that can be contrasted with the distance of individuals who have no relation to each other at all.

In Brown and Gilman's paradigm, the key to power is asymmetry, but it is often thought to be formality. This is seen in the following anecdote. I once entitled a lecture "The Paradox of Power and Solidarity." The respondent to my talk appeared wearing a three-piece suit and a knapsack on his back. The audience was amused by the association of the suit with power, the knapsack with solidarity. There was something immediately recognizable in this semiotic. Indeed, a professor wearing a knapsack might well mark solidarity with students at, for example, a protest demonstration. And wearing a three-piece suit to the demonstration might mark power by differentiating the wearer from the demonstrators, perhaps even reminding them of his dominant position in the institutional hierarchy. But wearing a three-piece suit to the board meeting of a corporation would mark solidarity with other board members, whereas wearing a knapsack in that setting would connote not solidarity but disrespect, a move in the power dynamic.

The Ambiguity of Linguistic Strategies

As the preceding example shows, the same symbol—a three-piece suit—can signal either power or solidarity, depending on, at least, the setting (e.g., board meeting or student demonstration), the habitual dress style of the individual, and the comparison of his clothing with that worn by others in the interaction. (I say "his" intentionally; the range of meanings would be quite different if a man's three-piece suit were worn by a woman.) This provides an analogue to the ambiguity of linguistic strategies, which are signals in the semiotic system of language. As I have demonstrated at length in previous books, all linguistic strategies are potentially ambiguous. The power-solidarity dynamic is one fundamental source of ambiguity. What appear as attempts to dominate a conversation (an exercise of power) may actually be intended to establish rapport (an exercise of solidarity). This occurs because (as I have worded it elsewhere) power and solidarity are bought with the same currency: The same linguistic means can be used to create either or both.

This ambiguity can be seen in the following fleeting conversation. Two women were walking together from one building to another in order to attend a meeting. They were joined by a man they both knew who had just exited a third building on his way to the same meeting. One of the women greeted the man and remarked, "Where's your coat?" The man responded, "Thanks, Mom." His response framed the woman's remark as a gambit in a power exchange: a mother tells a child to put on his coat. Yet the woman might have intended the remark as showing friendly concern rather than parental caretaking. Was it power (condescending, on the model of parent to child) or solidarity (friendly, on the model of intimate peers)? Though the man's uptake is clear, the woman's intention in making the remark is not.

Another example comes from a letter written to me by a reader of *You Just Don't Understand: Women and Men in Conversation.* A woman was at home when her partner arrived and announced that his archrival had invited him to contribute a chapter to a book. The woman remarked cheerfully how nice it was that the rival was initiating a rapprochement and an end to their rivalry by including her partner in his book. He told her she had got it wrong: because the rival would be the editor and he merely a contributor, the rival was actually trying to solidify his dominance. She interpreted the invitation in terms of solidarity. He interpreted it as an expression of power. Which was right? I don't know. The invitation was ambiguous; it could have "meant" either.

The Polysemy of Power and Solidarity

The preceding examples could be interpreted as not only ambiguous but polysemous. The question "Where's your coat?" shows concern *and* suggests a parent-child constellation. The invitation to contribute a chapter to a book brings editor and contributor closer *and* suggests a hierarchical relationship.

One more example will illustrate the polysemy of strategies signaling power and solidarity. If you have a friend who repeatedly picks up the check when you dine together, is she being generous and sharing her wealth, or is she trying to flaunt her money and remind you that she has more of it than you? Although the intention may be to make you feel good by her generosity, her repeated generosity may nonetheless make you feel bad by reminding you that she has more money. Thus both of you are caught in the web of the ambiguity of power and solidarity: it is impossible to determine which was her real motive, and whether it justifies your response. On the other hand, even if you believe her motive was purely generous, your response is nonetheless justified because the fact that she has this generous impulse is evidence that she has more money than you, and her expressing the impulse reminds you of it. In other words, both interpretations exist at once: solidarity—she is paying to be nice—and power—her being nice in this way reminds you that she is richer. In this sense, the strategy is not just ambiguous with regard to power and solidarity but polysemous. This polysemy explains another observation that initially surprised me: Paules (1991) reports that waitresses in a restaurant she observed over time are offended not only by tips that are too small, but also by tips that are too large. The customers' inordinate beneficence implies that the amount of money left is insignificant to the tipper but significant to the waitress.

Brown and Gilman are explicit in their assumption that power is associated with asymmetrical relationships in which the power is held by the person in the one-up position. This is stated in their definition: "One person may be said to have power over another to the degree that he is able to control the behavior of the other. Power is a relationship between at least two persons, and it is nonreciprocal in the sense that both cannot have power in the same area of behavior" (p. 254). I have called attention, however, to the extent to which solidarity in itself can be a form of control. For example, a young woman complained about friends who "don't let you be different." If the friend says she has a particular problem and the woman says, "I don't have that problem," her friend is hurt and accuses her of putting her down, of acting superior. The assumption of similarity requires the friend to have a matching problem (Tannen 1990b).

Furthermore, although Brown and Gilman acknowledge that "power superiors may be solidary (parents, elder siblings)" and "power inferiors, similarly, may be as solidary as the old family retainer" (p. 254), most Americans are inclined to assume that solidarity implies closeness, whereas power implies distance.[2] Thus Americans regard the sibling relationship as the ultimate in solidarity: "sister" or "brother" can be used metaphorically to indicate closeness and equality.[3] In contrast, it is often assumed that hierarchy precludes closeness: employers and employees cannot "really" be friends. But being linked in a hierarchy necessarily brings individuals closer. This is an assumption underlying Watanabe's (1993) observation, in comparing American and Japanese group discussions, that whereas the Americans in her study saw themselves as individuals participating in a joint activity, the Japanese saw themselves as members of a group united by hierarchy. When reading Watanabe, I was caught up short by the term "united." My inclination had been to assume that hierarchy is distancing, not uniting.

The anthropological literature includes numerous discussions of cultural contexts in which hierarchical relationships are seen as close and mutually, not unilaterally, empowering. For example, Beeman (1986) describes an Iranian interactional pattern he dubs "getting the lower hand." Taking the lower-status position enables an Iranian to invoke a protector schema by which the higher-status person is obligated to do things for him or her. Similarly, Yamada (1992) describes the Japanese relationship of *amae*, typified by the parent-child or employer-employee constellation. It binds two individuals in a hierarchical interdependence by which both have power in the form of obligations as well as rights vis-à-vis the other. Finally, Wolfowitz (1991) explains that respect/deference is experienced by Suriname Javanese not as subservience but as an assertion of claims. The Suriname Javanese example is particularly intriguing because it calls into question the association of asymmetry with power and distance. The style Wolfowitz calls respect-politeness is characterized by both social closeness and negative politeness.[4] It is hierarchical insofar as it is directional and unequal; however, the criterion for directionality is not status but age. The prototypical relationship characterized by respect politeness is grandchild-grandparent: a relationship that is both highly unequal and very close. Moreover, according to Wolfowitz, the Javanese assume that familial relations are inherently hierarchical, including age-graded siblings. Equality, in contrast, is associated with formal relationships that are also marked by social distance.

We can display these dynamics as a multidimensional grid of at least (and, potentially and probably, more) intersecting continuua. The closeness/distance dimension can be placed on one axis and the hierarchy/equality one on another. (See Figure 7.1.) Indeed, the intersection of these dimensions—that is, the co-incidence of hierarchy and closeness—may account, at least in part, for what I am calling the ambiguity and polysemy of power and solidarity.

Similarity/Difference

There is one more aspect of the dynamics of power and solidarity that bears discussion before I demonstrate the relativity of linguistic strategies. That is the similarity/difference continuum and its relation to the other dynamics discussed.

For Brown and Gilman solidarity implies sameness, in contrast to power, about which they observe, "In general terms, the *V* form is linked with differences between persons" (p. 256). This is explicit in their definition of "the solidarity semantic":

> Now we are concerned with a new set of relations which are symmetrical; for example, *attended the same school* or *have the same parents* or *practice the same profession*. If A has the same parents as B, B has the same parents as A. Solidarity is the name we give to the general relationship and solidarity is symmetrical. (257; italics in original)

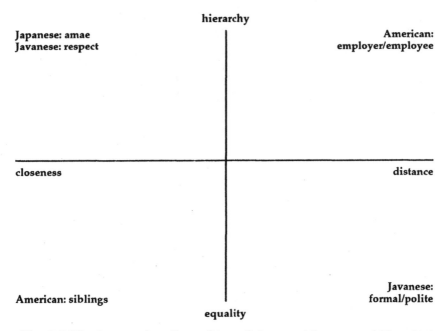

Fig. 7.1 The intersecting dimensions of closeness/distance and hierachy/equality.

The similarity/difference continuum calls to mind what I have discussed elsewhere (Tannen 1984, 1986) as the double bind of communication.[5] In some ways, we are all the same. But in other ways we are all different. Communication is a double bind in the sense that anything we say to honor our similarity violates our difference, and anything we say to honor our difference violates our sameness. Thus a complaint can be lodged: "Don't think I'm different." ("If you prick me, do I not bleed?" one might protest, like Shylock.) But a complaint can also be lodged: "Don't think I'm the same." (Thus, for example, women who have primary responsibility for the care of small children will be effectively excluded from activities or events at which day care is not provided.) Becker (1982:125) expresses this double bind as "a matter of continual self-correction between exuberance (i.e., friendliness: you are like me) and deficiency (i.e., respect: you are not me)." All these formulations elaborate on the tension between similarity and difference, or what Becker and Oka (1974) call "the cline of person," a semantic dimension they suggest may be the one most basic to language: that is, one deals with the world and the objects and people in it in terms of how close (and I would add, similar) they are to oneself.

As a result of these dynamics, similarity is a threat to hierarchy. This is dramatized in Harold Pinter's play *Mountain Language*. Composed of four brief scenes, the play is set in a political prison in the capital city of an unnamed country that is under dictatorial siege. In the second scene, an old mountain woman is finally allowed to visit her son across a table as a guard stands over them. But whenever she tries to speak to her son, the guard silences her, telling the prisoner to tell his mother that it is forbidden to speak their mountain language in the capital. Then he continues:

GUARD

. . . And I'll tell you another thing. I've got a wife and three kids. And you're all a pile of shit.

Silence.

PRISONER

I've got a wife and three kids.

GUARD

You've what?

Silence.

You've got what?

Silence.

What did you say to me? You've got what?

Silence.

You've got *what?*

He picks up the telephone and dials one digit.

Sergeant? I'm in the Blue Room ... yes ... I thought I should report, Sergeant ... I think I've got a joker in here.

The Sergeant soon enters and asks, "What joker?" The stage darkens and the scene ends. The final scene opens on the same setting, with the prisoner bloody and shaking, his mother shocked into speechlessness. The prisoner was beaten for saying, "I've got a wife and three kids." This quotidian statement, which would be unremarkable in casual conversation, was insubordinate in the hierarchical context of brutal oppression because the guard had just made the same statement. When the guard said, "I've got a wife and three kids. And you're a pile of shit," he was claiming, "I am different from you." One could further interpret his words to imply, "I'm human, and you're not. Therefore I have a right to dominate and abuse you." By repeating the guard's words verbatim, the prisoner was then saying, "I am the same as you."[6] By claiming *his* humanity and implicitly denying the guard's assertion that he is "a pile of shit," the prisoner challenged the guard's right to dominate him.[7] Similarity is antithetical to hierarchy.

The ambiguity of closeness, a spatial metaphor representing similarity or involvement, emerges in a nonverbal aspect of this scene. In the performance I saw, the guard repeated the question "You've got what?" while moving steadily closer to the prisoner, until he was bending over him, nose to nose. The guard's moving closer was a kinesic/proxemic analogue to the prisoner's statement, but with opposite effect: he was "closing in." The guard moved closer and brought his face into contact with the prisoner's not as a sign of affection (which such actions could signify in another context) but as a threat. Closeness, then, can mean aggression rather than affiliation in the context of a hierarchical rather than symmetrical relationship.

The Relativity of Linguistic Strategies

The potential ambiguity of linguistic strategies to mark both power and solidarity in face-to-face interaction has made mischief in language and gender research, wherein it is tempting to assume that whatever women do results from, or creates, their powerlessness and whatever men do results from, or creates, their dominance. But all the linguistic strategies that have been taken by analysts as evidence of dominance can in some circumstances be instruments of affiliation. For the remainder of this chapter I demonstrate the relativity of linguistic strategies by considering each of the following strategies in turn: indirectness, interruption, silence versus volubility, topic raising, and adversativeness, or verbal conflict. All of these strategies have been "found" by researchers to express or create dominance. I will demonstrate that they are ambiguous or polysemous with regard to dominance or closeness. Once again I am not arguing that these strategies *cannot* be used to create dominance or powerlessness, much less that dominance and powerlessness do not exist. Rather, my purpose is to demonstrate that the "meaning" of any linguistic strategy can vary, depending at least on context, the conversational styles of participants, and the interaction of participants' styles and strategies. Therefore we will have to study the operation of specific linguistic strategies more closely to understand how dominance and powerlessness are expressed and created in interaction.

Indirectness

Lakoff (1975) identifies two benefits of indirectness: defensiveness and rapport. Defensiveness refers to a speaker's preference not to go on record with an idea in order to be able to disclaim, rescind, or modify it if it does not meet with a positive response. The rapport benefit of indirectness results from the pleasant experience of getting one's way not because one demanded it (power) but because the other person wanted the same thing (solidarity). Many researchers have focused on the defensive or power benefit of indirectness and ignored the payoff in rapport or solidarity.

The claim by Conley, O'Barr, and Lind (1979) that women's language is really powerless language has been particularly influential. In this view women's tendency to be indirect is taken as evidence that women don't feel entitled to make demands. Surely there are cases in which this is true. Yet it can easily be demonstrated that those who feel entitled to make demands may prefer not to, seeking the payoff in rapport. Furthermore, the ability to get one's demands met without expressing them directly can be a sign of power rather than of the lack of it. An example I have used elsewhere (Tannen 1986) is the Greek father who answers, "If you want, you can go," to his daughter's inquiry about going to a party. Because of the lack of enthusiasm of his response, the Greek daughter understands that her father would prefer she not go and "chooses" not to go. (A "real" approval would have been "Yes, of course, you should go.") I argue that this father did not feel powerless to give his daughter orders. Rather, a communicative system was conventionalized by which he and she could both preserve the appearance, and possibly the belief, that she chose not to go rather than simply obeying his command.

Far from being powerless, this father felt so powerful that he did not need to give his daughter orders; he simply needed to let her know his preference, and she would accommodate to it. By this reasoning, indirectness is a prerogative of the powerful. By the same reasoning, a master who says, "It's cold in here," may expect a servant to make a move to close a window, but a servant who says the same thing is not likely to see his employer rise to correct the situation and make him more comfortable. Indeed, a Frenchman who was raised in Brittany tells me that his family never gave bald commands to their servants but always communicated orders in indirect and superpolite form. This pattern renders less surprising the finding of Bellinger and Gleason (1982, reported in Gleason 1987) that fathers' speech to their young children had a higher incidence than mothers' of both direct imperatives (such as "Turn the bolt with the wrench") *and* implied indirect imperatives (for example, "The wheel is going to fall off").

The use of indirectness can hardly be understood without the cross-cultural perspective. Many Americans find it self-evident that directness is logical and aligned with power whereas indirectness is akin to dishonesty as well as subservience. But for speakers raised in most of the world's cultures, varieties of indirectness are the norm in communication. In Japanese interaction, for example, it is well known that saying "no" is considered too face-threatening to risk, so negative responses are phrased as positive ones: one never says "no," but initiates understand from the form of the "yes" whether it is truly a "yes" or a polite "no." And this applies to men as well as women.

The American association of indirectness with female style is not culturally universal. Keenan (1974) found that in a Malagasy-speaking village on the island of Madagascar, women are direct and men indirect. But this in no way implies that the women are more powerful than men in this society. Quite the contrary, Malagasy men are socially dominant—and their indirect style is more highly valued. Keenan found that women were widely believed to debase the language with their artless directness, whereas men's elaborate indirectness was widely admired. In my own research (Tannen 1981) I compared Greeks and Americans with regard to their tendency to interpret a question as an indirect means of making a request. I found that whereas American women were more likely to take an indirect interpretation of a sample conversation, Greek men were as likely as Greek women, and more likely than American men *or women,* to take an indirect interpretation. Greek men, of course, are not less powerful vis-à-vis women than American men.

Indirectness, then, is not in itself a strategy of subordination. Rather, it can be used by either the powerful or the powerless. The interpretation of a given utterance and the likely response to it depend on the setting, on individuals' status and their relationship to each other, and also on the linguistic conventions that are ritualized in the cultural context.

Interruption

That interruption is a sign of dominance has been as widespread an assumption in research as in conventional wisdom. Most frequently cited is West and Zimmerman's (1983) finding that men dominate women by interrupting them in conversation. Tellingly, however, Deborah James and Sandra Clarke (this volume), reviewing research on gender and interruption, do not find a clear pattern of males interrupting females. Especially significant is their discovery that studies comparing amount of interruption in all-female versus all-male conversations find more interruption, not less, in all-female groups. Though initially surprising, this finding reinforces the need to distinguish linguistic strategies by their interactional purpose. Does the overlap show support for the speaker, or does it contradict or change the topic? I explore this phenomenon in detail elsewhere (Tannen 1989b) but I will include a brief summary of the argument here.

The phenomenon commonly referred to as "interruption," but more properly referred to as "overlap," is a paradigm case of the ambiguity of power and solidarity. This is clearly demonstrated with reference to a two and a half hour dinner table conversation that I have analyzed at length (Tannen 1984). My analysis makes clear that some speakers consider talking along with another a show of enthusiastic participation in the conversation (solidarity, creating connections); others, however, assume that only one voice should be heard at a time, so for them any overlap is an interruption (an attempt to wrest the floor, a power play). The result, in the conversation I analyzed, was that enthusiastic listeners who overlapped cooperatively, talking along to establish rapport, were perceived by overlap-resistant speakers as interrupting. This doubtless contributed to the impression reported by the overlap-resistant speakers that the cooperative overlappers had "dominated" the conversation. Indeed, the tape and transcript also give the impression that the cooperative overlappers had dominated, because the overlap-aversant participants tended to stop speaking as soon as another voice began.

It is worth emphasizing the role of balance in determining whether an overlap becomes an interruption in the negative or power-laden sense. If one speaker repeatedly overlaps and another repeatedly gives way, the resulting communication is asymmetrical, and the effect (though not necessarily the intent) is domination. But if both speakers avoid overlap, or if both speakers overlap each other and win out equally, there is symmetry and no domination, regardless of speakers' intentions. Importantly, though, and this will be discussed in the last section under the rubric of adversativeness, the very engagement in a symmetrical struggle for the floor can be experienced as creating rapport, in the spirit of ritual opposition analogous to sports. Further, an imbalance can result from differences in the purpose for which overlap is used. If one speaker tends to talk along in order to show support, and the other chimes in to take the floor, the floor-taking overlapper will tend to dominate.

Thus, to understand whether an overlap is an interruption, one must consider the context (for example, cooperative overlapping is more likely to occur in casual conversation among friends than in a job interview), the speakers' habitual styles (for example, overlaps are more likely not to be interruptions among those with a style I call "high-involvement"), and the interaction of their styles (for example, an interruption is more likely to occur between speakers whose styles differ with regard to pausing and overlap). This is not to say that one cannot use interruption to dominate a conversation or a person, only that it is not self-evident from the observation of overlap that an interruption has occurred, or was intended, or was intended to dominate.

Silence Versus Volubility

The excerpt from Pinter's *Mountain Language* dramatizes the assumption that powerful people do the talking and powerless people are silenced. This is the trope that underlies the play's title and its central theme: By outlawing their language, the oppressors silence the mountain people, robbing them of their ability to speak and hence of their humanity. In the same spirit, many scholars (for example, Spender 1980) have claimed that men dominate women by silencing them. There are obviously circumstances in which this is accurate. Coates (1986) notes numerous proverbs that instruct women, like children, to be silent.

Silence alone, however, is not a self-evident sign of powerlessness, nor volubility a self-evident sign of domination. A theme running through Komarovsky's (1962) classic study, *Blue Collar Marriage*, is that many of the wives interviewed said they talked more than their husbands: "He's tongue-tied," one woman said (p. 13); "My husband has a great habit of not talking," said another (p. 162); "He doesn't say much but he means what he says and the children mind him," said a third (p. 353). Yet there is no question that these husbands are dominant in their marriages, as the last of these quotes indicates.

Indeed, taciturnity itself can be an instrument of power. This is precisely the claim of Sattel (1983), who argues that men use silence to exercise power over women. Sattel illustrates with a scene from Erica Jong's novel *Fear of Flying,* only a brief part of which is presented here. The first line of dialogue is spoken by Isadora, the second by her husband, Bennett. (Spaced dots indicate omitted text; unspaced dots are a form of punctuation included in the original text.)

"Why do you turn on me? What did I do?"

Silence.

"What did I do?"

He looks at her as if her not knowing were another injury.

"Look, let's just go to sleep now. Let's just forget it."

"Forget what?"

He says nothing.

. . .

"It was something in the movie, wasn't it?"

"What, in the movie?"

". . . It was the funeral scene. ... The little boy looking at his dead mother. Something got you there. That was when you got depressed."

Silence.

"Well, *wasn't* it?"

Silence.

"Oh come on, Bennett, you're making me *furious*. Please tell me. Please."

The painful scene continues in this vein until Bennett tries to leave the room and Isadora tries to detain him. The excerpt certainly seems to support Sattel's claim that Bennett's silence subjugates his wife, as the scene ends with her literally lowered to the floor, clinging to his pajama leg. But the reason his silence is an effective weapon is her insistence that he tell her what's wrong. If *she* receded into silence, leaving the room or refusing to talk to him, his silence would be disarmed. The devastation results not from his silence alone but from the combination of his silence and her insistence on talking, in other words, the interaction of their differing styles.[8]

Researchers have counted numbers of words spoken or timed length of talk in order to demonstrate that men talk more than women and thereby dominate interactions. (See James and Drakich [this volume] for a summary of research on amount of talk.) Undoubtedly there is truth to this observation in some settings. But the association of volubility with dominance does not hold for all settings and all cultures. Imagine, for example, an interrogation, in which the interrogator does little of the talking but holds all the power.

The relativity of the "meaning" of taciturnity and volubility is high-lighted in Margaret Mead's (1977) discussion of "end linkage," a concept developed jointly by Mead, Gregory Bateson, and Geoffrey Gorer. Their claim is that universal and biologically constructed relationships, such as parent-child, are linked to different behaviors in different cultures. One of their paradigm examples is the apportionment of spectatorship and exhibitionism. In middle class American culture, children, who are obviously the weaker party in the constellation, are expected to exhibit while their more powerful parents are spectators; in contrast, in middle- and upper-class British culture, exhibition is associated with the parental role and spectatorship with children, who are expected to be seen and not heard.

Furthermore, volubility and taciturnity, too, can result from style differences rather than speakers' intentions. As I (Tannen 1984, 1985) and others (Scollon & Scollon 1981, Scollon 1985) have discussed at length, there are cultural and subcultural differences in the length of pauses expected between and within speaking turns. In my study of the dinner table conversation, those who expected shorter pauses between conversational turns began to feel an uncomfortable silence ensuing while their longer-pausing friends were simply waiting for what they regarded as the "normal" end-of-turn pause. The result was that the shorter pausers ended up doing most of the talking, another sign interpreted by their interlocutors as dominating the conversation. But their intentions had been to fill in what to them were potentially uncomfortable silences, that is, to grease the conversational wheels and ensure the success of the conversation. In their view, the taciturn participants were uncooperative, failing to do their part to maintain the conversation.

Thus silence and volubility, too, cannot be taken to "mean" power or powerlessness, domination or subjugation. Rather, both may imply either power or solidarity, depending on the criteria discussed.

Topic Raising

Shuy (1982) is typical in assuming that the speaker who raises the most topics is dominating a conversation. However, in a study I conducted (Tannen 1990a) of videotaped conversations among friends of varying ages recorded by Dorval (1990), it emerged that the speaker who raised the most topics was not always dominant, as judged by other criteria (for example, who took the lead in addressing the investigator when he entered the room). In a twenty-minute conversation between a pair of sixth-grade girls who identified themselves as best friends, Shannon raised the topic of Julia's relationship with Mary by saying, "Too bad you and Mary are not good friends anymore." The conversation proceeded and continued to focus almost exclusively on Julia's troubled relationship with Mary.

Similarly, most of the conversation between two tenth-grade girls was about Nancy, but Sally raised the topic of Nancy's problems. In response to Nancy's question "Well, what do you want to talk about?" Sally said, "Your mama. Did you talk to your mama?" The ensuing conversation focuses on happenings involving Nancy's mother and boyfriend. Overall, Sally raised nine topics, Nancy seven. However, all but one of the topics Sally raised were questions focused on Nancy. If raising more topics is a sign of dominance, Sally controlled the conversation when she raised topics, although even this was subject to Nancy's collaboration by picking them up. It may or may not be the case that Sally controlled the conversation, but the nature of her dominance is surely other than what is normally assumed by that term if the topics she raised were all about Nancy.

Finally, the effect of raising topics may also be an effect of differences in pacing and pausing, as discussed with regard to my study of dinner-table conversation. A speaker who thinks the other has no more to say on a given topic may try to contribute to the conversation by raising another topic. But a speaker who was intending to say more and was simply waiting for the appropriate turn-exchange pause will feel that the floor was taken away and the topic aggressively switched. Yet again, the impression of dominance might simply result from style differences.

Adversativeness: Conflict and Verbal Aggression

Research on gender and language has consistently found male speakers to be competitive and more likely to engage in conflict (for example, by arguing, issuing commands, and taking opposing stands) and females to be cooperative and more likely to avoid conflict (for example, by agreeing, supporting, and making suggestions rather than commands). (Maltz & Borker [1982] summarize some of this research.) Ong (1981:51) argues that "adversativeness" is universal, but "conspicuous or expressed adversativeness is a larger element in the lives of males than of females."

In my analysis of videotapes of male and female friends talking to each other (Tannen 1990a), I have begun to investigate how male adversativeness and female cooperation are played out, complicated, and contradicted in conversational discourse. In analyzing videotapes of friends talking, for example, I found a sixth-grade boy saying to his best friend,

> Seems like, if there's a fight, me and you are automatically in it. And everyone else wants to go against you and everything. It's hard to agree without someone saying something to you.

In contrast, girls of the same age (and also of most other ages whose talk I examined) spent a great deal of time discussing the dangers of anger and contention. In affirming their own friendship, one girl told her friend,

> Me and you <u>never</u> get in fights hardly,

and

> I mean like if I try to talk to you, you'll say, "Talk to me!" And if you try to talk to me, I'll talk to you.

These examples of gendered styles of interaction are illuminated by the insight that power and solidarity are mutually evocative. As seen in the statement of the sixth-grade boy, opposing other boys in teams entails affiliation within the team. The most dramatic instance of male affiliation resulting from conflict with others is bonding among soldiers, a phenomenon explored by Norman (1990).

By the same token, girls' efforts to support their friends necessarily entail exclusion of or opposition to other girls. This emerges in Hughes's (1988) study of girls playing a street game called foursquare, in which four players occupy one square each and bounce a ball into each other's squares. The object of the game is to eliminate players by hitting the ball into their square in such a way that they fail to hit it back. But this effort to "get people out" is at odds with the social injunction under which the girls operate, to be "nice" and not "mean." The girls resolved the conflict, and formed "incipient teams" composed of friends, by claiming that their motivation in eliminating some players was to enable others (their friends) to enter the game, since eliminated players are replaced by awaiting players. In the girls' terms "getting someone out" was "nice-mean," because it was reframed as "getting someone [a friend] in." This dynamic is also supported by my analysis of the sixth-grade girls' conversation: Most of their talk was devoted to allying themselves with each other in opposition to another girl who was not present. So their cooperation (solidarity) also entails opposition (power).

For boys power entails solidarity not only by opposition to another team, but by opposition to each other. In the videotapes of friends talking, I found that all the conversations between young boys (and none between young girls) had numerous examples of teasing and mock attack.[9] In examining preschool conversations transcribed and analyzed by Corsaro and Rizzo (1990:34), I was amazed to discover that a fight could initiate rather than preclude friendship. In the following episode, a little boy intrudes on two others and an angry fight ensues. This is the way Corsaro and Rizzo present the dialogue:

> Two boys (Richard and Denny) have been playing with a slinky on the stairway leading to the upstairs playhouse in the school. During their play two other boys (Joseph and Martin) enter and stand near the bottom of the stairs.

> Denny: Go!

> (Martin now runs off, but Joseph remains and he eventually moves halfway up the stairs.)

> Joseph: These are big shoes.

Richard: I'll punch him right in the eye.

Joseph: I'll punch you right in the nose.

Denny: I'll punch him with my big fist.

Joseph: I'll- I- I-

Richard: And he'll be bumpety, bumpety and punched out all the way down the stairs.

Joseph: I- I- I'll- I could poke your eyes out with my gun. I have a gun.

Denny: A gun! I'll- I- I- even if-

Richard: I have a gun too.

Denny: And I have guns too and it's bigger than yours and it poo-poo down. That's poo-poo.

(All three boys laugh at Denny's reference to poo-poo.)

Richard: Now leave.

Joseph: Un-uh. I gonna tell you to put on- on the gun on your hair and the poop will come right out on his face.

Denny: Well.

Richard: Slinky will snap right on your face too.

Denny: And my gun will snap right-

Up until this point I had no difficulty interpreting the interaction: the boys were engaged in a fight occasioned by Joseph's intrusion into Richard and Denny's play. But what happened next surprised and, at first, perplexed me. Corsaro and Rizzo describe it this way:

> At this point a girl (Debbie) enters, says she is Batgirl, and asks if they have seen Robin. Joseph says he is Robin, but she says she is looking for a different Robin and then runs off. After Debbie leaves, Denny and Richard move into the playhouse and Joseph follows. From this point to the end of the episode the three boys play together.

At first I was incredulous that so soon after their seemingly hostile encounter, the boys played amicably together. Finally I came to the conclusion that for Joseph picking a fight was a way to enter into interaction with the other boys, and engaging him in the fight was Richard and Denny's way of accepting him into their interaction—at least after he acquitted himself satisfactorily in the fight. In this light, I could see that the reference to poo-poo, which occasioned general laughter, was the beginning of a reframing from fighting to playing.[10]

Folklore provides numerous stories in which fighting precipitates friendship among men. One example is the Sumerian Gilgamesh epic, as recounted by Campbell (1964:87–92). Enkidu, a hairy man who lives with wild animals, is created by the mother-goddess to tame Gilgamesh, a god-king who has grown too arrogant and tyrannical. A hunter who encounters Enkidu appeals to Gilgamesh for help in subduing him. Gilgamesh sends the temple prostitute to lure Enkidu away from his wild animal companions. When the prostitute tells Enkidu about Gilgamesh,

> his heart grew light. He yearned for a friend. "Very well!" he said. "And I shall challenge him."

When they meet:

> They grappled, locked like bulls. The doorpost of the temple shattered; the wall shook. And, at last, Gilgamesh relented. His fury gone, he turned away. And the two, thereafter, were inseparable friends. (p. 89)

When Enkidu dies, Gilgamesh is distraught. In this legend, fighting each other is the means to establishing lifelong friendship.[11]

A modern-day academic equivalent is to be found in the situation of fruitful collaborations that began when an audience member publicly challenged a speaker after his talk. Finally, Penelope Eckert (p.c.) informs me that in her research on high school students (Eckert 1990) she was told by boys, but never by girls, that their close friendships began by fighting.

These examples call into question the correlation of aggression and power on one hand, and cooperation and solidarity on the other. Again the cross-cultural perspective provides an invaluable corrective to the temptation to align aggression with power as distinguished from solidarity. Many cultures of the world see arguing as a pleasurable sign of intimacy. Schiffrin (1984) shows that among lower-middle-class men *and women* of East European Jewish background, friendly argument is a means of being sociable. Frank (1988) shows a Jewish couple who tend to polarize and take argumentative positions, but they are not fighting; they are staging a kind of public sparring, where both fighters are on the same team. Byrnes (1986) claims that Germans find American students uninformed and uncommitted because they are reluctant to argue politics with new acquaintances. For their part Americans find German students belligerent because they provoke arguments about American foreign policy with Americans they have just met.

Greek conversation provides an example of a cultural style that places more positive value, for both women and men, on dynamic opposition. Kakava (1989) replicates Schiffrin's findings by showing how a Greek family enjoy opposing each other in dinner table conversation. In another study of modern Greek conversation, Tannen and Kakava (1992) find speakers routinely disagreeing when they actually agree and using diminutive name forms and other terms of endearment—markers of closeness—precisely when they are opposing each other.[12] These patterns can be seen in the following excerpt from a conversation that took place in Greece between an older Greek woman and me. The woman, whom I call Ms. Stella, has just told me that she complained to the police about a construction crew that illegally continued drilling and pounding through the siesta hours, disturbing her nap:

Deborah: Echete dikio.
Stella: Ego echo dikio. Kopella mou, den xero an echo dikio i den echo
               dikio. Alla ego yperaspizomai ta symferonta mou kai ta
               dikaiomata mou.

Deborah: You're right.
Stella: I am right. My dear girl, I don't know if I'm right or I'm not
               right. But I am watching out for my interests and my rights.

My response to Ms. Stella's complaint is to support her by agreeing. But
she disagrees with my agreement by reframing my statement in her own
terms rather than simply accepting it by stopping after "I am right." She
also marks her divergence from my frame with the endearment "kopella
mou" (literally, "my girl," but idiomatically closer to "my dear girl").

In another conversation, one which, according to Kakava, is typical of
her family's sociable argument, the younger sister has said that she cannot
understand why the attractive young woman who is the prime minister
Papandreou's girlfriend would have an affair with such an old man. The
older sister, Christina, argues that the woman may have felt that in having
an affair with the prime minister she was doing something notable. Her
sister replied,

Poly megalo timima re Christinaki na pliroseis pantos.

It's a very high price to pay, *re* Chrissie, anyway.

I use the English diminutive form "Chrissie" to reflect the Greek diminutive ending *-aki,* but the particle *re* cannot really be translated; it is simply a
marker of closeness that is typically used when disagreeing, as in the
ubiquitously heard expression "Ochi, re" ("No, *re*").

Conclusion

The intersection of language and gender provides a rich site for analyzing
how power and solidarity are created in discourse. But prior research in
this area evidences the danger of linking linguistic forms with interactional
intentions such as dominance. In trying to understand how speakers use
language, we must consider the context (in every sense, including at least
textual, relational, and institutional constraints), the speakers' conversational styles, and, most crucially, the interaction of their styles with each
other.

Attempts to understand what goes on between women and men in
conversation are muddled by the ambiguity of power and solidarity. The
same linguistic means can accomplish either, and every utterance combines elements of both. Scholars, however, like individuals in interaction,
are likely to see only one and not the other, like the picture that cannot be
seen for what it is—simultaneously a chalice and two faces—but can only
be seen alternately as one or the other. In attempting the impossible task of

keeping both images in focus at once, we may at least succeed in switching from one to the other rapidly and regularly enough to deepen our understanding of the dynamics underlying interaction such as power and solidarity as well as gender and language use.

NOTES

This chapter is a significantly revised, rewritten, and enlarged version of a paper entitled "Rethinking power and solidarity in gender and dominance," in Kira Hall, Jean-Pierre Koenig, Michael Meacham, Sondra Reinman, & Laurel A. Sutton (Eds.) *Proceedings of the 16th Annual Meeting of the Berkeley Linguistic Society* (519– 529). Berkeley: Linguistics Department, University of California, 1990. The rethinking and rewriting were carried out while I was in residence at the Institute for Advanced Study in Princeton, New Jersey, for which I am grateful to Clifford Geertz and the other faculty members of the Institute's School of Social Science.

1. I use the term "strategy" in its standard sociolinguistic sense, to refer simply to a way of speaking. No implication is intended of deliberate planning, as is the case in the common parlance use of such expressions as "military strategy." Neither, however, as Gumperz (1982) observes, are linguistic strategies "unconscious." Rather they are best thought of as "automatic." That is, people speak in a particular way without "consciously" thinking it through, but are aware, if questioned, of how they spoke and what they were trying to accomplish by talking in that way. This is in contrast to the "unconscious" motives of Freudian theory about which an individual would be unaware if questioned. (For example, most men would vigorously deny that they want to kill their fathers and marry their mothers, but a Freudian might claim that they do, only this wish is unconscious.)

2. I myself have made the observation that asymmetry is distancing whereas symmetry implies closeness, for example, with regard to the ritual of "troubles talk" and the way it often misfires between women and men (Tannen 1990b). Many women talk about troubles as a way of feeling closer, but many men frequently interpret the description of troubles as a request for advice, which they kindly offer. I have observed that this not only cuts off the troubles talk, which was the real point of the discourse, but also introduces asymmetry: if one person says she has a problem and another says she has the same problem, they are symmetrically arrayed and their similarity brings them closer. But if one person has a problem and the other has the solution, the one with the solution is one-up, and the asymmetry is distancing—just the opposite of what was sought by initiating the ritual.

3. This assumption is made explicit by Klagsbrun (1992:12), who writes, in a book about sibling relationships, "Unlike the ties between parents and children, the connection among siblings is a horizontal one. That is, sibs exist on the same plane, as peers, more or less equals." This comes immediately after she gives a pivotal example of how frustrated she was as a child by always being bested by her older brother. It is clear from the example that she and her brother were not equals: that he was older, and that he was male, were crucial factors in their rivalry and in his unbeatability. Much of the rest of Klagsbrun's book illustrates the fundamental inequality of siblings.

4. Negative politeness, as discussed by Brown and Levinson ([1978]1987), entails honoring others' needs not to be imposed on.

5. Scollon (1982:344–345) explains that all communication is a double bind because one must serve, with every utterance, the conflicting needs to be left alone (negative face) and to be accepted as a member of society (positive face). The term "double bind" traces to Bateson (1972).

6. I have demonstrated at length (Tannen 1987, 1989a) that repeating another's words creates rapport on a metalevel: It is a ratification of the other's words, evidence of participation in the same universe of discourse.

7. After the oral presentation of this paper both Gary Holland and Michael Chandler pointed out that the prisoner may be heard as implying the second part of the guard's statement: "and you're a pile of shit."

8. This scene illustrates what Bateson (1972) calls "complementary schismogenesis": each person's style drives the other into increasingly exaggerated forms of the opposing behavior. The more he refuses to tell her what's wrong, the more desperate she becomes to break through his silence. The more she pressures him to tell her, the more adamant he becomes about refusing to do so.

9. Some examples are given in Tannen (1990a, 1990b). Whereas the boys made such gestures as shooting each other with invisible guns, the girls made such gestures as reaching out and adjusting a friend's headband.

10. Elsewhere (Tannen 1990b:163–165) I discuss this example in more detail and note the contrast that the boys fight when they want to play, and the girl avoids disagreeing even when she does in fact disagree.

11. I was led to this legend by Bly (1990:243–244). In Bly's rendition, Gilgamesh is motivated by a desire to befriend Enkidu, the wild man.

12. Sifianou (1992) independently observes the use of diminutives as solidarity markers in Greek conversation.

REFERENCES

Bateson, Gregory (1972). *Steps to an ecology of mind*. New York: Ballantine.

Becker, A. L. (1982). Beyond translation: Esthetics and language description. In Heidi Byrnes (Ed.). *Contemporary perceptions of language: Interdisciplinary dimensions. Georgetown University Round Table on Languages and Linguistics 1982* (pp. 129–138). Washington, DC: Georgetown University Press.

Becker, A. L. & Oka, I Gusti Ngurah (1974). Person in Kawi: Exploration of an elementary semantic dimension. *Oceanic Linguistics* 13:229–255.

Beeman, William O. (1986). *Language, status, and power in Iran*. Bloomington: Indiana University Press.

Bellinger, David & Gleason, Jean Berko (1982). Sex differences in parental directives to young children. *Sex Roles* 8:1123–1139.

Bly, Robert (1990). *Iron John: A book about men*. Reading, MA: Addison-Wesley.

Brown, Roger & Gilman, Albert (1960). The pronouns of power and solidarity. In Thomas Sebeok (Ed.) *Style in language* (pp. 253–276). Cambridge, MA: M.I.T. Press.

Brown, Penelope & Levinson, Stephen ([1978]1987). *Politeness: Some universals in language usage*. Cambridge: Cambridge University Press.

Byrnes, Heidi (1986). Interactional style in German and American conversations. *Text* 6:189–206.

Campbell, Joseph (1964). *The masks of god: Occidental mythology*. New York: Viking.

Coates, Jennifer (1986). *Women, men and language*. London: Longman.

Conley, John M., O'Barr, William M., & Lind, E. Allen (1979). The power of language: Presentational style in the courtroom. *Duke Law Journal* Vol. 1978, No. 6.

Corsaro, William & Rizzo, Thomas (1990). Disputes in the peer culture of American and Italian nursery school children. In Allen Grimshaw (Ed.) *Conflict talk* (pp. 21–65). Cambridge: Cambridge University Press.

Dorval, Bruce (Ed.) (1990). *Conversational coherence and its development.* Norwood, NJ: Ablex.

Duranti, Alessandro & Brenneis, Donald (Eds.) (1986). *The audience as co-author.* Special issue of *Text* 6:239–247.

Erickson, Frederick (1986). Listening and speaking. In Deborah Tannen (Ed.) *Languages and linguistics: The interdependence of theory, data, and application. Georgetown University Round Table on Languages and Linguistics 1985* (pp. 294–319). Washington, DC: Georgetown University Press.

Erickson, Frederick & Shultz, Jeffrey (1982). *The counselor as gatekeeper: Social interaction in interviews.* New York: Academic Press.

Fasold, Ralph W. (1990). *The sociolinguistics of language.* Oxford: Basil Blackwell.

Frank, Jane (1988). Communicating "by pairs": Agreeing and disagreeing among married couples. Manuscript, Georgetown University.

Friedrich, Paul (1972). Social context and semantic feature: The Russian pronominal usage. In John J. Gumperz & Dell Hymes (Eds.) *Directions in sociolinguistics* (pp. 270–300). New York: Holt, Rinehart & Winston.

Gleason, Jean Berko (1987). Sex differences in parent-child interaction. In Susan U. Philips, Susan Steele & Christine Tanz (Eds.) *Language, gender, and sex in comparative perspective* (pp. 189–199). Cambridge: Cambridge University Press.

Gumperz, John J. (1982). *Discourse strategies.* Cambridge: Cambridge University Press.

Hughes, Linda A. (1988). "But that's not *really* mean": Competing in a cooperative mode. *Sex Roles* 19:669–687.

Kakava, Christina (1989). Argumentative conversation in a Greek family. Paper presented at the Annual Meeting of the Linguistic Society of America, Washington, DC.

Keenan, Elinor (1974). Norm-makers, norm-breakers: Uses of speech by men and women in a Malagasy community. In Richard Bauman & Joel Sherzer (Eds.) *Explorations in the ethnography of speaking* (pp. 125–143). Cambridge: Cambridge University Press.

Klagsbrun, Francine (1992). *Mixed feelings: Love, hate, rivalry, and reconciliation among brothers and sisters.* New York: Bantam.

Komarovsky, Mirra (1962). *Blue-collar marriage.* New York: Vintage.

Lakoff, Robin (1975). *Language and woman's place.* New York: Harper and Row.

Maltz, Daniel N. & Borker, Ruth A. (1982). A cultural approach to male-female miscommunication. In John J. Gumperz (Ed.) *Language and social identity* (pp. 196–216). Cambridge: Cambridge University Press.

McDermott, R. P. & Tylbor, Henry (1983). On the necessity of collusion in conversation. *Text* 3:277–297.

Mead, Margaret (1977). End linkage: A tool for cross-cultural analysis. In John Brockman (Ed.) *About Bateson* (pp. 171–231). New York: Dutton.

Norman, Michael (1990). *These good men: Friendships forged from war.* New York: Crown.

Ong, Walter J. (1981). *Fighting for life: Contest, sexuality, and consciousness.* Ithaca: Cornell University Press; Amherst: University of Massachusetts Press.

Paules, Greta Foff (1991). *Dishing it out: Power and resistance among waitresses in a New Jersey restaurant.* Philadelphia: Temple University Press.

Philips, Susan Urmston (1983). *The invisible culture: Communication in classroom and community on the Warm Springs Indian reservation.* New York and London: Longman; rpt. Waveland Press.

Pinter, Harold (1988). *Mountain language.* New York: Grove Press.

Sattel, Jack W. (1983). Men, inexpressiveness, and power. In Barrie Thorne, Cheris Kramarae & Nancy Henley (Eds.) *Language, gender and society* (pp. 119–124). Rowley, MA: Newbury House.

Schegloff, Emanuel (1982). Discourse as an interactional achievement: Some uses of 'uhuh' and other things that come between sentences. In Deborah Tannen (Ed.) *Analyzing discourse: Text and talk. Georgetown University Round Table on Languages and Linguistics 1981* (pp. 71–93). Washington, DC: Georgetown University Press.

Schegloff, Emanuel (1988). Discourse as an interactional achievement II. An exercise in conversation analysis. In Deborah Tannen (Ed.) *Linguistics in context: Connecting observation and understanding* (pp. 135–158). Norwood, NJ: Ablex.

Schiffrin, Deborah (1984). Jewish argument as sociability. *Language in Society* 13:311–335.

Scollon, Ron (1985). The machine stops: Silence in the metaphor of malfunction. In Deborah Tannen & Muriel Saville-Troike (Eds.) *Perspectives on silence* (pp. 21–30). Norwood, NJ: Ablex.

Scollon, Ron & Scollon, Suzanne B. K. (1981). *Narrative, literacy and face in interethnic communication.* Norwood, NJ: Ablex.

Shuy, Roger W. (1982). Topic as the unit of analysis in a criminal law case. In Deborah Tannen (Ed.) *Analyzing discourse: Text and talk. Georgetown University Round Table on Languages and Linguistics 1981* (pp. 113–126). Washington, DC: Georgetown University Press.

Sifianou, Maria (1992). The use of diminutives in expressing politeness: Modern Greek versus English. *Journal of Pragmatics* 17:155–173.

Spender, Dale (1980). *Man made language.* London: Routledge and Kegan Paul.

Tannen, Deborah (1981). Indirectness in discourse: Ethnicity as conversational style. *Discourse Processes* 4:221–238.

Tannen, Deborah (1984). *Conversational style: Analyzing talk among friends.* Norwood, NJ: Ablex.

Tannen, Deborah (1985). Silence: Anything but. In Deborah Tannen & Muriel Saville-Troike (Eds.) *Perspectives on silence* (pp. 93–111). Norwood, NJ: Ablex.

Tannen, Deborah (1986). *That's not what I meant!: How conversational style makes or breaks your relations with others.* New York: Ballantine.

Tannen, Deborah (1987). Repetition in conversation: Toward a poetics of talk. *Language* 63:574–605.

Tannen, Deborah (1989a). *Talking voices: Repetition, dialogue and imagery in conversational discourse.* Cambridge: Cambridge University Press.

Tannen, Deborah (1989b). Interpreting interruption in conversation. In Bradley Music, Randolph Graczyk & Caroline Wiltshire (Eds.) *Papers from the 25th Annual Regional Meeting of the Chicago Linguistic Society. Part Two: Parases-*

sion on Language in Context (pp. 266–287). Chicago: Chicago Linguistic Society. Rpt. in *Gender and discourse*. New York and Oxford: Oxford University Press, in preparation.

Tannen, Deborah (1990a). Gender differences in conversational coherence: Physical alignment and topical cohesion. In Bruce Dorval (Ed.), *Conversational coherence and its development* (pp. 167–206). Norwood, NJ: Ablex. Rpt. in *Gender and discourse*. New York and Oxford: Oxford University Press, in preparation.

Tannen, Deborah (1990b). *You just don't understand: Women and men in conversation*. New York: Ballantine.

Tannen, Deborah & Kakava, Christina (1992). Power and solidarity in modern Greek conversation: Disagreeing to agree. *Journal of Modern Greek Studies* 10:12–29.

Watanabe, Suwako (1993). Cultural Differences in Framing: American and Japanese Group Discussions. In Deborah Tannen (Ed.) *Framing in discourse*. New York and Oxford: Oxford University Press, 1993.

Wolfowitz, Clare (1991). *Language style and social space: Stylistic choice in Suriname Javanese*. Urbana and Chicago: University of Illinois Press.

West, Candace & Zimmerman, Don H. (1983). Small insults: A study of interruptions in cross-sex conversations between unacquainted persons. In Barrie Thorne, Cheris Kramarae, & Nancy Henley (Eds.) *Language, gender and society* (pp. 103–117). Rowley, MA: Newbury House.

Yamada, Haru (1992). *American and Japanese business discourse: A comparison of interactional styles*. Norwood, NJ: Ablex.

8

Who's Got the Floor?

CAROLE EDELSKY

Introduction

Though originating as and concluding with an analysis of gender and language, this study is primarily an initial investigation into that interactional structure known as "the floor." As such, it also entails a re-view of "turn." Using inferred participants' meanings rather than technical definitions, "floor" and "turn" were defined and two kinds of floors were identified in five informal committee meetings. One was the usual orderly, one-at-a-time type of floor; the other, a collaborative venture where two or more people either took part in an apparent free-for-all or jointly built one idea, operating "on the same wavelength."

The present chapter will follow an order that reveals how a piece of sociolinguistic research was conducted when both variables and hypotheses were allowed to emerge from the data (Glaser & Strauss 1967). It will also demonstrate that data analysis begins well before the traditional "data analysis stage" in research; that is, that transcribing data is at once problematic, intuition-producing, and fraught with often unreported yet important decisions. The sequence of presentation will be: (a) the original reasons for and initial procedures in the study; (b) the impetus (transcription display problems and the existence of collaborative floors) for the eventual research questions (defining the floor and describing two types, and investigating gender differences in relation to floor types); (c) a critical review of the literature dealing with floors and turns; (d) answers to the definitional questions regarding floor (and turn); (e) procedures for preparing the data for various frequency counts; and (f) a description of objective features of two floor types and related gender differences.

Theoretical Prods for the Study

At the time these date were collected (1978–79) there was a considerable discrepancy between theoretical notions about people and their behavior and research that investigates that behavior. On the one hand, according to certain *theory* people act toward categories of objects, ideas, other people, events—in short, toward the world—on the basis of the meanings they attribute to these categories. As they construct and verify these meanings through social interaction they, in essence, "produce culture" (Stokes & Hewitt 1976). Numerous writers advocated (as they still do) this view of jointly produced social "facts," "of a world that is both of our making and beyond our making" (Mehan 1978:60–61), wherein finely tuned, locally managed everyday events provide evidence of shared interpretations on the part of participants (Blumer 1969, Brown & Levinson 1978, Cicourel 1980, Garfinkel 1972, Goody 1978, Mehan 1974, 1978, O'Keefe, Delia, & O'Keefe 1980, Schegloff 1972a, Stokes & Hewitt 1976). For the sociolinguistic researcher such a theoretical stance implies a methodology that would allow variables and hypotheses to emerge, to some extent at least, from naturalistic data and that would account for the interpretive character of peoples' language interactions.

On the other hand, much early *research* on gender differences in language viewed women and men as almost mechanical entities often acting in contrived settings, and used variables that were designated a priori (see bibliographic examples in Dubois & Crouch 1976, Eakins & Eakins 1978, Edelsky 1978, Kramer, Thorne, & Henley 1978). Conflicting findings were rarely explained in ways that account for the interpretive or even contextual character of interaction (see Kramer, Thorne & Henley 1978, Nichols 1978, McConnell-Ginet, Furman, & Borker 1980, for exceptions). Until the middle to late 1970s the variables studied were rarely above the level of syntax. Only since the late 1970s has there begun to be anything resembling a trend in language/sex investigations focusing on discourse or pragmatic variables such as interruptions (West 1977) or topic control (Fishman 1978) in naturally occurring interactions. (See Soskin & John 1963 for an earlier example of an investigation of gender and conversational role.)

Thus in 1978 I began a "fishing expedition" to discover what gender differences might exist at a discourse level in English in the Southwest. This was based on the following beliefs: (a) that gender differences in speech are not evident in every word (Hymes 1977:168); (b) that power imbalances are both reflected and constructed anew not primarily through words or syntax but through aspects of the structuring of discourse (Fishman 1978); and (c) that although research questions don't ever totally emerge "on their own," they can nevertheless gain precision from particular data (Erickson 1977). Though aware at the outset that, indirectly at least, control of the floor and length of turns had been an issue in previous research on gender and language (Thorne & Henley 1975), I did not anticipate at the start the extent to which this study would temporarily forsake the gender/language issue for an investigation into the *nature* of the floor and exactly how this would then lead back to the original question concerning gender differences.

Initial Procedures

I audiotape-recorded five entire meetings of a standing committee that dealt with program and scheduling issues pertaining to a subarea within a university department. The committee was composed of seven women (of whom I was one) and four men. Different members could be classified as anything from familiar colleagues to very close friends. For the many years of its existence the committee membership had changed only with retirements and new hires; that is, by the time of taping the members constituted a stable collegial group. The recorded meetings ranged from one and one quarter to two hours in length with some members present at all meetings for the entire time and some present at only a few and for only part of the time. At one meeting a pair of visitors (one male and one female) were also present for one half hour. At all meetings dessert and coffee were always available, people sat around two round tables pushed together, and each meeting actually began with loud, joking pre-meeting conversation that either "slid" into or was explicitly terminated by the meeting talk. Although each meeting had a different character depending on those present, agenda topics, contemporaneous events in the department, and so on, all presumably shared characteristics with each other and with other kinds of multiparty talk (Atkinson, Cuff, & Lee 1978).

I transcribed the tapes by hand during one academic year, requiring about five hundred hours of transcription time. In addition, I took dated notes of my perceptions as I transcribed. The intended procedure was to let the intensive immersion in the data, a by-product of so many hours of transcribing, along with the possibility of recurring perceptions in the notes, engender specific hypotheses related to the focus of sex differences in discourse.

A Funny Thing Happened on the Way to the Focus

Partway through the transcribing it became clear that problematic aspects of transforming data to a written record would have to divert the study's focus to a different topic: structural aspects of interaction itself. That is, the question of the relation between gender and language could not be addressed until certain interactional concepts were clarified.

The original mode of transcribing was a simplified version of the Sacks, Schegloff, and Jefferson model (Schenkein 1978), listing speakers vertically and indicating overlaps as in (1) where Rafe (the committee chair) was trying to find the best time for holding meetings.

(1)

1 Rafe: OK, let's talk about Tuesday=
2 Len: =Well=
3 Carole: =OK, Tuesday
                         [
4 Sally: as long as we're out by four-thirty
                                           [
5 Carole: is my day from seven-forty in=
6 Marion: (   )
7 Carole: =the morning until six at night
8 Len: Well I'm here from   eight
                       [   ]
9 Carole: I   have
                       [   ]
10 Rafe: that's a little hard ((laugh))
11 Carole: Yeah. Now I've got three classes=
12 Rafe: =((whistles))
13 Carole: =And I usually use the in-between times to make sure for the
14 Rafe: OK
                 [[   ]]
15 Len: Yeah that's my problem
                       [   ]
16 Carole: the night times and it's the same thing for Thursday also
                                         [
17 Rafe: so Tuesday is out

Transcribing this way, I experienced an increasingly gnawing feeling that
what was "really" going on was not being visually captured. For instance,
it appears, if one overlooks the syntax, in lines 4 and 5 that Carole may be
overlapping Sally, and yet, if one knows Carole's normally slow and pause-
ful manner of talking, one knows that lines 3 and 5 constitute one, not
two, of Carole's utterances. The same discrepancy between the impression
created by the transcription display and the felt sense of what really constituted one person's full turn can be seen in lines 15 and 16. Here what
seems to be a case of Carole overlapping Len is actually an example of Len
and Rafe talking within a pause in Carole's utterance which begins in line
11. Similarly line 17 was part of a turn begun in line 14 rather than an
overlap begun in line 17.

Example (2), taken from the same negotiation over optimal meeting
times, appears to be visually similar to (1), especially in lines 9 through 18,
but there is a qualitative difference when listening to it; that is, one gets
the impression of more raucousness and overlapping in (2). While in (1),
lines 3, 5, 7, 9, 11, 13, and 16 were actually part of a single turn (in the
sense of participants' meanings for what counts as a turn rather than in an

"objective" or speaker-change sense), in (2), lines 6 and 7, lines 10 and 11, and lines 13, 14, 16, and 18 are three separate turns.

(2)

```
 1 Marion:   I'll see if I can (st- )
 2 Carole:            ┌─ Oh, I have        office hours=
 3 Len:               │  Yeah that's (    ) three of em
 4 Rafe:              └─ Is that OK? Could we try that
 5 Carole:   =but I'm here. I mean office hours doesn't count
             [                                          ]
 6 Len:      Oh yeah I could schedule my eating during office hours;=
 7 Len:      =(double      )
             [            ]
 8 Rafe:     (            )
             [            ]
 9 Sally:    That was the day I was gonna stay home and write but
             that's=
10 Len:      that was=
11 Len:      =my day to stay home and write
12 Sally:    =gone by the boards.      Scratch that idea
                                       [       ]
13 Len:                                Well did you see awright=
14 Len:      =did you see what happened. Every Thursday. Same=
             [                                          ]
15 Rafe:     Now see you got a good           excuse.
16 Len:      =thing. That's every Thursday. I try to keep that home=
                         [             ]
17 Sally:                every Thursday
18 Len:      =to write
```

It gradually became apparent that I could even deliberately bias the perception of the number of turns someone took by how much was typed onto one line. Compare the impression of a single turn for Sally in lines 9 and 12 in (2) with the impression of two turns for Sally in lines 1, 2, and 5 in example (3), depending on the length of the lines and the order in which the speakers are listed.

(3)

```
 1 Sally:    That was the day I was gonna stay home=
 2 Sally:    =and write but that's gone by the boards.
                    [
 3 Len:                     that was my day to stay home and=
 4 Len:      =write
                 [
 5 Sally:        Scratch that idea.
```

The effect of the transcript display on the understanding or (mis)per-ception of a phenomenon has been occasionally noted by others (Aleguire 1978, Jefferson 1973; see Ochs 1979 for a detailed discussion of this problem in relation to transcribing child-adult interactions). Usually it is ignored, however, sometimes to the point of "hiring out" the transcription process so that the researcher is not even privy to particular transcribing decisions that have been made.

In order to overcome the problem of bias stemming from the amount of type on a line or the order in which speakers were listed, I attempted to transcribe as though on a musical staff. Since all present have an effect on interaction, whether speaking or not, I constructed a fixed staff, with each line representing a participant, and with the leftmost type being that which was heard first. Example (4), from a discussion about how to title and grade a proposed new course, shows the difficulty such a display presents. Not only does this mode still fail to capture "felt" turn bound-aries, but it makes the content hard to follow and suggests that timing (or rhythm) is the basic interactional issue.

(4)

```
 ┌ Rafe:                                       498 and that could be
 │  Mary:                                                        call it a
 │  Carole:  They're only allowed one                       course that's
 │  Len:     it to be
 │  Anne:
 │  Karen:
 │  Sally:
 └ Nelly:
 ┌ Rafe:             Y                     Composition workshop
 │  Mary:    composition workshop              why don't we
 │  Carole:  a Y
 │  Len:
 │  Anne:
 │  Karen:                                        that's better. Credit
 │  Sally:             no they- must be a more- cause four eighty-one  is  a
 └ Nelly:
 ┌ Rafe:
 │  Mary:
 │  Carole:
 │  Len:
 │  Anne:
 │  Karen:   no credit I mean that would be so much better
 │  Sally:   is a Y, four sixty-six is a Y, that's two right there
 └ Nelly:
```

There were obviously important events that were not being captured: for example, did a speaker complete a turn (that one can feel "he never let me finish" despite one's having arrived successfully at a transition-relevant place [Sacks et al., 1974] is evidence that a participant's sense of what counts as a turn is not necessarily the same as a research definition of a turn as ending with the speech of another participant or the end of a unit type)? For example, was a speaker chimed in on and helped or was s/he interrupted? With mounting distress over the inhospitality of the traditional down-the-page, line-by-line transcription to these important events, I turned the paper sideways in order to try to capture the multidimensional, interrelated (as opposed to linear) character of the talk. I intended to place the offering of the speaker who had the floor in the center of the page and show any simultaneous talk, encouraging remarks, and so on, on either side. At this point I was still assuming that, even for periods of simultaneous talk, there would be one turn taker who was actually holding the floor. Example (5) is thus a retranscription in this new mode of what was shown in (1). It provides a display of a participant's sense of who had the floor, of how long a turn was, and of what happened to or concurrently with that turn.[1] It did not indicate that speaker change necessarily provided the boundaries for turns or for floor control. It also seemed to eliminate the problem of a display that could be biased by the amount typed on a line.

(5)

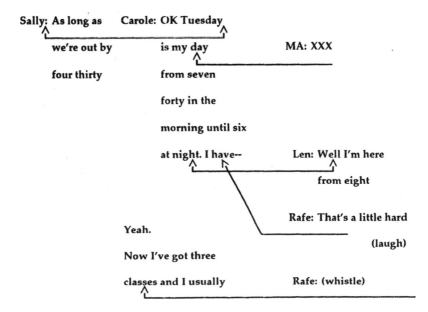

use the in-between time to

make sure for the   Rafe: OK so Tuesday]   [Len: Yeah that's

                                    is out   my problem

night times and it's

the same thing for Thursday also.

One very difficult problem remained, however, relating to the intention to present the floor holder in the center. Despite my participation in
the meetings and my ability, on hearing the tapes, to remember my impressions of what had generally been happening at any moment during the
meetings, there were frequent stretches of talk, lasting from 1.8 to 45.9
seconds in the first meeting at least, for which I could not determine who
had the floor. I referred to these as collaboratively developed floors, as
opposed to singly-developed floors which were held primarily by one
person at a time. There were two main types of collaborative floors:
seeming free-for-alls and, more frequently, cases of several people being
"on the same wavelength." The free-for-alls were stretches similar to example (6), an excerpt from a section when Rafe was introducing the topic of
what to do about students who were poor writers. He began by citing the
case of an administrator at an elite university who was notorious for his
poor writing. In (6) the enclosed area is the free-for-all; it shows much
simultaneity, joint building of an answer to a question, collaboration on
developing ideas (appreciation of irony and the minor scandal involved),
and laughter.

(6)

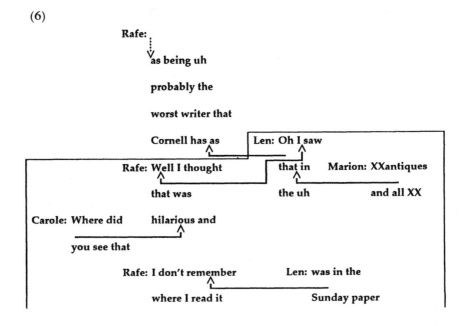

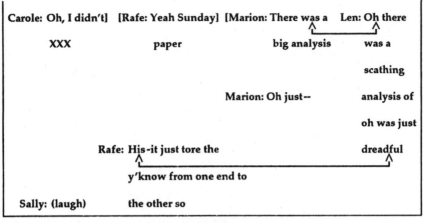

Carole: Oh, I didn't]   [Rafe: Yeah Sunday]   [Marion: There was a   Len: Oh there

XXX   paper   big analysis   was a

scathing

Marion: Oh just--   analysis of

oh was just

Rafe: His-it just tore the   dreadful

y'know from one end to

Sally: (laugh)   the other so

Carole: (laugh)   Marion: I looked at my

students' papers

Other collaborative stretches of talk, however, seemed more "orderly" and less "noisy"; yet it still was not possible to say that any one person had the floor. Rather, the impression was that several people were "on the same wavelength," even if in a sequence, sharing in the creation of an idea or a function (joking, suggesting, etc.), as they were in (7) when the committee began joking about having to name a laboratory after the members who were donating their "complimentary" publisher-supplied materials to that lab.

(7)

Rafe: That'd be fantastic.

Yeah it could. Look, the

idea is that we'll work these   Marion: Then we'll

materials in to these   have to call

Sally: Then it'd   it Seybrook

have to be the

Hudson Seybrook

Carole: Oh now listen,   Room   Marion: (laugh)

Rafe: That's--   I just donated

a big box full

of   Rafe: Oh my god,   Sally: Of Piaget

now we've   stuff?

done it

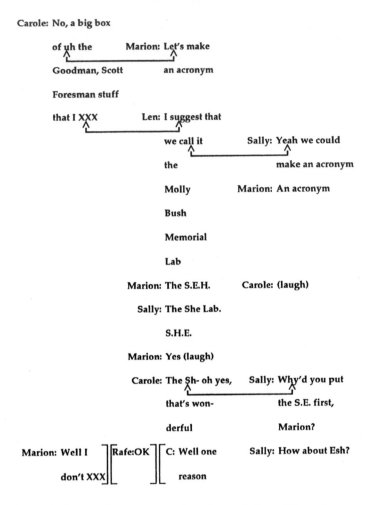

Carole: No, a big box

of uh the   Marion: Let's make

Goodman, Scott   an acronym

Foresman stuff

that I XXX   Len: I suggest that

we call it   Sally: Yeah we could

the   make an acronym

Molly   Marion: An acronym

Bush

Memorial

Lab

Marion: The S.E.H.   Carole: (laugh)

Sally: The She Lab.

S.H.E.

Marion: Yes (laugh)

Carole: The Sh- oh yes,   Sally: Why'd you put

that's won-   the S.E. first,

derful   Marion?

Marion: Well I   Rafe:OK   C: Well one   Sally: How about Esh?

don't XXX   reason

Sometimes, being on the same wavelength was inferred from long overlapping turns which each simultaneously developed the same entire idea or answered the same question (8) and where neither turn yielded to the other, as though in a fugue or a variation on a theme. (Example [8] is a two-person rebuttal to someone else's idea that an entire project be planned in great detail. The end of the overlapping in [8] has been marked by double lines so the reader can see the extent to which the two turns co-occurred and the absence of any attempt to repair the simultaneity.)

(8)

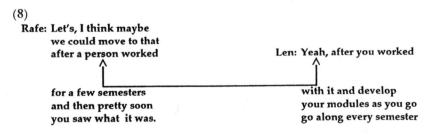

Rafe: Let's, I think maybe
we could move to that
after a person worked

for a few semesters
and then pretty soon
you saw what it was.

Len: Yeah, after you worked

with it and develop
your modules as you go
go along every semester

But we can't precon-	develop one or two
ceive what it is	more. By the third
	semester // you'd have them.

There were other times, as (9) shows, when this collaboration was achieved both through attention to the same function (answering) and topic and also through matching and marked rhythm and intonation.

(9)

Carole: What was it? It was

kids who came and

Len: Who came and-   wrote?   Rafe: :What'd you have? Nine

Len: Nine hundred   hundred or something?

or something

Len: They came and   Carole: But they wrote? In

shared each   front of XXX?

other's

writings and   Carole: Oh, oh   ] [Rafe: Yeah

y'know, this   Rafe: Bill Martin was there

kind of thing   and he did a thing

                  Len: And this year they've already   and he-

got a list of people that

they're considering

Note Len "singing":

                    ting,
              wri
        each other's

Rafe's echoing with:

                  ng,
            thi
        he did a

and Len completing the collaboration:

                ar
          this ye
      and

after Carole had tried to get clarification of something Len and Rafe had referred to as a "Young Author's Day."

Elsewhere, joint development of meaning and/or function was accomplished by individuals contributing pieces of one idea. There were even same-wavelength episodes where two or more people built one hedge, aborting their turns on their own, uninterrupted, and unoverlapped.

A New Focus

With so many instances where who had the floor was problematic, with the existence of two kinds of floors rather than one—one developed singly and one jointly [see examples (6) through (9)]—and with the repeated complaint in my notes ("I can't tell who has the floor here") and the frequent suspicion ("the women seem to outdo the men in the free-for-alls but not the holding forths"), I finally came to three realizations. First, I could no longer equate taking a turn and having the floor. Second, the interactional conduct of the sexes, often reflecting differentially accorded nonlinguistic rights and privileges, might also be related to an interaction of the type of floor in progress and those unequal rights. And third, a careful look at the nature of *floor* would have to precede an examination of gender and language.

Two research questions had thus emerged:

1. What is "the floor" (what definition will cover the kinds of floors discovered in these data: are there objective ways of differentiating the subjectively perceived collaborative floors from singly developed floors? is the contest metaphor—winning/losing the floor— always appropriate? how is having a turn related to having the floor, etc.)?
2. Are there gender differences in language use depending on the type of floor that is occurring (do women really outdo the men in collaborative floors?)?

Turns and Floors in the Literature

One-At-A-Time

The one-at-a-time character of conversation is the conceptual basis for the insightful and useful work on turn taking generally (Goffman 1971), turn-allocating mechanisms (Sacks et al. 1974), sequencing in speech acts or events (Schegloff 1972b), precise timing in verbal interaction (Jefferson 1973), turn-yielding and claiming signals (Duncan 1972), displays of power (West 1977) or other factors (Aleguire 1978) through interruption, and objectively defined formality (McHoul 1978). This characterization of one-at-a-time-ness has several possible sources. Many (Aleguire 1978, Duncan 1972, 1973, Duncan & Niederehe 1974, Kendon 1967, Meltzer, Morris, & Hayes 1971, Shapiro 1976, West 1977, Yngve 1970), though certainly not all studies making extensive use of the concept of turns have depended on data from dyads. In addition, the speech situations in many of the studies, regardless of the number of participants, have been relatively formal and have not always consisted of what natives would call "conversations": that is, therapy sessions, classes, experimenter-requested conversations between strangers (Duncan 1972, Jefferson 1973, Kendon 1967, Mchoul 1978, Mehan 1974, Shapiro 1976, Stephan & Mishler 1952, Yngve 1970) have provided the data for many "conversational" analyses. If not the source of the proposition that the fundamental normative structure as well as the statistical norm is that one party talks at a time, data from dyads or from situations where participant statuses are institutionally defined would most likely legitimate that proposition. A primary justification for why conversation should proceed in this fashion is that simultaneous talk would not permit much communication (Meltzer et al. 1971) since it is potentially unhearable (Jefferson 1973).

Though one-at-time has proved to be a useful premise for studies of speaker change, it has attendant problems. Its raison d'être, that people can only process a message from one source at a time, was found to be not necessarily true in a laboratory study of language processing (Spelke, Hirst, & Neisser 1976). There is also at least one speech community where naturally occurring simultaneous talk is frequent, expected, and processed (Reisman 1974). One-at-a-time is therefore not a conversational universal nor is it essential for the communication of messages. More seriously than the existence of exceptions, the unquestioning adoption of this premise causes researchers to see more-than-one-at-a-time as degenerate (Goffman 1967:40), as a breakdown (Duncan 1973:33), or as something requiring repair (Mchoul 1978:199). It causes one not only to avoid looking for alternative explanations for and characterizations of the well-attested existence of simultaneous talk but also to discredit the possible importance of this presumably less frequent phenomenon.[2] As this study demonstrates, instances of more-than-one-at-a-time are not always brief, repaired, or degenerate.

Turns

One-at-a-time is usually taken to mean one *turn* at a time. How turns are defined explicitly or implicitly varies from study to study, but the common thread is that some dimension I will call "technical" or mechanical is used as the basis for that definition. One notable exception is Yngve's (1970) work, which took what I call a "participant's or intentional sense" as a basis for determining a turn. (This technical/participant sense distinction is the same one alluded to by Aleguire [1978] when he criticized the use of researcher's rather than speaker's definitions for what counts as an interruption.) To Yngve, it was often hard to tell "who 'really' has the turn, if there is any such thing" (568). Though he never defined a turn, he did indicate that *having* a turn was a state of mind in addition to the display of particular behaviors.

The polar opposite of Yngve's basis for describing turns and the clearest example of the use of a technical or mechanical basis can be found in a technique called chronography, attributed to Jaffe and Feldstein (Burke 1979). Chronography can be done by machine, requires no researcher interpretations, and defines a turn as solo talk, beginning the instant one person starts to talk and ending prior to the instant someone else begins to talk alone. Obviously any overlaps are not considered part of anyone's turn. Duncan (1973), in somewhat less mechanistic but still technical fashion, tried to minimize the role of researcher organization of talk by looking for signals that themselves organize the stream of talk and that thus accomplish the smooth exchange of turns. Using a unit of analysis "between the clause and the turn," his analysis led him to define a turn as a unit of interaction with an end boundary marked by turn-claiming responses from the auditor. Mehan (1978) sometimes used turn synonymously with "who is speaking"; lack of precision here is understandable since turns and turn taking were not the primary concern of this piece of work. To Ochs (1978) and Sacks, Schegloff, and Jefferson (1974), turns are defined at one level as they are defined in *Webster's Third New International Dictionary of the English Language* (1971)—as a right, duty, or opportunity that occurs in a certain order. At another level, with a focus on distribution (exchange) of a "good" (turns), Sacks, Schegloff, and Jefferson (1974) use a "technical, nonintuitive characterization" of turns (Jefferson & Schenkein 1978:163). What occupies a turn slot in this work is a turn unit containing one or more (turn) transition-relevance places. For Schegloff (1972b), a turn is neither a "natural message" nor an activity but a slot in adjacency pairs.

Turns are not the only way conversational units have been categorized, nor are they the only unit which displays discrepant bases for categorization. Talk has been separated into turns and back channel responses (Duncan 1973, Duncan & Niederehe 1974, Sacks et al. 1974, Yngve 1970), planned and habitual responses (Kendon 1967), conversation and side sequences (Jefferson 1972), first pair parts and second pair parts of adjacency pairs (Schegloff & Sacks 1973), floor holdings and assenting utterances (Shapiro 1976), in- and out-of-meeting talk (Atkinson, Cuff & Lee 1978), pretherapy and therapy talk (Turner 1972). The turn versus back channel distinction is the one showing least agreement both among researchers and within the same piece of research.

To Duncan (1973) and Duncan and Niederehe (1974), back channels are short utterances not accompanied by speaker-state signals (postural, paralinguistic, and inhalation cues). In their research back channels included sentence completions, questions of clarification, brief restatements, nods, and *mmhm*'s. Duncan and Niederehe (1974) forsook their reliance on technical definitions (brevity plus claim signals), however, with an indication that there were some longer back channels that intuitively seemed to have the quality of a turn yet were unaccompanied by speaker-state signals. Shapiro (1976) and Sacks, Schegloff, and Jefferson (1974), on the other hand, believe that *any* change of speaker constitutes a trade of turns (with the exception of brief assents). Short questions and restatements were, then, not back channels as they were for Duncan and his colleagues. Yngve (1970:574–576) claimed that since long back channeled utterances could themselves be back channeled by other speakers, they could be considered turns. Earlier in the same article (568), however, his stance was that back channel talk does not count as a turn.

The cited implicit or explicit definitions of "turn" (and back channel talk) sometimes equate turns with speakers, sometimes require lone speech as a criterion, often include other participants' behaviors for determining boundaries, but do not include the turn taker's intentions as part of the definition.

The problem with defining turns simply on the basis of speaker exchange is that this does not account for either a participant's sense of what constitutes a turn or the intention of the turn taker. One is thus led away from an attempt to distinguish ratified from unratified talk (Goffman 1976, Philips 1976). One also misses the fact that some transcribed interruptions are not "felt" as interruptions while some transcribed one-at-a-time "turns" are (Aleguire 1978). This is related to a general inclination to disregard the completeness of a turn's content in favor of the structural features of that content. Such an inclination leads to defining a turn as finished even if the speaker did not feel the message was completed and so either added an afterthought or silently suffered an interpreted but not a technical cut-off. (Though Sacks, Schegloff, and Jefferson's [1974] notion that "possible completions" are what is oriented-to is extremely helpful for studies of speaker change, it distracts one from noticing that such places do not always co-occur with speaker's felt-to-be completed messages. Felt completion has consequences for social meaning, if not for syntax or timing.)

To use the signals of speakers or auditors as the determination of what counts as a turn and deliberately avoid the use of categories such as turns and topics that participants themselves perceive as meaningful (i.e., to take the role of cultural klutz) may be extremely useful for revealing certain features of synchronized speaker change. It provides little help, however, in understanding that the meaning and categorization of behavior do not reside in the behavior. For instance, the banging of a gavel can be the opening of a meeting or a joke (Atkinson, Cuff & Lee 1978); a speaker's gaze away may mean a "touchy" topic rather than a turn completion (Kendon 1967).

This is certainly not a new idea. Other writers (some of whom are the same ones who use a technical way to delimit turns) have either explicitly noted that what counts as "conversation," "topic," "floor," "turn," "gap" (all structural terms) is problematic for researchers (though not necessarily for participants) or have simply used a participant's sense to determine the category without directly mentioning it. Topics, for instance, are not self-evident; *what happened to the salt,* as a request at the table, is not a topic, whereas *what happened to the car* is (Speier 1972). Neither does all talk count as conversation. *Are you busy,* as an opener, is prior to "the conversation" in conversation (Schegloff & Sacks 1973). Nor are "conversation," "turn taking," and "floor holding" useful concepts for looking at perfunctory exchanges such as *take out the garbage/OK* (Yngve 1970). Gaps are not silences determined technically but rather "audibly unfilled slots" determined by participants' expectations that someone should be talking (McHoul 1978). There is thus a history of recognizing the problem in eliminating participant interpretations from analyses of units in the organization of conversation. Nevertheless the majority of the work on the mechanisms in turn taking appears to derive its definitions of "turn" and "floor" from a technical perspective and to presume tacitly that the primary goal in conversation is to conduct the event rather than to make meanings (Cicourel n.d.).

Floor

Not only does the literature reveal an absence of extensive analysis of entire speech events where turns include participants' perspectives, but it also reveals hardly any work which has as its major focus the concept of the floor or an explicit definition of "floor." There are some exceptions. Philips (1983) devotes an entire chapter to analyzing ways to get the floor in classrooms on the Warm Springs Indian Reservation. She maintains that in the official (versus the infrastructural) organization of classroom interaction, the teacher always sustains "one end of the floor." While she carefully and vividly describes participant structures that entail different means for getting the floor, she does not explicitly define "floor" itself. Using Philips's notion of participation structure, Shultz, Florio, and Erickson (1982) identify four such structures at family dinners. In these events the four different patterns in allocation of interactional rights and obligations produced four corresponding floor types. Shultz, Florio, and Erickson suggest that better questions than "who has the floor?" are "where is it?" and "how many kinds are there?"

A few other pieces of work make incidental statements or devote part of their attention to a distinction between floor and turn. Goffman (1976, 1981) discusses the use of asides, quips, and so forth, by listeners who remain in the "role of listeners" even as they speak (i.e., they do not gain the floor), while speakers who listen to such kibbitzing do not as a result lose the "role of speaker" (i.e., floor holder). His emphasis is on the options and resources a speaker can use while having the floor, rather than on "what is had" when one has it. Yngve (1970) claimed that having the floor was not the same as having the turn, on the basis of examples where several turns had been taken "before someone [had] the floor" and where one person had the floor while the other took "an occasional turn to ask him a question" (575). Possibly Yngve's definition of the floor was something like "official attention." Atkinson, Cuff & Lee (1978) called *right-e:r,* which occurred while others were taking *turns* during coffee break conversations, a *floor holder* for the beginning of a meeting. Schegloff and Sacks (1973) could perhaps be considered to have distinguished the two terms when they said that certain (but not all?) utterances "occupy the floor for a speaker's turn" (304), and Philips's (1976) notion of ratified and unratified talk may have been a start in separating turn from floor. West (1977) differentiated the two by proposing that interruptions "appear to acquire the floor if not the turnspace" for male speakers (13). In that study floor might have meant control over the conversation.

With these exceptions the literature either ignores an examination of the floor or uses "turn" and "floor" interchangeably. Duncan (1972) stated that turn boundaries were marked by floor-yielding cues which elsewhere were called turn-yielding cues. In writing about overlapping turns in one speech community, Reisman (1974) referred to the lack of a process for deciding "who is to have the floor" (113). Speakers "hold or release the floor when it is their turn," according to Speier (1972:400). Kendon (1967) reported that a speaker signaled when she was offering her partner the floor, signals which were later referred to as turn offerings. In writing about rules for turn taking, Mehan (1978) alternated between labeling them as rules for taking turns and rules for gaining access to the floor. Goodwin (1980) referred to floor-yielding signals as turn-yielding signals (440). Meltzer, Morris & Hayes (1971) equated the lone turn with the floor in their study of outcomes in contests for the floor. Shultz, Florio, and Erickson (1982) defined floor as access to a turn at speaking. (Goffman [1976] reversed that and defined turn as an opportunity to hold the floor.) Citing Goffman, Sacks, Schegloff, and Jefferson (1974) claim that what is organized in conversation is turns at talk which are accompanied by cues for requesting the floor and giving it up. Their entire article, concerning cues and mechanisms involved in the exchange of turns, could also be taken, therefore, as a proposal for cues involved in an exchange of having the floor.

In sum, then, the floor is variously and indirectly defined as a speaker, a turn, and control over part of a conversation. Metaphorically the floor (if not always "a turn") is viewed as the site of a contest where there is one winner and loser(s) (Meltzer, Morris & Hayes 1971, West 1977).

Interestingly dictionary definitions both do and do not equate turns with the floor (Webster's 1971). Turn is applied to a place, time right, or opportunity to do or receive anything (not just talk) which occurs in due rotation (both a slot and sequence). "Floor," a term more frequently a part of the language of meetings than of conversations, is used to mean a space (that part of a chamber occupied by members), participants (members of an assembly), and a right to be heard. The spatial and membership meaning of floor is not related to the meaning of turn; the right-to-be-heard meaning is. The tendency to equate these terms is therefore widespread in ordinary usage.

It could be, of course, that all of the cited works are using turn in two senses: a turn [at speaking] and a turn [at holding the floor]; that they simply delete what is in brackets; and that there is no equation of turn with floor. However, there is often careful and explicit attention to distinguishing speaking (or an utterance) from turn taking (or a turn). The absence of general efforts toward warning the reader that a turn at speaking is not the same as a turn at holding the floor coupled with the rarity of any separate definition for "floor" leads me to reject this possibility.

A possible source of the equation of turn, floor, and lone speaker is actual experience: that is, much interaction probably does consist of one speaker speaking in turn and also having the floor in turn. Experience with non-co-occurrence of turn, floor, and lone speaker and with extended simultaneous talk may simply not be considered, just as multiple topics and twists and turns to conversation are not considered when people tend to think of "a conversation" as having been monotopical (Schegloff & Sacks 1973). In addition, Goffman (1971) proposed that the body is a marker of various preserves such as space and turns. Thus a speaking turn, meaning an order, could easily come to be associated with the body that takes that turn. Rosch's theory of cognitive prototypes cited by Cicourel (n.d.) may also be functioning here with clear-cut prototypes being produced for each of these conversational categories. The prototypes might then merge as a result of one's experience with their frequent co-occurrence.

Regardless of the source the existence of that merger of turn, floor, and lone speaker embedded in a metaphor of competition presents several problems for research on face-to-face interaction. First, and most obviously, it discourages a separate analysis of speaking turn and floor turn. As the data will show, the two are not the same. Because separate analyses are discouraged, a careful search for how to *define* the floor apart from a turn also becomes unlikely. As one example some imply a definition of the floor as the focus of attention, so that a client's turn in a therapy session has the floor while the therapist's *mmhm*'s do not. It is certainly conceivable that in some cases, the *mmhm*'s are as much the focus of the client's attention as the client's long speaking turn is to the therapist (and the researcher). How to define the floor is not self-evident, but what should be evident from several of the examples shown earlier and the data to be presented later is that one person taking one turn at a time is only one way having the floor is accomplished, that lone control is a feature of only certain floor holdings. Lumping turn and floor together tends to discourage acknowledgment and investigation of the regular (and not necessarily brief) occurrence of other ways to have the floor.

Passing mention of "other ways" does occur sporadically, but in true "equational" fashion, these are considered collaboratively constructed *turns* rather than *floors*. Aleguire (1978) noted that turns could be shared, could operate in tandem, and did not necessarily transfer "possession" (of the floor? of the turn?). Yngve (1970) mentioned that there were cases in his data where each member thought s/he had the turn and where this was not merely due to an afterthought on the part of the first speaker. (Were these jointly produced turns or were they jointly developed floors accomplished through overlapping turns?) Speier (1972) and Jefferson (1973) cited Sacks's mention of the existence of collaborative sentences. (Who has the floor when all are taking these short turns to make one long turn?)

A metaphor of competition may also be appropriate for one but not all ways of having the floor.

Partial Answer to the First Research Question: What Is the Floor?

Turn and Floor Defined

Turn. Using intuitions gained from having been present as a participant, I developed definitions that are the opposite of Jefferson and Schenkein's (1978): that is, they are intuitive and *non*technical. I define turn as *an on-record "speaking"* (which may include nonverbal activities) *behind which lies an intention to convey a message that is both referential and functional.*

As others have emphasized, just any talk does not count as a turn. A turn is taken among particular participants. Therefore, what is truly off-record and is said to one or a few persons rather than to all, usually in a subdued voice, is considered a *side comment* (like the "counter conversations" of Atkinson, Cuff & Lee [1978] or Goffman's [1967] modulated messages that are not part of the officially accredited flow), since the participant makeup of the group which is addressed has now changed. Example (10) shows Len, Rafe, and Sally making side comments (Len is jokingly asking for sympathy for a broken university-issued pen; Rafe teases that his works; Sally asks Carole to pass her a cookie). Note especially that chairperson Rafe also takes a turn, shifting voice tone and topic as he moves from side commenting to taking a turn. He even marks this with a preface, *uh, in this lab,* to his on-record topic-shifting turn.

(10)

Rafe: (the topic has been scheduling)	
other than that	
it stays where it is	**Len:** Is there a doctor here?
Sally: Awright	**Marion:** (laugh)
	Rafe: (to Len) It's OK
	I've tried mine.
	It works well=
Rafe: =Uh in this lab, this	**Sally:** (to Carole) I need
lab is going to be	one of those
named the Hudson	cookies
Room	

The definition of turn also attempts to incorporate the turn taker's intentions in relation to making meaning, conveying referential as well as functional messages. That requires, then, that utterances where the speaker intends to provide only a feedback but not a referential message—*mhm, yeah,* and so on—not be considered turns. Rather, they are encouragers (Sacks, Schegloff, & Jefferson [1974] call them back channel responses). *That's right,* in this data, was categorized as a turn if it was said with a loudness and intonation pattern that would make it heard as *I agree with you entirely* or as an encourager if it was said more like *'ts right,* was placed in a particular way, and was heard as *go on*. Example (11) shows Rafe first making an encouraging remark and then immediately taking a turn at the same time Manny is taking a turn. Manny's turn, a disparaging report about a campus sports figure inserted into the agenda item concerning allegations of poor writing ability of some (usually minority) students, is considered a floor-holding turn while Rafe's is not. This distinction will soon be described in more detail.

(11)

Manny: . . . in racist comments he made in

his hour commentary on

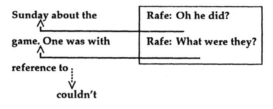

Sunday about the

game. One was with

reference to

couldn't

see him very well

Rafe: Oh he did?

Rafe: What were they?

The definition of turn not only demands that one differentiate a content from a feedback message but that one try to account for the speaker's intention regarding the boundaries of that message. If one were to take a speaker exchange perspective, one would transcribe *to improve himself* in (12) in the second position in which it is shown. If one used a participant's sense of where this phrase belongs, one would consider it an afterthought which belongs at the end of Manny's long turn about proposed procedures to help poor writers, as is shown in the first position in (12).

(12)

Manny: S'posing you identify

one student who needed

some help. Then what

recommendations, what

alternative do you have

```
                        to make recommendations

Carole: Well we        to that student │ to improve himself │
        _____^_____└────────────────────┘
        were talking                       (OR)

        about setting                  ┌─────────────────────────┐
              ^_____             │ Manny: To improve himself │
        up a clinic                    └─────────────────────────┘
```

This obviously has implications for who is interrupting whom (Aleguire 1978) and for why some "speaker exchange" interrupters are felt to be "participant sense" interruptees.

If one attempted but managed to convey no part of a referential message (*I-I-I-; Yeah, but see-*), that was considered an aborted utterance (rather than an aborted turn) because no message was revealed.

Floor. The floor is defined as *the acknowledged what's-going-on within a psychological time/space.* What's going on can be the development of a topic or a function (teasing, soliciting a response, etc.) or an interaction of the two. It can be developed or controlled by one person at a time or by several simultaneously or in quick succession. It is official or acknowledged in that, if questioned, participants could describe what's going on as "he's talking about grades" or "she's making a suggestion" or "we're all answering her."

There can thus be messages which are meant for public hearing (on record, not side comments), have both propositional and functional content (not merely encouragers), and are therefore turns but which do not constitute the official what's-going-on. Such *non-floor-holding turns* can be seen in (13) with my question of clarification as Rafe describes a party to a bad situation, in (14) with Len's wisecrack as Rafe introduces a new topic, and in (15) with Sally's addition of a detail to Len's report on how to fund Young Author Days. (These are examples taken from single floor episodes.)

(13)

```
Rafe: and y'know Fran's just a very

      nice person and to her it is

      in terrible shape and      ┌──────────────────────────┐
                    ^_____ │ Carole: Fran's the blonde? │
Rafe: No, dark hair and uh, oh my god,  └──────────────────────┘

      it was just bad
```

(14)

```
Rafe: Uh y'know there's uh

      something that uh
```

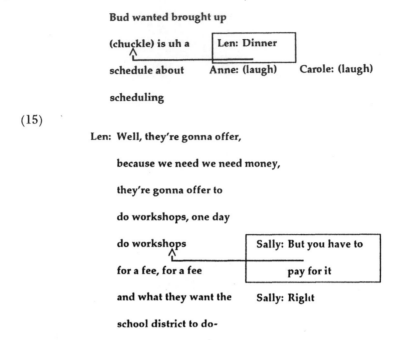

Bud wanted brought up

(chuckle) is uh a   Len: Dinner

schedule about   Anne: (laugh)   Carole: (laugh)

scheduling

(15)

Len: Well, they're gonna offer,

because we need we need money,

they're gonna offer to

do workshops, one day

do workshops   Sally: But you have to

for a fee, for a fee   pay for it

and what they want the   Sally: Right

school district to do-

In other words, it is possible to take a turn without having the floor.

It is also possible to have the floor while one is not talking. The clearest example of this from the present data is a case where what was going on was that Carole was making a report about students who needed help with writing. In the midst of the report she began to recount papers sorted into various categories. That her silence and counting did not change the official what's-going-on can be seen in example (16). Len and Sally took turns: that is, they made on-record comments addressed to the whole group, but they used low voices as a show of "respect" for the fact that Carole was still controling the floor even though she was not taking a turn. Moreover there were *long* silences when no one took a turn, when there was no rush to fill them, and when the silence was not heard as noticeably absent talk.

(16)

                                        Carole: ↓ (11.3 seconds while counting)
        Len: (low voice)
                Commit to memory
                if you will these
                elements of style.
                Read this XXX

                                        So out of twenty five
                                        there's eight in that
                                        group
                                        Sally: (whisper) Oh my gosh

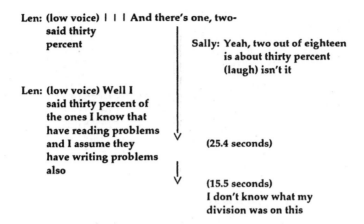

The floor happens within a psychological time and sometimes space. Turns that jointly build one floor can be separated in real time by another turn as Sally's is from Len's and Marion's in (17) around the start of the meeting.

(17)

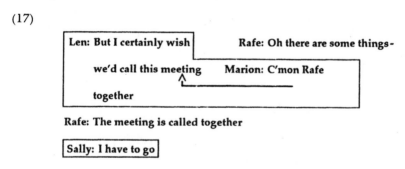

Here, Sally, Len, and Marion are heard as collaborating in producing what's going on: directing/prodding Rafe to hurry. There were instances that I believe exemplified the claim that a floor also occurs within a psychological space. At those times, the floor was being jointly produced, many turns were occurring at once, and, as I remember, the gazes of the turn takers were converging on a spot somewhere in the middle of the circular seating about a foot above the surface of the table. Unfortunately since there is no videotape record, I can supply nothing but this remembrance as evidence.

Turns occur among particular participants. So does what's going on. That means there is a possibility that, for more than an instant, nothing is going on for a given group—that there is no floor. In one case, (18), the original group temporarily dissolved in favor of the formation of different groupings in the midst of planning a retirement party for a department member. All the utterances were thus side comments in relation to the original set of people but turns in relation to the temporary smaller sets. A singly developed floor was accomplished among Mary, Sally, and Marion, but no floor was occurring in the total group of participants.

Marion: Maybe a dinner, a little

dinner I don't know

Mary: (to Sally) (low voice)	Bud: (to Rafe) (low voice)
I wonder if we should	well you know--
talk to Martha and see	
Sally: (to Mary) (low voice)	
Is that his wife?	
Marion: (to Sally) (low voice)	
Yeah	
Mary: (to Sally and Marion) (low voice)	
Shall I go call her?	

Rafe: Well let's see what

we'd like to do

Procedure for Analyzing the Data Objectively

Preparing the Data for Analysis

Once the research questions and the definitions were developed, the transcripts were divided into topical and/or functional episodes.[3] Conversational contributions were categorized as turns, side comments, or encouraging remarks.[4] The function(s) of each turn was then noted. Again I used my sense as a participant coupled with the perspective of an outside-reader-of-the-transcript to assign functions to contributions. That is, if it can be assumed that most talk conveys to intended recipients what the speaker wanted to get across (Goffman 1976), then as one of the recipients I should have been able to detect the functional intent (feeling tone, demand type, verbal activity) of a contribution as it was being made. As a check (perhaps at the time of the event and certainly as a later transcript reader and coder), I could wait to see how a "speaking" was responded to, getting help "quietly . . . from someone who [had] already read the situation for [me]" (Goffman 1976:179).[5] The functions thus identified were informing/

explaining; soliciting response; giving a positive or negative opinion, criticising, praising; reporting; arguing or disagreeing; joking/teasing; agreeing/validating; complying/acknowledging; warning/announcing; analyzing/interpreting; chiming in/hitching on; complaining; suggesting; summarizing; initiating a topic; offering; apologizing; using ritual politeness or greeting formulae.

At first an attempt was made to identify collaboratively constructed floors on an "objective" basis by circling only episodes which contained the same meaning units produced by two or more people, and later by circling only episodes which contained identical function notations produced by more than one speaker. Neither approach worked. Segments were circled that did not sound like collaborative floors and some were missed which sounded like clear collaborations. Ultimately, I used my subjective impression to isolate those episodes that sounded like either free-for-alls or two-or-more-on-the-same-wavelength. What remained were either singly produced floors or a very small number of uncategorized episodes which will be eliminated from further discussion.

Inducing the Variables

Following Glaser and Strauss (1967) and Bleiberg and Churchill (1975), I found the data had generated two major categories of floors. I selected prime exemplars of each and then attempted to induce/discover the elements or properties that distinguished them. That the presence of these elements would not be an artifact of the procedure for sorting the data into the two categories can be seen from the failure I had experienced earlier in trying to separate single from collaborative floors on the basis of more than one speaker's production of utterances with similar meanings or identical functions. Although I had thought they would, these hypothesized features clearly had not separated all collaborative floors from singly developed ones. (Another example of a lack of one-to-one correspondence between impression and actual production will be demonstrated in the section on results regarding sex differences. My feeling that women had participated more in collaborative floors than in single ones was not borne out by objective counts.)

As I relistened to the prime examples, I hypothesized a number of variables which might be characteristic of the two types of floors in varying proportions rather than in all-or-nothing terms. The variables were the following:

1. Quantity of participation (how long was each turn)
2. Frequency of participation (how many turns were taken in each type of floor episode)
3. Shared functions (how often did single or collaborative-floor episodes contain more than one turn used for identical functions)

4. Shared meaning units (how often did episodes contain messages which were very similar in content)
5. Shared function and shared meaning units (how often did episodes contain turns used for the same purpose and carrying the same message)
6. What percentage of similar messages were also shared in functions
7. Predominant functions depending on floor type
8. Amount of laughter (any laugh from one person on one occasion)
9. Number of "deep" overlaps over several phrases where each person continued without re-start-ups
10. Frequency of long, unfilled pauses (1.5+ seconds) within a turn
11. Frequency of long, unfilled pauses (1.5+ seconds) between turns
12. Instances of long pauses within a turn or a floor holding filled by a sotto voce turn of another person
13. Number of blocked or self-stopped utterances
14. Number of other nonturn utterances
15. Instances of use of the past tense (excluding modals since *might, could*, etc., are indicators of politeness as well as pastness)

Variables 1–12 were derived from attempts to articulate the base of my subjective impressions. Variables 13–15 were "logically" derived: that is, on the basis of the turn-allocation model of Sacks, Schegloff & Jefferson (1974) it seemed likely that in a one-at-a-time constructed floor, there would be more avoidance of potentially overlapping turns and thus more aborted utterances. When the speakership responsible for developing what's going on was more distributed, there might be fewer off-record asides and encouraging remarks from the sidelines since fewer would remain in the "gallery." With seemingly more solemn, orderly, and slower paced floors, there might be more monologues containing references to past events.

Data Analysis

Each meeting had a different character: One was more formal due to the presence of certain members; one seemed bizarre to almost everyone present (verified by postmeeting gossip); one was concerned almost totally with planning a party, and so on. It seemed unfaithful to the data to combine them and treat them as one set. Instead I analyzed the September meeting in its entirety and a different fifteen minutes of each of the remaining four meetings. In a few cases, however, for statistical reasons, data from all five meetings were combined.

Besides counting words, turns, functions, pauses, and so forth, I examined each episode, regardless of floor type, to see what began or preceded it. This included noting such elements as laughter; topic; functions; A (speaker knows about the event) versus B (addressee knows about the event) versus AB (both know about the event) events—extending Labov's

(1972) classification of who knows about the topic of *reported* events to who knows about any kind of topic; and first or second pair parts of adjacency pairs.

In addition to trying to describe features of the two kinds of floors in some numerical way to help answer an aspect of the first research question (are there objective ways of differentiating the subjectively perceived differences in floor type), I also analyzed the data in relation to quantity and language function according to sex of participant to answer the second research question (are there sex differences in language use depending on the type of floor that is occurring).

Counted Results

Differences Between the Two Types of Floors

Singly developed floors were far more prevalent than collaborative ones, whether one considers the amount of time devoted to them (from five to fourteen times the number of minutes) or the number of episodes so categorized (a total of 192 single floors and 96 collaborative ones). In most meetings, there were at least twice as many single floors, and each single-floor episode was considerably longer than most collaborative-floor episodes. Multiple analyses of variance (MANOVA) comparing floor type and sex of speaker showed that people took significantly (beyond the .01 level of probability) longer and fewer turns in singly developed than in collaboratively developed floors.

Rather than turns decreasing in size as a result of changing numbers of participants, as Sacks, Schegloff, and Jefferson (1974) posit (the same number of people were usually present for contiguous single and collaborative-floor episodes), they became shorter when the organization of the floor shifted. Episodes were longer when the floor was developed by single speakers in a sequence, then, not because more people took more turns but because people used single floors for holding forth. Related to this is the fact that reporting functions occurred during single but not collaborative floors. And related to the reporting function is the fact that past tense usage in single floors was two to three times what it was in collaborative ones. In other words, the induced variables are not totally discrete.

More turns in collaborative floor episodes contained the same meaning units, were used for the same functions, or were shared in both meaning units and functions. Example (17) earlier was an instance of shared function (prodding/directing Rafe) with different meaning units (Len's *wish we'd call this meeting together,* Marion's *c'mon Rafe,* and Sally's *I have to go*). Example (19) shows Rafe and Marion producing similar meaning units but with different functional intent (in the discussion about what to do about students' writing problems someone has suggested a need to also consider handwriting, Marion is arguing that that is out of the question; Rafe is both agreeing with and teasing her).

(19)

> Marion: Mm no, there's nothing
>
> you can do about people's
>
> cursive at this point.
>
> Y'can teach them
>
> manuscript, OK, but   Rafe: OK, the manuscript
>
> no one's going to   Maybe. Yeah. The
>
> change anybody's   cursive is over?
>
> cursive.   No chance for cursive

Episodes containing turns conveying the same meaning and the same function message are shown in examples (20) (where three people answer a question with the same simultaneously supplied answer) and (21) (where Marion and Rafe tease Carole as she admits ignorance of a friend's whereabouts).

(20)

> Jon: Which word are you talking about?

| Marion: Individualize] [Rafe: Individualize] [Carole: Individualize |

> Jon: Oh

(21)

> Len: Isn't that   ] [Carole: I don't know. I
>
> awful?   don't see him
>
> I don't know (laugh)   Marion: Oh, it's
>
> called
>
> off
>
> Rafe: Oh my god,   (laugh)
>
> it's called off   Marion: Yeah

In collaborative floors, from 22% to 38% of the turns shared the same meaning units, while fewer than 15% of the turns in single-floor episodes were alike in this way. There was less of a gap between the floor types regarding turns that were used for the same function (in one meeting, 60% of collaborative-floor turns shared functions while 53% of single-floor turns did). Listening to several people in succession informing or analyzing or reporting was not so likely, then, to result in the impression that these people were collaborating on developing what was going on. Hearing several contribute the same ideas was more likely to produce that impression. An even more likely source for a subjectively perceived collaborative floor were turns that shared ideas *and* functions. Such turns occurred five to ten times as often in collaborative-floor episodes.

There was a different "functional feel" to the two floor types. When actually counted, certain functions predominated in single floors but not collaborative ones (reporting, soliciting response, and validating/agreeing) or collaborative floors but not single ones (joking, hitching on/chiming in). Managing the agenda (reporting on items, seeking opinions and information, etc.) was the predominant (but not sole) activity when single floors were occurring. Time-outs from the agenda more often (but not always) coincided with collaborative floors. It is reasonable, then, that the distribution of functions was as it was. However, it is important to note that this is not simply the difference between meeting talk and conversations. There were collaborative floors that concerned and constituted the agenda, were not time-outs, and should be considered part of the meeting proper (see examples [8] and [9]); there were also single floors during conversations that occurred as pre-meeting talk.

My impression that collaborative floors were marked by more laughter must have been related to the greater amount of joking/teasing/wisecracking functions since there was a near equivalence of instances of laughter in the two floor types in most meetings.

The perception of more pauses in single-floor episodes and more instances where a non-floor-holding turn was delivered in a low voice out of respect for the single-floor holder who was not currently speaking was validated.

More nonturn utterances, side comments and encouragers, occurred in single floors. In fact, in some meetings, none of these occurred in collaborative ones. Regarding side comments, when the topic was being attended to by at least two people in a singly developed floor (a speaker and a listener), others were more free to do something else. In collaborative floors, the participation was so widely distributed that there was hardly anyone left to make a side comment to. As for encouraging remarks when many were developing an idea, an activity which could occupy everyone and which intrinsically displayed understanding/I'm-with-you/appreciation, what need would there be for additional encouragement?

Deep overlaps, a source of the impression of a free-for-all character to some collaborative floors, did occur more often in collaborative-floor episodes. By definition deeply overlapping turns did not contain stops and restarts; they were continuous, fluent contributions. That these occurred from four to sixteen times as often in collaborative floors as in single ones is evidence for the lack of concern for interruption in collaborative floors. Perhaps, as Reisman (1974) proposed for contrapuntal conversations in Antigua, people could rely on the repetition and redundancy (indicated by sharedness of meaning units/functions) of these overlapping messages to help in their processing.

The reasoning behind the guess that singly developed floors would contain more blocked or self-stopped utterances that never even developed into turns may not have been faulty but neither did it lead to an accurate prediction. As with laughter, the floors did not seem to be differentiated on the basis of aborted utterances. Self-stopped contributions, however, are intriguing phenomena in themselves. Some were cut off (interrupted) by other speakers. Many, though, were begun once another's turn was under way, were apparently stopped by their initiators, and might be considered unsuccessful interruptions. A label related to interruptions does not capture their complexity, however. Content, floor type, speaker's degree of involvement in the event, and speaker's role may all be related to self-stopped utterances.

In singly developed floors self-stops often seemed to be the beginning of an idea that did not mesh well with the ongoing message. Sometimes these may have been preludes to new topics (*OK, now what about* _____); at other times they were incipient rebuttals (*but* _____). In collaborative floors, they seemed more likely to be the beginning of an addition than a new direction (*sure, it's* _____). In both floor types some could have been actual demonstrations of the message "speaker-is-aghast" (*that's such a* _____*! what a* _____*!*), where the incomplete utterance might make a stronger statement about the speaker's feelings about the content than a complete one would.

A speaker's perception of the content match between his/her utterance and the current flow (being in or out of "synch") as the source of many aborted contributions is still not the whole story. Another factor is the perception of what kind of floor is occurring and what kind the speaker needs. If one is about to rebut or initiate a new topic, one needs lone floor space. An overlap might not have the desired impact. A self-stop (or a series of them, as often happened) could then be a signal that one is reserving a spot to develop an idea alone. If, however, one's idea is already being expressed (in a collaborative floor) and all a speaker has to offer is an addition, s/he can allow another to complete the message, can either overlap or stop without fearing that the contribution will go unheard. Thus, the meaning of the collaborative-floor self-stop may be quite different from that of the single-floor self-stop.

A consideration of both content and floor organization is still insufficient to account for all the factors behind an aborted utterance. There seems to have been a relationship between self-stops and deep overlaps, almost as though these were two sides of the same coin. Those who self-stopped most often (Len, Rafe, and Carole) also took part in most of the deep overlaps. Additionally they were among the most frequent turn takers. It is possible, then, that a high degree of involvement in each step of the progression of a speech event results in many signals for entrance to a single floor, many contributions that others can finish in a collaborative floor, and also many full, yet overlapped, contributions in the latter. (I am unable to explain why speakers would stop themselves on one single-floor occasion, yet deliver the full message on another.)

Content, floor organization, and a desire to be in on all the action still do not totally explain self-stopped contributions. Rafe, the chairperson, stopped himself in collaborative floors as often as he did in single ones, even if he began his speaking first. Perhaps, in his role as chair, he saw himself as being responsible for ensuring wide participation. When someone else would start, then as a "good chair/host," he could relax, stop himself, and clear the way for that person.

When looking for what began the collaborative-floor episodes, I found very few answers. They did not especially start with laughter or pauses or any particular function. Although there were more AB "events," topics several participants knew about, at the opening of collaborative- than single-floor episodes, this kind of topic was also present for many opening turns in single-floor episodes. It was apparently not the case, then, that when people spotted a topic they knew about, they always jumped in. The one consistent finding in relation to counted instances of a variable was that second pair parts of adjacency pairs (primarily, answers in question/answer sequences) were more often the openers of collaborative episodes. Apparently a question, for example, often appeared legitimately answerable by many at once. Second pair parts, however, accounted for only 19–44%, not 100%, of the opening turns in collaborative episodes. Most likely some combination of verbal and nonverbal signals invited a cooperatively developed floor. Videotapes might help give insight into what starts such floors. A topical analysis might also help. For instance, sex was mentioned once and obscenities were uttered twice in the five portions of analyzed transcriptions. All three cases were followed by collaborative floors. Obviously that still does not account for the other 93 collaborative episodes that grew out of other topics. There seemed to be no pattern, in these audiotaped data, to account for what occurred at the very beginning of or just before these episodes.

Gender Differences

What is immediately striking about some of the variables counted by gender as well as by floor is the shift that the men made in terms of sheer quantity. My impression during transcribing had been that women participated more in collaborative floors than they did in single ones and more than men did. Actually, it was men who participated less. The MANOVA referred to earlier not only dealt with the difference in words per turn and turns per minute depending on the type of floor being constructed; it also related these factors to speaker sex. In singly developed floors, the men held forth, took longer turns though not more of them—dominated the construction of the floor by virtue, at least, of the time they took talking. In collaborative floors, men talked less than they did in single ones and occasionally even less than the women in collaborative floors, a rare finding given the usual one of men as the "big talkers" (Edelsky 1978).

More specifically in all meetings men's turns were one and one fourth to nearly four times longer than women's in single-floor episodes (e.g., in the November meeting, 32.87 words per turn for men and 8.58 for women). By contrast, collaborative-floor episode turns for both women and men averaged about 6.5 words. Here is evidence then, given my admission that I perceived women talking more in collaborative than single floors and more than men in collaborative floors, for Kramer's (1975) proposal that perhaps our subjective impression of a talkative woman is simply one who talks as much as the average man. In any case, collaborative-floor episodes appeared to be quantity equalizers.

Not only was sheer quantity equalized, but so was the use of certain language functions usually associated with the "male domain," such as joking (Coser 1960). Collaborative floors found women joking, arguing, directing, and soliciting responses more and men less, while the reverse was true for single ones. Thus, not only was there a different functional "feel" to the two floor types, but women and men each had a somewhat different "style" and were differentially responsible for the "feel" of episodes depending on floor type.

Of course, it was always people, in roles, who produced whatever data were counted (turns, floors, functions, etc.). The chair, a male, was the leading user of the soliciting response function but only in singly developed floors. In collaborative ones, talk to solicit responses was uttered primarily by women. That women took the role of questioners (reactors, conversational ball carriers, etc.) is hardly a new finding and not one that is particularly an indicator of either control or equality. That the phenomenon of woman as questioner varies with the organization of talk, however, is new information. In these meetings, single-floor solicitations of responses seemed connected more to planning and clarifying points of information than to showing interest in another's topic as they were in Fishman's (1978) data. Response solicitations of this type in single-floor episodes were made more often by Rafe, the chair. Response solicitations in collaboration-floor episodes too were connected to plans, but they were also often combined with teases, word playing, arguing; often uttered in tandem; and often produced by women.

What seemed to happen, then, was that when what's-going-on was collaboratively constructed (as were many personal stories in women's rap groups studied by Kalčik 1975) and characterized by either a "happy babble of disorganized sound" (Goffman 1967:40) or a demonstration of being on the same wavelength, women and men interacted more as equals on many dimensions. A possible explanation for women's having outstripped men in the increase of certain language functions in collaborative floors (joking, arguing, suggesting, soliciting responses, validating, directing) and thus being more proactive and on center stage in collaborative floors and reactive and on the sidelines in single ones can be found in Brown and Levinson's (1978) work. They propose that people, and therefore women, are "rational" beings, choosing from their repertoires those strategies that best serve their interests. Singly developed floors, characterized by monologues, single party control, and hierarchical interaction where turn takers stand out from non–turn takers and floors are won or lost, share features with other contexts in which women have learned they had best not assert themselves. Collaborative floors, however, are inherently more informal, cooperative ventures which provided both a cover of "anonymity" for assertive language use and a comfortable backdrop against which women can display a fuller range of language ability.

The same general explanation, with different details, could have accounted for the men's decrease in quantity and thus dominance over the talking time in collaborative floors. Men too are "rational" beings and, like women, are able to respond to and accomplish moment-to-moment shifts in interaction to suit their purposes. If participation in collaborative floors does in fact provide the high levels of communicative satisfaction (interest, a sense of "we"-ness, excitement, fun, etc.) they appeared to engender, it would seem that people would be desirous of being a part of such activity. What men would get out of collaborative floors, then, would not be the joint benefits of both a forum for fuller expression of their functional talents as well as an opportunity for experiencing high involvement, synergistic, solidarity-building interaction. Rather it would be the single benefit mentioned last. A signal that such a conversational structure was available, then, would be an offer hardly anyone could refuse.

Conclusions

Previously it would have seemed that the appropriate general question about gender and language was, How do women and men carry out their socially designated and differentiated power positions as they carry on oral discourse? That is, do the sexes negotiate interactional space and time as equals, and if not, what differences obtain? On the basis of this study's giant detour to analyze the floor, that question now seems too simple. A better one is, *Under what conditions* do men and women interact (e.g., hold the floor) more or less as equals and under what conditions do they not?

As was stated at the beginning, the unpremeditated detour consisted of an investigation into "the floor" that was initial and exploratory. As such, it has been necessarily global and has certainly generated many new questions. Most obviously, does the definition of "floor" fit other speech events and other data?

The definition that was developed here has been implicitly proposed as applicable to a variety of speech events. That is, while the types of floors identified and their proportionate use may be peculiar to these informal meetings, the definition itself of "floor" should apply to floors in conversations, formal meetings, debates, informal meetings, classroom discussions, group therapy sessions, and so on. One problem (mentioned earlier in the section *One-at-a-time*) with many "conversational" analyses is that they have often drawn their data from events that are not strictly conversations[6]: experimental sessions, service encounters, therapy sessions, classroom lessons, and so forth. Characteristics of these nonconversations are then generalized to conversations as well as a range of speech events. The present study would be subject to the same criticism if it claimed that *holding* the floor at a formal debate, an informal meeting, a lunch date, and so on, entailed the same privileges; that the different *ways floors were developed* in informal meetings are the same ways they are developed in anything from coffee klatches to seminars. Instead, the proposal here is that *what is had* when having the floor (but *not* how one gets it or what one does with it or what consequences follow from having it or what it means to have it) is a constant.

A question for future research is, Does it?

Another obvious question is whether the two ways of developing the floor in these data appear with different numbers, gendered combinations, statuses, and so on, of participants in different speech events; that is, the study cries out for both replication and replication with variation.

Additionally, what other contextual factors besides floor structure contribute to interpretations of what counts as a turn, an interruption, and so on? For instance, the particular interactional histories of specific participants may be such a factor. In the present study one participant was somewhat bitter about personal consequences of past events in the department. Other participants "bent over backward" to show that person respect and lift the person's spirits. Consequently this member's side comments, regardless of their content or the low voice with which they were delivered, were responded to as though they had been on-record; they were treated as turns.

Other questions include: What are the cues and mechanisms which invite a collaboratively developed floor? What are the speaker-change signals, turn-allocation devices, and oriented-to features that accompany them? Are there different turn-tying and cohesion strategies in collaborative floors (and, if so, do these require a reexamination of conversational maxims or postulates)? Is there a difference in communicative satisfaction in or attitudes toward the floor types? Is there a relationship between types and content of contributions (aborted utterances, moves of various kinds, etc.) and floor type?

Regardless of the answers, it is clear that the floor might be taken as a worthwhile object of research.

NOTES

I wish to thank Cheris Kramarae for her encouragement and help during the project and Terri Rosegrant, Sarah Hudelson, Vera John-Steiner, Betty Lou DuBois, Keith Walters, and Erving Goffman for their comments on an earlier draft.

Special appreciation goes to my colleagues for their willingness to be taped while being themselves. This chapter originally appeared in *Language in Society* 10 (1981):383–421. An earlier version of one part of this study, "How to Have the Floor: Two General Ways," appears in C. Edelsky (Ed.) *Conversational Analysis: New Perspectives*, 1981, a special issue of the *Journal of the Linguistic Association of the Southwest*.

1. Presentation of more than one speaker's talk on the same line indicates the start of simultaneous talk. Brackets indicate simultaneous starts; arrows are used for overlaps beginning unevenly. Double-direction arrows show where the floor holder's talk was overlapped by talk directed to the general topic or the group at large; single-direction arrows show someone being both overlapped and addressed directly. Since by this time I was interested in the start of overlapping turns but not in the synchrony of talk, I made no attempt to indicate the end of simultaneity in talk.

2. In child language research, had frequency been the criteria for study of a phenomenon, simplification rather than rule overgeneralization would have been the focus of attempts to explain the process of language acquisition (Hakuta & Cancino 1977).

3. "Episode" is not a precise term. It is unrelated to the episodes of Esau and Bristol-Poth (1981), conversational chunks characterized by within-chunk states of tension and resolution. It is somewhat related to Gumperz and Cook-Gumperz's notion of "speech activity" (cited by Shultz, Florio & Erickson 1982), a unit of discourse that may consist of one or more connected topics and an action, such as "chatting about the weather," "trying to get someone's attention," or "lecturing about linguistics." Just as the speech activity idea does not use a single standard to decide on the size of activities (embedded within lecturing about linguistics, there might also be the activity of trying to get someone's attention), neither did I make episode-dividing decisions in a way that would ensure that all episodes were at the same level of generality. I was aware of the problem during data analysis but am still unable to resolve it.

4. I made no attempt to examine moves within or across turns directly, even though *move* as a unit is probably more basic than *turn* for considerations of the sequencing and cohesiveness of interactions (Goffman 1976). In this study, however, I was interested in types of "speakings" or contributions and their "legitimacy," rather than the sequence of contributions and their cohesion. I was especially interested in sorting out *turn* from *floor* (I have never seen *move* and *floor* conflated in the literature).

Since one turn can contain two moves and thus be perceived as two back-to-back turns for the same speaker just as two contributions by different people can constitute one move and be perceived as one jointly built turn, it is clear that the turn count for this study would not be identical with one that takes account of moves. Multiple moves within turns were implicitly acknowledged when functions were noted. That is, a contribution which responded to another's query and then asked a new question was coded as accomplishing both informing and soliciting response functions. However, one contribution could also be a vehicle for several functions that were not separate moves, for example, complaining in a teasing mode was coded as both complaining and teasing. The instances of all functions together thus exceeds slightly the number of all turns taken (e.g., in one fifteen-minute segment, there were a total of 234 turns taken and 268 functions noted) and probably exceeds the numbers of moves made. If future work should emphasize the "move"-ment of interaction as it relates to ways of having the floor, it would do well to incorporate notions of *move* as well as *turn*.

5. Most likely, to identify the function(s) of turns, both as participant and as analyzer, I tacitly used my knowledge of the structure of the utterance, paralanguage, my history with the speakers, and general pragmatics (van Dijk 1977).

6. Since the exact nature of "conversations" was not the focus of this study, and since previous research either collapses a variety of speech events under the umbrella term "conversation" or differentiates these only according to a turn-allocation system (Sacks et al. 1974), any definition I could propose would be premature.

REFERENCES

Aleguire, David (1978). Interruptions as turn-taking. Paper presented at Ninth World Congress of Sociology, Uppsala, Sweden.

Atkinson, M. A., Cuff, E. C. & Lee, R. E. (1978). The recommencement of a meeting as a member's accomplishment. In Jim Schenkein (Ed.) *Studies in the organization of conversational interaction* (pp. 133–153). New York: Academic Press.

Bleiberg, Susanne & Churchill, Lindsey (1975). Notes on confrontation in conversation. *Journal of Psycholinguistic Research* 4(3):273–378.

Blumer, Herbert (1969). *Symbolic interactionism: Perspective and method.* Englewood Cliffs, NJ: Prentice-Hall.

Brown, Penelope & Levinson, Stephen (1978). Universals in language usage: Politeness phenomena. In Esther Goody (Ed.) *Questions and politeness: Strategies in social interaction.* Cambridge: Cambridge University Press.

Burke, J. (1979). Interruptions and overlap. Department of Speech Communication, University of Illinois, Urbana. Unpublished manuscript.

Cicourel, Aaron (1980). Three models of discourse analysis: The role of social structure. *Discourse Processes* 3.101–132.

Coser, Rose (1960). Laughter among colleagues. *Psychiatry* 23:81–95.

Dubois, Betty Lou & Crouch, Isabel (1976). *Proceedings of the conference on the sociology of the languages of American women.* San Antonio, TX: Trinity University.

Duncan, Starkey (1972). Some signals and rules for taking speaking turns in conversations. *Journal of Personality and Social Psychology* 23(2):283–293.

Duncan, Starkey (1973). Toward a grammar for dyadic conversation. *Semiotica* 9:29–46.

Duncan, Starkey, Jr., & Niederehe, George (1974). On signalling that it's your turn to speak. *Journal of Experimental Social Psychology,* 10:234–247.

Eakins, Barbara & Eakins, Gene (1978). *Sex differences in human communication.* Boston: Houghton Mifflin.

Edelsky, Carole (1978). *Genderlects: A brief review of the literature.* ERIC Document Reproduction Service no. ED 165187.

Erickson, Frederick (1977). Some approaches to inquiry in school-community ethnography. *Anthropology and Education Quarterly* 8(2):58–69.

Esau, Helmut & Bristol-Poth, Annette (1981). Contextual constraints on conversational turn-taking. In Carole Edelsky (Ed.) *Conversational analysis: New perspectives.* Special issue of *Journal of the Linguistic Association of the Southwest* 4:1.45–55

Fishman, Pamela (1978). Interaction: The work women do. *Social Problems* 24:397–406.

Garfinkel, Harold (1972). Remarks on ethnomethodology. In John J. Gumperz & Dell Hymes (Eds.) *Directions in sociolinguistics.* New York: Holt Rinehart & Winston. Rpt. Oxford: Basil Blackwell.

Glaser, Barney & Strauss, Anselm (1967). *The discovery of grounded theory: Strategies for qualitative research.* New York: Aldine.

Goffman, Erving (1967). *Interaction ritual: Essays on face-to-face behavior.* Garden City, NY: Anchor Books.

Goffman, Erving (1971). *Relations in public.* New York: Harper & Row.

Goffman, Erving (1976). Replies and responses. *Language in Society* 5(3):257–311.

Goffman, Erving (1981). *Forms of talk.* Philadelphia: University of Pennsylvania Press.

Goodwin, Charles (1980). Review of Starkey Duncan and Donald Fiske, *Face to face interaction: Research, methods, and theory. Language in Society* 8(3):439–444.

Goody, Esther (1978). Towards a theory of questions. In Esther Goody (Ed.) *Questions and politeness: Strategies in social interaction*(pp. 17–43). Cambridge: Cambridge University Press.

Hakuta, Kenji & Cancino, Herlinda (1977). Trends in second language acquisition research. *Harvard Educational Review* 47(3):294–316.

Hymes, Dell (1977). Qualitative/quantitative research methodologies in education: A linguistic perspective. *Anthropology and Education Quarterly* 8(2): 165–176.

Jefferson, Gail (1972). Side sequences. In David Sudnow (Ed.) *Studies in social interaction* (pp. 294–338) New York: The Free Press.

Jefferson, Gail (1973). A case of precision timing in ordinary conversation: Overlapped tag-positioned address terms in closing sequences. *Semiotica* 9:47–96.

Jefferson, Gail & Schenkein, Jim (1978). Some sequential negotiations in conversation. In Jim Schenkein (Ed.) *Studies in the organization of conversational interaction.* New York: Academic Press.

Kalčik, Susan (1975). ". . . like Ann's gynecologist or the time I was almost raped": Personal narratives in women's rap groups. *Journal of American Folklore,* 88:3–11.

Kendon, Adam (1967). Some functions of gaze-direction in social interaction. *Acta Psychologica* 26:22–63.

Kramer, Cheris (1975). Women's speech: Separate but unequal? In Barrie Thorne & Nancy Henley (Eds.), *Language and sex: Difference and dominance.* Rowley, MA: Newbury House.

Kramer, Cheris, Thorne, Barrie, & Henley, Nancy (1978). Perspectives on language and communication. *Signs: Journal of Women in Culture and Society* 3(3):638–651.

Labov, William (1972). Rules for ritual insults. In David Sudnow (Ed.), *Studies in social interaction* (pp. 120–169). New York: Macmillan.

McConnell-Ginet, Sally, Furman, Nelly, & Borker, Ruth (1980). *Women and language in literature and society.* New York: Praeger.

McHoul, Alexander (1978). The organization of turns at formal talk in the classroom. *Language in Society* 7:183–213.

Mehan, Hugh (1974). Accomplishing classroom lessons. In Aaron V. Cicourel,

Kenneth H. Jennings, Sybillyn H. M. Jennings, Kenneth C. W. Leiter, Robert MacKay, Hugh Mehan, David R. Roth, *Language use and school performance,* (pp. 76–142). New York: Academic Press.

Mehan, Hugh (1978). Structuring school structure. *Harvard Educational Review* 48(1):32–64.

Meltzer, Leo, Morris, William N. & Hayes, Donald P. (1971). Interruption outcomes and vocal amplitude: Explorations in social psychophysics. *Journal of Personality and Social Psychology* 18(3):392–402.

Nichols, Patricia (1978). Dynamic variation as a model for the study of language and sex. Paper presented at Ninth World Congress of Sociology, Uppsala, Sweden.

Ochs, Elinor (1979). Transcription as theory. In Elinor Ochs and Bambi B. Schieffelin (Eds.) *Developmental pragmatics.* New York: Academic Press.

O'Keefe, B., Delia, J. & O'Keefe, D. (1980). Interaction analysis and the analysis of interactional organization. In Norman K. Denzin (Ed.) *Studies in symbolic interaction, III.* New York: Johnson Associates.

Philips, Susan (1976). Some sources of cultural variability in the regulation of talk. *Language in Society* 5:81–95.

Philips, Susan (1983). "Getting the floor" in the classroom. In *The invisible culture: Communication in classroom and community on the Warm Springs Indian Reservation.* White Plains, NY: Longman. Rpt. Prospect Heights, IL: Waveland Press.

Reisman, Karl (1974). Contrapuntal conversations in an Antiguan village. In Richard Bauman & Joel Sherzer (Eds.) *Explorations in the ethnography of speaking* (pp. 110–124). Cambridge: Cambridge University Press.

Sacks, Harvey, Schegloff, Emanuel & Jefferson, Gail (1974). A simplest systematics for the organization of turn-taking for conversation. *Language* 50:696–735.

Schegloff, Emanuel (1972a). Notes on a conversational practice: Formulating place. In Pier Paolo Giglioli (Ed.) *Language and social context* Baltimore: Penguin Books.

Schegloff, Emanuel (1972b). Sequencing in converstional openings. In John J. Gumperz & Dell Hymes (Eds.) *Directions in sociolinguistics.* New York: Holt, Rinehart & Winston.

Schegloff, Emanuel & Sacks, Harvey (1973). Opening up closings. *Semiotica* 8:283–327.

Schenkein, Jim (Ed.) (1978). *Studies in the organization of conversational interaction.* New York: Academic Press.

Shapiro, D. (1976). Conversational structures and accurate empathy: An exploratory study. *British Journal of Social and Clinical Psychology* 15:213–215.

Shultz, Jeffrey, Florio, Susan, & Erickson, Frederick (1982). Where's the floor?: Aspects of the cultural organization of social relationships in communication at home and at school. In Perry Gilmore & Alan Glatthorn (Eds.) *Children in and out of school: Ethnography and education* (pp. 88–123) Washington DC: Center for Applied Linguistics.

Soskin, William & John, Vera P. (1963). The study of spontaneous talk. In Roger Barker (Ed.) *The stream of behavior* (pp. 228–281). New York: Appleton-Century-Crofts.

Speier, Matthew (1972). Some conversational problems for interactional analysis. In David Sudnow (Ed.) *Studies in social interaction* (pp. 297–427). New York: The Free Press.

Spelke, Elizabeth, Hirst, William, & Neisser, Ulric (1976). Skills of divided attention. *Cognition* 4:215–230.

Stephan, Frederick F. & Mishler, Elliot G. (1952). The distribution of participation in small groups: An exponential approximation. *American Sociological Review* 17:598–608.

Stokes, Randall, & Hewitt, John P. (1976). Aligning actions. *American Sociological Review* 41:838–849.

Thorne, Barrie & Henley, Nancy (1975). *Language and sex: Difference and dominance.* Rowley, MA: Newbury House.

Turner, Roy (1972). Some formal properties of therapy talk. In David Sudnow (Ed.) *Studies in social interaction.* New York: Macmillan.

van Dijk, Teun (1977). Context and cognition: Knowledge frames and speech act comprehension. *Journal of Pragmatics* 1:211–232.

Webster's Third New International Dictionary of the English Language, Unabridged. (1971). Springfield, MA: G & C Merriam Company.

West, Candace (1977). Against our will: Male interruptions of females in cross-sex conversations. In Judith Orasanu, Mariam K. Slater & Leonore Loeb Adler (Eds.) *Language, sex, and gender.* Annals of the New York Academy of Sciences, vol. 327:81–97.

Yngve, Victor (1970). On getting a word in edgewise. *Papers from the Sixth Regional Meeting of the Chicago Linguistic Society*, pp. 567–578.

IV
CRITICAL
REVIEWS OF
THE LITERATURE

9

Women, Men, and Interruptions:
A Critical Review

DEBORAH JAMES
and
SANDRA CLARKE

Overview of Research Results: Questions in Need of Answers

Within the language and gender literature one of the findings most widely cited as well established is that men interrupt women more than women interrupt men. For example, Rosenblum (1986:160) states that "men are more likely to interrupt and overlap women's speech than the reverse." Aries (1987:152) observes that "men have frequently been found to interrupt women more than women interrupt men." And Holmes (1991:210) concludes that "the balance of evidence [seems] to confirm the view that men interrupt others more often than women do, and that, more specifically, men interrupt women more than women interrupt men."

This chapter will show that a review of studies appearing between 1965 and 1991 and dealing with gender differences in the use of interruptions does not support this conclusion; most research has found no significant difference between the genders in number of interruptions initiated, in either cross-sex or same-sex interaction. It will be argued that this result is unsurprising, given the multifunctional nature of simultaneous talk. The question then arises of whether women and men differ in the functions for which they use simultaneous talk. Potential ways of determining whether men use simultaneous talk as a means of dominating interactions to a greater extent than do women are surveyed; it is shown that the research to date provides no firm evidence for such a gender difference when any such criterion is taken into account. However, since no criterion approaches being a fully adequate measure of whether an instance of simultaneous talk constitutes a dominance attempt, it cannot be definitively concluded that no gender differences exist in this respect. Some evidence is then provided that women are more likely than men to use simultaneous talk to show involvement and rapport, a fact that would be consistent with other findings in the literature on gender differences in conversational behavior. Finally, the potential effects of various subject and situational variables on women's and men's use of simultaneous talk are discussed; it is noted that existing research provides comparatively little information with respect to these. Further, a number of methodological problems are noted which may have led to misleading results, and to which future researchers should be alert.

The research on interruptions deals, broadly speaking, with instances in which one person initiates talk while another person is already talking. Most researchers in the area of language and gender, in the area of family interaction, and in the psychological literature in general have assumed that the basic function of such behavior is to prevent the first speaker from being able to finish what he or she wants to say, and to allow the second speaker to take over the floor. Mishler and Waxler (1968:140), for example, state that "a person-control strategy such as an interruption [says] 'Stop talking' or 'I am no longer listening to what you say.'" Interruption is interpreted as violating normal conversational rules, as being negative or undesirable behavior, and as constituting an attempt to exercise power and to dominate and control the interaction through control of the floor and of the topic of conversation. Thus, for example, West (1984:55) states that "an interrupting speaker is engaged in violation of the current speaker's right to be engaged in speaking"; Octigan and Niederman (1979:52) observe, "An interruption or overlap is taken as a violation and a sign of conversational dominance." Given this assumption, the commonly cited finding that males interrupt females more than the reverse has been seen as unsurprising, since males have more power and status than females. Males are therefore likely, it has been supposed, to presume that they have a right to take the floor from females, whereas females will not make the same assumption with respect to males. Perhaps, too, because of their higher status, males are assumed by both sexes to be more likely to be right about things than are females, so that it would be seen by both sexes as more legitimate for males to interrupt females than the reverse (this would be the prediction of status characteristics theory—Berger, Rosenholtz, and Zelditch [1980], and see James and Drakich [this volume]—an approach which takes into account how status differences can affect expectations and beliefs about oneself and others).

An alternative theoretical approach to accounting for gender differences in verbal behavior posits that females and males, because of their differing socialization in sex-separate peer groups, come to have different interactional goals and to use different verbal strategies to attain those goals (e.g., Maltz and Borker 1982, Tannen 1990). This approach, too, would predict that males would interrupt more (assuming the preceding interpretation of the role of interruptions to be correct), since males learn that an important goal for them is to assert their status, to appear a leader, to "win"; frequently seizing and holding the floor provides a means of achieving this goal. Females, on the other hand, appear to learn to focus instead on establishing and maintaining harmonious relationships with others; this would militate against their violating conversational rules by interrupting others.

Contrary to these predictions, a review of the studies which have examined the use of interruptions in mixed-sex interaction (whether dyadic or group) reveals that it is not, in fact, the case that most have found men to interrupt women more than the reverse. Indeed, the majority of studies have found no difference between the sexes in this respect. The findings of these studies are summarized in Table 9.1.[1] We consider here only the results in terms of the relative number of interruptions initiated (one complication being that different studies have used different measures of interruption; this point will be discussed shortly). Of twenty-one studies which have compared the number of interruptions initiated by females and by males in dyadic interaction, only six, or fewer than a third, have found men to interrupt women more than the reverse. Thirteen studies have found no significant difference between the sexes in total number of interruptions, and two have found women to interrupt men more. In addition, twelve studies have examined interruptions in groups of more than two. Of these, five have found men to initiate more interruptions overall; four have found no significant difference between the genders in this respect; and three have found women to initiate more interruptions. Of course, to determine whether males interrupt females more than the reverse, one must also, for group studies, factor in the sex of the person interrupted (since, for example, a finding of men's interrupting more overall could conceivably result from their interrupting other men with particular frequency; there might be no significant difference in quantity between men's interruptions of women and women's interruptions of men). Only seven of the studies of groups have done this systematically. In all but one of these cases, the results have correlated with the findings with respect to who interrupted more overall; for example, if the study found men to interrupt more than women overall, it also found men to interrupt women more than the reverse. (The one exception is Kennedy and Camden [1983], in which women were found to interrupt others more than men overall, but women and men were found to interrupt each other to an equal extent.) Studies of groups which took into account the sex of the person interrupted are indicated by an asterisk in Table 9.1.[2]

These studies—along with those to be presented in Table 9.2—have most frequently employed as subjects unacquainted college students; the great majority of studies of dyads have been set in an experimental laboratory, while most of those examining groups have dealt with naturally

Table 9.1 The Relationship Between Gender and Number of Interruptions
Initiated in Mixed-Sex Interaction
(A = studies of dyads; B = studies of groups)

A (1) Studies Which Found No Significant Difference Between the Genders in Number of Interruptions
Bilous & Krauss 1988
Dindia 1987
Duncan & Fiske 1977
Frances 1979
Jose, Crosby, & Wong-McCarthy 1988
Kollock, Blumstein, & Schwartz 1985
Leet-Pellegrini 1980
Leffler, Gillespie, & Conaty 1982
Marche 1988
Martin & Craig 1983
Roger & Nesshoever 1987
Simkins-Bullock & Wildman 1991
Welkowitz, Bond, & Feldstein 1984

(2) Studies Which Found Males to Interrupt Females Significantly More Than the Reverse[3]
Bohn & Stutman 1983
Esposito 1979
Octigan & Niederman 1979
Peterson 1986
West 1979, West 1982, West & Zimmerman 1983 (all three describe the same study)
Zimmerman & West 1975

(3) Studies Which Found Females to Interrupt Males Significantly More Than the Reverse
Sayers 1987
Shaw & Sadler 1965

B (1) Studies Which Found No Significant Difference Between the Genders in Total Number of Interruptions
Beattie 1981*
Smith-Lovin & Brody 1989*[4]
Willis & Williams 1976
Woods 1989

(2) Studies Which Found Males to Interrupt Significantly More Than Females Overall
Brooks 1982
Case 1988
Craig & Pitts 1990*
    (significantly more successful[5] interruptions of students by male rather than female tutors; more successful interruptions of female students by male students than the reverse; no statistics provided for relative overall number of [successful] interruptions produced by male and female students)

(continued)

Table 9.1   (*Continued*)

Eakins & Eakins 1976
McMillan, Clifton, McGrath, & Gale 1977

(3) Studies Which Found Females to Interrupt Significantly More Than Males Overall
Connor-Linton 1987*
Kennedy & Camden 1983*
Murray & Covelli 1988*[6]

occurring interaction. Virtually all of these studies have been conducted in the United States or Britain. (For a discussion of the possible relevance of such variables, see pp. 260–265.)

Also of interest here is the question of whether males differ from females in interruption behavior when same-sex interaction is compared. If the major determinant of interruptive behavior is simply having more status or power than others with whom one is interacting, there is indeed no reason to expect differences between all-male and all-female interaction with respect to number of interruptions. If, on the other hand, learned differences in goals and verbal strategies are an important determinant, and if asserting a leadership role by taking the floor is an important strategy for males but not for females, then one would expect there to be more interruptions in all-male than in all-female interaction.

The results of studies which have compared number of interruptions in same-sex interaction are presented in Table 9.2. The great majority— seventeen of twenty-two—found no gender differences. This might appear to suggest that status or power, rather than gender differences in interactional goals, is the more important determinant; nevertheless we will see that the situation cannot be assumed to be as simple as this. Two further studies found more interruptions in all-male interaction, and three studies, contrary to both types of prediction just made, found more interruptions in all-female interaction.

Our survey of the gender-related interruptions literature, then, poses several important questions. First of all, why is it that the majority of studies have not found men to interrupt women more than the reverse in mixed-sex interaction? Second, why has there been so much variation in the results of studies? Third, why is it that some studies have found women to interrupt more than men, in both mixed-sex and same-sex interaction? And fourth, are there aspects of interruption behavior other than simply the relative number of interruptions initiated by women and men which would be more revelatory of gender differences?

With respect to the first question, one explanation for the lack of significant gender differences may lie in the fact that the commonly held assumption that interruptions serve primarily to dominate and control conversations is overly simplistic. A considerable body of recent research

Table 9.2   All-Female Versus All-Male Interaction
with Respect to Number of Interruptions

(All are studies of dyads, except Smith-Lovin and Brody [1989]
and Dabbs and Ruback [1984], which examined three-person
and five-person groups respectively.)

**(1) Studies Which Found No Significant Difference in
Number of Interruptions**
Dabbs & Ruback 1984
Dindia 1987
Duncan & Fiske 1977
Esposito 1979
Frances 1979
LaFrance & Carmen 1980/LaFrance 1981 (these describe the
    same study)
Marche 1988
Martin & Craig 1983
McLachlan 1991
Octigan & Niederman 1979
Peterson 1986
Roger & Schumacher 1983
Rogers & Jones 1975
Simkins-Bullock & Wildman 1991
Smith-Lovin & Brody 1989
Trimboli & Walker 1984
Welkowitz, Bond, & Feldstein 1984

**(2) Studies Which Found Significantly More Interruptions
in All-Male Interaction**[7]
Bohn & Stutman 1983
de Boer 1987

**(3) Studies Which Found Significantly More Interruptions
in All-Female Interaction**
Bilous & Krauss 1988
Crosby 1976
Street & Murphy 1987

suggests that simultaneous talk may frequently be unrelated to dominance.
A later section on the functions of interruptions (pp.238–247) reviews
this literature and surveys the ways in which "interruptions" can and do
perform useful, healthy functions in conversation; it also surveys evidence
suggesting that the majority of interruptions in casual conversation may
not be dominance-related, and that the proportion of dominance-related
interruptions may be highest in certain types of context. In addition,
that section examines so-called successful and unsuccessful interruptions,
showing that the former are sometimes more strongly associated with
dominance than the latter, but that no simple correlation can be assumed.
A section on gender and the use of dominance-associated interruptions

(pp. 247–258) focuses on types of criteria which might shed light on the question of whether men are indeed more likely to use interruptions to dominate interactions than are women and shows that no reliable conclusion may be drawn. A section on gender and cooperative interruptions (pp. 258–260) presents some evidence that women are more likely to use simultaneous talk for supportive and rapport-building functions than are men. Lastly, a section on miscellaneous factors affecting gender-related interruptions (pp. 260–268) reviews possible explanations for the inconsistencies in the findings of different studies, examining different variables which may affect the number of interruptions initiated by each gender and other aspects of the methodologies employed which might also have contributed to the variations in the results found.

The Use of the Term "Interruption" in This Review

A comment must be made before continuing with respect to our use of the term "interruption." First, while interruptions are normally thought of as involving simultaneous talk, an utterance may perform the same types of function as an interruption without simultaneous speech actually occurring; for example, the interruptor may begin to speak immediately upon the interruptee's completing the utterance of a word while in midturn, and the interruptee may consequently cease speaking and relinquish the turn. Such phenomena have been noted by Meltzer, Morris, and Hayes (1971) and Ferguson (1977), among others; they are most commonly referred to (after Ferguson) as "silent interruptions." Although relatively few researchers have investigated the latter,[8] we include these as part of the phenomena of concern here. In effect, this survey deals with all those instances in which the switch between speakers is not completely "smooth," in the sense of Ferguson (1977); in "smooth speaker switches" the first speaker completes his/her turn and there is no simultaneous speech. In order to refer to these, a term is needed which refers to this set of phenomena and which is at the same time free of connotation as to the role or function of the second speaker's utterance, since, as noted previously, such an utterance may not necessarily be disruptive. Unfortunately no such term exists in English. The word "interruption," both in ordinary usage and in the usage of most researchers, has negative connotations, implying violation of another's right to speak. The term "overlap" has been used by Tannen (1983 and subsequent works) and by some others to indicate simultaneous talk without any negative connotation; however, this term is problematic for our purposes in that it does not allow for "silent interruptions," and in that it has been commonly used in the interruptions literature in two different specific technical senses.[9] Moreover, in colloquial usage the word "overlap" carries the implication that the first speaker completes his/her utterance without ceding the floor, and the term needed for our purposes should not be restricted to these cases alone.

There is, however, a precedent in the literature for the use of the term "interruption" to mean simply "any deviation from a smooth speaker switch." Ferguson (1977) and those researchers who have adopted her classification of types of interruption (e.g., Beattie 1981, Marche 1988, Craig & Pitts 1990) use it with this interpretation (see also Beattie 1989:334 for further discussion of this point). Under the circumstances, and in the absence of any clearly more satisfactory alternative, we have chosen to follow this precedent in our general comments on the research in this area; in this context, then, "interruption" should be understood as meaning "any deviation from a smooth switch between speakers," with no implication as to whether speaking rights are violated.

One point should be kept in mind, however: since the great majority of researchers have been concerned with interruption behavior as a measure of dominance, most have attempted to exclude from consideration those instances which they viewed as non-dominance-related (these constituting, usually, only a very small class of cases); thus they have counted interruptions in such a way as to exclude such instances. This will be commented on further in the next section (see pp. 238, 240–241, and note 11). Thus, when the term "interruption" is used in reports of the results of specific studies, the precise set of phenomena included is determined by the individual study.

The Functions of Interruptions

Interruptions as Supportive and Cooperative Speech Acts

There exists one type of simultaneous utterance which has long been recognized by most researchers as supportive rather than disruptive in nature. This category is most commonly referred to (after Yngve 1970) as "back channel utterances" or "back channel responses"[10]; these consist of one-word utterances such as "mhm," "yeah," "uh-huh," and "right" (and nonverbal equivalents such as nods) and are uttered by a listener primarily to indicate interest and attention to what the speaker is saying. They need not be, but frequently are, uttered simultaneously with the speaker's talk. The great majority of studies have explicitly excluded these from their count of interruptions (the only clear exceptions are Willis & Williams [1976], Shaw & Sadler [1965], and Welkowitz, Bond, & Feldstein [1984]).

It has been widely assumed in the past, however, that aside from back channel utterances, simultaneous talk is relatively rare in conversation, and that the basic rule is that only one person speaks at a time. Sacks, Schegloff, and Jefferson (1974:700–701), in setting out what has become the most widely accepted theory of turn taking in conversation, state: "Overwhelmingly, one party talks at a time. . . . Transitions from one turn to the next occur, for the most part, with little or no gap and little or no overlap." Given this assumption, it is not surprising that it has been supposed that instances of simultaneous talk other than back channels and very brief overlapping between turns necessarily constitute negative and dysfunctional acts. However, it has become increasingly apparent in more recent research that such simultaneous talk is, in fact, common and, far from being necessarily disruptive, may even function to signal and promote solidarity between speakers. One of the first to comment on this was Kalčik (1975), who noted in an examination of communication in two women's rap groups that interruptions were frequent, rarely seemed to be objected to, and were primarily supportive or collaborative in nature, often produced as the women worked out a topic or a story together as a group. Other researchers who have noted that simultaneous talk frequently has a supportive function include Bennett (1981), Edelsky (1981, this volume), Beattie (1982), Shultz, Florio & Erickson (1982), Kennedy & Camden (1983), Murray (1985, 1987), Tannen (1983, 1984, 1987, 1989, 1990), Testa (1988), Moerman (1988), Coates (1989), Goldberg (1990), and Herman (1991). Edelsky (1981, this volume), for example, in a well-known study of faculty committee meetings, argued that two types of "floor" could be distinguished, singly developed floors and collaboratively developed floors. In single floors, in which the discussion was highly task-oriented (focusing on such matters as reporting on items), the "one speaker at a time" rule was followed, and there were few interruptions. In collaborative floors, however, this rule no longer applied, and simultaneous speech was normal. In this type of floor, through talking simultaneously, participants developed an idea together, produced a joint answer to a question, or shared in joking. Edelsky notes that a high degree of involvement in the interaction characterized the use of simultaneous speech in collaborative floors.

Similar observations are made by Coates (1989), in a study of conversations among a group of women friends. She found that simultaneous speech was very common, but that it normally consisted of "work[ing] together to produce shared meanings" (p. 113), rather than attempts to take the floor from another speaker. Most commonly one speaker would make a comment or ask a question during another speaker's turn, this functioning simply as a sign of active listenership; a speaker would complete another's utterance, without in any way attempting to obtain the floor; or two or more speakers would contribute simultaneously to the same theme, in a manner very similar to that described by Edelsky.

Tannen (1983 and later works) has also argued that simultaneous talk can have a cooperative function; she suggests, indeed, that it can serve as a way of indicating that one is interested in, enthusiastic about, and highly involved in the conversation. This is particularly true, she suggests, of a certain type of conversational style characteristic of some cultural groups (for example, New York Jewish speech). In this style, which is also characterized by a rapid pace, expressive phonology, exaggerated intonation contours, frequent back channel utterances, and other features, Tannen argues that higher priority is placed on honoring the positive face of others (their need to know that others like them and are involved with them) (Brown &

Levinson 1987) than on honoring others' negative face (their need not to be imposed upon) (Tannen 1989:272). Thus, in this style interruptions are very frequent and serve to carry a metamessage of interpersonal rapport; indeed, failure to interrupt is interpreted as indicating lack of interest.

Thus it is evident that far from being disruptive in nature, interruptions may frequently be supportive, collaborative, and rapport-building.[11]

Other Circumstances in Which Interruptions Do Not Violate the Speaking Rights of Others

Various researchers have pointed out other uses of interruptions which, while not being particularly associated with collaboration and rapport, nevertheless do not constitute violations of conversational rules. For example, one might interrupt because of a problem with the communicative process. For example, if one is failing to understand what the speaker is trying to communicate because one did not catch or did not understand a word used, one might legitimately break in to ask for clarification; or, if one realizes that the speaker, in answering a question one has posed, has not properly understood it, one might legitimately interrupt in order to rephrase the question in a clearer way. Goldberg (1990) and Bull and Mayer (1988), among others, discuss the existence of such "relationally neutral" uses (the term is Goldberg's). Similarly, certain types of situation may require immediate speech, and here too interruptions are obviously appropriate (e.g., "Fire!"; "Don't touch that, it's hot!") (see, e.g., Tannen 1989:268–269 and Goldberg 1990:886–888). As one further type of example Testa (1988) contends that if A is explaining something to B and in the middle of the explanation B gets A's point, it is appropriate and not disruptive for B to interrupt A. Jefferson (1973) makes a similar point. (There may be cultural and individual variation as to the acceptability of such types of interruption as these last.)

A particularly common circumstance in which simultaneous talk, while not supportive in function, is also obviously not disruptive, is the case of the simple mistiming error. For example, B may recognize that A is about to finish her or his turn and begin to speak slightly before A has stopped; or B may make a mistake in judgment about whether A is ready to finish and begin to speak when A is not, in fact, ready to relinquish the turn. Usually in the latter case the interruptor stops speaking after realizing that the current speaker is continuing. (Coates [1989] suggests that enthusiasm is particularly likely to lead to such errors, Dindia [1987], that they may result from nervousness or awkwardness.)[12]

It is relevant to note here that a number of studies adopting the Sacks, Schegloff, and Jefferson (1974) theory of turn allocation in conversation have attempted to exclude systematically such mistiming errors from their count of interruptions (all remaining simultaneous talk, other than back channels, is normally then assumed—unjustifiably, as is clear from the rest of the discussion in this section—to be disruptive). Following Schegloff (1973) cases of mistiming in this approach are termed "overlaps," as opposed to interruptions; these are defined as occurring at or just before a "transition-relevant place" (that is, a possible completion point, defined as the end of any "unit-type") in the current speaker's talk. As a mechanical measure for distinguishing mistiming errors from other types of simultaneous talk, this is quite problematic and has been extensively criticized; see pp. 266–267.[13]

In actual fact, the extent to which an interruption is interpreted as negative and disruptive is probably not a black-and-white matter, but rather a matter of degree. Murray (1987), arguing for this point, suggests a number of factors which may contribute to degree of disruptiveness; these include whether the interruptee has made her/his first point, whether s/he has finished what s/he wanted to say, whether s/he has been unduly monopolizing the floor, and whether the interruptor has a special claim to be heard (this being the case if, e.g., the interruptee has previously not allowed the interruptor to answer a third person's question or has been attacking the interruptor and not letting him/her respond to the attack).

The Extent to Which Interruptions Are Likely to Be Dominance-Related in Different Types of Interaction

To evaluate the results of the studies dealing with the relationship between interruptions and gender accurately, it is necessary to consider what proportion of the interruptions in an interaction are likely to be of the disruptive, dominance-related type, and whether the proportion is likely to be higher in some kinds of interaction than in others.

It is possible that in casual conversations between friends, many of the interruptions are cooperative and rapport-building. Some support for this is provided by Coates (1989), who reports that only a minority of the simultaneous speech in her data could be analyzed as representing attempts to take over the floor, and by Tannen (1989), who states that when students in her course counted "overlaps" in half-hour casual conversations they had taped, roughly 75% of these were judged to be cooperative rather than obstructive.[14] It is possible, however, that the proportion of interruptions which are dominance-related might be higher in other types of interaction.

One approach which might potentially shed light on these matters involves classifying interruptions in terms of their content relative to the interruptee's talk. A few studies have made such a classification. Kennedy and Camden (1983), in a study of graduate students interacting in seminars and work programs, classified 38% of the interruptions in the data as instances of agreement and 11% as instances of clarification (here, the interruptor attempts to understand the interruptee's message). The remaining interruptions constituted disagreement, changes of subject, and tangential remarks.[15] Insofar as agreement and clarification can be assumed to be supportive and cooperative, half of the interruptions in these contexts, then, would not have been of the disruptive type. Kennedy and Camden note (p. 58), "In many cases, the interruptions seem to serve a healthy, functional and confirming communicative role." Sayers (1987), in a study of unstructured conversation in dyads, found similar results: approximately half the interruptions constituted agreement, elaboration, or requests for clarification. In Willis and Williams (1976), a study of high school students' speech in class discussions and casual conversation, 34% of interruptions (in total; setting was not taken into account) were found to constitute agreement, and 51% disagreement; the remainder were not classified.

These results, then, in particular those of Kennedy and Camden and of Sayers, appear to provide further support that a significant percentage of interruptions in interactions may not be dominance-related. The difference between unstructured conversation (Sayers 1987) and conversation in seminars or work groups (Kennedy & Camden 1983) appears not to have affected results.

However, some caution is called for in interpreting the findings of these studies. It does not necessarily follow that when one interrupts to agree or ask for clarification, such interruptions never constitute attempts to seize the floor; for example, as is pointed out by Dindia (1987) and by Smith-Lovin and Brody (1989), one can agree with what is being said as a precursor to taking over the floor. Further, interruptions involving disagreement are not necessarily disruptive; even in collaborative, rapport-building simultaneous talk, one speaker may be gently disagreeing with another. Examples of this can be found in the data provided by Coates (1989) (e.g., p. 112). Thus, a more adequate analysis of what an interruptor may have been attempting to do must take into account not simply the content of an interruption, but also the larger context in which the interruption is used.

A quite different type of approach to the role of interruptions in interactions, specifically directed toward determining the extent to which the interruptions in an interaction are likely to be dominance-related, is provided by eight studies which have attempted to test the relationship between interruption use and dominance by indirect means. Six of these studies examined experimentally the relationship between an individual's use of interruptions and his or her predisposition toward dominance over others, as measured by a psychological test;[16] one examined the relationship between interruptions and relative power in intimate couples, where power was measured by a questionnaire dealing with relative influence over day-to-day decision making (Kollock, Blumstein & Schwartz 1985); and one examined the relationship between interruptions and overall "domineering behavior," the latter being measured in terms of the proportion of messages transmitted which attempted to assert relational control (Courtright, Millar, & Rogers-Millar 1979:180–181).

Of these studies the three which found the clearest link between interruptions and dominance all examined interactions in which competition and conflict were present, and indeed, it is plausible to suppose that this would be a context particularly likely to elicit dominance-related interruptions.[17] In Kollock, Blumstein & Schwartz (1985), a study of heterosexual and homosexual intimate couples, partners had to decide jointly how to resolve a hypothetical conflict about which they had been given differently slanted versions of the facts; thus, they were "set up" to argue with each other. In couples in which one partner was more powerful than the other in terms of relative influence over day-to-day decision making, the more powerful partner attempted more interruptions; in couples where the partners were equal in power, they did not differ in number of interruptions. The initiating of interruptions, then, was linked with being more powerful. This suggests that a significant percentage of interruptions were of the dominance-related, disruptive type, as there is no reason to expect the initiation of other types of interruptions to be associated with power. In two other studies, Roger and Schumacher (1983) and Roger and Nesshoever (1987), subjects were assigned topics for discussion on which they were known to disagree and were instructed to try to convince their partners of their own point of view. These two studies were concerned not with total number of interruptions but with "successful" interruptions (to be discussed in more detail on pp. 244–246), in which the interruptee yields the floor to the interruptor; both studies found that individuals with personalities high in dominance initiated significantly more such interruptions than those with personalities low in dominance.

In two further studies the interaction was less obviously conflictual, but involved a formal task (Rogers & Jones 1975, Aries, Gold, & Wiegel 1983). In a formal task, participants come together to accomplish a specific instrumental goal such as making a joint decision or working out a joint solution to a problem. Since there is evidence that status differences are more likely to affect interaction in situations involving formal tasks than in those involving informal tasks (in which no collective decision is required) or in non–task-oriented situations (Berger, Rosenholtz & Zelditch 1980), it would be reasonable to hypothesize that a higher proportion of interruptions would be dominance-related in formal task settings. On the other hand, however, the situation is complicated by the fact that even in a formal task setting, some segments of the interaction may be less task-oriented than others, and this may affect interruption behavior. For example, it will be recalled that in her study of faculty meetings—a formal task setting—Edelsky (1981, this volume) found that in the second of the two types of floor that she distinguished (collaborative floors), the interaction became less task-oriented. While collaborative floors took up only a small part of the interaction, the bulk of the simultaneous talk took place in this type of floor, and this talk was primarily cooperative rather than disruptive. Thus even with a formal task context it appears that it is possible for the majority of the simultaneous talk to be nondisruptive in nature. What, then, were the results of the work of Rogers and Jones

(1975) and Aries, Gold, and Weigel (1983)? Both observed a relationship between interruptions and a high dominance predisposition, but this did not hold for all types of subject or all types of setting. Rogers and Jones, studying same-sex dyads, found a positive link between number of interruptions and high dominance for male dyads but not for female dyads; and Aries et al., studying same-sex and mixed-sex groups, found such a link for all-male groups but not all-female or mixed-sex groups. (The relevance of these findings to gender is discussed on pp. 251–253.)

In two other studies, Courtright, Millar and Rogers-Millar (1979) and Marche (1988), subjects were instructed to discuss assigned problems; while they were not required to reach a collective decision, it is nevertheless possible that such a context would be more likely to elicit dominance-related interruptions than would unstructured, non–task-oriented friendly conversation. Courtright et al., in a study of married couples, did find that the more "domineering" the spouse, or the greater the proportion of messages s/he transmitted that attempted to assert relational control, the more likely s/he was to interrupt the other partner. Marche, studying two age groups averaging fourteen and nineteen years old, found that in the case of the fourteen-year-olds, high-dominance subjects initiated significantly more interruptions overall than low-dominance ones; however, no such pattern was present in the case of the nineteen-year-olds.

Of the eight studies under review that have explored the relationship between dominance and interruption use, only one (Ferguson 1977) examined unstructured conversation between friends. This was the only study of the group which found comparatively little correlation between interruptions and dominance predisposition;[18] this provides some additional support for the hypothesis that dominance-related interruptions are less likely to occur in casual conversation between friends than in other contexts.

It would appear, then, that a significant percentage of interruptions in casual conversation may be non-dominance-related. The proportion of interruptions which are dominance-related may be higher in contexts involving formal tasks, and highest in interactions involving competition and conflict. However, much more research is needed to determine the facts in this area.[19]

"Successful" Interruptions and Dominance

It has been assumed by some researchers that one specific type of interruption event, defined in terms of formal observational criteria, is particularly strongly associated with dominance. Clearly, if correct, this must be taken into account in any consideration of the relationship between interruption use and gender. This approach to investigating the link between interruptions and dominance recognizes that conversation is jointly produced: not only is the behavior of the interruptor relevant, but so also is the behavior of the interruptee. Of central importance is the distinction between a situation in which, on being interrupted by B, A yields the floor to B (here, the interruption is called, in the most commonly used terminology, "successful"); and a situation in which A continues speaking and B, the interruptor, stops speaking without gaining the floor (here, the interruption is termed, most commonly, "unsuccessful").[20] This distinction appears to have been first made in family interaction studies such as Farina (1960) and Mishler and Waxler (1968). It has been generally assumed that successful interruptions constitute a much clearer manifestation of dominance on the part of the interruptor than do unsuccessful interruptions (e.g., Smith-Lovin & Brody 1989:427, Kollock, Blumstein, & Schwartz 1985:40, Natale, Entin, & Jaffe 1979:875).

There is obviously a certain amount of plausibility in the idea that interruptions in which the first speaker yields the turn are particularly likely to be associated with dominance. One type of evidence for this hypothesis is provided by McLaughlin (1984), who found that when asked to rate speech samples, subjects rated successful interruptions as more domineering than unsuccessful ones (unless there was a readily apparent reason why the interruption had occurred). In addition, several of those studies mentioned earlier (see pp. 242–244) which have dealt with the relationship between use of interruptions and dominance predisposition or power have also examined whether this link is stronger for successful interruptions than for unsuccessful ones, and/or whether it is stronger for those interruptions which are successful than for total attempted interruptions. Results have been mixed. Both Roger and Schumacher (1983) and Roger and Nesshoever (1987) did indeed find a positive correlation between successful interruptions and dominance predisposition, but no correlation between unsuccessful interruptions and dominance. However, both studies note that this latter result may have been due to the fact that there were relatively few unsuccessful interruptions in their data. Kollock, Blumstein, and Schwartz (1983) found that the more powerful partner in a couple produced a greater number of successful interruptions; however, unsuccessful interruptions were not examined separately and it is possible that this finding was simply a result of the fact that the more powerful partner initiated more interruptions overall. Aries et al. (1983) concluded that for all-female groups, while there was no link between dominance predisposition and total attempted interruptions, there was indeed a positive correlation between dominance predisposition and successful interruptions; for all-male groups the correlation held for both but was stronger in the case of successful interruptions. For mixed-sex groups, however, no correlation was found for either attempted or successful interruptions. Marche (1988) concluded that for her fourteen-year-old subjects, there was a positive correlation between dominance predisposition and successful interruptions, but a negative correlation between dominance and unsuccessful interruptions. However, no such pattern held for nineteen-year-olds, and indeed some results were the opposite of what might be expected: for example, for nineteen-year-old females, the less dominant they were, the more successful interruptions they initiated. Further, Ferguson (1977) found no correlation between dominance predisposition and either successful interruptions or unsuccessful interruptions. And while Rogers and Jones (1975) found a positive correlation between total attempted interruptions and dominance predisposition, they found no link between successful interruptions and dominance.

These findings suggest that while successful interruptions are sometimes more strongly associated with dominance than unsuccessful ones, this is far from universally true. We will not attempt here to sort out the reasons for the variations in the findings of these studies. It should, however, be noted that clearly no one-to-one relationship exists between successful interruptions and dominance. Perusal of examples of simultaneous talk given in Tannen (1989:271, 273, 278), in Edelsky (this volume:196–198), and in Coates (1989:112), for example, reveals a number of instances of what are technically successful interruptions, but which are clearly both intended and perceived as collaborative and rapport-building. Similarly, "neutral" interruptions of the types discussed earlier (see pp. 240–241) are normally successful (the interruptee is expected to cease speaking, as noted by Goldberg [1990:888]), yet are not dominance-associated. Further, it does not follow that unsuccessful interruptions are necessarily unrelated to dominance. Edelsky (this volume:218), for example, notes that in more task-oriented floors or contexts, "self-stops," as she calls them, were sometimes preludes to new topics ("OK, now what about—") and sometimes incipient rebuttals ("but—"), and that speakers often produced a series of these in close sequence; she suggests that these may act as signals that the speaker is "reserving a spot" to develop an idea alone. While not violating others' right to the floor, in the appropriate context such behavior could be perceived as intimidating by other participants. It is overly simplistic, then, to assume that those instances of interruption which are manifestations of dominance can be accurately and straightforwardly identified in terms of the successful versus unsuccessful distinction.

The Functions of Interruptions: Conclusions

It is clear then that while interruptions may function to prevent others from completing their talk and to allow the interruptor to take over the floor, this is only one of various functions which they can perform. What proportion of interruptions are likely to be of this disruptive type in any given conversation is probably affected by various aspects of the interaction, including such factors as the degree of conflict present. It may well be that in many conversations only a relatively small proportion of the interruptions are of the disruptive type (it must be kept in mind, too, that there is no simple dividing line between disruptive and nondisruptive interruptions, as pointed out by Murray [1987]). Lastly there is some evidence that "successful" interruptions tend to be more strongly associated with dominance and disruptiveness than "unsuccessful" ones; however, it is clear that no simple one-to-one relationship is involved here.

Clearly, a central problem in analyzing the function of interruptions is that there exist no simple, objective ways of determining the function of an interruption. Only an analysis which takes into account the larger context in which the interruption takes place, including the semantic content of the interruption, the general trend and content of the conversation up to that point, and the relationship between the participants—and which also considers the conversational style employed by the interruptor, given that individual's cultural background—is likely to ascertain adequately the role which an interruption was intended to perform.[21]

Gender and the Use of Dominance-Associated Interruptions

The preceding discussion helps to shed light on why the majority of studies listed in Tables 9.1 and 9.2 have not found males to interrupt more than females. While there are reasons to expect that males would initiate more interruptions of the disruptive, dominance-related type, as was discussed earlier (see pp. 232–233), here is no reason to expect that they would initiate more interruptions of other types than would females. If many interruptions, perhaps even the great majority in many interactions, are not intended or perceived as disruptive, it is not surprising that females and males have, in most cases, been found not to differ in number of interruptions.[22]

Certain questions, however, remain. First, is it in fact the case that males' interruptions are more likely to constitute dominance-related attempts to seize the floor than are those of females? Ways of approaching this question exist other than that of comparing the relative number of interruptions produced; some of these have already been touched on earlier. The five sections that follow will investigate these.

A second question of interest is: Are males'—and, indeed, females'—interruptions more likely to be dominance-associated when the interruptees are female than when they are male? Since females have lower status, it may be viewed as more legitimate to attempt to seize the floor from females than from males (Berger, Rosenholtz & Zelditch 1980). On the other hand, given that the male interactional style stresses competing and winning (e.g., Maltz & Borker 1982, Tannen 1990), and given that various studies have found more sex-stereotypic behavior in same-sex than in mixed-sex interaction (e.g., Piliavin & Martin 1978, Carli 1989), and that levels of dominance behavior have been found to be higher in all-male than in all-female groups (e.g., Ridgeway & Diekema 1989), it is also conceivable that the highest levels of dominance-associated interruptions might occur between males. Interruptee gender will be touched on where relevant in the four sections to follow (see pp. 248–253). The fifth section (see pp. 253–258) will survey research on the extent to which females and males discriminate on the basis of coparticipants' gender in their overall interruption attempts and will discuss possible interpretations of the results.

Semantic Content as a Gauge of Gender Differences with Respect to Dominance-Related Interruptions

As was mentioned earlier (see pp. 241–242), a few studies have classified interruptions into different types on the basis of their content relative to the interruptee's talk (e.g., agreement, disagreement, support). It has been noted there that no one-to-one relationship can be assumed between these categories and the relative disruptiveness of an interruption; for example, one can agree but still be attempting to seize the floor, and one can disagree but in a context in which the interruption nevertheless has a collaborative function. Still, any common patterns in gender differences running through these studies could be relevant to the question of whether males produce more interruptions of the disruptive type, and to the question of whether females are more likely to receive interruptions of this type than are males.

Five studies have compared the genders with respect to the content of interruptions. (Four of these found the genders not to differ in relative number of interruptions; one, Sayers 1987, found females to interrupt more.) Kennedy and Camden (1983), Sayers (1987), and Dindia (1987) classified interruptions as agreement, clarification, disagreement, and disconfirmation (in disconfirmation the interruption either changes the subject or in some way minimizes or makes light of the interruptee's talk). None of these three studies observed any gender differences with respect to the semantic content of interruptions when the sex of the interruptor alone was taken into account. Kennedy and Camden, studying mixed-sex groups, did not investigate the effects of interruptee gender. Sayers studied mixed-sex dyads only. Dindia, investigating mixed and same-sex dyads, did find interruptee gender to be relevant in some respects: males made more disconfirming interruptions toward females than they did toward males or than females did toward either sex; at the same time, however, both genders produced more agreeing interruptions when addressing members of the opposite sex than when addressing members of the same sex. Males also used more disagreeing interruptions when addressing other males than any other sex combination. A further study dealing with interruption content, Willis and Williams (1976), classified interruptions in mixed-sex groups as agreement, disagreement, irrelevant to the speaker's topic, and miscellaneous. Female interruptors used more agreeing interruptions with males than with other females, and more disagreeing interruptions with other females than with males; no other gender differences were observed. Lastly, Smith-Lovin and Brody (1989), examining mixed-sex and same-sex groups, classified interruptions as supportive, negative, or neutral. The only gender difference found was that males were more likely to initiate a supportive interruption toward another male when in an all-male group than when in a mixed-sex group.[23]

Even assuming, oversimplistically, a correlation between disruptiveness and aspects of content such as disagreement, these studies clearly fail to provide any convincing support for the hypothesis that males initiate more interruptions of the dominance-related type than do females. Overall, comparatively few differences were discovered. Dindia's finding that males used more disagreeing interruptions with other males than any other sex combination is partially supportive of a pattern of more competition, and thus possibly more disruptive interruptions, in all-male interaction; however, Smith-Lovin and Brody's results appear to contradict this. Some of Dindia's and Willis and Williams's results suggest that more disruptive interruptions may be directed against women than against men, but other results—such as Dindia's finding that men use more agreeing interruptions toward women than toward men—do not support such a conclusion.

Type of Context as a Gauge of Gender Differences with Respect to Dominance-Related Interruptions

It was suggested earlier (see pp. 241–244) that the proportion of interruptions which represent dominance attempts may be particularly low in casual, friendly conversation; may possibly be higher in formal task contexts (although this is unclear); and may be particularly high in interactions which involve competition and conflict. If it were the case that in casual, unstructured conversation the sexes were most likely not to differ in relative number of interruptions initiated, and in competitive, conflictual contexts males were frequently found to initiate more interruptions than females, this would provide some support for the hypothesis that males' interruptions are more likely to be dominance-related than are those of females. Is this, then, the case?

Five studies listed in Tables 9.1 and 9.2 have investigated interruptions in a context involving a relatively high degree of competition or conflict. Three of these are Kollock, Blumstein, and Schwartz (1985), Roger and Nesshoever (1987), and Roger and Schumacher (1983). As was discussed earlier (see pp. 242–243), these studies also tested whether individuals who were the more powerful member of a couple (in the case of Kollock et al.) or who had a high predisposition toward dominance in their personalities (in the case of the other two studies) initiated more interruptions, attempted or successful, than individuals of whom this was not the case; the results supported this hypothesis in all three studies. None of these studies found the sexes to differ in relative frequency of interruptions (Roger and Nesshoever examined mixed-sex dyads, Roger and Schumacher same-sex dyads, and Kollock et al. both types). However, subjects were preselected in such a way that an equal number of females and males represented the more powerful member of their couple or had a high predisposition toward dominance (see note 16 and p. 242); thus, power or a high dominance tendency may have simply outweighed gender as a determinant of interruption behavior in these studies. In real life males and females are not equally likely to be high in power or dominance predisposition.

Two other studies compared interruption behavior in competitive and in more cooperative contexts (e.g., Trimboli and Walker [1984] compared, on the one hand, friendly chats dealing with topics on which subjects held similar views and, on the other, arguments dealing with topics on which subjects held opposite views). Trimboli and Walker found that while there were more interruptions in the competitive situation, all-male, all-female, and mixed-sex dyads did not differ in overall number of interruptions in either type of context; behavior of the sexes in mixed-sex dyads was not compared. Jose, Crosby, and Wong-McCarthy (1980), examining mixed-sex dyads, reported with respect to gender only that females were interrupted more often in the more cooperative setting than any other gender and context combination. Clearly, then, these studies are not supportive of the hypothesis that competitive contexts would be particularly likely to elicit findings of males exceeding females in the extent to which they interrupt others. Equally clearly, however, more research is needed in this area.

A comparison of studies of unstructured conversations and studies involving a formal task also reveals no clear difference between these two types of context in the proportion of cases in which males were found to interrupt more than females, for either same or mixed-sex interaction. However, as was noted earlier (see p. 243), it is not in fact obvious that more interruptions of the disruptive type are to be expected in formal task contexts than in unstructured, friendly conversation. Thus, we find here, as previously, no evidence to support the hypothesis that males initiate more interruptions of the dominance-related type, either against females or against males.

"Successful" Interruptions as a Gauge of Gender Differences with Respect to Dominance-Related Interruptions

In a previous section (see pp. 244–246) it was observed that "successful" interruptions may be more likely to be associated with attempts to seize the floor from others than are "unsuccessful" interruptions, although not all the relevant evidence is supportive of this hypothesis, and successful interruptions certainly need not be dominance-related. Despite the fact that there are some problems here, one obvious avenue to pursue, in attempting to determine whether males initiate more interruptions which represent dominance attempts than do females, is to survey the results of studies which have compared the genders with respect to the number of successful interruptions initiated. In addition, if successful interruptions are particularly likely to occur when the interruptee is female, this would suggest that females are more willing to yield the floor than are males, whether because of differences in female and male interactional styles, or because of males' higher status (in the case of cross-sex interruptions) or both.

Eleven studies have examined gender in relation to the initiation of successful interruptions. Nine have dealt with mixed-sex interaction. Of these Woods (1989), studying three-person groups of colleagues interacting at their place of work, found males to initiate a greater number of successful interruptions than females; Craig and Pitts (1990), dealing with tutorials, found male students to initiate a greater number of "successful speaker switches" involving interruption of females than the reverse. The remaining seven studies found no gender differences (Beattie 1981, Roger & Nesshoever 1987, Kollock et al. 1985, Welkowitz et al. 1984, Smith-Lovin & Brody 1989, Marche 1988, and Natale et al. 1979). In addition the last five of these, plus two further studies (Rogers & Jones 1975 and Roger & Schumacher 1983), examined same-sex interaction. Here, Kollock et al. (1985) found—contrary to what might have been predicted—that there were more successful interruptions in female than in male homosexual couples. No other study found a gender difference. However, with respect to the "no difference" findings of Kollock et al. (1985) and Roger and Nesshoever (1987) for mixed-sex interaction, and of Roger and Schumacher (1983) for same-sex interaction, having higher power or being high in dominance may have outweighed gender here as a factor in interruption behavior; see the previous comments on pp. 249–250 (this would, however, leave the results of Kollock et al. for same-sex pairs unexplained). In any case the same-sex results clearly fail to provide any support for the notion that there might be more dominance-associated interruptions in all-male than in all-female interaction. Of the mixed-sex results, where a difference exists males were found to initiate the greater number of successful interruptions; this difference appears only in a small minority of the studies, however.

Three studies—West (1979), Kennedy and Camden (1983), and Dindia (1987)—have also examined in detail the responses of males and females to being interrupted. None found either sex to be more likely to yield the floor to an interruptor.

Overall then there appears to be no convincing evidence that males initiate a greater number of successful interruptions than females toward either gender, and little evidence that females are more likely to be successfully interrupted than are males. Thus, this criterion, like those in the two immediately preceding sections (see pp. 248–250), does not support either the hypothesis that males surpass females in the use of dominance-related interruptions or the hypothesis that females more often have dominance-related interruptions directed at them. However, it should be kept in mind that the connection between "successful" interruptions and dominance is, in any case, neither simple nor straightforward.

Dominance Predisposition and Power as Gauges of Gender Differences with Respect to Dominance-Related Interruptions

We have seen that a small number of studies have dealt with the extent to which the number of interruptions initiated correlates with having a high dominance predisposition or having greater power in a relationship. For three studies—Kollock et al. (1985), Roger and Schumacher (1983), and Roger and Nesshoever (1987)—having a high dominance predisposition affected the interruption behavior of males and of females in the same way and to the same extent: both genders produced significantly more interruptions (or in the case of the latter two studies, successful interruptions) than low-dominance individuals. However, the four other studies which have investigated the relationship between interruptions and dominance predisposition and which employed subjects of both sexes (Rogers & Jones 1975, Aries et al. 1983, Courtright et al. 1979, and Marche 1988) have all found some gender differences with respect to this relationship: having a high dominance predisposition was found not to affect the interruption behavior of males and females in exactly the same way (these results will be discussed later). If the hypothesis that males initiate more interruptions of the dominance-associated type than do females were correct, we might expect that where a difference in the behavior of high-dominance males and females were found, it would take the following form: having a high dominance predisposition would be more likely to prompt males to interrupt a great deal than it would females. Such a result might follow from the different interactional goals which males and females acquire; for instance, females' focus on harmonious relationships with others may cause females to be more reluctant than males to use interruptions as dominance-related attempts to seize the floor even when they have high dominance predispositions themselves. The type of context, however, could also be relevant here; for example, particularly competitive and conflictual situations such as those investigated in Kollock et al. (1985), Roger and Schumacher (1983), and Roger and Nesshoever (1987) could conceivably cause males' and females' behavior to be more alike.

Turning then to the results of studies in which differences in the interruption behavior of high-dominance males and females were observed, let us begin with the findings with respect to same-sex interaction. Rogers and Jones (1975) discovered that high-dominance partners attempted significantly more interruptions than low-dominance ones only in male dyads; also, there was a nonsignificant tendency for high-dominance partners to initiate a greater number of successful interruptions in male dyads only. This study did indeed find, then, that high-dominance predisposition prompted males to interrupt more, but not females. Aries et al. (1983) similarly found a positive correlation between high-dominance predisposition and attempted interruptions in all-male groups, but not in all-female groups.[24] However, another finding of this study was in the opposite direction from that anticipated: with respect to successful interruptions, not only was there a positive correlation between these and high-dominance predisposition in both all-female and all-male groups, but the correlation was, in fact, stronger in all-female groups.

With respect to mixed-sex interaction, Aries et al. observed no correlation between high dominance predisposition and interruptions in mixed-sex groups, for either men or women. And, contrary to what might have been anticipated, Courtright et al. (1979), studying married couples, found that the wife's "domineeringness" score (see p. 242) was more strongly associated with interruptions than was the husband's. One relevant factor in this last finding, however, might be the topics assigned for discussion, all of which—unlike those in the other studies examined—dealt with interpersonal relationships (e.g., "How does a couple develop and maintain a strong marital and family relationship?"). There is much evidence from studies that interpersonal relationships are perceived by both genders as a female area of expertise; thus, this may have given the wives in this study a status as "experts" which had the effect of making them feel more justified than their husbands in making dominance-associated interruptions. If this is part of the explanation, it points to the importance of the topic of conversation as a factor affecting the number of interruptions of the dominance-associated type which an individual may produce.

One last study, Marche (1988), dealt with both same-sex and mixed-sex dyadic interaction; here, all findings held independently of the sex of the addressee. High-dominance males and females did not differ with respect to overall number of interruptions in this study, in either of the two age groups studied (fourteen- and nineteen-year-olds); however, some gender differences were found which do not form a readily interpretable pattern. For example, the higher in dominance nineteen-year-old females were, the fewer—rather than the more, as might have been expected—"simple" interruptions (in Ferguson's [1977] terminology, i.e., successful interruptions involving simultaneous speech in which the interruptee fails to complete his/her turn) they produced, while for male nineteen-year-olds no relationship existed between these and dominance. Conversely for male, but not female, nineteen-year-olds, the higher in dominance they were, the fewer—again, rather than the more—"silent" interruptions (successful interruptions in which no simultaneous speech occurs) they produced. Results such as these suggest strongly that the relationships among various types of interruption, dominance, and gender may be more complex than has usually been assumed.

These studies, then, provide no evidence that high-dominance males produce more interruptions than high-dominance females in mixed-sex interaction. With respect to same-sex interaction, some evidence is supportive of this hypothesis, but other evidence fails to support it or even appears to contradict it. Explanations for some of the gender differences observed remain obscure. As in the three previous sections, we also find here no clear evidence that males do indeed initiate more interruptions of the dominance-associated variety than do females.

Discrimination on the Basis of Gender of Interruptee as a Gauge of Gender Differences with Respect to Dominance-Related Interruptions

As pointed out earlier (see p. 247), one issue of concern is that of whether interruptions are more likely to constitute dominance-related attempts to seize the floor when interruptees are female than when they are male, a result that might follow from females' lower status relative to males. Alternatively, it is also possible that the highest number of dominance-related interruptions might be directed by males against other males. It has been shown in the four previous sections that from the perspective of the criteria there dealt with, although the results of some individual studies have matched the predictions of one or the other of these hypotheses, research results taken as a whole provide no clear support for either hypothesis. However, as was previously noted, the criteria employed in these sections may not be completely reliable. A number of researchers have addressed the question of whether either sex is more likely to have dominance-related interruptions directed at them simply by comparing the frequency with which females and males are interrupted; most of these have also factored in the sex of the interruptor. The results are summarized in Table 9.3; nine studies of mixed-sex groups and twelve studies which compared same-sex and mixed-sex dyads are surveyed here. This section will review and evaluate this research.

Perusal of Table 9.3 reveals one striking pattern. In thirteen of these twenty-one studies females were interrupted more than males by either one or both sexes (those studies listed in [2]–[6]; in the case of Craig and Pitts [1990], this was true of student-student interruptions only, as noted in [1] and [2]). However, males were interrupted more by either sex in only two studies (those in [5]; in the case of Brooks [1982], male students, but not male professors, were interrupted more than females [by females], as noted in [2] and [5]). Clearly, the hypothesis that dominance-related interruptions are generally more likely to be directed against females than against males, as a result of the status difference between them, would provide one explanation for this discrepancy in numbers. Also of interest are the results by sex of interruptor, summarized from the nineteen studies listed in (1)–(5) in Table 9.3. In a significant subportion of these studies (eight) males interrupted females more than they did males, and in one further study (Craig & Pitts 1990) males interrupted females more in the case of student-student interruptions, although they interrupted both sexes equally in the case of tutor-student interruptions. In the remaining ten studies males interrupted both sexes to an equal extent. In the case of female interruptors, the majority of studies (twelve) found them to interrupt both sexes to an equal extent. In only four studies did females interrupt other females to a greater extent overall than they did males. In one study, they interrupted males more; in two studies the results were mixed—in Craig and Pitts (1990), females students interrupted other female students more than they did male students but interrupted both sexes equally in the case of tutor-student interruptions, while Brooks (1982) found (by contrast) that female students interrupted male students more than they did other female students but interrupted female professors more than male professors.

It is noteworthy that in no study have males interrupted other males more than they have females. This would initially appear to weigh against

Table 9.3   Studies Which Have Examined Whether Each Gender Interrupts
Females or Males More

(1) Studies in Which Both Females and Males Interrupted Females and Males to an Equal Extent
Beattie 1981
Craig & Pitts 1990
    (with regard to successful interruptions of students by tutors, or the reverse; cf. [2])
Duncan & Fiske 1977
Frances 1979
Greif 1980[25]
Leffler, Gillespie, & Conaty 1982[26]
Martin & Craig 1983
Murray & Covelli 1988
Simkins-Bullock & Wildman 1991

(2) Studies in Which Both Sexes Interrupted Females More Than They Did Males
Brooks 1982
    (with regard to students' interruption of professors; professors' interruptions of students not tabulated; cf. [5])
Craig & Pitts 1990
    (with regard to successful interruptions of students by other students; cf. [1])
McMillan et al. 1977
Peterson 1986

(3) Studies in Which Males Interrupted Females More Than They Did Other Males, But Females Interrupted Both Sexes to an Equal Extent
Octigan & Niederman 1979
Smith-Lovin & Brody 1989
Willis & Williams 1976
Zimmerman & West 1975

(4) Studies in Which Females Interrupted Other Females More Than They Did Males, But Males Interrupted Both Sexes to an Equal Extent
Bilous & Krauss 1988
Marche 1988

(5) Studies in Which Males Interrupted Females More Than They Did Other Males, and Females Interrupted Males More Than They Did Other Females
Brooks 1982
    (with regard to students' interruption of other students; cf. [2])
Dindia 1987

(6) Studies in Which Females Were Interrupted More, But It Is Not Reported Whether They Were Interrupted More By Males, Females, or Both Males and Females[27]
Eakins & Eakins 1976
Kennedy & Camden 1983

the hypothesis that the highest number of dominance-related interruptions would be directed by males against other males; however, this begs the question of the functions being performed by the interruptions, a point to which we will return again.

It is also significant that male interruptors appear to have "discriminated against" females to a somewhat greater extent than female interruptors did in these nineteen studies; they did this in nine studies, as opposed to only six in the case of female interruptors (if we include both Craig and Pitts [1990] and Brooks [1982] as studies in which at least some group of females was "discriminated against"). One possible interpretation of this result is that males' interruptions are, in general, more likely to be dominance-related attempts to seize the floor than are females', because it is only in this case that the status of the interruptee should make a difference. There is no reason to expect interruptions which are intended as cooperative or supportive, or such types of interruption as mistiming errors, to be more frequently directed toward lower-status individuals (females) than toward higher-status individuals (males). If male interruptors "discriminate against" females more than female interruptors do, this could mean that males' interruptions are more frequently attempts to seize the floor.

However, other possible explanations for the findings must also be explored. For example, with respect to the issue just raised, Smith-Lovin and Brody (1989), who found males to interrupt females more than other males but females to interrupt both sexes equally, propose that cross-sex conflict explains this apparent inconsistency between male and female behavior. In this account both males' and females' interruptions are held to be primarily dominance attempts. Smith-Lovin and Brody, noting that some studies have yielded indirect evidence that there is more conflict in mixed-sex than in same-sex interaction (e.g., South et al. 1987),[28] suggest that while in the case of males, the status difference and the element of cross-sex conflict both work in the same direction, leading them to interrupt females more than other males, in the case of females the two factors lead in opposite directions; status differences lead women to defer to men while interrupting other women, but adversarial conflict leads them to interrupt men while respecting or supporting the speech of others of their own sex. If the two effects were roughly equal in strength, these authors point out, they could cancel each other out, causing women to interrupt both sexes equally.

This account offers an explanation for the results of the four studies listed under (3) in Table 9.3, and it might also serve to explain the findings of the two studies listed under (5), in which both sexes interrupted the opposite sex more than their own, if we assume that for female interruptors some factor caused cross-sex conflict to outweigh deference to males in these two studies. The results of the remaining studies listed under (1), (2), and (4), however, would not be readily explained by this account.

Moreover, it is also possible that factors unrelated to dominance were at work in these studies. For example, in Dindia (1987) (one of the studies under [5]), more than half the interruptions in mixed-sex dyads were instances of agreement. This suggests that these interruptions may not have been of the disruptive type, and thus that cross-sex conflict may not provide the best interpretation of these data; Dindia proposes as an alternative that mixed-sex conversations—at least among strangers, presumably, as in her study—may be more "awkward" than same-sex conversations, leading to more mistiming errors.[29] It is also possible that in the studies comparing same- and mixed-sex dyads in which females interrupted other females more than males, the reason was not that females felt it was more legitimate to attempt to take the floor from other females, but rather that interruptions of the rapport-building, cooperative type are particularly characteristic of all-female interaction; that is, the increase may have involved an increase in supportive, rather than disruptive, interruptions. Evidence for this will be discussed later (see pp. 258–260), where it will be suggested that this best explains the findings of the two studies listed under (4) in Table 9.3. (This type of highly rapport-building interaction may, however, be more appropriate in some contexts than in others; this may explain why some dyadic studies did not find females interrupting other females more than males.)

Consideration of the cooperative function of interruptions, in turn, raises the issue of whether males might initiate more interruptions of the cooperative type when talking to females than when talking to males; could this be at least part of the explanation for the fact that so many studies have found males to interrupt females more than they did other males? As noted earlier, various studies have shown males' behavior to be less sex-stereotypic in mixed-sex than in same-sex interaction; also, Bilous and Krauss (1988) found that both males and females manifested some speech accommodation in the direction of the other gender's style. If cooperative interruptions are more characteristic of the female than of the male verbal style, it is possible that males may tend to increase their use of these when interacting with females. In the absence of detailed comparisons of the roles of males' interruptions in same and mixed-sex interaction, however, this must remain speculation.

In sum, then, one possible interpretation of the findings of the twenty-one studies listed in Table 9.3 is that interruptions tend to be more likely to constitute dominance-related attempts to seize the floor when interruptees are female than when they are male, and that males' interruptions are somewhat more likely to represent dominance attempts than are those of females. However, these findings could also be interpreted in other ways. To the extent that cross-sex conflict is an issue, perhaps females' interruptions are equally as intentionally disruptive as those of males. On the other hand, perhaps the increases in interruptions observed do not in fact represent dominance attempts, but rather nondisruptive types of interruption triggered by such factors as gender differences in verbal style and speech accommodation.[30] In evaluating the findings, then, we come up once more against the problem of how to interpret the roles and functions of interruptions.

Gender and Dominance-Associated Interruptions: Conclusions

No clear conclusions, then, can be drawn at this time from the existing research findings as to whether males' interruptions are more likely to constitute attempts to seize the floor than are those of females, or as to whether females are more likely than males to have dominance-related interruptions directed against them. It may simply not be the case that males and females differ significantly overall with respect to the use of dominance-associated interruptions; but given the fact that none of the criteria discussed in the preceding five sections constitute truly reliable gauges of whether or not an interruption constitutes a dominance attempt, this cannot be concluded with any certainty.

The central problem, of course, as noted earlier (see pp. 246–247), is that there exist no simple, objective criteria to determine whether or not an interruption constitutes a dominance-related attempt to seize the floor (and indeed, as observed earlier, there is in any case unquestionably no hard-and-fast line between interruptions which are and are not dominance-associated; a continuum is involved). The only approach to determining the role of the interruptions in a given interaction which is likely to approach adequacy is the type of analysis undertaken by such researchers as Tannen, Edelsky, and Coates (see pp. 239–240), which takes into detailed account the larger context in which the interruptions occur. However, determination of the extent to which the interruptions in any given interaction represent dominance attempts is inherently problematic, in that this involves ascertaining the intentions of the interruptor, and these can only ultimately be guessed. (Having the participants contribute to the analysis, as has been done by Tannen and also by, e.g., Roger and Nesshoever [1987], is no doubt a useful tactic here.) In addition, as noted earlier, a further potentially difficult aspect of any such analysis is that the conversational style normally used by the interruptor must also be taken into account; for example, speakers of the style described by Tannen (1983 and later works), as discussed earlier (see pp. 239–240), must be identified and judged differently from speakers of styles in which interruptions may be less widely regarded as rapport-building in function.

Gender and Cooperative Interruptions

We have seen that not only are instances of interruption not necessarily disruptive in nature, but they can function to indicate support, collaboration, and solidarity. There is considerable evidence, however, that women tend to perform more positive socioemotional behavior of this kind in interactions than do men. For example, many studies have found women to do more agreeing and showing of support, in both same- and mixed-sex interaction (e.g., Leet-Pellegrini 1980, Aries 1982, Wood & Karten 1986, Carli 1989); the majority of studies which have examined the use of back channel responses by listeners have found women to use more (e.g., Bilous & Krauss 1988, Roger & Nesshoever 1987, Edelsky & Adams 1990); and several studies have found women to be more likely to express interest in another's opinions or feelings by such means as asking questions or using tags (Fishman 1983, Holmes 1984, Cameron, McAlinden, and O'Leary 1989).

Given the preceding findings, one might hypothesize that women would be more likely than men to use interruptions to indicate interest and rapport. Three studies which have examined all-female groups— Kalčik (1975), Coates (1989), and Booth-Butterfield and Booth-Butterfield (1988)—have all reported the interruptions in the groups studied to be primarily of this kind. Coates (1989), indeed, suggests that this is the most typical function of simultaneous talk in all-female interaction. However, virtually no studies have applied the same kind of detailed analysis to interruptions in all-male groups so that comparisons might be made between the genders in these respects. One exception is McLachlan (1991), a study which provides some support for the hypothesis under discussion: McLachlan reported that when tackling a problem in which they were in agreement as to the solution (as determined by a pretest), female dyads produced more simultaneous speech classified by coders as nondisruptive than did male dyads.

Moreover there exists one type of indirect evidence which suggests that interruptions may tend to be more commonly of the collaborative, supportive type in all-female than in all-male interaction. As shown in Table 9.2, three studies (Bilous & Krauss 1988, Street & Murphy 1987, Crosby 1976) found significantly more total interruptions in all-female pairs than in all-male pairs. In addition, although Marche (1988) observed no gender difference overall in number of interruptions, in this study of three age groups averaging nine, fourteen and nineteen years old[31] there were significantly more interruptions in female than in male pairs in the fourteen-year-old group; further, across all three age groups, females were significantly more likely to interrupt other females than they were males. One further study, Dabbs and Ruback (1984), reported a tendency for all-female groups to produce more interruptions than all-male groups. What is of particular interest in all five of these studies is that each reports in addition other findings for all-female talk which, together with the interruption findings, suggest a pattern remarkably reminiscent of the conversational style described by Tannen (1983 and later works) and mentioned earlier (see pp. 239–240). To recap, in this "high-involvement" style, interruptions are frequent and serve a primarily positive socioemotional function, indicating interest and enthusiasm. Other characteristics of this style include frequent and expressive back channel responses, a fast rate of speech, and fast pacing with respect to turn taking; Tannen notes that the overall effect of one of intensity and rapid pace (1983:120–121). The

findings of all these studies suggest that this type of speech style characterizes all-female, but not all-male talk. For example, Bilous and Krauss
(1988) report of their study that female pairs not only interrupted more
than male pairs, but also produced more back channel responses, paused
less, produced more total words, produced shorter utterances, and
laughed more; they note that this suggests a higher involvement level in
female than in male pairs (p. 190). Similarly, Marche (1988) notes that not
only did females interrupt other females more than they did males, but
female pairs also produced more brief, multiple, and repeated back channel
responses; laughed more; and made more brief restatements of the partner's previous utterance (this last is also noted by Tannen as typical of this
high-involvement, rapport-building style). Such findings suggest that the
relatively high level of interruptions observed in female interaction in these
five studies was probably primarily associated with the expression of interest, enthusiasm, and rapport. No study that we know of has reported
behaviors such as those mentioned as being more strongly characteristic of
male than of female interaction, or even as being equally characteristic of
male and female interaction.[32]

In addition, Bilous and Krauss (1988) and Marche (1988) examined
mixed-sex dyads as well as same-sex dyads. The features mentioned previously were found to be, in general, less prevalent in mixed-sex than in
female dyads in both studies, and Bilous and Krauss report that females
significantly reduced most of these behaviors, including interruptions,
when talking to males (representing accommodation to the male speech
style). Thus, this style may be particularly characteristic of all-female talk,
at least under some circumstances.

Other Factors Which May Have Affected Results in the Gender-Related Interruptions Literature

This chapter has reviewed a number of studies dealing with potential
gender differences in the use of interruptions and has pointed to considerable inconsistencies in the findings of different studies. What kinds of
factors might have given rise to these inconsistencies? Clearly, various
subject and situational variables may have been at work here. Beyond this,
however, other aspects of the methodology employed may also have contributed to the variations in the findings; methodological considerations,
moreover, render the research results of questionable reliability in a percentage of cases. This section will first review subject and situational variables which may have affected results and then turn to methodological
problems.

Effects of Subject and Situational Variables

Most of the gender-related research on interruptions has involved unacquainted or minimally acquainted college students interacting in dyads;

the setting has most commonly been that of the experimental laboratory. The effects of such factors as age, degree of intimacy, type of setting, and topic of conversation have rarely been systematically addressed in this literature. We will review here various factors which might potentially affect the results of studies with respect to gender differences in interruption use and comment on the existing evidence as to any such effects, dealing first with subject and then with situational variables.

(1) Age. While, as we have seen, most research on adults has involved no significant gender differences in interruption behavior, the only two studies of very young children—Esposito (1979) and Peterson (1986), which examined three- and four-year-olds—both found that boys interrupted girls significantly more than the reverse in mixed-sex pairs. Obviously, one possible explanation is that these young children are not yet sufficiently socialized to initiate interruptions of the supportive or cooperative type (given that these involve some degree of awareness of the needs of others), and that very young boys are more likely than girls to initiate dominance-related interruptions. However, further research is needed to warrant such a conclusion. With respect to older preadolescent children, Marche (1988) found no significant gender differences in interruption behavior in nine-year-olds, and Welkowitz et al. (1984) found only one gender difference for eight-year-olds: the interruptee was more likely to retain the floor in female dyads than in male or mixed-sex dyads. This may imply fewer disruptive interruptions in the female dyads. Both studies also compared different age groups. The only major age-based difference found by Marche was that for fourteen-year-olds, but not for nine- or nineteen-year-olds, there were more interruptions in female than in male same-sex dyads; it is not clear how this age effect might be best explained. Welkowitz et al. found that the interruptee was more likely to retain the floor in dyads of male twenty-year-olds than in dyads of male eight-year-olds (there was no such effect for female dyads) and was more likely to retain the floor in mixed-sex dyads of twenty-year-olds than in mixed-sex dyads of eight-year-olds. This may imply fewer dominance-related interruptions by the older males and the older mixed-sex dyads than by the younger ones.[33]

(2) Degree of Intimacy. Research suggests that unacquainted individuals are more likely than those who know each other well to rely on characteristics such as sex to define status/power relationships; close friends and intimates may transcend this to create their own personal division of power (Maccoby & Jacklin 1974, Drass 1986). Consistent with this are the findings of Kollock et al. (1985), in which relative power, but not gender, affected interruption use in intimate couples. We might anticipate, then, that in mixed-sex interaction males would be more likely to exceed females in the initiation of dominance-associated interruptions when participants are unacquainted or not well acquainted than when they are intimates. Three studies have systematically examined the relationships among interruptions, degree of intimacy, and gender. Two found no evi-

dence for such an effect (although it should be kept in mind that both studies dealt only with the raw number of interruptions, and of course it is not clear what proportion of these would have been dominance-associated): Shaw and Sadler (1965), who concluded that females interrupted more than males in mixed-sex pairs, found that they interrupted to an equal extent whether the partner was a husband, a boyfriend, or a stranger, and Crosby (1976) similarly found that whether a (same-sex) dyad partner was a friend or a stranger did not affect number of interruptions. The third study, McLachlan (1991), comparing same-sex interaction between friends and between strangers in a problem-solving task, reported two significant triple interactions involving disagreement, gender, and familiarity for successful interruptions and back channel responses; however, "the cell means were not readily interpreted" and "the results were not considered sufficiently robust for further comment" (p. 210).

Further, a comparison of those studies from Tables 9.1 and 9.2 which involved unacquainted subjects and those which involved friends or acquaintances (no studies other than those mentioned have involved intimate couples) reveals no clear pattern of gender-related differences.

(3) Personality Factors. The relationship between gender and a tendency toward high dominance predisposition as factors in interruption behavior—including the extent to which dominance predisposition may differently affect males' and females' interruption behavior—has been discussed (see pp. 251–253). There is in addition a certain amount of research on the effects of sex-role self-concept on interruption use (e.g., LaFrance & Carmen 1980, Jose et al. 1980, Drass 1986, Marche 1988). Results have been mixed; we will not attempt to review these here. A useful discussion of the problems involved in studying sex-role self-concept in relation to conversational behavior is provided in Crosby, Jose & Wong-McCarthy (1981). In addition, a few studies have examined the relationship between interruption use and such qualities (of interruptor and/or interruptee) as need for social approval, emotional maturity, and degree of extroversion (Natale et al. 1979 [see note 13], Feldstein et al. 1974, Rim 1977). Only Natale et al. examined whether the effects found held equally for males and for females; no gender differences were observed.

(4) Status/Power in the Interaction Resulting From Some Source Other Than Gender. To the extent that interruptions are associated with dominance, it might be expected that individuals with higher status or power in the interaction deriving from some source other than gender would interrupt lower-status, lower-power individuals more than the reverse, and that this might outweigh any effects on interruption use which might otherwise be produced by gender. As previously noted, this may help to explain the findings of no gender differences in Kollock et al. (1985 [see pp. 249–250]), Leffler et al. (1982 [see notes 19 and 26]), and, in part, Craig and Pitts (1990 [see note 19]).

(5) Degree of Conflict Present, and the Extent to Which the Interaction Is Task-Oriented. The possible differential effects of these factors on females' and males' use of interruptions, and the conclusions which can be drawn from existing research with respect to this, have been discussed (see pp. 249–250).

(6) Natural Versus Laboratory Setting. It has sometimes been suggested (e.g., Smith 1985) that a laboratory setting is particularly conducive to the display of control-related behaviors, and thus might favor male dominance displays, although this is a controversial point. However, comparison of studies on interruptions in these two types of setting reveal no systematic differences in the results as they relate to gender. (Thirty-one of the forty-three studies listed in Tables 9.1 and 9.2 involved a laboratory experiment; twelve—for the most part studies of groups—examined naturally occurring speech.)

(7) Dyad Versus Group. Kennedy and Camden (1983:55) suggest that since the amount of speech time and floor access available per person is less in a group than in a dyad, this leads to an increased demand for speeches of shorter duration and a relaxation of turn-taking protocol, and thus interrupting may become a more legitimate means of gaining the floor in a group than in a dyad. (Beattie [1981:29–30] makes a similar point.) If this is true, one might expect that there would be fewer findings of males interrupting more than females in studies of mixed-sex groups than in those of mixed-sex dyads. Indeed, a somewhat higher percentage of studies of mixed-sex groups have found females to interrupt more than males than is the case in studies of dyads (three out of twelve, or 25%, as opposed to only two out of twenty-one, or 9.5%); however, contrary to expectation, slightly more studies of mixed-sex groups than studies of dyads have found males to interrupt more (five out of twelve, or 42%, as compared to six out of twenty-one, or 29%).

(8) Topic of Conversation. If the topic of conversation is perceived as representing a male or a female area of expertise, the gender in question may feel more of an "authority" in that area and thus may feel more justified in making dominance-associated interruptions. It was suggested earlier (see pp. 252–253) that this may explain the finding of Courtright et al. (1979) that wives' "domineeringness" scores were more strongly associated with interruptions than were those of husbands. In most of the studies in Tables 9.1 and 9.2 no information is provided as to the topic(s) discussed; in thirteen, however, the topic is described (in each case, it was assigned for discussion by the experimenter). These topics were sex-neutral in all but two cases, in both of which they dealt with a "female area of expertise." It is noteworthy that one of these two studies (Shaw & Sadler 1965) is also one of the few in which females were found to interrupt males more than the reverse (the topic here dealt with interper-

sonal relationships, as in Courtright et al. [1979]). In the remaining study, however (Leet-Pellegrini 1980), in which subjects were asked to discuss the possible effects of TV violence on children—since it deals with children, arguably a topic on which women would perceive themselves and be perceived by men as particularly competent—the genders were not found to differ significantly in number of interruptions.

(9) Change in Gender Behavior Over the Years. It is also conceivable that the influence of the women's movement might, over time, have brought about changes in women's and men's beliefs and assumptions about their own and the other sex, and consequently changes in their behavior. In fact, when one conducts a comparison of the findings of studies in chronological order, an interesting result emerges. Restricting ourselves here to research on mixed-sex interaction, the single study done during the 1960s (Shaw & Sadler 1965) found females to interrupt males more than the reverse. Of the ten studies published in the 1970s (all between 1975 and 1979; we include here West [1979], the results of which were also published later in West [1982] and West & Zimmerman [1983]), fully seven found males to interrupt more, while three others found no gender difference. Of the twenty-three studies published between 1980 and 1991, however, fourteen found no gender difference, five found males to interrupt more, and four found females to interrupt more. Thus, while 70% of the studies published between 1975 and 1979 found males to interrupt more, only 22% of those conducted between 1980 and 1991 found this (the distribution is similar for the first and second halves of the decade).

Caution is called for, however, in drawing the conclusion that women must have interrupted men more in the 1980s and 1990s than they did in the 1970s. It is not inconceivable that in the years immediately following the publication of Zimmerman and West's enormously influential 1975 study, the expectation of similar results (i.e., that men interrupted women far more than the reverse) may have caused some element of experimenter bias to enter into the design and/or analysis of some studies. That such bias may affect results is illustrated by the fact that two surveys of studies on gender differences in, respectively, influenceability (Eagly & Carli 1981) and performance in task groups (Wood 1987) have found a significant relationship between the sex of the researcher and the generation of results flattering to that sex. Some ways in which such a bias might enter into analysis will be discussed in the next section. Expectations of researchers that males would interrupt females more than the reverse may have been somewhat reduced in the early 1980s by the publication of such widely cited studies in the interruptions literature as Beattie (1981), which found the sexes not to differ in interruption use.

All of these variables, then, are potentially germane to women's and men's use of interruptions, and at least some may help to account for the inconsistencies in the findings of different studies. There are also, of course, other variables which may be relevant, for example, the subjects' socioeconomic class, cultural and/or ethnic group, and amount of education. Existing research, however, provides virtually no information about the possible effects of these factors on women's and men's use of interruptions. Clearly, there is much scope for future research into the effects of all these factors on interruption use as it interrelates with gender.

Methodological Considerations

Other aspects of the methodology employed in studies of interruptions may also have contributed to the inconsistencies in their results. One important factor here is undoubtedly the way in which interruptions have been counted; studies have differed in this, rendering their results not truly comparable. Moreover, more seriously, the method of counting used may sometimes have led to misleading or unreliable results. Further, unrepresentatively small subject samples, absence of statistical testing, and faulty statistical methods render the results of some studies of questionable reliability.

Let us being with a consideration of the measures by which interruptions have been counted. While most studies have simply counted instances of interruption in raw numbers, some have instead divided the number of interruptions by the amount of time that the other participant(s) spoke, to produce a rate.[34] This latter way of measuring interruptions takes into account differences in the opportunities afforded to the two participants to interrupt. For example, suppose that A and B, talking together, each initiate the same raw number of interruptions toward the other, but A talks twice as much as B; in that case, B has interrupted at only half of A's rate, since B has had twice as much opportunity to interrupt as A. Thus, a study counting raw numbers of interruptions would conclude that there was no difference between A and B with respect to interruptive behavior, while a study measuring interruption rate would conclude that A interrupted B twice as much as B interrupted A. Measurement of interruptions as a rate would appear to be a more accurate gauge of interruption behavior.

Nine studies dealing with gender have measured rate rather than raw number of interruptions;[35] none of these found a significant difference between the sexes in their rate of interruption. Five of these studies also report results on the amount that women and men spoke. Of these, four found no significant difference (Duncan & Fiske 1977, Frances 1979, Martin & Craig 1983, and Leffler et al. 1982); the remaining study, Kollock et al. (1985), had mixed results. Nevertheless one is led to wonder whether some studies which measured interruptions in terms of raw numbers and found no difference between the genders might not have found a difference if interruptions had been measured as a rate; in view of the fact that most studies have found men to talk more than women in mixed-sex interaction (either overall or under at least some circumstances) (see James & Drakich, this volume), this raises the possibility that men might have interrupted women at a more frequent rate than the reverse in these studies.

It is also possible that in the five studies listed in Table 9.1 in which females were found—in each case, by the raw numbers measure—to interrupt significantly more than males in mixed-sex interaction, the sexes may not in fact have differed significantly in the rate at which they interrupted each other, if males spoke more than females did in these studies. Males were indeed found to talk significantly more than females in two of these studies, Connor-Linton (1987) and Sayers (1987), and in the case of the latter, there does exist evidence that the female and male subjects did not differ in the rate at which they interrupted.[36]

There have also been, of course, other kinds of differences among studies in how interruptions have been measured, as noted earlier; these too raise questions of comparability with respect to the results of different research. Thus while most studies have excluded back channel utterances from their count of interruptions, a few have not (see p. 238); while some studies have excluded other types of simultaneous talk perceived as supportive rather than disruptive in function, others have not (see note 11); while some have excluded the type of mistiming error termed an "overlap" by Schegloff (1973), others have not (see pp. 240–241 and note 13); and while most studies have ignored the existence of "silent" interruptions, a few have included them in their interruptions count (see note 8). Clearly, differences of these kinds could affect results. As just one kind of example, "silent" interruptions, in which the interruptor begins speaking during a slight pause in the interruptee's talk—so that no simultaneous speech occurs (see p. 237)—are of course one form of "successful" interruption; to the extent that successful interruptions are more strongly associated with dominance than unsuccessful ones, to exclude "silent" interruptions might conceivably reduce the extent to which the counted interruptions constituted attempts to seize the floor.

Yet another problem is that the way in which instances of interruption are counted can sometimes be subject to errors in interpretation, and, moreover, susceptible to experimenter bias. One often-cited example of this is to be found in the research which has attempted to separate "overlaps" in the Schegloff (1973) sense from "interruptions." As was noted earlier (see pp. 240–241), the distinction between the two types is based on whether the simultaneous speech initiated is or is not near a "transition-relevant place" (that is, a possible completion point); this is defined simply as the end of any "unit-type," that is, any word, phrase, clause, or sentence (Sacks et al. 1974:702). But, of course, the crucial criterion with respect to whether or not an instance of simultaneous speech is simply a mistiming error is really whether the interruptor believes that the interruptee is about to reach a point which can reasonably be taken as the end of his/her turn; and this, in fact, requires taking into account not only syntactic criteria, but also the semantic content of the interruptee's speech, the larger communicative context, prosodic and nonverbal turn-yielding signals (Duncan 1973), and even knowledge of the personality of the interruptee.[37] (These problems have been pointed out by a number of researchers, e.g., Bennett [1981], McLaughlin [1984], Wilson, Wiemann & Zimmerman [1984], Murray [1985, 1987], Murray & Covelli [1988], Tannen [1989].) These then are also the criteria the analyst must use in deciding whether a given instance of simultaneous talk is likely to have been a simple mistiming error. A further problem here too is that the common use of written transcripts of conversations, as opposed to videotapes, makes unavailable prosodic and nonverbal turn-yielding signals. Thus, in practice the decision of the analyst as to whether instances of simultaneous talk should be classified as "interruptions" or merely "overlaps" must involve a large subjective component, and as a result errors can be made, and biased expectations can influence judgment.

Further, the use of written transcripts in the usual format originated by Sacks et al. (1974) may also lead to other types of error in interpretation. Edelsky (1981, this volume), in a nice discussion of this, points out that the way in which participants' contributions are displayed on the page can give a misleading impression of who interrupted whom. Other researchers who have commented on the fact that the transcript display can affect interpretation include Alcguire (1978), Jefferson (1973), and Ochs (1979). Comparable problems can arise when a mechanized means such as a computer system that records simultaneous speech is used (as in, e.g., Natale et al. 1979).

Other aspects of the methodology used may also render of questionable reliability the results of some studies. The pioneering study of Zimmerman and West (1975), for example, which found men to interrupt women overwhelmingly more than the reverse, has been criticized not only on the grounds that bias may have been present in the counting of instances of interruption (Murray & Covelli 1988, Murray 1988), but also on the grounds that the relatively small number of interruptions identified render the results unrepresentative (Marche 1988), on the grounds that the number of subjects was small and over a quarter of the male interruptions in the mixed-sex conversations were attributable to a single subject (Beattie [1981], who also points out that if just one other male subject was relatively voluble, this would have caused the gender difference to be significant), and on the grounds that the effects of speech setting were not controlled for (Murray & Covelli 1988). Similar criticisms could also be made of other studies. A telling discussion of how research on interruptions has often employed faulty statistical methods is provided by Dindia (1987), who points out that studies have often tested only for the sex of the interruptor, ignoring the effect of the sex of the interruptee and the interaction of sex of interruptor and sex of interruptee; she notes that if the correlation between the two is ignored, results may be reported as significant which in fact are not, or vice versa. Statistical tests used in studies of simultaneous speech, then, she argues, have often ignored the fact that interruption behavior in one member of a group or dyad is not independent of that of other members; typically, researchers in this area have incorrectly applied statistical tests that assume independent observations. In addition, not all studies have even employed statistical testing (e.g., Eakins & Eakins 1976, Woods 1989).

Clearly not only do methodological differences among studies create problems when it comes to comparing their results, but more seriously, because of faulty methodology, real gender differences in interruption use may be obscured, or gender differences may be reported which are not in fact present. It is vital that these problems be ironed out in future research, if reliable results are to be obtained.

Conclusions

Males have been hypothesized to be more likely than females to use interruption as a means of dominating and controlling interactions. It has been widely cited that, consistent with this hypothesis, most research has found males to interrupt females more than the reverse. This review has pointed out that such a conclusion is incorrect; the majority of studies have found no significant difference between the sexes in this respect. This may be a consequence of the fact that a large proportion of the simultaneous talk in an interaction may not represent attempts to dominate or control the interaction. Various efforts have been made by researchers to find simple, objective criteria by which those instances of interruption which constitute attempts to dominate can be reliably distinguished from those which do not. It is clear, however, that no such criteria exist.

There also exist approaches other than that of simply comparing the overall number of interruptions initiated which serve as potential means of testing whether males are more likely than females to use dominance-associated interruptions, and of testing whether such interruptions are more likely to be directed against females than against males. These include examination of the semantic content of females' and males' interruptions as directed toward each sex and comparison of the number of "successful" interruptions initiated by and toward each sex. Overall no clear-cut gender differences have emerged from the research by any of these criteria. Because none is an entirely reliable gauge of dominance in interruption behavior, however, it cannot be definitively concluded that males and females do not differ with respect to the use of dominance-associated interruptions.

A small amount of evidence exists that females may use interruptions of the cooperative and rapport-building type to a greater extent than do males, at least in some circumstances. However, definitive conclusions as to whether males and females differ in the ways in which they use interruptions, whether of the cooperative or dominance-related type, must probably be dependent on analyses of conversations which take into detailed account the larger context in which the interruptions occur—

although, as noted earlier (see p. 258), this approach is also in some ways problematic.

In addition, little evidence exists as to the effects of a number of different subject and situational variables on the interruption behavior of females and males; clearly this constitutes a further area for future research. And lastly, it is essential that future researchers be alert to ways in which the methodology employed can contribute to misleading and unreliable results in the area of gender and interruption use.

NOTES

1. We have omitted from Tables 9.1 and 9.2 unpublished papers of which we have been unable to obtain a copy (e.g., Hirschman 1973 and Ofshe 1981, cited in the bibliographies in Thorne & Henley 1975 and Thorne, Kramarae, & Henley 1983), and a few papers dealing with interruptions and gender in which the results reported were insufficiently clear or insufficiently specific with respect to our concerns in this review (e.g., McCarrick et al. 1981, van Alphen 1987, Pieper 1984, Greif 1980). All of the studies reported on involved adult interaction, with the exception of Esposito (1979) and Peterson (1986), which examined three- and four-year-olds; also, two studies (Welkowitz, Bond, & Feldstein 1984, Marche 1988) examined eight- or nine-year-olds in addition to adults.

2. Also of relevance here are two studies of parent-child dyads, Greif (1980) and Pieper (1984), both of which failed to find a significant difference between the number of interruptions initiated by mothers and by fathers but found a tendency for fathers to produce more. Greif also discerned a nonsignificant trend for boys to interrupt parents more than girls did.

3. In addition, Natale, Entin, and Jaffe (1979), in a study of same-sex and mixed-sex dyads, found that males initiated more interruptions overall than females. However, since the sex of the partner was not taken into account, it is not possible to tell whether males interrupted females more than the reverse in this study.

4. Smith-Lovin and Brody (1989), Willis and Williams (1976), and Woods (1989), while they found no difference between males and females in relative number of interruptions, report other findings with regard to the use of interruptions which they argue reflect male dominance. These will be discussed in a later section.

5. Craig and Pitts excluded from consideration cases in which the interruption did not result in the interruptor gaining single control of the floor. See pp. 244–246 for a further discussion of this distinction.

6. Murray and Covelli (1988) studied, along with three mixed-sex groups, two same-sex and two mixed-sex dyadic interviews; their results are collapsed across all these.

7. In addition, in Natale, Entin, and Jaffe (1979) (see note 3), it is possible that there may have been more interruptions in male than in female dyads; however, since the sex of the interruptee was not taken into account in this study, it is not possible to determine whether or not this was the case.

8. Those studies from Tables 9.1 and 9.2 which included "silent interrup-

tions" in their investigation are Beattie (1981), Craig and Pitts (1990), Marche (1988), Roger and Schumacher (1983), Roger and Nesshoever (1987), and Trimboli and Walker (1984).

9. See pp. 240–241 for one commonly used definition of "overlap." A second definition is that employed in research adopting Ferguson's (1977) method of classifying deviations from smooth speaker switches; it here refers to an instance in which both speakers continue talking simultaneously, neither yielding to the other.

10. Other names include "assent terms" (Schegloff 1972), "listener responses" (Dittman & Llewellyn 1967), "minimal responses" (Zimmerman & West 1975), "accompaniment signals" (Kendon 1967), and "reinforcers" (Wiemann & Knapp 1975).

11. A few of the studies listed in Tables 9.1 and 9.2 have recognized that some specific types of simultaneous talk other than back channel responses are likely to be primarily supportive and have excluded these from their count of interruptions (in an attempt to isolate those instances of simultaneous talk which are disruptive from those which are not). Woods (1989) and Leffler et al. (1982) excluded cases in which a word or phrase was repeated; West and Zimmerman (1983) excluded "saying the same thing at the same time;" and Duncan and Fiske (1977), Roger and Schumacher (1983), Roger and Nesshoever (1987), Marche (1988), and Smith-Lovin and Brody (1989) excluded phrases such as "I agree" or "that's right," requests for clarification, brief restatements of another speaker's utterance, and completions of another speaker's sentence. It is certainly, however, not safe to assume that once such types of simultaneous talk as these last are excluded, all remaining cases will then be genuinely disruptive. For example, instances of simultaneous talk in which participants are jointly developing an idea or sharing in a joke (as described in, e.g., Coates [1989] or Edelsky [1981, this volume]) might well not be excluded by these measures; nor would types of interruption such as those illustrated in on pp. 240–241, which are not supportive in nature but are nonetheless not disruptive.

In addition, in one last study, de Boer (1987) (see Table 9.2), instances of simultaneous talk were classed as "interruptions" (as opposed to "overlaps") apparently on a purely subjective basis, that of whether they manifested "competition."

12. This discussion of mistiming errors is primarily applicable to conversational styles which do not value fast pacing as a sign of involvement and rapport. In cultural groups in which such a style is the norm, pauses between turns are perceived as indicating lack of rapport; overlapping talk of the type described is normal, both because speakers wish to prevent pauses and because overlapping itself is seen as evidence of positive involvement in the conversation (see Tannen 1984).

13. Twelve studies from Tables 9.1 and 9.2 have excluded "overlaps," in this definition, from their count of interruptions: Dindia (1987), Kollock et al. (1985), Esposito (1979), Octigan and Niederman (1979), West (1979, 1982)/West and Zimmerman (1983), Zimmerman and West (1975), Sayers (1987), Smith-Lovin and Brody (1989), Woods (1989), Eakins and Eakins (1976), Kennedy and Camden (1983), and Murray and Covelli (1988).

14. Some further support for the notion that most interruptions are not dominance-related in unstructured conversation is provided by Natale, Entin, and Jaffe (1979), who found that the frequency with which individuals interrupted

others in this context correlated positively with their "desire for social approval" on a standard test, a result which would not be expected if most interruptions are manifestations of a disregard for others' right to speak.

15. This classification is based on the work of Watzlawick, Beavin, and Jackson (1967).

16. These six studies each used an established psychological dominance test involving subject self-rating; Ferguson (1977) additionally employed a dominance rating based on the interviewer's personal judgment. While the choice of test differed from study to study, testing was in general designed to measure the extent to which subjects tend to influence or control the behavior of others in their interpersonal interactions (cf. Ferguson 1977:299).

17. In addition, three studies which have compared competitive interactions with less competitive ones have found there to be significantly more interruptions in the former than in the latter (Jose et al. 1980, Trimboli & Walker 1984, Stephens & Beattie 1986).

18. Dominance was observed to be correlated only with "overlaps," defined as instances of interruption in which both speakers completed their utterances. This finding has not been duplicated in other studies.

19. Also relevant here are a few studies in which individuals differing in status on a basis other than that of gender were compared with respect to the number of interruptions they initiated. Wiens, Thompson, Matarazzo, Matarazzo, and Saslow (1965) found that higher-status nurses interrupted an interviewer more than lower-status nurses did; West and Zimmerman (1977), that parents interrupted children more than the reverse; West (1985), that doctors interrupted patients more than the reverse; and Leffler et al. (1982), that when dyad members were assigned the role of "teacher" or "student," "teachers" interrupted "students" more than the reverse. In addition, Craig and Pitts (1990) found that tutors interrupted students "successfully" (see pp. 244–245) more than the reverse in tutorials; however, Beattie (1981) found the opposite to be the case. It may well be pertinent here that except in the case of the study on parents and children, all these involved formally structured interaction, rather than casual friendly conversation. In addition, however, it is possible that factors independent of status considerations may have been relevant in some cases; for instance, the nature of children's conversation may tend to be more provocative of interruptions than that of adults, and the requirements of the pedagogical role may tend to lead to more interruptions by teachers or tutors than by students.

20. Some researchers include as part of the definition of "successful interruption" that the interruptee does not complete his or her utterance (e.g., Kollock et al. 1985, Roger & Schumacher 1983, Roger & Nesshoever 1987, Smith-Levin & Brody 1989, Welkowitz et al. 1984). Other researchers use a slightly broader definition, in which the crucial factor is simply that the interruptor ends by gaining single control of the floor—the interruptee may or may not complete his or her utterance (e.g., Natale et al. 1979, Rogers & Jones 1975, Beattie 1981, Craig & Pitts 1990). See also Ferguson (1977) for an often-cited four-way classification of interruptions which takes into account the response of the interruptee and Roger, Bull, and Smith (1988) for a still more detailed classification of interruptions along these lines.

21. Goldberg (1990) proposes a heuristic to determine whether an interruption is dominance-related, rapport-related, or neutral, based on the semantic con-

tent of the interruption (the focus here is primarily on whether the interruption shares a topic with the interrupted talk). This proposal constitutes a useful contribution to the problem but does not provide a full explanation; for example, it does not account for differences in the use and interpretation of simultaneous talk as a result of conversational style differences (Tannen 1983 and later works).

22. As noted earlier, some studies have omitted from their interruptions count some types of interruption (beyond simply "back channel" responses, which have been almost always omitted) which they believed likely to be not dominance-related. Of these too, however, only a minority found males to interrupt more than females. Of the eight studies mentioned in note 11 which excluded types of interruption thought to be supportive, two found males to interrupt more (West & Zimmerman 1983, de Boer 1987); the rest found no difference. Of the twelve studies listed in note 13 which excluded the type of mistiming error identified by the criteria of Schegloff (1972) (see pp. 240–241), four found no difference, five found males to interrupt more, and three found females to interrupt more. Of course, in these cases, many of the remaining interruptions which were counted still may not have been disruptive.

23. In addition, de Boer (1987), as noted in note 11, classified instances of simultaneous talk as "interruptions" only if they manifested "competition," apparently judged on a subjective basis. By this criterion, male pairs were found to produce more interruptions than female pairs. (However, de Boer also notes that one particular conversation between two men might have caused this difference to be significant.) Further, Lamothe (1989) classified interruptions as positive, negative, or "other" and found that when female, male, and mixed-sex pairs were compared, female pairs produced the largest number of positive interruptions and male pairs the largest number of negative interruptions. (However, Lamothe's definition of "interruption" is unclear; unfortunately, we have been unable to obtain the full text of this paper.)

24. It may also be relevant that in Ferguson (1977), in which all the subjects were female, comparatively little relationship was found between interruptions and high dominance predisposition. However, as was previously noted (see p. 244), the fact that this study involved informal conversation between friends may also be a factor.

25. In this study of parent-child dyads both parents tended to interrupt daughters more than sons, but this did not reach significance.

26. As was previously noted (see note 19), in this study subjects were assigned the roles of "teacher" and "student," and either the higher status or the pedagogical function associated with the "teacher" role may have outweighed the impact of gender on interruption behavior.

27. In addition, Woods (1989) found that subordinate females in three-person work groups were more often successfully interrupted than subordinate males. No statement is made, however, as to whether females were more often successfully interrupted than males overall, or as to the results with respect to attempted interruptions.

28. Going beyond the research cited by Smith-Lovin and Brody (1989), some studies have found women to show more competitive behavior with men than with other women (e.g., Hogg 1985, Carli 1989). However, the results of some other studies contradict this (e.g., Leet-Pellegrini 1980, Aries 1976).

29. The findings of Welkowitz et al. (1984), in which there were a greater number of unsuccessful interruptions in mixed-sex than in same-sex dyads, are also

consistent with this suggestion. No other studies have produced results obviously consistent with this particular proposal, however.

30. One further illustration of the fact that discrimination in interruption attempts on the basis of gender may not necessarily involve issues of status and dominance is provided by Brooks (1982), in which students in college classes interrupted female professors more than male professors. Brooks also reports that students participated twice as much in female professors' classes and suggests that female professors encouraged class participation more; thus, the reason why students interrupted female professors more than male professors may have been simply that they had more opportunities to interrupt female professors.

31. While Marche studied the number and type of interruptions used in all three age groups, the relationship between interruption use and dominance predisposition was examined only for the fourteen- and nineteen-year-olds. For this reason, references to this work earlier in the chapter have mentioned only these two age groups.

32. Several other studies echo the same theme. Thus Hirschman (1973) observed that female pairs interrupted each other more than male pairs, but that "the females when talking to each other tended to elaborate on each others' utterances, the males to argue" (cited in Thorne & Henley 1975:249). Also LaFrance (1981) found that significantly more of the interruptions in female pairs constituted questions than in male pairs and noted that these are "more responsive in character" than other types of interruptions. (However, Dindia [1987] did not find the sexes to differ in number of interruptive questions.) In addition, the finding of Ofshe (1981, cited in Thorne, Kramarae, & Henley 1983:276), that not only were there much higher rates of simultaneous speech in all-female than in all-male groups, but the difference was greater during social than during task activity, suggests that here too, females may have been using interruptions for rapport-building purposes to a greater extent than males.

33. Greenwood (1989, cited in Tannen 1989:270, 1990:192–195), however, found that a high rate of interruption was a sign of social comfort among preadolescent children; this suggests that by this age the use of interruptions as collaborative and rapport-building acts is already well developed.

34. It has sometimes been suggested that conversing with a very talkative partner is likely to increase the amount of interruptions an individual initiates, because of the need to "get a word in edgewise." Findings with respect to this have been mixed, however. Natale et al. (1979) observed that the more an individual talked, the more likely s/he was to be interrupted, and Drass (1986) found that for males, but not for females, the more time the subject spent listening, the more likely it was that he would initiate an interruption. However, Kennedy and Camden (1983) and Dindia (1987) both found lengthy speech by a partner to have no effect on interruption use.

35. These are Duncan and Fiske (1977), Roger and Nesshoever (1987), Roger and Schumacher (1983), Martin and Craig (1983), Leffler et al. (1982), LaFrance and Carmen (1980)/LaFrance (1981) (describing the same study), Smith-Lovin and Brody (1989), Frances (1979) (this study employed both measures), and Kollock et al. (1985) (this last study, however, measured interruption rate by dividing the number of interruptions individuals produced by the amount they spoke themselves, rather than by the amount their partner spoke). As an additional note Beattie (1981) and Craig and Pitts (1990) employed neither measure; both studies measured interruptions as a percentage of all speaker switches.

36. In an earlier (1984) version of this paper Sayers did measure interruptions as a rate and reported no significant gender difference.

37. For example, Coates (1989:108) points out that certain individuals have a tendency to "tail off" (*sic*) without finishing their sentences.

REFERENCES

Aleguire, David (1978). Interruptions as turn-taking. Paper presented at Ninth World Congress of Sociology, Uppsala, Sweden.

Aries, Elizabeth (1976). Interaction patterns and themes of male, female, and mixed groups. *Small Group Behavior* 7:7–18. Reprinted in 1977 as: Male-female interpersonal styles in all male, all female and mixed groups. In Alice Sargent (Ed.) *Beyond sex roles* (pp. 292–298). St. Paul, MN: West.

Aries, Elizabeth (1982). Verbal and nonverbal behavior in single-sex and mixed-sex groups: Are traditional sex roles changing? *Psychological Reports* 51:127–134.

Aries, Elizabeth (1987). Gender and communication. In Phillip Shaver & Clyde Hendrick (Eds.) *Sex and gender* (pp. 149–176). Newbury Park, CA: Sage Publication.

Aries, Elizabeth, Gold, Conrad & Weigel, Russell H. (1983). Dispositional and situational influence on dominance behavior in small groups. *Journal of Personality and Social Psychology* 44:779–786.

Beattie, Geoffrey W. (1981). Interruption in conversational interaction and its relation to the sex and status of the interactants. *Linguistics* 19:15–35.

Beattie, Geoffrey W. (1982). Look, just don't interrupt! *New Scientist* 95:859–860.

Beattie, Geoffrey W. (1989). Interruptions in political interviews: A reply to Bull and Mayer. *Journal of Language and Social Psychology* 8:327–336.

Bennett, Adrian (1981). Interruptions and the interpretation of conversation. *Discourse Processes* 4:171–188.

Berger, Joseph, Rosenholtz, Susan J. & Zelditch, Morris Jr. (1980). Status organizing processes. *American Sociological Review* 6:479–508.

Bilous, Frances R. & Krauss, Robert M. (1988). Dominance and accommodation in the conversational behaviours of same- and mixed-gender dyads. *Language and Communication* 8:183–194.

Bohn, Emil & Stutman, Randall (1983). Sex role differences in the relational control dimension of dyadic interaction. *Women's Studies in Communication* 6:965–104.

Booth-Butterfield, Melanie & Booth-Butterfield, Steve (1988). Jock talk: Cooperation and competition within a university women's basketball team. In Barbara Bate & Anita Taylor (Eds.) *Women communicating: Studies of women's talk* (pp. 177–198). Norwood, NJ: Ablex.

Brown, Penelope & Levinson, Stephen C. (1987). *Some universals in language usage*. Cambridge: Cambridge University Press.

Brooks, Virginia R. (1982). Sex differences in student dominance behavior in female and male professors' classrooms. *Sex Roles* 8:683–690.

Bull, Peter & Mayer, Kate (1988). Interruptions in political interviews: A study of Margaret Thatcher and Neil Kinnock. *Journal of Language and Social Psychology* 7:35–45.

Cameron, Deborah, McAlinden, Fiona, & O'Leary, Kathy (1989). Lakoff in context: The social and linguistic functions of tag questions. In Jennifer Coates & Deborah Cameron (Eds.) *Women in their speech communities* (pp. 74–93). London and New York: Longman.

Carli, Linda L. (1989). Gender differences in interaction style and influence. *Journal of Personality and Social Psychology* 56:565–576.

Case, Susan (1988). Cultural differences, not deficiencies: An analysis of managerial women's language. In Suzanna Rose & Laurie Larwood (Eds.) *Women's Careers: Pathways and Pitfalls* (pp. 41–63). New York: Praeger.

Coates, Jennifer (1989). Gossip revisited: Language in all-female groups. In Jennifer Coates & Deborah Cameron (Eds.), *Women in their speech communities* (pp. 94–122), London and New York: Longman.

Connor-Linton, Jeff (1987). Gender differences in politeness: The struggle for power among adolescents. *Southern California Occasional Papers in Linguistics* pp. 64–98. Los Angeles: University of Southern California.

Courtright, John A., Millar, Frank E. & Rogers-Millar, L. Edna (1979). Domineeringness and dominance: Replication and expansion. *Communication Monographs* 46:179–192.

Craig, D. & Pitts, M. K. (1990). The dynamics of dominance in tutorial discussions. *Linguistics* 28:125–138.

Crosby, Faye (1976). The effects of mode of interaction, sex and acquaintance on conversation management. Ph.D. diss., Boston University.

Crosby, Faye, Jose, Paul & Wong-McCarthy, William (1981). Gender, androgyny, and conversational assertiveness. In Clara Mayo and Nancy Henley (Eds.) *Gender and nonverbal behavior* (pp. 151–169). New York: Springer-Verlag.

Dabbs, James M. Jr. & Ruback, R. Barry (1984). Vocal patterns in male and female groups. *Personality and Social Psychology Bulletin* 10:518–525.

de Boer, Mieke (1987). Sex differences in language: Observations of dyadic conversation between members of the same sex. In Dede Brouwer & Dorian de Haan (Eds.) *Women's language, socialization and self-image* (pp. 148–163). Dordrecht: Foris.

Dindia, Kathryn (1987). The effects of sex of subject and sex of partner on interruptions. *Human Communication Research* 13:345–371.

Dittman, Allen T. & Llewellyn, Lynn G. (1967). The phonemic clause as a unit of speech decoding. *Journal of Personality and Social Psychology* 6:341–348.

Drass, Kriss A. (1986). The effect of gender identity on conversation. *Social Psychology Quarterly* 49:294–301.

Duncan, Starkey (1973). Toward a grammar for dyadic conversation. *Semiotica* 9:29–47.

Duncan, Starkey & Fiske, Donald W. (1977). *Face-to-face interaction.* Hillsdale, NJ: Lawrence Erlbaum Associates.

Eagly, Alice H. & Carli, Linda L. (1981). Sex of researchers and sex-typed communications as determinants of sex differences in influenceability: A meta-analysis of social influence studies. *Psychological Bulletin* 90:1–20.

Eakins, Barbara & Eakins, R. Gene (1976). Verbal turn-taking and exchanges in faculty dialogue. In Betty Lou Dubois & Isabel M. Crouch (Eds.), *The Sociology of the languages of american women* (pp. 53–62). San Antonio, Texas: Trinity University.

Edelsky, Carole (1981). Who's got the floor? *Language in Society* 10:383–421.

Edelsky, Carole & Adams, Karen (1990). Creating inequality: Breaking the rules in debates. *Journal of Language and Social Psychology* 9:171–190.

Esposito, Anita (1979). Sex differences in children's conversation. *Language and Speech* 22:213–220.

Farina, A. (1960). Patterns of role dominance and conflict in parents of schizophrenic patients. *Journal of Abnormal and Social Psychology* 61:31–38.

Feldstein, Stanley, Alberti, L., BenDebba, M. & Welkowitz, Joan (1974). Personality and simultaneous speech. Paper presented at the annual meeting of the American Psychological Association, New Orleans. Cited in Stanley Feldstein and Joan Welkowitz (1978), A chronography of conversation: In defense of an objective approach. In Aron W. Siegman & Stanley Feldstein (Eds.) *Nonverbal behavior and communication*. New Jersey: Lawrence Erlbaum.

Ferguson, Nicola (1977). Simultaneous speech, interruptions and dominance. *British Journal of Social and Clinical Psychology* 16:295–302.

Fishman, Pamela M. (1983). Interaction: The work women do. In Barrie Thorne, Cheris Kramarae & Nancy Henley (Eds.) *Language, gender and society* (pp. 89–102). Rowley, MA: Newbury House.

Frances, Susan J. (1979). Sex differences in nonverbal behavior. *Sex Roles* 5:519–535.

Goldberg, Julia A. (1990). Interrupting the discourse on interruptions: An analysis in terms of relationally neutral, power- and rapport-oriented acts. *Journal of Pragmatics* 14:883–904.

Greenwood, Alice (1989). Discourse variation and social comfort: A study of topic initiation and interruption patterns in the dinner conversation of preadolescent children. Ph.D. diss., City University of New York.

Greif, Esther Blank (1980). Sex differences in parent-child conversations. *Women's Studies International Quarterly* 3:253–258.

Herman, Vimala (1991). Dramatic dialogue and the systematics of turn-taking. *Semiotica* 83:97–121.

Hirschman, Lynette (1973). Female-male differences in conversational interaction. Paper given at annual meeting of the Linguistic Society of America, San Diego, California, December 1973.

Hogg, Michael A. (1985). Masculine and feminine speech in dyads and groups: A study of speech style and gender salience. *Journal of Language and Social Psychology* 4:99–112.

Holmes, Janet (1984). Women's language: A functional approach. *General Linguistics* 24:149–178.

Holmes, Janet (1991). Language and gender. *Language Teaching* 24:207–220.

Jefferson, Gail (1973). A case of precision timing in ordinary conversation: Overlapped tag-positioned address terms in closing sequences. *Semiotica* 9:47–96.

Jose, Paul, Crosby, Faye & Wong-McCarthy, William (1980). Androgyny, dyadic compatibility and conversational behavior. In Howard Giles, W. Peter Robinson & Philip M. Smith (Eds.) *Language: Social psychological perspectives* (pp. 115–119). New York: Pergamon Press.

Kalčik, Susan (1975). ". . . like Ann's gynecologist or the time I was almost raped": Personal narratives in women's rap groups. *Journal of American Folklore* 88:3–11. (Reprinted in Claire R. Farrer (Ed.) *Women and folklore*, 3–11. Austin: University of Texas Press, 1975).

Kendon, Adam (1967). Some functions of gaze direction in social interaction. *Acta Psychologica* 26:22–63.

Kennedy, Carol W. & Camden, Carl (1983). A new look at interruptions. *Western Journal of Speech Communication* 47:45–58.

Kollock, Peter, Blumstein, Philip & Schwartz, Pepper (1985). Sex and power in interaction. *American Sociological Review* 50:34–46.

LaFrance, Marianne (1981). Gender gestures: Sex, sex-role and nonverbal communication. In Clara Mayo & Nancy M. Henley (Eds.) *Gender and nonverbal behavior* (pp. 129–150). New York: Springer-Verlag.

LaFrance, Marianne & Carmen, Barbara (1980). The nonverbal display of psychological androgyny. *Journal of Personality and Social Psychology* 38:36–49.

Lamothe, Jacqueline (1989). La conversation des femmes: pratique et perception. Paper presented at the Annual Meeting of the Canadian Women's Studies Association, Quebec City, Quebec, Canada.

Leet-Pellegrini, Helena M. (1980). Conversational dominance as a function of gender and expertise. In Howard Giles, W. Peter Robinson & Philip M. Smith (Eds.) *Language: Social psychological perspectives* (pp. 97–104). New York: Pergamon Press.

Leffler, Ann, Gillespie, Dair & Conaty, Joseph C. (1982). The effects of status differentiation on nonverbal behavior. *Social Psychology Quarterly* 45:153–161.

Maccoby, Eleanor E. & Jacklin, Carol N. (1974). *The psychology of sex differences*. Stanford, CA: Stanford University Press.

Maltz, Daniel & Borker, Ruth (1982). A cultural approach to male-female miscommunication. In John J. Gumperz (Ed.) *Language and social identity* (pp. 195–216). Cambridge, England: Cambridge University Press.

Marche, Tammy A. (1988). The developmental and gender related use of listener responsiveness and interruption behaviour. M.Sc. thesis, Department of Psychology, Memorial University of Newfoundland.

Martin, Judith N. & Craig, Robert T. (1983). Selected linguistic sex differences during initial social interactions of the same-sex and mixed-sex student dyads. *Western Journal of Speech Communication* 47:16–28.

McCarrick, Anne K., Manderscheid, Ronald W. & Silbergeld, Sam (1981). Gender differences in competition and dominance during married-couples group therapy. *Social Psychology Quarterly* 44:164–177.

McLachlan, Angus (1991). The effects of agreement, disagreement, gender and familiarity on patterns of dyadic interaction. *Journal of Language and Social Psychology* 10:205–212.

McLaughlin, Margaret L. (1984). *Conversation: How talk is organized*. Beverly Hills, CA: Sage.

McMillan, Julie R., Clifton, A. Kay, McGrath, Diane & Gale, Wanda S. (1977). Women's language: Uncertainty, or interpersonal sensitivity and emotionality? *Sex Roles* 3:545–559.

Meltzer, Leo, Morris, William N. & Hayes, Donald P. (1971). Interruption outcomes and vocal amplitude: Explorations in social psychophysics. *Journal of Personality and Social Psychology* 18:392–402.

Mishler, Elliot G. & Waxler, Nancy E. (1968). *Interaction in families: An experimental study of family processes and schizophrenia*. New York: Wiley.

Moerman, Michael (1988). *Talking culture: Ethnography and conversation analysis*. Philadelphia: University of Pennsylvania Press.

Murray, Stephen O. (1985). Toward a model of members' methods for recognizing interruptions. *Language in Society* 14:31–41.

Murray, Stephen O. (1987). Power and solidarity in interruption: A critique of the Santa Barbara School conception and its application by Orcutt and Harvey (1985). *Symbolic Interaction* 10:101–110.

Murray, Stephen O. & Covelli, Lucille H. (1988). Women and men speaking at the same time. *Journal of Pragmatics* 12:103–111.

Natale, Michael, Entin, Elliot & Jaffe, Joseph (1979). Vocal interruptions in dyadic communication as a function of speech and social anxiety. *Journal of Personality and Social Psychology* 37:865–878.

Ochs, Elinor (1979). Transcription as theory. In Elinor Ochs & Bambi Schieffelin (Eds.) *Developmental Pragmatics,* (pp. 43–72). New York: Academic Press.

Octigan, Mary & Niederman, Sharon (1979). Male dominance in conversations. *Frontiers* 4:50–54.

Ofshe, Richard (1981). Gender-linked norms for speech regulation in discussion groups: An application of two-process theory. Unpublished paper, Department of Sociology, University of California, Berkeley, 1981.

Peterson, Carole (1986). Sex differences in conversational interruptions by pre-schoolers. *Journal of the Atlantic Provinces Linguistic Association* 8:23–28.

Pieper, Ursula (1984). Is parental language sexually differentiated? *Studia Anglia Posnaniensia* 17:71–80.

Piliavin, Jane A. & Martin, Rachel R. (1978). The effects of the sex composition of groups on style of social interaction. *Sex Roles* 4:281–2996.

Ridgeway, Cecilia & Diekema, David (1989). Dominance and collective hierarchy formation in male and female task groups. *American Sociological Review* 54:79–93.

Rim, Y. (1977). Personality variables and interruptions in small discussions. *European Journal of Social Psychology* 7:247–251.

Roger, Derek B., Bull, Peter E. & Smith, Sally (1988). The development of a comprehensive system for classifying interruptions. *Journal of Language and Social Psychology* 7:27–34.

Roger, Derek B. & Schumacher, Andrea (1983). Effects of individual differences on dyadic conversational strategies. *Journal of Personality and Social Psychology* 45:700–705.

Roger, Derek B. & Nesshoever, Willfried (1987). Individual differences in dyadic conversational strategies: A further study. *British Journal of Social Psychology* 26:247–255.

Rogers, William T. & Jones, Stanley E. (1975). Effects of dominance tendencies on floor holding and interruption behaviour in dyadic interaction. *Human Communication Research* 1:113–122.

Rosenblum, Karen E. (1986). Revelatory or purposive? Making sense of a 'female register'. *Semiotica* 59:157–170.

Sacks, Harvey, Schegloff, Emanuel & Jefferson, Gail (1974). A simplest systematics for the organization of turn-taking for conversation. *Language* 50:696–735.

Sayers, Frances (1984). Interaction involvement, gender role, and selected conversational behaviors. Paper presented at the National Women's Studies Association, Douglass College, New Brunswick, NJ.

Sayers, Frances (1987). Sex and conversational control. Paper presented at the 10th Annual Communication, Language, and Gender Conference. Marquette University.

Schegloff, Emanuel (1972). Sequencing in conversational openings. In John Gumperz & Dell Hymes (Eds.) *Directions in sociolinguistics*. New York: Holt, Rinehart & Winston.

Schegloff, Emanuel (1973). Recycled turn beginnings. Public lecture at the Summer Linguistic Institute, Linguistic Society of America, Ann Arbor, MI.

Shaw, Marvin E. & Sadler, Orin W. (1965). Interaction patterns in heterosexual dyads varying in degree of intimacy. *Journal of Social Psychology* 66:345–351.

Shultz, Jeffrey, Florio, Susan & Erickson, Frederick (1982). Where's the floor? Aspects of the cultural organization of social relationships in communication at home and at school. In Perry Gilmore & Alan Glatthorn (Eds.), *Children in and out of school: Ethnography and education* (pp. 88–123). Washington, DC: Center for Applied Linguistics.

Simkins-Bullock, Jennifer A. & Wildman, Beth G. (1991). An investigation into the relationships between gender and language. *Sex Roles* 24:149–160.

Smith, Philip M. (1985). *Language, the sexes, and society*. Oxford: Basil Blackwell.

Smith-Lovin, Lynn & Brody, Charles (1989). Interruptions in group discussions: The effects of gender and group composition. *American Sociological Review* 54:424–435.

South, Scott J., Markham, William T., Bonjean, Charles M. & Corder, Judy (1987). Sex differences in support for organizational advancement. *Work and Occupations* 14:261–285.

Stephens, Jane & Beattie, Geoffrey (1986). On judging the ends of speaker turns in conversation. *Journal of Language and Social Psychology* 5:119–134.

Street, Richard L., Jr. & Murphy, Thomas J. (1987). Interpersonal orientation and speech behavior. *Communication Monographs* 54:42–62.

Tannen, Deborah (1983). When is an overlap not an interruption? One component of conversational style. In Robert J. DiPietro, William Frawley & Alfred Wedel (Eds.) *The First Delaware Symposium on Language Studies* (pp. 119–129). Newark, DE: University of Delaware Press.

Tannen, Deborah (1984). *Conversational style: Analyzing talk among friends*. Norwood, NJ: Ablex.

Tannen, Deborah (1987). Repetition in conversation: Toward a poetics of talk. *Language* 63:574–605.

Tannen, Deborah (1989). Interpreting interruption in conversation. In *Papers from the 25th Annual Meeting of the Chicago Linguistics Society. Part 2. Parasession on language and context,* (pp. 266–287). Chicago: University of Chicago. Rpt. in Deborah Tannen, *Gender and discourse*. New York: Oxford University Press, in preparation.

Tannen, Deborah (1990). *You just don't understand: Women and men in conversation*. New York: Ballantine.

Testa, Renata (1988). Interruptive strategies in English and Italian conversation: Smooth versus contrastive linguistic preferences. *Multilingua* 7:285–312.

Thorne, Barrie, & Henley, Nancy (Eds.) (1975). *Language and sex: Difference and dominance*. Rowley, MA: Newbury House.

Thorne, Barrie, Kramarae, Cheris, & Henley, Nancy (Eds.) (1983). *Language, gender and society*. Rowley, MA: Newbury House.

Trimboli, Carmelina & Walker, Michael (1984). Switching pauses in cooperative and competitive conversations. *Journal of Experimental Social Psychology* 20:297–311.

van Alphen, Ingrid (1987). Learning from your peers: The acquisition of gender-specific speech styles. In Dede Brouwer & Dorian de Haan (Eds.) *Women's language, socialization and self-image* (pp. 58–75). Dordrecht: Foris.

Watzlawick, Paul, Beavin, Janet & Jackson, Don (1967). *Pragmatics of human communication*. New York: WW Norton.

Welkowitz, Joan, Bond, Ronald N. & Feldstein, Stanley (1984). Conversational time patterns of Japanese-American adults and children in same and mixed-gender dyads. *Journal of Language and Social Psychology* 3:127–138.

West, Candace (1979). Against our will: Male interruptions of females in cross-sex conversations. In Judith Orasanu, Mariam K. Slater & Leonore Loeb Adler (Eds.) *Language, sex and gender* (pp. 81–97). New York: Annals of the New York Academy of Sciences 327.

West, Candace (1982). Why can't a woman be more like a man? An interactional note on organizational game-playing for managerial women. *Work and Occupations* 9:5–29.

West, Candace (1985). *Routine complications: Troubles with talk between doctors and patients*. Bloomington, IN: Indiana University Press.

West, Candace & Zimmerman, Don H. (1977). Women's place in everyday talk: Reflections on parent-child interaction. *Social Problems* 24:521–528.

West, Candace & Don H. Zimmerman (1983). Small insults: A study of interruptions in cross-sex conversations between unacquainted persons. In Barrie Thorne, Cheris Kramarae, & Nancy Henley (Eds.) *Language, gender and society* (pp. 102–117). Rowley, MA: Newbury House.

Wiemann, John & Knapp, Mark (1975). Turn-taking in conversations. *Journal of Communication* 25:75–92.

Wiens, Arthur N., Thompson, Shirley M., Matarazzo, Joseph D., Matarazzo, Ruth G. & Saslow, George (1965). Interview interaction behavior of supervisors, head nurses and staff nurses. *Nursing Research* 14:322–329.

Willis, Frank N. & Williams, Sharon J. (1976). Simultaneous talking in conversation and sex of speakers. *Perceptual and Motor Skills* 43:1067–1070.

Wilson, Thomas P., Wiemann, John M. & Zimmerman, Don H. (1984). Models of turn-taking in conversational interaction. *Journal of Language and Social Psychology* 3:159–183.

Wood, Wendy (1987). Meta-analytic review of sex differences in group performance. *Psychological Bulletin* 102:53–71.

Wood, Wendy & Karten, Stephen J. (1986). Sex differences in interaction style as a product of perceived sex differences in competence. *Journal of Personality and Social Psychology* 50:341–347.

Woods, Nicola (1989). Talking shop: Sex and status as determinants of floor apportionment in a work setting. In Jennifer Coates & Deborah Cameron (Eds.) *Women in their speech communities* (pp. 141–157). London and New York: Longman.

Yngve, Victor H. (1970). On getting a word in edgewise. *Papers from the Sixth Regional Meeting of the Chicago Linguistic Society* (pp. 567–578). Chicago: University of Chicago.

Zimmerman, Don H. and West, Candace (1975). Sex roles, interruptions and silences in conversation. In Barrie Thorne & Nancy Henley (Eds.) *Language and sex: Difference and dominance* (pp. 105–129). Rowley, MA: Newbury House.

10

Understanding Gender Differences in Amount of Talk: A Critical Review of Research

DEBORAH JAMES
and
JANICE DRAKICH

*When both husband and wife wear pants it is not difficult to tell them
apart—he is the one who is listening.*
—Anonymous

The belief that women talk more than men is firmly entrenched in Western culture. However, the investigation of gender differences in amount of talk has not supported this widely held stereotype: the bulk of research findings indicate that men talk more than women. Results have, however, been far from consistent on the question of which gender talks more: some studies have found that women talk more than men, at least in some circumstances, and a number of studies have found no difference between the sexes in amount of talk. In this chapter we examine the inconsistent research findings and attempt to demonstrate that they are, in fact, more consistent than they might initially appear. We argue that in order to make sense of these findings, it is necessary to consider carefully the context and structure of social interaction within which gender differences are observed.

The Research Findings on Amount of Talk

Sixty-three studies that we know of which appeared between 1951 and 1991 have addressed the question of gender differences in amount of talk

281

in adult interaction.[1] Fifty-six of these studies, the great majority, deal with mixed-sex interaction (see Table 10.1); in addition, ten of these fifty-six, plus a further seven studies, have compared male and female talk in same-sex interaction.[2] Our review focuses on those studies which have examined mixed-sex interaction. Virtually all of these have used as their subjects middle-class English-speaking Americans; consequently the conclusions we report can only be viewed as holding for this group, although we contend that our consideration of the context and structure of social interaction can also be applied to explanations for observed behavior in other cultural groups.

Studies have varied as to how amount of talk has been measured; these measures have included the total number of words, the total number of seconds spent talking, the number of turns at talk taken, and the average length of a turn. In the case of six studies different measures produced discrepant results; in these cases the measure used to classify the study in Tables 10.1–10.4 is that of the number of seconds spent talking or words

Table 10.1   An Overview of Studies Dealing with Gender Differences in Amount of Talk in Mixed-Sex Adult Interaction

---

Studies in Which Men Were Found to Talk More Than Women Overall
Argyle, Lalljee, & Cook 1968
Aries 1976
Bernard 1972
Caudill 1958
Doherty 1974
Eakins & Eakins 1976
Eubanks 1975
Heiss 1962
Hilpert, Kramer, & Clark 1975
Karp & Yoels 1976
Kelly, Wildman, & Urey 1982
Kenkel 1963
Latour 1987
Mulac 1989
Parker 1973
Sayers 1987
Simkins-Bullock & Wildman 1991
Smith-Lovin, Skvoretz, & Hudson 1986
Strodtbeck 1951
Strodtbeck, James, & Hawkins 1957
Strodtbeck & Mann 1956
Swacker 1976
Wood & Karten 1986
Woods 1989

(*continued*)

Table 10.1   (*Continued*)

Studies in Which Men Were Found to Talk More Than Women in Some Circumstances, But No Difference Was Found in Other Circumstances
Boersma, Gay, Jones, Morrison, & Remick 1981
Brooks 1982
Cornelius & Gray 1988
Cornelius, Gray, & Constantinople 1990
Craig & Pitts 1990
Edelsky 1981, this volume
Kollock, Blumstein, & Schwartz 1985
Nemeth, Endicott, & Wachtler 1976
Soskin & John 1963
Sternglanz & Lyberger-Ficek 1977

Studies in Which in Some Circumstances Men Were Found to Talk More Than Women, But in Others Women Were Found to Talk More Than Men
Dovidio, Brown, Heltman, Ellyson, & Keating 1988
Hershey & Werner 1975
Kajander 1976

Studies in Which Sometimes Men Were Found to Talk More, Sometimes Women, and Sometimes Neither, Depending on the Circumstances
Leet-Pellegrini 1980

Studies in Which Women Were Found to Talk More Than Men Overall
Aries 1982
Askinas 1971

Studies in Which No Difference Was Found Between the Genders in Amount of Talk
Bilous & Krauss 1988
Case 1988
Crosby, Jose, & Wong-McCarthy 1981
Crouch & Dubois 1977
Duncan & Fiske 1977
Frances 1979
Hirschman 1973
Hirschman 1974
Leffler, Gillespie, & Conaty 1982
Manber 1976
Markel, Long, & Saine 1976
Martin Craig 1983
McLachlan 191
McMillan, Clifton, McGrath, & Gale 1977
Robertson 1978
Shaw and Sadler 1965

uttered. The only exception is that of Edelsky (1981, this volume), which examined only number of turns taken and average length of a turn. Since this study found no gender difference in number of turns but that males' turns were longer (in one type of "floor"), and this would presumably lead to males' taking up more overall talking time, we have classified this study as finding males to talk more (in that type of floor).[3] Some comments will be made on problems associated with the use of different measures of amount of talk, and on the cases in which discrepant results were found for different measures.

To summarize, of these fifty-six studies dealing with adult mixed-sex interaction males were found to talk more than females overall in twenty-four, or 42.9%, of the studies. In a further ten studies (17.9%) it was found that males talked more than females in some circumstances, with there being no difference in other circumstances. In three studies (5.4%) sometimes males and sometimes females talked more, depending on the circumstances, and in one further study sometimes males, sometimes females, and sometimes neither talked more, again depending on the circumstances. Sixteen studies (28.6%) found no difference between the sexes overall in amount of talk; only two studies (3.6%) found females to talk more overall. The interesting questions here are, then, first, why have the majority of studies found males to talk more than females, either overall or under at least some circumstances? Second, how is the variation in the findings of different studies to be explained? And third, why does the stereotype that women talk more exist, given that there is extraordinarily little empirical support for it? We will concentrate here on the first and second questions and will return to the third at the conclusion of the chapter.

The Approach to Understanding the Research Findings

We begin by reviewing the main explanations which have been proposed within the language and gender literature as to why most studies have found men to talk more than women in mixed-sex interaction. Many researchers have attributed this in a straightforward way to the fact that men have greater status and power than do women. Holding the floor at length, it is held, is a way in which men exploit this greater power and exercise dominance over women. Dale Spender argues (1980) that men control language and determine the norms by which it can be used, and that they attempt to prevent women from speaking from lack of respect for women and as a way of legitimating their own primacy. "In a male supremacist society where women are devalued, their language is devalued to such an extent that they are required to be silent" (pp. 42–43). It has further been suggested that men use specific mechanisms to discourage women from speaking, such as interruptions and inattention to the topics women raise (Spender 1980:87, Thorne, Kramarae, & Henley 1983:17). (It might be noted, however, that the majority of studies dealing with gender differences in interruptions have not, in fact, found males to interrupt females more than the reverse; see James and Clarke [this volume].) This approach makes a contribution to our understanding of gender differences in talk but offers no explanation for the fact that many studies have found no difference between the genders in amount of talk, or for the fact that a few studies have found women to talk more.

Another approach to explaining why most studies have found men to talk more than women, first proposed in Maltz and Borker (1982), focuses on the idea that women and men tend to learn, through socialization, to approach conversational interaction with different goals and to use different verbal strategies in interacting with others. Much evidence suggests that men learn that it is important for them to assert status and to appear a leader in interactions, while women learn to concentrate on using talk in such a way as to establish and maintain harmonious relationships with others. It has been suggested that taking and holding the floor for long periods follows logically from this as a male speech strategy, since this can function as a way of gaining attention and asserting status, while by contrast, being careful not to take up a disproportionate amount of talking time follows logically from the female speech style, since this emphasizes cooperation, support, and equality among interactants. Thus, Coates (1986:117), for example, comments that "the differences between the competitive, assertive male style and the co-operative, supportive female style mean that men will tend to dominate in mixed-sex interaction."[4] Moreover, Tannen (1990) proposes reasons why men might not always talk more than women, from the point of view of this approach: she suggests that men tend to talk more than women in "public" situations, whereas women tend to talk more than men in "private" situations. In a public situation, she suggests, there are typically more participants than in a private situation, they know each other less well, and there are more status differences among them; therefore, participants are more likely to feel that they will be appraised by others in the group. Men will thus talk more because they feel the need to establish or maintain their status in the group, whereas women will talk less because they do not use talk to assert status and because they fear that their talk will be judged negatively. In a private situation, on the other hand, one is with individuals with whom one feels close; since women view talk as crucial in maintaining close relationships whereas men do not, women will tend to talk more than men in private settings. This approach, too, has played a dominant role in our understanding of gender differences in talk.

We propose here, however, an alternative approach to making sense of the findings in the area of amount of talk which we will argue is a particularly fruitful one. This approach offers, we suggest, significant further insights both into why so many studies have found men to talk more and into why there has been so much variation in the findings in this area. In this viewpoint, careful consideration is taken of the exact context and structure of social interaction. Berger, Rosenholtz, and Zelditch (1980), among others, argue that differences in behavior result primarily from differences in expectations and beliefs about oneself and others. This approach, we suggest, is crucial to an understanding of gender differences in amount of talk. Differences in how much women and men talk in different contexts, we maintain, can be explained in terms of the differential cultural expectations about women's and men's abilities and areas of competence—which are associated with the difference in status between women and men—in interrelationship with specific factors in particular situations which can affect these expectations. In taking this approach, we adopt the sociological perspective of status characteristics (or expectation states) theory (Berger, Fizek, Norman, & Zelditch 1977). Status characteristics theory provides us with a framework and a cumulative body of research which help us to understand the processes that connect gender to observable inequalities in face-to-face interaction. To clarify our subsequent discussion, we briefly introduce the central concepts of status characteristics theory—"self-other performance expectations" and "status characteristics."

Status Characteristics Theory

Status characteristics theory focuses on how status differences organize interaction. The theory argues that in social interaction individuals evaluate themselves relative to the other individuals with whom they are participating and come to hold expectations as to how, and how well, they will perform in relation to every other participant in the interaction. These "self-other performance expectations" provide the structure of the interaction which then determines subsequent interaction. The formulation of these "self-other performance expectations" is based on the "status characteristics" possessed by the participants in the social interaction. A status characteristic is any characteristic that is socially valued, is meaningful, and has differentially evaluated states which are associated directly or indirectly with beliefs about task performance ability—"performance expectations." Examples of status characteristics are race, sex, education, or organizational office. People's social expectations as to how well and in what way the different participants in an interaction will perform are crucially associated with whether individuals possess the high or the low state of the relevant status characteristic (particularly when participants do not know each other well, so that other information which might override the influence of these status characteristics is unavailable to them). Thus, for example, individuals who have high status with regard to a status characteristic are viewed as being in general more intellectually competent and able than are individuals who have low status with regard to that status characteristic. Consequently the high-status individual is not only expected to perform better but is also given more opportunity to perform than the lower-status individual. It is important to note that status characteristics and their associated performance expectations are relational; that is, we do not speak of performance expectations for women, but rather we speak of performance expectations associated with women in relation to those performance expectations associated with men. "Because status characteristics involve relational expectations females do not in this conception carry sex-related characteristics around with them in every situation; or, put in other words, sex-related characteristics are not assumed to be part of their character, they are assumed to be beliefs about certain kinds of situations" (Berger et al. 1977:35).

The power of this theory lies in its explanation of how external status characteristics structure the status hierarchy of face-to-face interaction. This theoretical approach for explaining the data, then, places particular importance on social structure, which sociologists have defined as patterned relationships.

The fruitfulness of this approach will become more evident as we analyze the findings. Let us now turn to a more careful examination of the research and research findings on amount of talk.

The Relevance of the Research Activity to Amount of Talk

The research on amount of talk focusing on face-to-face interaction has examined talk within the context of a variety of different kinds of activities. These activities, we argue, can be held to form a continuum. At one end are "formal tasks"; at the other are informal non-task-oriented activities. In between the two are "informal tasks" and activities such as interaction in a college or university classroom which occur within formal structures but are not task-oriented.

Formal task activities are defined in sociology as activities in which a pair or group of individuals come together to accomplish specific instrumental goals such as solving a problem together or making a joint decision. These tasks require participants to exchange ideas, to take each other's opinions into account as they work at the task, and to complete the task successfully by producing a single, collective outcome such as a committee decision. By comparison, neither informal task activities nor non-task-oriented activities require the accomplishment of a specific goal such as joint decision making or problem solving. An example of an informal task is a situation in which subjects have been brought together and asked by an experimenter simply to "get to know one another"; an example of a non-task-oriented activity is naturally occurring casual conversation. These different types of activity are associated with different rules, regulations, and requirements.

Since our position in examining the research findings is that the behavior observed is dependent on the requirements of the situation and the relative performance expectations that participants hold in a given situation, it is necessary to differentiate studies examining behavior within different contexts. For our purposes here we deal separately with the studies employing formal task activities, the studies involving informal activities (both task and nontask), and the studies involving formally structured but not task-oriented activities, such as college classroom interaction.[5]

Amount of Talk in Formal Task Contexts

Twenty-four of the fifty-six studies dealing with adult face-to-face interaction have employed formal task activities. As examples of these, three studies have examined talk in task-oriented committee meetings such as faculty meetings or hospital staff meetings (Eakins & Eakins 1976, Edelsky 1981, this volume, Caudill 1958); in two studies subjects were

Table 10.2 Studies Involving Formal Tasks

Studies Which Found Men to Talk More Overall
Caudill 1958
Eakins & Eakins 1976
Heiss 1962
Hilpert, Kramer, & Clark 1975
Kelly, Wildman, & Urey 1982
Kenkel 1963
Mulac 1989
Simkins-Bullock & Wildman 1991
Smith-Lovin, Skvoretz, & Hudson 1986
Strodtbeck 1951
Strodtbeck, James, & Hawkins 1957
Strodtbeck & Mann 1956
Wood & Karten 1986

Studies Which Found Men to Talk More in Some Circumstances, But No Difference in Other Circumstances
Edelsky 1981, this volume
Kollock, Blumstein, & Schwartz 1985
Nemeth, Endicott, & Wachtler 1976

Studies Which Found Men to Talk More in Some Circumstances, But Women to Talk More in Others
Hershey & Werner 1975

Studies in Which Sometimes Men Were Found to Talk More, Sometimes Women, and Sometimes Neither, Depending on the Circumstances
Leet-Pellegrini 1980

Studies Which Found Women to Talk More Overall
Aries 1982

Studies Which Found No Difference Between the Genders in Amount of Talk
Bilous & Krauss 1988
Crosby, Jose, & Wong-McCarthy 1981
McLachlan 1991
McMillan, Clifton, McGrath, & Gale 1977
Shaw & Sadler 1965

---

members of a mock jury who had to decide on the guilt or innocence of a defendant (Strodtbeck & Mann 1956, Strodtbeck, James, & Hawkins 1957); in one study small groups were asked to solve a murder mystery (McMillan, Clifton, McGrath, & Gale 1977); in another married couples were asked to come to a decision on such matters as how to spend money won in a lottery (Hershey & Werner 1975); and in still another small groups had to reach a consensus on the advisability of a doctor's prescribing amphetamines to a trusted student who wanted the drugs to help improve his or her performance on a medical school admission test (Aries 1982).

Of these twenty-four studies (see Table 10.2) thirteen found men to talk more than women overall, and three found men to talk more in certain circumstances, with there being no difference in other circumstances (in one of these, Edelsky [1981, this volume], men can in fact be presumed to have also talked more overall; see note 3). One study found that sometimes men and sometimes women talked more, depending on the circumstances; one study found that sometimes men, sometimes women, and sometimes neither talked more, again depending on the circumstances; and five studies found no difference between the genders in amount of talk. Only one study found women to talk more than men overall.

Understanding the Results

The analysis of these results begins with the question, Why did the great majority of these studies find men to talk more than women, either overall or in at least some circumstances?

Previous research has indicated that those who have high status with regard to a status characteristic such as race, organizational rank, or occupation participate more in task-oriented dyads or groups than do those who have low status with regard to that characteristic (e.g., Berger, Rosenholtz, & Zelditch 1980, Stein & Heller 1979, Slater 1966, Capella 1985). Thus, if gender is also a status characteristic, it is not surprising to find men talking more than women in such contexts. Why, however, should those of high status talk more than those of low status in formal task-oriented interactions? The answer to this question can be found in status characteristics theory; in fact, the finding that men talk more than women follows precisely the predictions of the theory. As was noted earlier, the theory holds that individuals who have high status with regard to some status characteristic will be viewed both by themselves and by others as more intellectually competent, and therefore likely to perform better, than individuals who have low status with regard to that characteristic. Higher-status individuals, then, since they feel more competent, will be more willing to contribute to the interaction than will lower-status individuals. They will also tend to be less tolerant of, and less willing to wait for, contributions from lower-status individuals, since they perceive those individuals as less competent at the task. Lower-status individuals, on the other hand, expect higher-status individuals to be more competent than they are themselves. Thus, they encourage the participation of the higher-status individuals, they tend to wait for them to make contributions, and they are less willing to contribute to the interaction themselves. The effect is, of course, that higher-status individuals make significantly more verbal contributions and consequently take up significantly more time talking.[6]

As a further point, studies of role differentiation in groups have shown that those of higher status in a group are normally assigned to and accept a specifically task-oriented role, while those of lower status are normally assigned to and accept instead a primarily (positive) socioemotional role (in performing a positive socioemotional role, one supports others, shows interest, works to relieve tension in the group, etc.) Occupants of task-oriented roles are expected to make more task-oriented contributions than are occupants of positive socioemotional roles, and moreover, task-oriented contributions (typically, information, opinions, and suggestions) normally take up more talking time than do positive socioemotional contributions (e.g., agreeing and giving indications of interest). This latter point is confirmed by research documenting that the majority of group interaction consists of task-oriented behaviors (Anderson & Blanchard 1982). This pattern of role differentiation, then, also contributes to the overall result that those of higher status talk more in a task-oriented setting than do those of lower status. (And indeed many studies have found men to give more information and opinions than women in mixed-sex dyads or groups [e.g., Piliavin & Martin 1978, Fishman 1983, Wood & Karten 1986] and have found women to perform more socioemotional acts in interactions [e.g., Fowler & Rosenfeld 1979, Burleson 1982, Wood 1987].)

Support for this general explanation of why men talk more than women in mixed-sex formal task-oriented settings is provided by the following. First, the theory would predict that women would talk more in same-sex than in mixed-sex interaction in such settings, since their status (all else being equal) would be equivalent to that of their coparticipants, and further, that the distribution of task and socioemotional behavior would be similar for both female and male same-sex groups. Two studies, Bilous and Krauss (1988) and Mulac (1989), have compared amount of talk in same-sex and mixed-sex formal task-oriented interaction; both found that women did indeed talk more in same-sex than in mixed-sex interaction.[7] In addition, Yamada, Tjosvold, and Draguns (1983) and Lockheed (1976) both found that females and males did not differ in number of task-oriented contributions in same-sex formal task groups, but that males produced significantly more such contributions than did females in mixed-sex groups.

Second, support for the theory is provided by Eskilson and Wiley (1976), who examined three-person groups performing a formal task. For half of these groups leaders were assigned by the drawing of lots. For the other half a test related to the task was administered, and one member of the group was announced to have performed best on this test. (In fact, however, s/he was selected at random). This individual was assigned to be the leader of the group and was in addition given information relevant to the task which other group members did not have. Status characteristics theory would predict that the women leaders in this second group would have high status in the group, regardless of its gender composition; would both perceive themselves and be perceived by others as relatively highly competent at the task; as a result would participate verbally to an extent similar to that of the equivalent male leaders; and would participate more than female leaders who were chosen by the drawing of lots. These were indeed the results found.

Thus when gender and associated expectations are nullified, males and females behave similarly with regard to amount of talk in task-oriented groups; it is only when gender influences the interaction that differences in amount of talk appear.

At this point we turn to the following question: Why, then, is it that eleven of these twenty-four studies dealing with amount of talk in formal task-oriented interaction did *not* find men to talk more than women overall?

An examination of these eleven studies in comparison with those which did find men to talk more overall reveals two methodological differences between them which help to explain the inconsistency in the findings: differences in the way in which amount of talk was measured and differences in the variables examined.

First, one source of the apparent inconsistency in findings lies in how amount of talk was measured. In Aries (1982), which found women to talk more, and Shaw and Sadler (1965) and McMillan, Clifton, McGrath, and Gale (1977), who found no difference between the genders in amount of talk, what was measured was not the total amount of talk (measured in seconds or in words) produced by men and women, nor the average length of verbal contributions, but rather (in the cases of Aries and of Shaw and Sadler) the number of verbal acts initiated by each gender, and (in the case of McMillan et al.) the number of sentences produced. The first two and the last two measures, however, do not necessarily produce identical results. For example, Craig and Pitts (1990), in a study of university tutorials, found that male and female tutors did not differ in average number of verbal acts initiated, but that male tutors nevertheless took up more overall talking time; the same was true of male and female students in male-led tutorials. Presumably this was because males were producing longer utterances (although this was not explicitly measured). Similarly, three studies, Edelsky (1981, this volume), Frances (1979), and Duncan and Fiske (1977), found that men and women did not differ in average number of verbal acts in mixed-sex interaction, but that the average length of an act was significantly greater for men. In all probability the reason why these different measures may produce different results has to do with the consistent finding of mixed-sex interaction studies (noted earlier) that a greater percentage of men's than of women's speech consists of specifically task-oriented behavior such as giving information, opinions, and suggestions, whereas a greater percentage of women's than of men's speech consists of positive socioemotional and "facilitating" behavior, such as agreeing, giving indications of interest in what others are saying, and trying to draw out others. (Indeed, one of the findings of Aries [1982] was that this was the case for her subjects.) Acts of the former type tend to take up significantly more talking time than acts of the latter type. Thus it is possible for the genders to initiate the same number of verbal acts or even for females to initiate more, but for males nevertheless to take up significantly more talking time. In the case of these three studies which measured only the number of acts initiated or sentences produced men may in fact have taken up more talking time overall than women; we do not know. Thus, it is important to be aware that different measures can produce different results in comparing studies of gender differences in amount of talk; all too often, the results of different measures have been assumed by researchers to represent the same behavior, when in fact they represent different types of behavior.[8]

A second source of the apparent inconsistency in the findings lies in the variables examined in particular studies. Hershey and Werner (1975) provide one illustration of this. This study of decision making by married couples found that wives who were not associated with a feminist organization spoke for a significantly shorter length of time than did their husbands, but wives who *were* associated with a feminist organization spoke for a *greater* length of time than did their husbands. Thus, in contrast with other researchers, Hershey and Werner introduce the variable of feminism; this nullifies the impact of gender for feminist couples. For those couples who held more traditional expectations about the genders, the results conformed to stereotypic expectations. However, for the feminist couples the results did not conform to gender expectations. Feminists are not likely to accept traditional sexist values nor adhere to traditional gender roles in interaction and are likely to choose as marriage partners men who have similar views. Thus, we might expect these women to make, and be allowed by their husbands to make, more task-oriented contributions than would otherwise be usual.

Similarly, Kollock, Blumstein, and Schwartz (1985) in a study of communicative patterns in heterosexual and homosexual couples introduced the variable of "relative power," measured in terms of relative influence over day-to-day decision making (as determined by a questionnaire completed by each partner). It was found that in heterosexual couples in which the male was the more "powerful" member, and in homosexual couples in which one member was more "powerful" than the other, the more powerful member took up significantly more talking time when the couple worked together on a formal task. However, in couples in which the members were rated as equal in power, there was no significant difference in amount of talk.[9]

Leet-Pellegrini (1980) examined the contribution of "expertise." While she found no difference between equally "nonexpert" men and women in amount of talk,[10] she found that when one member of a mixed-sex dyad was supplied with topically relevant information such that s/he took on the role of "expert" in the task assigned, women as well as men talked significantly more than their uninformed partner of the opposite sex. Having expertise is likely to make women as well as men perceive themselves, and be perceived by their partner, as relatively high in competence. (However, male "experts" were found to occupy significantly more talking space relative to uninformed female partners than did female "experts" relative to uninformed male partners; this is unsurprising, since status characteristics theory would predict that individuals would combine the performance expectations associated with their gender and their expertise status characteristics [diffuse and specific, respectively]. That is, individuals will add the positive expectations and subtract the negative expectations to formulate an averaged expectation. Thus, here, individuals would add the positive performance expectations for the male "experts" who held high status on both gender and expertise, but for the women "experts" would subtract the negative performance expectations associated with being female from the positive expectations associated with being an "expert.")

Edelsky (1981, this volume) examined a rather different kind of variable. In this study of five committee meetings Edelsky argued that it was possible to distinguish two kinds of "floors" ("singly developed floors" and "collaboratively developed floors"), where a floor is defined as "the acknowledged what's-going-on within a psychological time/space" (Edelsky, this vol.: 209). Single floors, which were by far the most prevalent type of floor, were characterized by single speakers taking turns in sequence and were highly task-oriented. Here men spoke significantly more than women, as we might expect. In collaborative floors, which were of relatively brief duration, two or more people spoke simultaneously in seeming "free-for-alls" or "jointly built one idea, operating on the same wavelength" (p. 189). This included, for example, jointly sharing in building an answer to a question or joking together about some matter. In collaborative floors the interaction was "high involvement, synergistic, solidarity-building" (p. 221). Collaborative floors were clearly overall less task-oriented than single floors; for example, Edelsky notes that "managing the agenda," such as reporting on items and soliciting responses, was the predominant activity in single floors but not in collaborative floors; "time-outs from the agenda more often . . . coincided with collaborative floors." (p. 217) (for example, joking was much more common). In collaborative floors, there was no difference in the amount of talking time taken up by men and women. But indeed our theory predicts a difference in this direction between single and collaborative floors. Since collaborative floors are typically less task-oriented, there is a lessened demand for the status-associated intellectual competence than is the case in single floors, and moreover, because collaborative floors are jointly developed, making a contribution is not perceived as an attempt to take single control of the floor. For both of these reasons, women are likely to feel less "on the spot" and thus more willing to speak in collaborative than in single floors (and men are likely to take a more tolerant attitude toward their contributions).

All of these studies point to the importance of social structure—the underlying pattern of social relationships and the underlying structure of self-other expectations—in explaining behavior.

Overall, then, we can conclude that the results of existing studies on amount of talk in mixed-sex formal task-oriented interaction are quite consistent with what one would predict if it is accepted that the expectations associated with high-status people are normally attached to men and the expectations associated with low-status people are normally attached to women, but that it is also the case that particular circumstances can affect or nullify the impact of gender on expectations.

Amount of Talk in Formally Structured but Not Formally Task-Oriented Interaction

Sixteen studies (see Table 10.3) have examined interaction in contexts which involve a relatively high degree of formal structure but are not formally task-oriented in the sense defined earlier: that is, in which there is no requirement that the group successfully complete a task by producing a single, collective outcome. Twelve of these studies have dealt with participation in college classrooms. The remaining four are Bernard (1972), a study of TV panel discussions; Swacker (1976), an examination of question-and-answer periods after papers were presented at three academic conferences; Woods (1989), a study of colleagues conferring at work; and Leffler, Gillespie, and Conaty (1982), in which subjects role-played being "teacher" or "student." Of these studies six found males to talk more overall; six found males to talk more in some circumstances, but no difference in other circumstances; one found males to talk more in one respect, but females to talk more in another; and three found no difference between the genders. None of these studies found females to talk more overall.

These results are consistent with those found for the studies involving formal tasks: the great majority of studies found men to talk more than women, either overall or in some circumstances. Since, as in the case of formal tasks, the contexts involved here are ones in which intellectual competence is perceived as important, it is to be expected that the results would be similar to those of the formally task-oriented studies.

As in the case of the studies examined earlier the presence of factors which serve to nullify the impact of the expectations associated with gender aids in explaining the variations in the findings. For example, in Leffler, Gillespie, and Conaty (1982), in which pairs of subjects role-played being "teacher" and "student" (and "teachers" were given extra

Table 10.3   Studies Examining Formally Structured,
but Not Formally Task-Oriented Interaction

Studies Which Found Men to Talk More Overall
Bernard 1972
Karp & Yoels 1976
Latour 1987
Parker 1973
Swacker 1976
Woods 1989

Studies Which Found Men to Talk More in Some Circumstances, But No Difference in Other Circumstances
Boersma, Gay, Jones, Morrison, & Remick 1981
Brooks 1982
Cornelius & Gray 1988
Cornelius, Gray, & Constantinople 1990
Craig & Pitts 1990
Sternglanz & Lyberger-Ficek 1977

Studies Which Found Men to Talk More in One Respect, But Women to Talk More in Another
Kajander 1976

Studies Which Found No Difference Between the Genders in Amount of Talk
Crouch & Dubois 1977
Leffler, Gillespie, & Conaty 1982
Robertson 1978

relevant information), it was found that the status and expertise associated with the "teacher" role outweighed the effects of gender, with the result that "teachers" talked more than "students" regardless of the gender of the subject.

Considerable variation exists in the results of the studies dealing with amount of participation in college classrooms. There appear to be several variables which are relevant here. Chief among these are the sex of the instructor and the subject matter of the course in question. Unfortunately, however, studies have not been consistent as to their findings concerning the relevance of these variables. For example, Sternglanz and Lyberger-Ficek (1977) and Craig and Pitts (1990) found that males spoke significantly more, proportionately, than females in male-taught classes, but that there was no difference in female-taught classes; Karp and Yoels (1976) and Parker (1973) found that males spoke more than females in both types of class, but that the difference was greater in male-taught classes. In contrast with all four of these studies, however, Brooks (1982) found that males participated more than females in female-taught classes, but that there was no difference in male-taught classes; and Boersma, Gay, Jones,

Morrison, and Remick (1981) found that males made more comments than females in female-taught nonscience classes but that there was no difference in male-taught classes or in science classes, and also found that male students were significantly more likely than females to speak more than once per interaction with a female instructor, but that this difference disappeared with a male instructor. (Sternglanz & Lyberger-Ficek [1977] also found that male students were more likely than females to speak more than once per interaction with an instructor but did not find the sex of the instructor to be relevant.) In addition, Cornelius and Gray (1988) found that the highest participation rates were those of male students in female-taught classes in the arts and social sciences. Sorting out the effects of these and other possible variables is beyond the scope of this review; further research is clearly needed in this area.[11]

Nevertheless, the fact that most of these studies found males to talk more than females, either overall or under some circumstances, is clearly consonant with what one would predict given the social structural factors discussed earlier.

Amount of Talk in Informal Task Contexts and Non–Task-Oriented Contexts

Let us now turn to those sixteen studies dealing with amount of talk which have not involved formal task-oriented activities or other formally structured interaction (see Table 10.4). Most of these studies have been experiments in which pairs or small groups of subjects were asked to "talk about anything" or "just get to know each other," or else were asked to discuss a topic such as how to grow vegetables (Dovidio, Brown, Heltman, Ellyson & Keating 1988) or who should control the money in a marriage (Eubanks 1975). Three studies, in addition, have involved the recording of naturally occurring speech: Soskin and John (1963) examined the speech of one couple for several days; Doherty (1974) observed a therapy group in a psychiatric hospital; and Case (1988) studied the speech of a group of managers at a management school who "worked together in an unstructured setting, observing and attempting to understand their own . . . behavior [as leaders], and coming face to face with issues of power, uncertainty, and normlessness" (p. 45). Of these sixteen studies five found males to talk more than females overall; one found males to talk more in some circumstances, and no difference in others; one found males to talk more in some circumstances, and females to talk more in another; eight found no difference between the genders in amount of talk; and one found females to talk more than males. (All the studies finding females to talk more or no difference measured the total amount of talking time, rather than the number of acts produced.)

Thus, even in these informal situations nearly a third of the studies found males to talk more than females overall. However, it is of interest to

Table 10.4 Studies Involving Informal Tasks and Non-Task-Oriented Activities

Studies Which Found Men to Talk More Overall
Argyle, Lalljee, & Cook 1968
Aries 1976
Doherty 1974
Eubanks 1975
Sayers 1987

Studies Which Found Men to Talk More in Some Circumstances, and No Difference in Others
Soskin & John 1963

Studies Which Found Men to Talk More in Some Circumstances, and Women to Talk More in Another
Dovidio, Brown, Heltman, Ellyson & Keating 1988

Studies Which Found Women to Talk More Overall
Askinas 1971

Studies Which Found No Difference Between the Genders in Amount of Talk
Case 1988
Duncan & Fiske 1977
Frances 1979
Hirschman 1973
Hirschman 1974
Manber 1976
Markel, Long, & Saine 1976
Martin & Craig 1983

compare these studies with those of formal task activities and other formally structured interaction: a much smaller percentage of these studies found males to talk more than females either overall or under some circumstances (37.5%, as opposed to 67% in the case of formal tasks and 75% in the case of formally structured but not task-oriented interaction; studies in which sometimes men and sometimes women talked more are ignored in this count). Thus, the amount that women talk appears to be much more likely to equal or exceed the amount that men talk in informal contexts than it does in formal task-oriented contexts or other formally structured contexts.

Understanding Talk in Informal Contexts

In attempting to account for these findings, we begin, as before, with a consideration of why men would be likely to talk more than women in informal task- and non-task-oriented interactions, from the point of view of status characteristics theory.

First, the kinds of cultural beliefs associated with gender which facilitate males' greater amount of talk in formal task-oriented groups can also affect informal interactions. In particular, we have observed that in formal task-oriented groups the nature of the task requires instrumental skills and competence at the task. If there is no objective information in the situation to assess participants, participants will rely on the status characteristics present in the situation, such as sex, to assess competence and to formulate self-other expectations. The differential evaluation of males and females is connected to the cultural belief that individuals who have higher status are more competent than are individuals of lower status. Given this, we might expect that even in informal interactions, men would tend to act, and be allowed to act, as "authorities" to a greater extent than women. Men would therefore make more statements, give more information, and offer more expressions of opinion than do women. And, as noted earlier, a number of studies have indeed found that men do give more statements, information, and opinions than do women, even in informal interactions (e.g., Fishman 1983, Aries 1976, Kaplan 1976). This will tend to increase the amount of talking which men do relative to that which women do.

Why, then, has there been a much lower incidence of findings of males talking more in studies of informal task- and non–task-oriented interaction than in studies of formal-task or other formally structured interaction? It would seem from this that informal situations must differ from more formal ones in significant ways. One important respect in which they differ is that while both types of interactions require instrumental and socioemotional skills, informal interactions require more socioemotional skills. The success of informal interactions is based on facilitating and maintaining harmonious interpersonal relations rather than on completing a task. To achieve this end, socioemotional rather than instrumental skills are required. The cultural beliefs and expectations associated with the relative competence of males and females in these skills are that women would be socioemotional experts. Therefore, both men and women in informal interaction would expect women to engage in talk which would move the interaction along.

It is not surprising, then, that many studies have found that women's speech is significantly more "affiliative" and "facilitating" than is men's (toward both sexes). As noted earlier, women contribute more positive socioemotional acts, such as agreeing and showing support (e.g., Aries 1982, Leet-Pellegrini 1980, Piliavin & Martin 1978, Wood & Karten 1986). Women work harder than do men at keeping conversations going and keeping them running smoothly (Fishman 1983, McLaughlin, Louden, Cashion, Altendorf, Baaske, & Smith 1985). More specifically, compared to men, women have been found to give more indications of interest in and attention to what other people are saying. For example, women make supportive remarks, explicitly acknowledge what has been said by others, and make comments which develop or elaborate on what others have said (Kalčik 1975, Jones 1980, Roger & Schumacher 1983, Coates 1989). Women tend to be more likely to try to draw out another person's opinions or feelings, for example, by asking questions or using tags (Fishman 1983, Holmes 1984, Sayers 1987, Cameron, McAlinden, & O'Leary 1989). They are more likely to take up and build on topics introduced by someone else and to initiate new topics when a conversation flags (Fishman 1983).[12]

This is relevant to amount of talk in that the "facilitative" types of speech function just described do in themselves take up a certain amount of talking time, and that certain types of interaction require them to a greater extent than other types. Fishman (1983:99) notes that "sometimes women are required to sit and 'be a good listener' because they are not otherwise needed [to work at keeping the conversation going]. At other times women are required to fill silences and keep conversation moving, to talk a lot."

In particular, these types of speech function are required more in informal conversations than in formal task ones or in other types of formally structured interaction. In formal task interaction, participants (especially, of course, male participants) are expected and are well motivated to make contributions, and therefore it is less necessary for someone to talk simply to keep the conversation going or to try to draw out others. Similarly, in situations such as a college classroom or a panel discussion, where participation is governed by formal rules, these speech functions are called for far less than in informal conversations. Probably, also, the more casual the conversation and the fewer the participants, the more these "facilitative" uses of speech are required.[13] This then is one factor which might help to explain why males have been more frequently found to talk more than females in studies of formal tasks and formally structured activities than in studies of informal activities.[14]

Another related factor which may contribute to the social structure of interactions is the topic of conversation. Men and women differ in the areas in which they are expected to be knowledgeable and in which they consequently tend to be knowledgeable; for example, if the topic of discussion were how to build a table, men would be expected to, and would thus be likely to, know more, but if the topic of discussion were how to set a table, women would be expected to, and would be likely to, know more. It is reasonable, then, to conclude that in mixed-sex interaction, the topic may have an effect on the verbal output of each gender depending on the gender bias in topic competency. And indeed, there is evidence from studies that this is the case. For example, in Dovidio et al. (1988) it was found that when mixed-sex dyads were asked to discuss either a neutral topic (vegetable gardening) or a topic in which males are expected to be more knowledgeable than females (automotive oil changing), males spoke more than females, but when they were asked to discuss a topic in which females are expected to be more knowledgeable than males (pattern sewing), females spoke more than males. As another example, in Kelly, Wild-man, and Urey (1982) small groups had to reach a decision on two issues, one involving a male-oriented topic (cars) and one involving a neutral topic (travel). While men talked more than women on both tasks, the difference was significantly greater in the case of the task involving the male-oriented topic. (This was also true in the case of the neutral versus male-oriented topics in Dovidio et al. [1988].) Similarly March (1953) found that in political discussion the more local the issue, the more women talked, presumably because local issues were seen as more female-appropriate. It is reasonable to suppose that topics in which females are expected to be more competent than males (and perhaps neutral topics as well) are more likely to arise in informal conversations than in formal task activities or formally structured interaction such as a college classroom. Researchers have tended to pay little attention to topic as a factor affecting amount of talk, and we suspect that in some studies, the findings may have been in part a result of the topic of conversation. One example of this has been given earlier with reference to Leet-Pellegrini (1980) (see note 10). As a further example Askinas (1971) found that in mixed-sex groups of college students from coeducational residences, women talked more than men when discussing coeducational versus single-sex housing. Women may have talked more because this topic involves a discussion of interper-sonal relationships with others, and since women are expected to be the socioemotional experts, they are in general more likely and willing to discuss such matters than are men (e.g., Aries & Johnson 1983, Davidson & Duberman 1982, Levin & Arluke 1985). In addition, women have more of a vested interest in this topic then men because of women's greater vulnerability in coeducational living in light of the prevalence of violence against women by men and the social stigma that may be attached to single women sharing residence with men. And, to take another exam-ple, in Hirschman (1973), a study of dyads in which no difference was found between the genders in amount of talk, the discussion topic as-signed was "love, sexuality, and marriage"; although this is of course a topic of significant interest to both genders, its high level of socioemo-tional content may have encouraged more talk by women than might otherwise have been the case.

More generally, contexts which involve in any way an area where one gender is believed to be and is likely to be more competent than the other can be expected to affect amount of talk. For example, Golinkoff and Ames (1979) and Stoneman and Brody (1981) found that when parents were asked to play with their child with a set of toys (both parents being present), mothers talked significantly more than fathers. Since mothers are given more responsibility for child care and since dealing with children is thus generally viewed as a female area of expertise, it is not surprising that women talked more (and were allowed by the men to talk more) in this situation.

Differences in cultural expectations about the areas in which men and women are competent determine men's and women's actual performances and, consequently, the amount of talk.

Conclusions

Research indicates that men and women often behave differently with regard to the amount that they talk in adult face-to-face interaction. Frequently men talk more than women; however, they do not necessarily do so. We have argued here that these behaviors are best explained in terms of the social structure of the interaction; this is informed by the difference in status between the genders and the differential cultural expectations about men's and women's abilities and areas of competence. As the social structure of the interaction changes, so also do expectations and consequently behavior; hence the apparent inconsistencies in the results of studies on amount of talk.

This review of the literature on amount of talk shows that in order to understand gender differences in interactional behavior, it is important to take into account the full range of findings in the area examined, and it is vital that the complexity of the contribution which social structure and social context can make to behavior be appreciated. Most previous accounts of gender differences in amount of talk within the language and gender literature have concentrated only on the common finding that men talk more than women in mixed-sex interaction. The reason most commonly suggested for this finding has been simply that men talk more as a way of exploiting their greater power and exercising dominance and control over women, and that they tend to attempt to prevent women from speaking because they devalue women. We hope to have shown here that such an account is limited. While it takes into account the emergence and maintenance of the status hierarchy of social interaction, it fails to appreciate the subtle interplay between the social structure of the interaction and the beliefs and expectations associated with the social context of the interaction. Our work complements and extends the power explanation by moving the discourse from gender dispositions of power to the shared set of performance expectations which differentiate individuals, and as a consequence both give rise to power differences and maintain and perpetuate status hierarchies in social interaction. An alternative approach to explaining gender differences in amount of talk has focused on the idea that women and men are socialized to have different goals in interactions and to use talk in different ways in order to attain these goals. While it takes account of the impact of social context on the amount of talk produced by each gender, and certainly contributes to our understanding of gender-related differences in amount of talk, this approach fails, in particular, to appreciate the importance of the status difference between the genders as a factor affecting expectations about females and males and consequently affecting their socialization and subsequent behavior.

This chapter has shown, then, that the range of results found by studies with respect to amount of talk, which cannot be adequately understood either from a power perspective or from the perspective of differential gender-based interactional styles, can be explained in a reasonably consistent and satisfactory way when given a careful analysis from the perspective of social structure and social context.

Epilogue: Stereotypes Revisited

As a final note, let us consider again the widely held stereotype that women talk more than men do. Why does this stereotype exist? One commonly cited suggestion is that of Spender (1980): "The talkativeness of women has been gauged in comparison not with men but with *silence*. Women have not been judged on the grounds of whether they talk more than men, but of whether they talk more than silent women" (p. 42). Kramarae (1981) expresses the same idea when she says, "the long tradition of male control of language, determining both the symbols that are developed and the norms for usage for women and men, means that women's speech will not be evaluated the same way as men's speech. . . . Women may talk less, but they still talk too much" (p. 116).[15]

Another suggestion has involved the fact that women and men tend to discuss different types of topics (e.g., Aries & Johnson 1983, Levin & Arluke 1985), along with the idea that men tend to judge "women's" topics as trivial or unimportant; Coates (1986:103), for example, comments, "The idea that women discuss topics which are essentially trivial has probably contributed to the myth of women's verbosity, since talk on trivial topics can more easily be labelled 'too much.'"

We suggest that a further useful approach to the question of why the stereotype exists is as follows. Because of the differential cultural expectations about women's and men's abilities and areas of competence, women and men use talk in different ways. In particular, women are expected to use and do use talk to a greater extent than do men to serve the function of establishing and maintaining personal relationships (this is not surprising, as the responsibility for interpersonal relationships primarily rests with women); for example, as we have observed, women, to a greater extent than men, are expected to talk, and do talk, simply in order to keep the interaction flowing smoothly and to show goodwill toward others, and they are expected to talk, and do talk, about personal feelings and other socioemotional matters relevant to interpersonal relationships to a greater extent than do men. (These types of talk are both more likely to occur in informal interactions; thus, one contributory factor to the stereotype is probably the fact that men have more frequently interacted with women in informal than in formal interactions.) Therefore, men have experienced women as talking at times when they would be less likely to choose to talk themselves, and about matters about which men would be less likely to choose to talk about themselves.[16] In addition, men may perceive women as more talkative than men as a consequence of observing women's interactions with other women. A number of studies have found that what is particularly important in female friendships is the sharing of intimate feelings and confidences through talk, whereas in male friendships the sharing of activities is more important (e.g., Caldwell & Peplau 1982, Aries & Johnson 1983, Lowenthal, Thurnher, & Chirrboga 1976). The fact that women spend significantly more time than men "just talking" with each other may be perceived by men as constituting unusual (and therefore, excessive) talkativeness. Moreover, as noted by previous researchers, because of the association of "women's talk" with talk which has socioemotional functions and consequently less value than instrumental talk, men may fail to appreciate the social value of this talk. Thus, women may be perceived by men as talking at times when no talk is necessary, and thus as talking too much.

NOTES

1. We ignore here studies which have dealt with interaction between children or between parents or teachers and children, and studies in which the genders were not compared within the same interaction (for example, those which examined the behavior of interviewees in separate interviews or which compared subjects' descriptions of pictures or other objects).

2. Thirteen of these seventeen studies––Aries (1976), Borgatta and Stimson (1963), Crosby (1976), Duncan and Fiske (1977), Frances (1979), Lamb (1981), Leet-Pellegrini (1980), Markel, Long, and Saine (1976), Martin and Craig (1983), McLachlan (1991), Mulac (1989), Simkins-Bullock and Wildman (1991), and Street and Murphy (1987)—found no gender differences in amount of talk between same-sex pairs or groups. Bilous and Krauss (1988) and Dabbs and Ruback (1984) found females to talk more than males in same-sex informal interaction, and Ickes and Barnes (1977) found female pairs to produce more utterances when left alone by the experimenter prior (as subjects believed) to the experiment. Rosenfeld (1966) found that when asked to pretend that they disliked and did not want closer acquaintanceship with their co-participant, female pairs spoke less than male pairs.

3. Since Edelsky reports that the type of "floor" in which males talked more was far more prevalent than the type of floor in which they did not (see further discussion later in the text), it is presumably also the case that males talked more overall in this study. Since she does not actually state this, however, we have included this study only under the heading "men talked more under some circumstances."

4. It should be commented here that analyses in which differential socialization has been invoked to explain gender differences in behavior have often in the past implicitly treated these behaviors as inherent properties of females and males; it has been assumed that sex-typed behaviors are absolute. Such analyses are fundamentally flawed in that they fail to recognize the importance of social structure to behavior; and as a consequence, behavior that does not conform to gender-role socialization goes unexplained (or, more seriously, the behavior is interpreted as spurious or a result of methodological weaknesses). Such assumptions constitute a disservice to intellectual inquiry and at the same time perpetuate stereotypical

images of women's and men's behavior. However, it should be noted that work within the language and gender literature since the 1970s which has ascribed gender differences in behavior to learned differential speech styles and strategies is not subject to this type of criticism; researchers have normally viewed these different styles/strategies as explicitly grounded in social context and social structure (e.g., "speech is a means for dealing with social and psychological situations. When men and women have different experiences and operate in different social contexts, they tend to develop different genres of speech and different skills for doing things with words" (Maltz & Borker 1982:200); "Women's speech strategies—for example, their "interaction work" . . . and styles of "politeness" . . .—may be understood, at least in part, as ways of coping with greater male power" (Thorne, Kramarae, & Henley 1983:15).

5. Most of the research on amount of talk has examined the behavior of subjects in a controlled experimental setting. One concern sometimes expressed by researchers is that behavior in such a setting does not constitute an accurate guide to natural behavior. Smith (1985:155), for example, suggests that no elicited conversation in an experiment can be characterized as informal, and that experimental studies in general are more likely to elicit a disproportionate amount of male speech than are studies of naturally occurring talk: "I personally doubt . . . that the relatively formal and task-related norms of laboratory settings in which people are aware of being observed and recorded can ever be overridden by simple instructions [e.g., 'just get acquainted']. If they cannot, then formal observational settings will always favour the display of control-related behaviours, and the apparent dominance of those for whom these settings have a facilitative effect—in this case, men." Whether the fact of being observed and recorded makes subjects particularly self-conscious is a debatable point; Wiemann (1981), for example, found that after the first minute, tape-recording did not make subjects self-conscious. In any case, we compared those studies out of these fifty-six which involved experiments with those which examined naturally occurring speech, with a view to seeing whether there was a systematic difference in the results along the lines suggested by Smith. In fact the differences were the opposite of those predicted by Smith: proportionately, more studies which examined naturally occurring speech found males to talk more, either overall or under some circumstances (fifteen of twenty-one studies, or 71%) than did studies involving experiments (twenty of thirty-five studies, or 57%). It is also the case, however, that a far higher proportion of the studies of naturally occurring speech dealt with a formally task-oriented or formally structured situation than was the case with the experimental studies (eighteen of twenty-one studies of naturally occurring speech, as opposed to twenty-three of thirty-five experimental studies). We present arguments in the text that formally task-oriented and formally structured settings are significantly more likely to elicit more speech by males than by females than are informal speech situations; thus, we propose that this is why the studies of naturally occurring speech and the experimental studies produced somewhat disparate results. (We do not dispute, however, that the ways in which an experimental setting may affect speech behavior would be a useful subject for future research.)

6. Tannen (1990) suggests that women tend to feel that a situation is more "public" when men (other than perhaps family members) are present, and that women are more likely to fear that their talk will be judged negatively in public settings than are men. Status characteristics theory provides an explanation for why the presence of men would tend to make women more concerned about how

their talk would be judged, since it predicts that women's lower status relative to men would cause them to view themselves as relatively less competent and knowledgeable.

7. The matter of whether men talk more when with women than when with other men in formal task-oriented interaction is complicated by the fact that there is considerable evidence that men tend to compete for status with other men; since holding the floor for long periods is one way of achieving this, this is likely to counterbalance the predicted tendency for men to talk more when with women than when with men. Mulac (1989) did find that men talked more when with women than with men, but Bilous and Krauss (1988) found that the sex of the partner made no difference to the amount of talk produced by men.

8. In Aries (1982:132) it is suggested that the reason why females were found to initiate more verbal acts than males has to do with changes in "the norms . . . regarding the acceptability and desirability of . . . verbal participation by women." We question this, however, since if this were the case, one would expect that an examination of the studies reviewed here in chronological order would reveal a gradual increase in the findings of no difference between the genders in amount of talk and in the findings of women talking more. However, no such pattern is discernable.

9. A further, more unexpected finding of this study was that in heterosexual couples in which the woman was rated as more powerful than the man, the man nevertheless talked more. Kollock, Blumstein and Schwartz note that other aspects of their findings "suggest that men are generally uncomfortable with role reversal in such realms as sexuality and income. . . . Perhaps this discomfort takes the form of increased loquaciousness. These men may feel it necessary to call attention to themselves as participants in the interaction, and to remind their partners that it is a dialogue" (Kollock et al. 1985:43).

10. The task assigned to subjects in this study was to discuss the negative effects of television violence on children and recommend ways for improving the quality of television programming. As will be discussed in more detail later in the chapter, the topic of conversation is another factor which can affect the relative amount of talk of the two genders; for example, when the topic involves an area which is expected to be of particular concern to women, women tend to talk more than they would otherwise. Since child care is seen as the particular responsibility of women, this may well explain why women talked as much as men in this study, as opposed to less than men as might otherwise have been expected, when neither partner was given extra relevant information.

11. For the information of the reader, Kajander (1976), which we have described as finding men to talk more in one respect but women to talk more in another, observed specifically that male students initiated more contact in the classroom, but that female students answered more questions, in particular "rote" questions. Kajander suggests that this is a result of personality differences between men and women which affect cognitive styles; she suggests that the cognitive style of males is predominantly characterized by problem solving, while the cognitive style of females is characterized by a more simplistic lesson learning, and that consequently males are more adept at handling material independently than are females. While we have no suggestions as to why females were found to answer more questions in this study (no other study found this result), we suggest that a social structural analysis offers a far more satisfactory explanation for why males would initiate more contact in the classroom than does Kajander's analysis.

12. Evidence indicates that even when women are functioning as leaders of a group, their speech is nevertheless more affiliative in orientation than is typically the case with men's speech. For example, Eskilson and Wiley (1976) found that while women leaders "showed intense involvement with the instrumental tasks of the group," they simultaneously "performed the expected encouraging and tension-relieving behaviour" (Eskilson & Wiley 1976:192). They conclude that women leaders do "double work" by meeting the instrumental expectations of their role as leaders and the socioemotional expectations of their role as women.

13. In addition, it has been suggested by some researchers that silence may sometimes function as a male speech strategy in informal conversations with women (particularly when the participants are intimate). Zimmerman and West (1975) and Fishman (1983) found that in informal conversation in male-female pairs silences and delayed minimal responses were much more commonly used by men than by women and argue that these function as ways of asserting a dominant role and controlling the overall direction of the conversation; similarly, Sattel (1983) notes that in disputes in male-female pairs, male silence and inexpressiveness—refusal to talk—can function as ways of controlling the situation. One consequence of such male silence would be that women would be forced to work harder and talk more in order to keep the conversation going.

14. As was noted earlier, Tannen (1990) proposes that women are likely to talk more in "private" contexts (which would presumably involve primarily informal activities) than in "public" contexts (into which formally task-oriented and formally structured activities would presumably tend to fall), and she suggests that one important reason for this is that women's socialization, to a significantly greater extent than men's, emphasizes talk as crucial to the maintenance of harmonious relationships. This conclusion is similar to the point made here. We might, however, note that status characteristics theory takes into account and helps to explain such gender-specific expectations. Berger et al. (1977:7) state that status characteristics are socially constructed and that what is learned is "translated into observable inequalities in face-to-face interaction." As noted earlier, research suggests that lower-status individuals are expected to engage in a greater amount of positive socioemotional behavior than are higher-status individuals. Thus, women's overall lower status in relation to men, together with the expectation that women will interact with men on a daily basis, leads to an expectation of greater involvement in positive socioemotional talk by women than by men.

15. Some evidence is provided for this hypothesis by Cutler and Scott (1990), who found that the contribution of female speakers to mixed-sex dyadic conversations was perceived by subjects to be greater than that of male speakers, although in fact the contributions were identical.

16. A similar observation has been made by Tannen (1990:78).

REFERENCES

Anderson, Lynn R. & Blanchard, P. N. (1982). Sex differences in task and socio-emotional behavior. *Basic and Applied Social Psychology* 3:109–139.

Argyle, Michael, Lalljee, Mansur, & Cook, Mark (1968). The effects of visibility on interaction in a dyad. *Human Relations* 21:3–17.

Aries, Elizabeth (1976). Interaction patterns and themes of male, female, and mixed groups. *Small Group Behavior* 7:7–18. Rpt. as: Male-female interpersonal styles in all male, all female, and mixed groups. In Alice Sargent (Ed.) *Beyond sex roles* (pp. 292–298). St. Paul: West, 1977.

Aries, Elizabeth (1982). Verbal and nonverbal behavior in single-sex and mixedsex groups: Are traditional sex roles changing? *Psychological Reports* 51:127–134.

Aries, Elizabeth & Johnson, Fern L. (1983). Close friendship in adulthood: Conversational content between same-sex friends. *Sex Roles* 9:12, 1185–96.

Askinas, Barry E. (1971). The impact of coeducational living on peer interaction. Ph.D. diss., Stanford University. *Dissertation Abstracts International* p. 32, 1634-A.

Berger, Joseph, Fizek, M. Hamit, Norman, Robert Z. & Zelditch, Morris Jr. (1977). *Status characteristics and social interaction.* New York: Elsevier.

Berger, Joseph, Rosenholtz, Susan J. & Zelditch, Morris Jr. (1980). Status organizing processes. *Annual Review of Sociology* 6:479–508.

Bernard, Jessie (1972). *The sex game.* New York: Atheneum.

Bilous, Frances R. & Krauss, Robert M. (1988). Dominance and accommodation in the conversational behaviors of same- and mixed-sex gender dyads. *Journal of Language and Communication* 8:183–194.

Boersma, P. Dee, Gay, Debora, Jones, Ruth A., Morrison, Lynn & Remick, Helen (1981). Sex differences in college student-teacher interactions: Fact or fantasy? *Sex Roles* 7:775–784.

Borgatta, Edgar F. & Stimson, John (1963). Sex differences in interaction characteristics. *Journal of Social Psychology* 60:89–100.

Brooks, Virginia R. (1982). Sex differences in student dominance behavior in female and male professors' classrooms. *Sex Roles* 8:683–690.

Burleson, Brant R. (1982). The development of comforting communication skills in childhood and adolescence. *Child Development* 53, 6:1578–1588.

Caldwell, Mayta A. & Peplau, Letitia Anne (1982). Sex differences in same-sex friendship. *Sex Roles* 8:721–732.

Cameron, Deborah, McAlinden, Fiona & O'Leary, Kathy (1989). Lakoff in context: The social and linguistic functions of tag questions. In Jennifer Coates & Deborah Cameron (Eds.) *Women in their speech communities* (pp. 74–93). London and New York: Longman.

Capella, Joseph N. (1985). Controlling the floor in conversation. In Aron W. Siegman & Stanley Feldstein (Eds.) *Multichannel integrations of nonverbal behavior* (pp. 69–103). Hillsdale, NJ: Erlbaum.

Case, Susan Schick (1988). Cultural differences, not deficiencies: An analysis of managerial women's language. In Suzanna Rose & Laurie Larwood (Eds.) *Women's Careers: Pathways and Pitfalls* (pp. 41–63). New York: Praeger.

Caudill, William A. (1958). *The psychiatric hospital as a small society.* Cambridge, MA: Harvard University Press.

Coates, Jennifer (1986). *Women, men, and language.* London and New York: Longman.

Coates, Jennifer (1989). Gossip revisited: Language in all-female groups. In Jennifer Coates & Deborah Cameron (Eds.) *Women in their speech communities* (pp. 99–122). London and New York: Longman.

Cornelius, Randolph R., & Gray, Janet M. (1988). The chilly climate: fact or artifact? *Journal of Higher Education* 59:527–550.

Cornelius, Randolph R., Gray, Janet M. & Constantinople, Anne P. (1990). Student-faculty interaction in the college classroom. *Journal of Research and Development in Education* 23:189–197.

Craig, D. & Pitts, M. K. (1990). The dynamics of dominance in tutorial discussions. *Linguistics* 28:125–138.

Crosby, Faye (1976). The effect of mode of interaction, sex, and acquaintance on conversation management. Ph.D. diss., Boston University.

Crosby, Faye, Jose, Paul, & Wong-McCarthy, William (1981). Gender, androgyny, and conversational assertiveness. In Clara Mayo & Nancy M. Henley (Eds.) *Gender and Nonverbal Behavior* (pp. 151–169). New York: Springer-Verlag.

Crouch, Isabel M. & Dubois, Betty Lou (1977). Interpersonal communication in the classroom: Which sex's speech is inferior? *Journal of the Linguistics Association of the Southwest* 2:129–141.

Cutler, Anne & Scott, Donia R. (1990). Speaker sex and perceived apportionment of talk. *Applied Psycholinguistics* 11:253–272.

Dabbs, James M., Jr. & Ruback, R. Barry (1984). Vocal patterns in male and female groups. *Personality and Social Psychology Bulletin* 10:4, 518–525.

Davidson, Lynne R. & Duberman, Lucile (1982). Friendship: Communication and interactional patterns in same-sex dyads. *Sex Roles* 8:809–822.

Doherty, Edmund G. (1974). Therapeutic community meetings: A study of communication patterns, sex, status, and staff attendance. *Small Group Behavior* 5:244–256.

Dovidio, John F., Brown, Clifford E., Heltman, Karen, Ellyson, Steve L. & Keating, Caroline F. (1988). Power displays between women and men in discussions of gender-linked tasks: A multichannel study. *Journal of Personality and Social Psychology* 55:580–587.

Duncan, Starkey Jr. & Fiske, Donald W. (1977). *Face-to-face interaction.* Hillsdale, NJ: Lawrence Erlbaum Associates.

Eakins, Barbara & Eakins, R. Gene (1976). Verbal turn-taking and exchanges in faculty dialogue. In Betty Lou Dubois & Isabel Crouch (Eds.) *The sociology of the languages of American women* (pp. 53–62). San Antonio: Trinity University.

Edelsky, Carole (1981). Who's got the floor? *Language in Society* 10:383–421.

Eskilson, Arlene & Wiley, Mary Glenn (1976). Sex composition and leadership in small groups. *Sociometry* 39:183–194.

Eubanks, Sheryle B. (1975). Sex-based language differences: A cultural reflection. In R. Ordoubadian & W. von-Raffler Engel (Eds.) *Views on language* (pp. 109–120). Murfreesboro, TN: Inter-University Publishers.

Fishman, Pamela M. (1983). Interaction: The work women do. In Barrie Thorne, Cheris Kramarae, & Nancy Henley (Eds.) *Language, gender and society* (pp. 89–102). Rowley, MA: Newbury House, 1983.

Fowler, G. D. & Rosenfeld, L. B. (1979). Sex differences and democratic leadership behavior. *Southern Speech Communication Journal* 45:69–78.

Frances, Susan J. (1979). Sex differences in nonverbal behavior. *Sex Roles* 5:519–535.

Golinkoff, Roberta Michnick & Ames, Gail Johnson (1979). A comparison of fathers' speech to mothers' speech with their young children. *Child Development* 50:28–32.

Heiss, Jerold S. (1962). Degree of intimacy and male-female interaction. *Sociometry* 25:197–208.

Hershey, Sibilla & Werner, Emmy (1975). Dominance in marital decision making in women's liberation and non-women's liberation families. *Family Process* 14:223–233.

Hilpert, Fred, Kramer, Cheris & Clark, Ruth A. (1975). Participants' perceptions of self and partner in mixed-sex dyads. *Central States Speech Journal* 26:52–56.

Hirschman, Lynette (1973). Female-male differences in conversational interaction. Paper presented at annual meeting of the Linguistic Society of America, San Diego, CA. Cited in Barrie Thorne, Cheris Kramarae & Nancy Henley (Eds.) *Language, gender and society.* Rowley, MA: Newbury House, 1983.

Hirschman, Lynette (1974). Analysis of supportive and assertive behavior in conversations. Paper presented at annual meeting of the Linguistic Society of America, San Francisco, CA. Cited in Barrie Thorne, Cheris Kramarae and Nancy Henley (Eds.) *Language, gender and society.* Rowley, MA: Newbury House, 1983.

Holmes, Janet (1984). Women's language: A functional approach. *General Linguistics* 24:149–178.

Ickes, William & Barnes, Richard D. (1977). The role of sex and self-monitoring in unstructured dyadic interactions. *Journal of Personality and Social Psychology* 35:315–330.

Jones, Deborah (1980). Gossip: Notes on women's oral culture. In Cheris Kramarae (Ed.) *The voices and words of women and men* (pp. 193–198). Oxford: Pergamon Press.

Kajander, Cheryl Ann (1976). The effects of instructor and student sex on verbal behaviors in college classrooms. Ph.D. diss., University of Texas at Austin. *Dissertation Abstracts International* 37 (5-A), 2743–2744.

Kalčik, Susan (1975). ". . . like Ann's gynecologist or the time I was almost raped": Personal narratives in women's rap groups. *Journal of American Folklore* 88:3–11. Rpt. in C. R. Farrer (Ed.) *Women and folklore* (pp. 3–11). Austin, Texas: University of Texas Press.

Kaplan, Susan L. (1976). The assertion of power: Ideals, perceptions, and styles. Paper presented at annual meeting of the American Psychological Association, Washington, DC. Cited in Barrie Thorne, Cheris Kramarae & Nancy Henley (Eds.) *Language, gender and society* (p. 272). Rowley, MA: Newbury House, 1983. 272.

Karp, David A. & Yoels, William C. (1976). The college classroom: Some observations on the meaning of student participation. *Sociology and Social Research* 60:421–439.

Kelly, Jeffrey A., Wildman, Hal E., & Urey, Jon R. (1982). Gender and sex role differences in group decision-making social interactions: A behavioral analysis. *Journal of Applied Social Psychology* 12:112–127.

Kenkel, William F. (1963). Observational studies of husband-wife interactions in family decision-making. In Marvin Sussman (Ed.) *Sourcebook in marriage and the family* (pp. 144–156). Boston: Houghton-Mifflin.

Kollock, Peter, Blumstein, Philip, & Schwartz, Pepper (1985). Sex and power in interaction: Conversational privileges and duties. *American Sociological Review* 50:34–46.

Kramarae, Cheris (1981). *Women and men speaking.* Rowley, MA: Newbury House.

Lamb, Theodore A. (1981). Nonverbal and paraverbal control in dyads and triads: Sex or power differences? *Social Psychological Quarterly* 44:49–53.

Latour, Trudi (1987). Language and power: Issues in classroom interaction. *Women and Language* X:29–32.

Leet-Pellegrini, Helena M. (1980). Conversational dominance as a function of gender and expertise. In Howard Giles, W. P. Robinson & Philip M. Smith (Eds.) *Language: social psychological perspectives* (pp. 97–104). New York: Pergamon Press.

Leffler, Ann, Gillespie, Dair & Conaty, Joseph C. (1982). The effects of status differentiation on nonverbal behavior. *Social Psychology Quarterly* 45:153–161.

Levin, Jack & Arluke, Arnold (1985). An exploratory analysis of sex differences in gossip. *Sex Roles* 12:281–286.

Lockheed, Marlaine E. (1976). The modification of female leadership behavior in the presence of males. ETS-PR-76-28. Princeton, NJ: Educational Testing Service.

Lowenthal, M., Thurnher, M., & Chirrboga, D. (1976). *Four stages of life*. San Francisco: Jossey-Bass.

Maltz, Daniel N. & Borker, Ruth A. (1982). A cultural approach to male-female miscommunication. In John J. Gumperz (Ed.) *Language and social identity* (pp. 195–216). Cambridge, MA: Cambridge University Press.

Manber, Michele R. (1976). Sex differences in perceived status as reflected in linguistic style. Unpublished ms., San Francisco State University. Cited in Barrie Thorne, Cheris Kramarae & Nancy Henley (Eds.) *Language, gender and society*. Rowley, MA: Newbury House, 1983.

March, James G. (1953). Political issues and husband-and-wife interaction. *Public Opinion Quarterly* 17:461–470.

Markel, Norman H., Long, Joseph J. & Saine, Thomas J. (1976). Sex effects in conversational interaction: Another look at male dominance. *Human Communication Research* 2:356–364.

Martin, Judith N. & Craig, Robert T. (1983). Selected linguistic sex differences during initial social interactions of same-sex and mixed-sex student dyads. *The Western Journal of Speech Communication* 47:16–28.

McLachlan, Angus (1991). The effects of agreement, disagreement, gender and familiarity on patterns of dyadic interaction. *Journal of Language and Social Psychology* 10:3, 205–212.

McLaughlin, Margaret L., Louden, A. D., Cashion, J. L., Altendorf, D. M., Baaske, K. T. & Smith, S. W. (1985). Conversational planning and self-serving utterances: The manipulation of topical and functional structures in dyadic interaction. *Journal of Language and Social Psychology* 4:233–251.

McMillan, Julie R., Clifton, A. Kay, McGrath, Diane & Gale, Wanda S. (1977). Women's language: Uncertainty or interpersonal sensitivity and emotionality? *Sex Roles* 3:545–559.

Mischel, Walter (1966). A social learning view of sex differences in behavior. In Eleanor E. Maccoby (Ed.) *The development of sex differences* (pp. 56–81). Stanford, CA: Stanford University Press.

Mulac, Anthony (1989). Men's and women's talk in same-gender and mixed-gender dyads: Power or polemic? *Journal of Language and Social Psychology* 8:249–270.

Nemeth, Charles, Endicott, Jeffrey & Wachtler, Joel (1976). From the 50's to the 70's: Women in jury deliberations. *Sociometry* 39: 305–336.

Parker, Angele M. (1973). Sex differences in classroom argumentation. M.S. thesis, Pennsylvania State University. Cited in Barrie Thorne, Cheris Kramarae & Nancy Henley (Eds.) *Language, gender and society* (p. 291). Rowley, MA: Newbury House, 1983.

Piliavin, Jane Allyn & Martin, Rachel Rosemann (1978). The effects of the sex composition of groups on style of social interaction. *Sex Roles* 4:281–296.

Preisler, Bent (1986). *Linguistic sex roles in conversation.* Berlin: Mouton de Gruyter.

Robertson, Angelika (1978). The relationship of class sex composition, teacher sex, and selected attitudinal variables to the verbal class participation of female college students. Ed.D. diss., University of Massachusetts. Cited in Barrie Thorne, Cheris Kramarae & Nancy Henley (Eds.) *Language, gender and society* (p. 291). Rowley, Mass.: Newbury House, 1983.

Roger, Derek B. & Schumacher, Andrea (1983). Effects of individual differences on dyadic conversational strategies. *Journal of Personality and Social Psychology* 45:700–705.

Rosenfeld, Howard M. (1966). Approval-seeking and approval-inducing functions of verbal and nonverbal responses in the dyad. *Journal of Personality and Social Psychology* 4:597–605.

Sattel, Jack W. (1983). Men, inexpressiveness, and power. In Barrie Thorne, Cheris Kramarae & Nancy Henley (Eds.) *Language, gender and society* (pp. 119–124). Rowley, MA: Newbury House.

Sayers, Frances (1987). Sex and conversational control. Paper presented at the Tenth Annual Communication, Language, and Gender Conference. Marquette University.

Schwartz, E. (1970). Sex roles and leadership dynamics: A study of attitudes toward the female sex role. Senior honors thesis, University of Pennsylvania. Cited in Barrie Thorne, Cheris Kramarae & Nancy Henley (Eds.) *Language, gender and society.* Rowley, MA: Newbury House, 1983.

Shaw, Marvin E. & Sadler, Orin W. (1965). Interaction patterns in heterosexual dyads varying in degree of intimacy. *Journal of Social Psychology* 66:345–351.

Simkins-Bullock, Jennifer A. and Wildman, Beth G. (1991). An investigation into the relationships between gender and language. *Sex Roles* 24:3/4. 149–160.

Slater, Philip E. (1966). Role differentiation in small groups. In Alexander P. Hare, Edgar F. Borgatta & Robert F. Bales (Eds.) *Small groups: Studies in social interaction* (pp. 610–647). New York: Knopf.

Smith, Philip M. (1985). *Language, the sexes, and society.* Oxford: Basil Blackwell.

Smith-Lovin, Lynn, Skvortez, John V. & Hudson, Charlotte G. (1986). Status and participation in six-person groups: A test of Skvoretz's comparative status model. *Social Forces* 64:992–1004.

Soskin, William F. & John, Vera P. (1963). The study of spontaneous talk. In Roger Barker (Ed.) *The stream of behavior* (pp. 228–281). New York: Appleton-Century-Crofts.

Spender, Dale (1980). *Man made language.* London, Boston, and Henley: Routledge and Kegan Paul.

Stein, R. Timothy & Heller, Tamar (1979). An empirical analysis of the correlations between leadership status and participation rates reported in the literature. *Journal of Personality and Social Psychology* 37:1993–2002.

Sternglanz, Sarah Hall & Lyberger-Ficek, Shirley (1977). Sex differences in student-teacher interactions in the college classroom. *Sex Roles* 3:345–362.

Stoneman, Zolinda & Brody, Gene H. (1981). Two's company, three makes a difference: An examination of mothers' and fathers' speech to their young children. *Child Development* 52:705–707.

Street, Richard L., Jr. & Murphy, Thomas J. (1987). Interpersonal orientation and speech behavior. *Communication Monographs* 54:42–62.

Strodtbeck, Fred L. (1951). Husband-wife interaction over revealed differences. *American Sociological Review* 18:141–145.

Strodtbeck, Fred L., James, Rita M. & Hawkins, Charles (1957). Social status in jury deliberations. *American Sociological Review* 22:713–719.

Strodtbeck, Fred L. & Mann, Richard D. (1956). Sex-role differentiation in jury deliberations. *Sociometry* 19:3–11.

Swacker, Marjorie (1976). Women's verbal behavior at learned and professional conferences. In Betty Lou Dubois & Isabel M. Crouch (Eds.) *The sociology of the languages of American women* (pp. 155–160). San Antonio: Trinity University.

Tannen, Deborah (1990). *You just don't understand: Women and men in conversation*. New York: Ballantine.

Thorne, Barrie, Kramarae, Cheris & Henley, Nancy (1983). Language, gender and society: Opening a second decade of research. In Barrie Thorne, Cheris Kramarae & Nancy Henley (Eds.) *Language, gender, and society*. Rowley, MA: Newbury House.

Wiemann, John M. (1981). Effects of laboratory videotaping procedures on selected conversational behaviours. *Psychological Abstracts* 67(5736):619.

Wood, Wendy (1987). Meta-analytic review of sex differences in group performance. *Psychological Bulletin* 102:53–71.

Wood, Wendy & Karten, Stephen J. (1986). Sex differences in interaction style as a product of perceived sex differences in competence. *Journal of Personality and Social Psychology* 50:341–347.

Woods, Nicola (1989). Talking shop: Sex and status as determinants of floor apportionment in a work setting. In Jennifer Coates & Deborah Cameron (Eds.) *Women in their speech communities* (pp. 141–157). London and New York: Longman.

Yamada, Elaine M., Tjosvold, Dean & Draguns, Juris G. (1983). Effects of sex-linked situations and sex composition on cooperation and styles of interaction. *Sex Roles* 9:541–553.

Zimmerman, Don H. & West, Candace (1975). Sex roles, interruptions and silences in conversation. In Barrie Thorne & Nancy Henley (Eds.) *Language and sex* (pp. 105–129). Rowley, MA: Newbury House.

Contributors

Penelope Brown is a researcher at the Max Planck Institute for Psycholinguistics in The Netherlands. She works in collaboration with the Cognitive Anthropology Research Group, which is currently engaged in cross-cultural and cross-linguistic research on language, cognition, and social interaction. She is the coauthor (with Stephen Levinson) of *Politeness: Some Universals in Language Usage* and, in addition to her work on interactional style in Tzeltal, is the author of a number of papers on spatial language and spatial conceptualization in Tzeltal.

Sandra Clarke is professor of linguistics at Memorial University of Newfoundland. Her research interests span quantitative sociolinguistics and Algonquian linguistics as well as language and gender. Her publications include "Phonological variation and recent language change in St. John's English" and *A Grammatical Sketch of North West River Montagnais*. She is president of the Canadian Linguistic Association and a former member of the editorial board of the *Canadian Journal of Linguistics*. She is currently editing a volume on Canadian English.

Janice Drakich is a feminist scholar and activist. She has published on women in academe, violence in the family, and on family law issues. Her most recent work is on fathers' rights groups and women during World War II in Windsor, Ontario. She is engaged in a collective writing project on "writing a feminist romance." Most recently her report on the *Status of Women in Ontario Universities* (written with Dorothy Smith, Penni Stewart, and Bonnie Fox) was published by the Ontario Ministry of Colleges and Universities. She is associate professor in the Department of Sociology and Anthropology at the University of Windsor, Ontario, Canada.

Carole Edelsky is professor of curriculum and instruction at Arizona State University. Her dissertation "Acquisition of an Aspect of Communicative Competence: Recognition of Sex of Speaker from Linguistic Cues—or—Knowing How to Talk Like a Lady," was one of the first to investigate gender and language. She is the author of several articles on conversational analysis—particularly conversation in classrooms—as well as gender and language. Her most recent work in the latter category is "Creating inequality: Breaking the rules in political debates."

Donna Eder is associate professor of sociology at Indiana University. She has published other research on adolescent peer culture and styles of talk, including research on gossip, insulting, teasing, and storytelling. She is currently completing a book entitled *Remember When: Gender, Talk, and Adolescent Culture*.

Marjorie Harness Goodwin is professor of anthropology at the University of South Carolina. She is a conversation analyst whose articles have dealt with topics ranging from gendered talk in children's interaction to the achievement of collaborative vocal and nonvocal interaction. She is the author of *He-Said-She-Said: Talk as Social Organization Among Black Children* and has been editor of linguistic anthropology for *American Anthropologist*. Her recent work has focused on multiparty talk in the workplace.

Deborah James is associate professor of linguistics at the Scarborough campus of the University of Toronto. She has published articles on English interjections, tense, and Algonquian linguistics—in particular on various aspects of the morphology and syntax of Cree. She is the coordinator of the Women's Studies Programme at the University of Toronto, Scarborough campus. Her current research focuses on language and gender.

Barbara Johnstone is associate professor of linguistics at Texas A&M University. She is the author of *Stories, Community, and Place: Narratives from Middle America* and *Repetition in Arabic Discourse: Syntagms, Paradigms, and the Ecology of Language*, as well as the editor of the two-volume *Repetition in Discourse: Interdisciplinary Perspectives*. She has published on Arabic syntax, semantics, and rhetorical style; on narrative; and on regional and individual variation in discourse in journals such as *American Speech, Studies in Language, Text, Linguistics, Anthropological Linguistics*, and *Language in Society*. Her current work concerns the individual voice and discourse in the American South.

Amy Sheldon is a linguist whose research has covered a variety of topics in child and adult language acquisition. Her work has been published in such journals as *Applied Psycholinguistics, Journal of Verbal Learning and Verbal Behavior, Language Learning,* and *Merrill-Palmer Quarterly.* She is currently writing a book about gender and children's conversations. She is an associate professor in the Department of Speech Communication at the University of Minnesota and is a member of the Graduate Faculty of the Program in Linguistics, the Center for Advanced Feminist Studies, and the Center for Learning, Perception and Cognition at the University of Minnesota.

Deborah Tannen is University Professor in the Linguistics Department at Georgetown University. Her books include: *Conversational Style: Analyzing Talk Among Friends; Talking Voices: Repetition, Dialogue, and Imagery in Conversational Discourse; You Just Don't Understand: Women and Men in Conversation;* and *That's Not What I Meant!: How Conversational Style Makes or Breaks Your Relations With Others.* Topics addressed in her other books and articles include spoken and written language, the relationship between conversational and literary discourse, cross-cultural communication, and doctor-patient communication. She is associate editor of *Language in Society* and *Text.*

Index

317

Printed in the United States
25168LVS00003B/209

9 780195 081947